QUEERYING PLANNING

This volume is dedicated to the memory of Sue Hendler, who served on the faculty of Queens University from 1987 until receiving a diagnosis of advanced metastatic breast cancer in January 2007. Her death came too early in September 2009. Well recognized for her work on feminist approaches to planning history and ethics, Sue's final project, with Gail Dubrow, was to bring together planners working on LGBT topics to produce the first published volume on the subject. When it was clear that Sue's focus needed to be redirected to her own health struggles, they passed it on to Petra L. Doan to edit. Sue lived her beliefs in all respects, from a passion for the natural world and related environmental concerns to a well-honed set of ethics that emphasized truth-telling. This volume is an extension of her wider vision of a wholly inclusive approach to planning.
Fortunately, this vision has many advocates.

Queerying Planning
Challenging Heteronormative Assumptions
and Reframing Planning Practice

Edited by

PETRA L. DOAN
Florida State University, Florida, USA

ASHGATE

© Petra L. Doan 2011

All rights reserved. No part of this publication may be reproduced, stored in a retrieval system or transmitted in any form or by any means, electronic, mechanical, photocopying, recording or otherwise without the prior permission of the publisher.

Petra L. Doan has asserted her right under the Copyright, Designs and Patents Act, 1988, to be identified as the editor of this work.

Published by
Ashgate Publishing Limited
Wey Court East
Union Road
Farnham
Surrey, GU9 7PT
England

Ashgate Publishing Company
Suite 420
101 Cherry Street
Burlington
VT 05401-4405
USA

www.ashgate.com

British Library Cataloguing in Publication Data
Queerying planning : challenging heteronormative
  assumptions and reframing planning practice.
  1. City planning--Social aspects. 2. Urban policy--Social
  aspects. 3. Sexual minorities--Social conditions. 4. Gay
  community. 5. Sociology, Urban.
  I. Doan, Petra L.
  307.1'216'08664-dc22

Library of Congress Cataloging-in-Publication Data
Queerying planning : challenging heteronormative assumptions and reframing planning practice / by Petra L. Doan.
    p. cm.
  Includes bibliographical references and index.
  ISBN 978-1-4094-2815-2 (hbk) -- ISBN 978-1-4094-2816-9 (ebk)
  1. Public spaces--Planning. 2. Sexual minorities. 3. Urban renewal. I. Doan, Petra L., 1955-
  HT185.Q44 2011
  307.1'21608664--dc23

2011015958

ISBN 978 1 4094 2815 2 (hbk)
ISBN 978 1 4094 2816 9 (ebk)

Printed and bound in Great Britain by
TJ International Ltd, Padstow, Cornwall.

Contents

List of Figures and Tables   *vii*
Notes on Contributors   *ix*
Acknowledgments   *xiii*

1   Why Question Planning Assumptions and Practices about Queer Spaces   1
    Petra L. Doan

PART I   PLANNING THEORY AND PRACTICE

2   Queerying Planning Practice: Understanding Non-Conformist Populations   21
    Ann Forsyth

3   Lavender Landmarks Revisited: Advancing an LGBT Preservation Agenda   53
    Gail Dubrow

4   Querying Planning (Theory): Alphabet Soup or Paradox City?   71
    Sue Hendler and Michael Backs

5   Queerying Identity: Planning and the Tyranny of Gender   89
    Petra L. Doan

6   Queering the Suburbs: Analyzing Property Values in Male and Female Same-Sex Suburbs in the United States   107
    Katrin B. Anacker

PART II   GOVERNANCE AND POLITICAL ISSUES

7   Queerying Planning in Australia: The Problems and Possibilities of Multiscalar Governance for LGBT Sexual Minorities   129
    Andrew Gorman-Murray

8   Queering the Political-Economy: Anti-discrimination Law and the Urban Regime in Orlando, Florida   145
    Thomas Chapman

| 9 | Queerying Creative Cities
Tiffany Muller Myrdahl | 157 |

PART III   REGULATING SEX IN THE CITY

| 10 | Planning for Sex/Work
Phil Hubbard | 169 |
| 11 | Queerying Urban Governance: The Emergence of Sex Industry Premises into the Planned City
Jason Prior and Penny Crofts | 185 |

PART IV   REFLECTIONS AND CONCLUSIONS

| 12 | Reflections on Classic Articles on Planning and LGBT Communities
Sy Adler, Johanna Brenner, Michael Frisch, Larry Knopp and Mickey Lauria | 211 |
| 13 | Conclusions and Reflections for the Future: Reframing Planning Practice
Petra L. Doan | 221 |

List of References *231*
Index *273*

List of Figures and Tables

Figures

11.1	Map Showing Central Sydney Local Government Areas, and Location of the Bathhouses Discussed in the Study	186
11.2	Cover of the Cumberland County Council Pamphlet	193

Tables

5.1	Dichotomous Sex/Gender and Space	93
5.2	Percent of Transgender Respondents Who Experienced Discrimination in Public Accommodations (N = 6450)	99
6.1	Regional Distribution of Census Tracts with at least One Reported Male or Female Same-Sex Household by Census Region with Home Ownership Above 50 percent	115
6.2	Descriptive Statistics for Census Tracts with Home Ownership Rate Above 50 percent	116
6.3	Regression Analyses for Census Tracts with Home Ownership Rate Above 50 percent	120

Notes on Contributors

Sy Adler is Professor in the Department of Urban Studies and Planning at Portland State University, Portland, Oregon, USA. He has a M.C.P. from Harvard and a PhD from Berkeley. He is the author of several books and has published numerous articles on planning and urban development issues. His research interests include comparative studies of planning institutions, theories and practices, and relationships between urban planning and public health.

Katrin B. Anacker is Assistant Professor at George Mason University, Arlington, Virginia, USA. She has a PhD from Ohio State University. Her research interests include housing, housing policy, race and public policy, and real estate markets. She is the author of the book, *Analyzing Mature Suburbs in Ohio Through Property Values*, and numerous articles including an article on Same Sex Households in *Urban Geography*.

Michael Backs is a former student of Sue Hendler and graduate of the planning program at Queens University in Kingston, Ontario, Canada. He is currently a graduate student in the Department of Geography and Program in Planning at the University of Toronto, Toronto, Ontario.

Johanna Brenner is Professor Emerita in the Department of Sociology at Portland State University, Portland, Oregon, USA. She has a PhD from UCLA. She has written several books on women and politics as well as numerous articles. Her research interests include class, race, gender, political sociology, and feminist theory.

Tom Chapman is Assistant Professor of Geography at Old Dominion University, Norfolk, Virginia, USA. Before earning his PhD at Florida State University in 2007, he was an urban planner for the city of Boston, Massachusetts. His research interests are in political and cultural geography, particularly intersections of the sexual citizen and the politics-of-place.

Penny Crofts is a Senior Lecturer at the Faculty of Law, University of Technology, Sydney, New South Wales, Australia. She earned her BEc, LLB (Honors) and LLM at the University of Sydney and a MPhil from the University of Canterbury. She has published in journals including *Current Issues in Criminal Justice*, *Public Spaces Law Journal*, and *Local Government Law*.

Petra L. Doan is Associate Professor at Florida State University, Tallahassee, Florida, USA. She earned a PhD from Cornell University in Urban and Regional Planning. She writes on both planning in developing areas as well as planning for queer spaces in North America. She has published numerous articles including several on LGBT issues in the *Journal of Planning Education and Research*, *Gender, Place, and Culture*, and *Environment and Planning A*.

Gail Dubrow is Professor in the Department of History at the University of Minnesota, Minneapolis, Minnesota, USA. She has a PhD in Urban Planning from UCLA and has written three books as well as numerous articles and book chapters, including "Blazing Trails with Pink Triangles and Rainbow Flags," in *Restoring Women's History Through Historic Preservation*, edited by Gail Dubrow and Jennifer Goodman.

Ann Forsyth is Professor in the Department of City and Regional Planning at Cornell University, Ithaca, New York, USA. She has a PhD in City and Regional Planning from Cornell University. She works mainly on the social aspects of physical planning and urban development and the success of planned alternatives to sprawl. She is author of three books and numerous articles, including "Sexuality and Space – Non-conformist Populations and Planning Practice," in the *Journal of Planning Literature*.

Michael Frisch is Associate Professor in the Department of Architecture, Urban Planning, and Design at the University of Missouri, Kansas City, Missouri, USA. He has a PhD in urban planning and policy development from Rutgers University. His research interests include: how twentieth century urban planning reinforces particular family models, how planning creates the necessary conditions for sustainable economic growth, evaluation of environmental, land use, and community development policies in Kansas City, New Orleans, and other cities.

Andrew Gorman-Murray is a Lecturer in Social Science (Geography) at the University of Western Sydney, New South Wales, Australia, with expertise in social, cultural and political geography. He has a PhD from Macquarie University. His major research foci are geographies of sexuality and gender. He examines the way gays and lesbians resist heteronormativity and affirm sexual difference. Dr Gorman-Murray also explores the constitution of gay and lesbian spatialities across rural, suburban and inner-city Australia. He is widely published and is currently working on the book *Geographies of Sexualities Down Under: Gay and Lesbian Spatialities in Australia* (Ashgate, forthcoming).

Sue Hendler was Associate Professor at Queens University, Kingston, Ontario, Canada. She received a PhD from the University of Waterloo, Ontario. Her research interests included environmental philosophy and policy, social issues, and professional (planning) ethics. She published articles on feminist approaches to planning, including the historical role(s) of women in early Canadian planning. Her untimely death in September of 2009 is a great loss to the profession.

Phil Hubbard is Professor of Urban Studies at the University of Kent, UK. He has a PhD from the University of Birmingham. His current research focuses on questions of social inclusion/exclusion and combines psychoanalytical and post-structuralist ideas to explore the ongoing and contested making of social identities at different scales, from the body to the city. He is author of numerous books and articles on the subject of city life and several with a focus on regulating adult business in the city.

Larry Knopp is Professor and Director of the Center for Interdisciplinary Arts and Sciences at the University of Washington–Tacoma, Washington, USA. He has a PhD in Geography from the University of Iowa. He is the author of numerous articles on the spatiality of sexuality, gender and class. He has explored links in the United States, United Kingdom, and Australia between urban land, housing and labor markets, regional economic change and the construction of place based gay identities, communities and political movements.

Mickey Lauria is Professor in the Department of City and Regional Planning, Clemson University, Clemson, South Carolina, USA. He has a PhD in Geography from the University of Minnesota. He has published four books and numerous articles on urban redevelopment, urban politics, and community-based development organizations in planning, geography, and urban studies journals. His research interests include race, housing, neighborhood change, and the practical implications of this research for planning in inner city minority areas.

Tiffany Muller Myrdahl is Assistant Professor of Women's Studies and an Associate Member of the Department of Geography at University of Lethbridge, Alberta, Canada. She has a PhD from the University of Minnesota and has published articles in the *Journal of Lesbian Studies*, *Gender, Place, and Culture*, and *Social and Cultural Geography*.

Jason Prior is a Senior Researcher at the Institute for Sustainable Futures, University of Technology, Sydney, New South Wales, Australia. He has a PhD from the University of New South Wales. Jason's research expertise builds on his cross-disciplinary background in architecture, urban studies, planning, sociology, geography and architecture. His research explores the interplay of built form, governance, planning and sexuality within Sydney in the twentieth century.

Acknowledgments

The germ of the idea for this book came literally in a bedroom meeting at a planning conference. Nothing inappropriate happened nor was it an illicit assignation. The event was a scheduled roundtable discussion on "LGBT issues and planning" organized by Sue Hendler. Most of us in the group felt that it was oddly appropriate that a discussion raising issues of sexual orientation and gender identity was scheduled by conference organizers in a room on the 11th floor of the hotel, well removed from the rest of the conference on the lower floors of the hotel. For whatever reason, the room we were assigned was on a floor devoted entirely to guest bedrooms. It was funny, but also somehow reflective of the current state of play in the academic discussion of LGBT issues in planning.

One of the best things to come out of that meeting was that there should be a book on queer issues and planning. Sue Hendler and Gail Dubrow agreed to take the lead in organizing and editing this project, and others of us agreed to write chapters (this initial group also included Michael Frisch, Ann Forsyth, Katrin Anacker, and myself). However, the unfortunate illness of Sue Hendler and a new administrative position for Gail Dubrow threatened to derail this project. At the request of Gail and Sue, I agreed to step in and complete the task which included soliciting a number of new chapters and locating a publisher. Because of my contacts with the Sexuality and Space group within the Association of American Geographers, I put out a call for geographers who combined experience in planning with an interest in queer space issues to participate and Tom Chapman, Andrew Gorman-Murray, Jason Prior, Tiffany Muller Myrdahl, and Phil Hubbard joined the project. My biggest regret is that Sue Hendler did not live long enough to see this project through to completion, though her chapter has been ably completed by one of her former students, Michael Backs, who stepped into the brink to complete their complex chapter linking planning theory to queer theory.

I am profoundly grateful for the indefatigable love and support of Elizabeth Kamphausen, who read every chapter and undertook the huge job of merging the references into a single bibliography. Her enthusiasm for the book and understanding of its importance has been part of the fuel that kept me and this project from foundering.

Petra L. Doan
Tallahassee
Florida

Chapter 1
Why Question Planning Assumptions and Practices about Queer Spaces

Petra L. Doan

This volume, *Queerying Planning: Challenging Heteronormative Assumptions and Reframing Planning Practice*, poses a set of queer questions ("queeries") for planning practitioners and scholars interested in urban development issues about the ways that current planning practices have neglected the needs of the Lesbian, Gay, Bisexual, and Transgender (LGBT) community for safe urban spaces in which to live, work, and play. The authors in this volume seek to redress this oversight by raising questions about the intentions of many urban redevelopment objectives, municipal land use regulations, and economic development strategies that fail to consider the requirements of the LGBT population for urban spaces.

Many LGBT neighborhoods that have developed over the past 50 years are experiencing severe development pressure that threatens the vitality of these places as centers of LGBT life in the city (Dubrow, Chapter 3). In 2007 the author of this introduction took a tour of key sites in the gay history of San Francisco, and found it quite sobering to find that many of the iconic gay spaces in the city from the 1950s and 1960s had disappeared. Most of these places have been obliterated by urban redevelopment and by the failure of historic preservation to consider the importance of these historic monuments for the LGBT community (Doan and Higgins, 2011). Although the Castro District in San Francisco remains a highly visible gay neighborhood (gayborhood) for those who can afford to live there, the high property values and rents have made living, working, and organizing in this area difficult for many in the LGBT community. In addition, the desirability of this gentrified space means many upper middle class people who do not identify as gay are moving into the neighborhood, sparking some serious reflections about "whether gays and lesbians should assimilate into mainstream culture as they gain acceptance or maintain a separate place" (Buchanan, 2007).

The contributions in this volume go beyond descriptive accounts of queer spaces and practices around the globe, and seek to interrogate planning practice and pose questions for academic and professional planners about the dynamic nature of the LGBT community. Several of the chapters seek to integrate queer theory with planning theory and practice in ways that highlight the fluid nature of this community's need for safe and welcoming spaces since the mid twentieth century. Although previous planning efforts often restricted the development of sexual minority communities in the name of order and public safety, several chapters highlight the ways that current planning policies have sometimes acted to exploit the "success" of gay villages and encourage the large scale commercialization of such spaces. The result of ill-considered commercialization is that well-financed developers receive large benefits and some of the most marginalized members of the urban community are left without a neighborhood (for example homeless, gender queer youth and retired LGBT people). Other chapters analyze the ways queer–friendly spaces are emerging in urban and suburban locations that stretch existing assumptions about what constitutes a gayborhood.

The over-arching theme of the book is that it is critical to examine the impacts of urban planning and development decisions on the LGBT community that are repeated in US cities as well as other countries, such as Canada, Australia, and the United Kingdom. In spite of claims that the field of planning has learned to value diversity and inclusivity, it is not clear whether some changes to planning codes and practice represent conscious acts of discrimination or are merely taken in ignorance of the needs of the LGBT population. The various contributors argue that it is essential to reframe planning practice to be more inclusive and to provide more direct support to the changing nature of the LGBT community and its evolving need for spaces in which to gather, reside and recreate.

Planning and Inclusion within the American Context

In order to understand how to reframe planning practice to be more inclusive of LGBT people it is useful to consider similar efforts to open the field of planning to women and minorities. There is by now fairly widespread agreement among planning theorists around the globe that concepts like multiculturalism, diversity, and inclusion must be integral components of current planning discourse. In the United Kingdom Healey (1997) has promoted a form of collaborative planning discourse that requires the recognition of difference among various stakeholders. Campbell (2006: 100) also in the UK context has urged that the process of planning include a broad concept of justice that is not restricted "to those with whom we share a common identity and/or encounter through face-to-face contact." In the Australian context Gleeson and Low (2000) argue that multiculturalism takes the form of cultural pluralization where culture is broader than ethnicity, but includes the expression of any human social identity. Finally, Sandercock (2003) adds the notion of justice suggesting that a just city is one that is socially inclusive, where difference is given recognition and respect.

However, for many years this was not a commonly held perspective. For instance, Sandercock has taken to task the narrowness of "mainstream planning" in the introduction to her edited volume on multiculturalism.

> At the most fundamental level there has been a failure to address two basic questions in these mainstream modernist planning histories. What is the object of planning history? And who are its subjects? (Sandercock, 1998: 6)

An important consequence of this failure has been the silencing of the contributions of women, people of color, and LGBT people. Historically the field of urban planning has been intellectually inclusive, drawing upon urban theories from the related fields of geography, economics and sociology as well as civil engineering and architecture. However, the practice of planning has been much less open to different perspectives, especially as they relate to minority communities and their particular needs. Because the ways in which planning has been opened to broader participation vary within different national contexts, this section will focus mainly on the American context.

Recently, urban planners in the United States celebrated the one hundredth anniversary of the first American city planning conference, held in May of 1909 in Washington, DC. This conference brought together representatives of two distinct movements with different visions of the city, the Social Reform and the City Beautiful Movements (Peterson, 2009). In the aftermath of this conference proponents of the City Beautiful Movement solidified their grasp on the profession, effectively muting the social reformers' concerns with the congestion and deplorable conditions experienced by inner city slum dwellers. Peterson describes the planning profession at that time as "mostly Protestant, upper and upper-middle class, college-educated, and active in local business and professional life and still beholden to late-Victorian social norms and genteel modes of taste" (2009: 124). Peterson does not mention gender or ethnicity in his description, because at the time there was no diversity since all of these early purveyors of urban order were white men.

This lack of inclusion is not surprising since the practice of planning is intricately interwoven with the exercise of power, primarily through the use of information (Forester, 1982), but also through the refusal to acknowledge information relevant to those who lack power. Although there are few academic planners who would claim that planning is a wholly technical and therefore unbiased field, the behavior of planners over the last century suggests otherwise. Fainstein and Fainstein (1971: 344) observed that, "traditional planning has as its principal goal the original aim of the planning movement: the creation of an orderly urban environment." Fainstein and Fainstein argued that the critical issue was who determined the definition of orderly (the goal) and the means of achieving that objective. Thirty years later Frisch (2002) argued that the "order" desired by many planning practitioners continued to be narrowly heterosexist, favoring white, male, and heterosexual conceptions of orderliness.

In the American context, Birch and Silver (2009) have provided a list of ten critical points for future planners. The first nine involve mostly technical skill development, but the tenth and final point highlights the fact that planners need to develop a different kind of proficiency:

> [to] identify and interact with diverse interests, mediate differences, and undertake negotiation and consensus building to help different constituencies

reach agreement in the face of new global energy and climate challenges. (Birch and Silver, 2009: 121)

This last skill recognizes the importance of diverse perspectives, although it has taken nearly a century for the profession to acknowledge so publicly the value of diversity. Unfortunately, there is less unity on how to achieve such diversity and who should be included in a set of diverse perspectives. In a review article for the one hundredth anniversary of the first planning conference, Dalton (2009) reviewed a list of the most influential books in planning submitted by the members of the Editorial Board of the *Journal of the American Planning Association* and concluded that much work remains to be done since issues of race, poverty, and gender were almost completely ignored.

Planning and Women

The struggle for full inclusion of women within the field of planning provides a number of important lessons for making planning more aware of and inclusive of LGBT people. In the United States the movement to incorporate women in planning took many years and only happened through determined advocacy, first around the right to vote, and later around the right to work. At the beginning of the last century women were not allowed to vote, cities were considered unsafe places for women, and planning was thought to be an unsuitable career for a woman (Hendler and Harrison, 2000). Wilson (1991) suggests that during this period urban reformers (who at the time happened to be almost exclusively male) viewed the presence of unaccompanied women in the city as a sign of moral turpitude and a cause of urban disorder. Spain (2001) provides a quite different account of the ways that women organized to make cities better places during the late nineteenth and early twentieth centuries by creating a variety of redemptive places such as settlement houses and women's organizations. Women like Catherine Bauer (Birch 1994a) and Mary Kingsbury Simkhovitch (Wirka, 1994) were not formally employed as planners but made significant contributions to the field of housing as well as broader social reform which at the time was labeled "municipal housekeeping" (Birch, 1994b).

The women's movement also demonstrated the importance of defining more precisely the link between planning and women's lives which has important ramifications for the contemporary struggle to include LGBT issues within mainstream planning. After the vast suburban expansion of the post-World War Two era feminist planners pointed out the sexist nature of cities and the planners who shaped them (Hayden, 1981). Others have argued persuasively that cities and their public spaces are distinctly gendered and that planning needs to expand to include a gender agenda (Sandercock and Forsyth, 1992). Some scholars have argued that it is important to first identify and then work to reduce the visible and invisible boundaries that constrain women's full participation in the life of the city

(Miranne and Young, 2000). Fainstein and Servon (2005) have suggested that a gendered lens provides a perspective that allows broad issues such as universal childcare, transportation solutions that relieve the double burden of home-making and paid labor, and housing design that makes life easier for families.

Furthermore, several scholars argued that in order to expand planning practice to include women's issues, more women needed to be included within the profession. Leavitt (1981) noted that during the 1950s the number of professional planners doubled from 1,000 to 2,000, but only 100 of these were women and by the 1970s less than fifteen percent of professional planners were women. The 1979 decision of the American Planning Association to create a Division of Women and Planning was a critical step in recognizing the importance of women's roles in the city and opening the field of planning to women. The formation of this Division generated considerable opposition from some APA board members who felt that it was not appropriate to create a division for the purposes of advocacy (Macris, n.d.). In response, the newly formed Division leadership opted to focus on "the impact of planning on the needs of women as clients, rather than on the status and needs of professional women planners" (Macris, n.d.: 3).

Opening the profession to women was a first step, but ensuring that more women were trained in the field of planning required more work within the planning academy. In 1986 a group of women who taught in planning schools held an initial meeting in which they noted the lack of women in faculty positions within the academy as well as difficulties in getting feminist oriented publications accepted by mainstream planning journals (Howe and Hammer, 2002). The subsequent creation of the Faculty Women's Interest Group (FWIG) within the Association of Collegiate Schools of Planning in 1991 marked another milestone in making the planning academy fully accessible to and sensitive to the perspectives of women.

Planning and People of Color

Similarly, there are important lessons for the inclusion of LGBT individuals and community concerns within the field of planning that can be drawn from the track record of planning with respect to race and ethnicity. First it is essential to acknowledge the pernicious effects of discrimination and racism both in local government and within the field of planning. Unfortunately persistent racism during much of the twentieth century complicated efforts by some planners to address issues of urban inequality. After the 1909 planning conference which emphasized the City Beautiful over the Social Reform movement, years of discrimination and neglect by municipal officials and planners resulted in inner cities that were characterized by poverty, violent crime, and despair. Urban policies such as restrictive covenants and redlining had also reinforced racially distinct neighborhood boundaries. Planners had contributed to this dysfunction by adopting zoning codes based on family definitions that pathologized the African-American family (Ritzdorf, 2000). The abuse of municipal regulations had created a separate and unequal society (Goldsmith and Blakeley, 1992), a virtual American version of apartheid (Massey and Denton, 1993).

This pattern of discrimination was met with organized and determined resistance by the African-American community through a variety of protest actions that demanded full civil rights. Though these marches and sit-ins attracted widespread attention, real change was slow in coming. During the long hot summers of the 1960s race riots erupted in the Watts neighborhood of Los Angeles, as well as neighborhoods in Detroit, Chicago, and Washington, DC, forcing urban officials and planners to sit up and begin to pay closer attention. Furthermore, the assassination of Dr. Martin Luther King touched off such widespread rioting in 168 US cities (Kweit and Kweit, 1998) and profoundly re-shaped the planning agenda with regard to the "inner city."

In the aftermath of these protests, local government officials began to take notice of conditions in the worst urban areas. Regrettably, there was little effort to gain detailed understanding of conditions in the inner city and few attempts to include minority community residents. For example, during slum clearance efforts in the West End of Boston in the 1960s, the failure of planning authorities to communicate with inner city residents during implementation exacerbated the negative impacts (Fincher and Iveson, 2008). June Thomas (1998: 201) suggested "that city improvement efforts, in the context of racial oppression, can be racially oppressive." Huw Thomas (2000) has suggested that the categories of race and ethnicity must be deconstructed to highlight their socially constructed nature. This confusion of identity categories certainly added to the failure of planners to grasp the dynamics of life in the inner city and the lack of sensitivity to issues of injustice.

> A greater understanding of the connections between the black urban experience and urban planning history could develop a higher level of awareness about racial injustice. Such awareness, combined with knowledge of practical tools for promoting equity, could go a long way toward allowing planners to help break the historic linkage between urban development and racial oppression. (J. Thomas, 1994: 9).

The above quote provides a critical lesson for increasing the inclusion of the LGBT community in planning decision-making. Although it is often acknowledged that planning requires the full participation of minority populations, the plethora of minority identity categories complicates the determination of who should participate. Early attempts to resuscitate the old Social Reform movement through "advocacy planning" (Davidoff, 1965) on behalf of minority groups had only limited success. A later effort to re-orient planning practice to promote "equity planning" with broader participation and more inclusive categories (Krumholz and Forester, 1990) was somewhat more successful.

Institutional support has been another critical step in bringing issues of race and ethnicity into sharper focus within planning discourse and the profession at large. For example the establishment of the Planning and the Black Community Division (PBCD) of the American Planning Association in 1989 provided a forum for planners, administrators, public officials, students, and other APA members to address issues of significance to communities of color and planners of color. However, there are still concerns about the low level of participation by minorities in planning. A recent PBCD newsletter promoted a conference to address the questions of "Why are so few people of color in the planning profession? Why are so few people of color APA members?" (PBCD Newsletter, November 2003: 6).

In recent years several other specialized divisions of the American Planning Association have been formed. In 2004 an Indigenous Planning Division was created followed in 2005 by the Latinos in Planning Division. This organizing by planners of color in a national institution has been an important element in raising critical issues from their various communities. Apparently minority planners do feel they have made a substantial contribution to enabling and empowering communities of color to engage with the planning process (J. Thomas, 2008), but there are not yet sufficient numbers to make a substantive impact. The formation of a Planners of Color Interest Group (POCIG) in 2008 within the Association of Collegiate Schools of Planning may reinforce the continuing need to recruit and train planners of color to work in the field of planning.

Some LGBT activists have argued that the experiences of women and people of color with respect to fighting discrimination should be the model for LGBT activists working for civil rights as well as for those who support increased inclusion in planning decisions that shape existing communities. This book takes the perspective that while these prior movements have important lessons for the inclusion of LGBT issues and needs within planning practice, there are also a number of important differences. Some queer theorists have criticized the LGBT civil rights movement as "minoritarian" (Corber and Valocchi, 2003) resulting in a set of fixed identity categories that may exclude other sexual and gender non-conforming minorities who do not identify as narrowly gay or lesbian, although they do challenge heteronormative expectations.

Resistance to Planning for the LGBT Community

The previous section on Planning and Inclusion makes clear that the planning agenda is in large part shaped by those in power, and does not readily expand to include other minority groups without sustained pressure from specific interest groups. It is therefore not surprising that there has been an ongoing struggle for the inclusion of the LGBT community into planning discourse as well as for the recognition that this minority community is affected by planning decisions. This continuing tension is evident from the controversy created after the American Planning Association (APA) first established a Gays and Lesbians in Planning Division (GALIP) in 1998. In response to the creation of this division, a number of planning practitioners expressed strong disapproval about an APA division oriented to LGBT planners through a series of "Letters to the Editor" in *Planning Magazine*, the official magazine of the American Planning Association (APA).[1] Although this dissent did not torpedo the newly formed GALIP Division, it did highlight the fact that there was, and possibly still is, a good deal of anger at the idea that LGBT issues deserve planning attention. The following excerpts from some of these letters are a sobering reminder of the strong resistance to LGBT issues from some individuals within the profession.

The negative comments about the creation of GALIP used several different types of argument. The first group of responses makes clear that some planners were deeply disturbed by the very presence of LGBT people within the organization.

> Any organization, particularly a professional one, should not pander to its members' race, gender, religious affiliation, or sexual preference. (R. Martin, Letters to the Editor, 2000. *Planning Magazine*, 66, 5: 27)

> There is absolutely no justification for APA endorsing *GALIP*. Theirs is a lifestyle choice, not a planning issue. Our efforts at providing good planning should be directed to people. Period. (R Fuller, Letters to the Editor, 1999. *Planning Magazine*, 65, 5: 26)

> It is unfortunate that *Planning* continues to publicize and support the gay lifestyle by publishing articles and letters ... People choose to become drug addicts. They also choose a criminal lifestyle, also moral issues. (R Betz, Letters to the Editor, 2000. *Planning Magazine*, 66, 5: 27)

The above comments are useful illustrations of the intensity of feelings about gays and lesbians within the planning profession and the nature of the discourse used to belittle or ignore these LGBT people. According to the Oxford English Dictionary (2009) the word pandering means "to gratify or indulge an immoral or distasteful desire, need, or habit or a person with such a desire." Applying the word pandering to issues like race, gender, religious affiliation, and sexual orientation suggests that each of these categories must be either immoral or highly distasteful, suggesting a profound intolerance for difference. In a similar vein, the above claim that good planners should only be planning for people, and not promoting "lifestyle choices" has a hidden sub-text that planning should only promote the status quo for people who are "normal." Linking gays and lesbians to drug users and criminals is an almost unbelievable demonization of LGBT people, indicating a powerful need to de-legitimize difference by labeling LGBT people as "other."

---

1 In fairness, a number of supportive and positive letters were also printed, so these views should not be taken as representative of the profession as a whole, but merely representative of those within the profession for whom the idea of a Gays and Lesbians in Planning Division is anathema.

The anti-LGBT bias in these letters, written ten years ago, reverberates in the recent wave of political ads aired in support of California's 2008 Proposition Eight which defined marriage as between one man and one woman. The depth and intensity of these feelings is reminiscent of the resistance to including women and minorities within the mainstream of political life, as well as in planning. The women's movement and the civil rights movement each first had to overcome similarly entrenched resistance before their demands for meaningful participation could be addressed. There is some reason for optimism because virulent anti-gay activism by the religious right has had a profound influence on the level and type of organizing by the LGBT community (Fetner 2008). Undoing this "othering" is not just the work of planners, but is being addressed more broadly by a variety of LGBT activists who are working to establish municipal anti-discrimination ordinances in more than 100 cities across the United States. There is a lot more work to do in this arena because obviously in many parts of the US and the rest of the world any behavior classified as other is immediately marginalized and silenced. Chapman (Chapter 8, this volume) argues that the struggle for LGBT equality involves a variety of competing discourses about citizenship at the level of counties and municipalities that has a direct impact on LGBT planners.

Two more recent excerpts from *Planning Magazine* in response to the GALIP controversy raise the issue of the infamous "Gay Agenda," an issue that seems to have some currency among contemporary planners.

> By endorsing and allowing the *GALIP* division to exist, APA is allowing this group as a platform to spread their agenda, not furthering the planning profession. (B. Spivey, Letters to the Editor, 2000. *Planning Magazine*, 66, 5: 27)

> We have compromised our objectivity by our association with specific liberal and environmental agendas that have no compelling message or call to accountability. Too often, planners have conceded opportunities for leadership in order to gain affirmation from some quarters, for instance by creating subdivisions such as Gays and Lesbians in Planning that offer little benefit to the broader community. (Lecount, 2003. "Viewpoint," *Planning Magazine*, 69, 6: 46)

Both of these critics suggest that by allowing the creation of GALIP, the APA was guilty of abetting some unspecified agenda which was clearly liberal and probably gay. Using the "gay" agenda in this way is a neo-conservative trope designed to link gayness with the worst images of infection and disease. The insistence on morality and the denial of any valid LGBT planning issues is an example of a not very subtle hegemonic masculinity (Connell 1995) that can understand no perspectives other than its own. Entrenched heteronormative planners who for years have taken for granted their ability to define the urban "agenda" seem quite fearful that they are losing control. Both the women's movement and the civil rights movement confronted similar claims that were aimed at undermining the legitimacy of the women's agenda and the various Black, Latino(a), Asian, and Native American agendas. From the experience of earlier movements, it seems like the best antidote to such attitudes is the kind of regular, responsible, and unavoidable presence at national conferences of the sort that GALIP provides.

The final set of writers provide the most salient critique in arguing that there are no legitimate planning concerns related to the LGBT community. It is comments like the following that have particularly inspired this volume, as a vehicle for elaborating precisely why planning should and must take into account the needs of the LGBT community.

> The last time I checked, good urban form, safe neighborhoods, and watershed protection had nothing to do with race, sex, or sexual orientation. (K. Templin, Letters to the Editor, 1999. *Planning Magazine*, 65, 11: 23)

> I do not see the need to form such a division. Do gays and lesbians require larger lot sizes, narrower road rights-of- way, faster GIS systems, or unique natural resources? (C. Bahr, 1998. Letters to the Editor, *Planning*. 64, 12: 29)

> I continue to be baffled as to the purpose of the Gays and Lesbians in Planning Division. One's sexual preference is no more relevant to his or her pursuits as a professional planner than if he or she were a vegetarian or a Baptist (R. Dunn, Letters to the Editor, 2000. *Planning Magazine*, 66, 5: 27)

> I propose that APA disband all three special interest divisions (women, African Americans, and gays) that have no basis in the planning profession and are "points of view" rather than disciplines. (A.Vansen, Letters to the Editor, 1999. *Planning Magazine*, 65, 8: 27)

It is interesting to note that none of these writers mentions any particular LGBT issue which is NOT legitimate as a planning subject. There is simply a blanket condemnation of any issue related to the LGBT community as illegitimate. Each of the critics above seems to define planning as a wholly technical field (lot sizes and road widths) that has little to do with the people who use these facilities. The suggestion that the identity based divisions (Women, and the Black Community) should be disbanded since they lack any legitimate planning issues is startling. It would seem that the commitment to inclusion of a diversity of perspectives in planning as described earlier (Birch and Silver 2009), is not as widespread as some would like to believe. The chapters in this volume will address each of these points directly.

It is worthy of note that sometimes critiques of LGBT issues come from the left. In the 1950 and 1960s many leftist groups struggled with issues of homosexuality, in part because of the echoes of the very strong anti-gay rhetoric of Stalinism (Thorstad, 1995). The increasing gay and lesbian political activism of the 1970s created some openings for LGBT people within the leftist movement, but for a number of years sexuality remained a source of contention. For example, noted trans activist Leslie Feinberg (1996) describes feeling isolated in the Workers World Party until 1976 when a pamphlet was published with the title "Marxist Interpretations of Gay and Lesbian Oppression." This tract helped Feinberg and others realize that openly queer people might be welcome in the movement. Apparently some of the prejudice against queer individuals remains in this movement as evidenced by an off hand comment by a leftist planning faculty member that gay liberation is nothing more than "making it safe for gay gentrifiers to buy up poor people's houses and make a huge profit when they sell them." While there is clearly a grain of truth to this statement as indicated previously in the Castro, to assume that all LGBT people are wealthy male gentrifiers is a massive over-generalization and simplification of LGBT issues within planning.

These types of comments from both conservative and radical planning perspectives demonstrate the need for a queer interrogation of the field. A recent example of the continuing resistance to anything queer in public in some localities is the summary dismissal of Susan Stanton, a city manager in the city of Largo, FL who announced her intention to transition from male to female and was fired shortly thereafter in March 2007. (For a more in depth discussion of the silencing effect of this action, see Doan, Chapter 5). In many smaller cities expressing a queer public presence remains problematic and creates a void in public discussion of LGBT issues, let alone among planners.

This sensitivity to public concern is a partial explanation of why planning lags behind other related disciplines such as sociology, history, and geography. Even the sub-discipline of international development planning has made considerable progress in the past decade in expanding heteronormative conceptualizations of gender and sexuality (see for example Jolly 2000, Lind 2009, 2010, and Lind and Share 2003). These fields have already made substantial efforts to integrate queer theoretic perspectives into their analysis. Unfortunately, as noted above, the planning literature is mostly silent on queer issues. The reluctance to engage with LGBT issues is partly linked to the professionalization of planning as a career. At the same time the breadth of the field of planning, incorporating a wide range of disciplinary backgrounds and professional perspectives, adds to the complexity of finding any consensus on the need for a planning voice for the LGBT community. Because many planners work directly or indirectly with either public or private sector institutions, they are often directly accountable to elected local officials like those who fired Susan Stanton. While many jurisdictions have adopted LGBT inclusive ordinances suggesting some measure of recognition and support, there are still many local governments across the US that have not yet and are not likely to adopt such protections, much less express public support for LGBT populations. Because local public visibility currently enforces a conservative influence on the profession, planners within the academy need to show the way forward.

The Evolution of Gay and Lesbian Spaces

One of the recurrent criticisms seen in the previous sections was that "special interest groups" have nothing to do with "real" planning issues. In response the women's movement took great pains to document how planning had an impact on women's lives. Planners of color continue to be engaged in the same type of work to link legitimate planning issues to their particular interest groups (Black Community, Indigenous, Latino/a communities, etc.). The following section aims to set the stage for the same kind of discourse vis-à-vis the LGBT community. This section uses a brief review of the evolution of LGBT neighborhoods and the sometimes queer discourse that surrounds their evolution to examine a number of important planning issues for the LGBT community.

Cities have been linked with homosexuality throughout history, but the modern city seems inextricably linked to the evolution of gays and lesbians (Abraham, 2009). In recent years there have been numerous historical analyses of the presence of gays and lesbians within cities. Prior to 1969 LGBT spaces were for the most part ephemeral and restricted to the most marginalized sex districts (Sides, 2006). Cities across the United States, including New York (Chauncey, 1994; Kaiser 1997), Philadelphia (Stein, 2000), Los Angeles (Kenney 2001), and San Francisco (Boyd, 2003) all had significant gay and lesbian populations that were for the most part hidden from public view, but nonetheless needed spaces in which to live, work, and seek entertainment.

Much of the early organizing in the United States was in response to overt harassment and discrimination against lesbian, gay, bisexual, and transgendered (LGBT) individuals. Because rural areas were perceived to be less tolerant, many LGBT people moved to cities where higher density created a measure of anonymity and also a critical mass of other non-conforming individuals. In the 1950s cities became the locus for more intensive organizing by LGBT groups. During this period in the United States two early gay rights groups were established, the Mattachine Society and the Daughters of Bilitis (D'Emilio, 1983) in Los Angeles and San Francisco. As the movement became more established other affiliated groups sprang up in cities across the nation. In spite of the organizing the LGBT community continued to experience numerous incidents of harassment, overt discrimination, and arrests for patronizing bars and other public venues. A violent street protest at Compton's Cafeteria in San Francisco by sexual and gender minorities may have been the first overt sign of resistance (Stryker, 2008). However, in 1969 a police raid on a gay bar in New York City known as the Stonewall Inn quickly grew into a three day uprising of lesbian, gay, bisexual, and transgendered (LGBT) citizens of New York City that is now known as the Stonewall rebellion (Kenney, 1998).

This high profile riot was the final straw that launched the movement for LGBT rights (D'Emilio, 1983). In the aftermath gay men across North America became more assertive of their rights to visibly exist in urban spaces, playing an important role in the gentrification of declining inner city neighborhoods (Lauria and Knopp, 1985). These neighborhoods, sometimes called gayborhoods, became important social gathering points for previously marginalized gay men (Whittle, 1994) as well as sites for capital accumulation through home investments (Knopp, 1990). In addition, they provided a key locus for political organizing and community building (Castells, 1983), ensuring a somewhat more inclusive alternative to the hetero-normative nature of most urban spaces (Bell et al. 1994). The election of Harvey Milk to the San Francisco Board of Supervisors was a watershed in the emergence of a gay political identity (Shilts, 1982). Other gay urban villages were often centered on a cluster of gay bars and bookstores that were marked by rainbow flags and other visible symbols of the emerging gay identity (Nash, 2006; Reed, 2003).

Lesbians also asserted their rights to space, though sometimes more quietly than gay men. Adler and Brenner (1992) suggested that lower incomes and a higher likelihood of child custody shifts their residential location choice towards less expensive areas with more attractive schools and other neighborhood amenities. Lesbian clusters also existed in places like Park Slope, Brooklyn (Rothenburg 1995) and in smaller cities like Northampton, Massachusetts (Forsyth, 1997). Lesbians were particularly sensitive to the heterosexing of urban spaces (Valentine 1993) and often did not create visibly marked territory in the built environment like gay villages (Peace 2001), but instead embodied their identity through clothing, hair style, or other symbols like pinkie rings, labris earrings, rainbows, or simply an overt gaze to signify spaces and to quietly proclaim an identify for themselves (Valentine, 1995, 1996). This subtlety has often meant that lesbian neighborhoods are not as visible as overtly gay areas but are often co-located in more bohemian "spaces of difference" (Podmore, 2001). Rooke (2007) suggested that lesbian bars exist not as fixed places, but as temporary (i.e. rotating) women's nights in various locations allowing communities of like-minded women to blend into the built environment (Wolfe, 1997). Dubrow (Chapter 3) notes the challenge of preserving such spaces for posterity, but provides examples of how some LGBT communities have been able to organize and preserve their history.

To date, there has been little discussion of these developments in the major planning journals with two notable exceptions. Forsyth's article (2001 and an updated version included as Chapter 2 in this volume) in the *Journal of Planning Literature* provides an overview of the implications for planning practice of the more visible role played by lesbian, gay, and bisexual individuals in cities and the surrounding areas. In the *Journal of Planning Education and Research* Frisch (2002) has written a trenchant critique of the heterosexist nature of many planning projects and highlights the need for a more inclusive planning practice. The important contributions of these two articles need to be updated and enhanced by recent advances in the field of queer studies which are included in this volume.

Queerying LGBT Spaces

As gay and lesbian neighborhoods became more visible, they became more recognizable as spaces of difference that some have called queer (cf. Bell and Valentine, 1995; Betsky, 1997; Ingram, et al. 1997; Binnie and Valentine, 1999). With visibility came commercialization and the rise of urban villages that function as cultural enclaves some of which are LGBT friendly (Bell and Jayne, 2004). Some of these new forms of cosmopolitan urbanism are globally diverse and highly tolerant spaces (Binnie et al. 2006), but other urban scholars began to question whether the idea of an inclusive queer space was merely a theoretical and often patriarchal construct (Nast 2002; Rushbrook, 2002). In fact many of these spaces excluded bisexuals (Hemmings, 2002), transgendered people (Namaste, 2000; Doan, 2001; Doan, 2007), and gender non-conformists in general (Whittle, 1996; Browne, 2006a).

These challenges to the notion of inclusive queer spaces were rooted in the development of an academic sub-discipline known as queer theory (for a more in depth treatment of this subject see Chapter 4 in this volume by Hendler and Backs). The field developed around the post-structuralist understanding that gender is a social construct which is not fixed but performative (Butler 1990). Queer theorists have recognized that fixed homosexual identities used by regulatory regimes use the homosexual "other" as a means of determining heteronormativity. Corber and Valocchi suggested that heteronormativity is:

> the set of norms that make heterosexuality seem natural or right and that organize homosexuality as its binary opposite. This set of norms works to maintain the dominance of heterosexuality by preventing homosexuality from being a form of sexuality that can be taken for granted or go unmarked. (2003: 4)

This understanding interrogated the notion that gay and lesbian identities are fixed and suggests instead that such identities as well as gender are in a state of flux (Jagose, 1996) that is contingent upon temporal, social, and cultural practices (Hines, 2006). Sullivan suggested that deconstructing identity in this way "aims to de-naturalize heteronormative understandings of sex, gender, sexuality, sociality, and the relations between them" (2003: 81). Doan (2010) argued that the heteronormative gendering of spaces creates a kind of gender tyranny that regulates gender non-conformists and especially transgendered people.

Understanding heteronormativity complicates the study of urban spaces and in particular the field of planning which attempts to understand and influence the form of the built environment. Some useful insights can be gained from a sister discipline, the geography of sexualities (Knopp and Brown, 2003; Knopp, 2007; Browne, Lim and Brown, 2007). Geographers working in this area have extended Butler's performativity to suggest that the performance of gender in space not only shifts with each instance, but in a very real way each performance also changes the space in which it is performed (Gregson and Rose, 2000;

Browne 2006b). Browne, et al. suggested that "space is not just the vessel in which things happen, but is actively constituted through the actions that take place" (2007: 9). This fluid performativity of space enabled some radical queer activists to create autonomous queer spaces that push the boundaries of both heteronormativity and homonormativity (Brown 2007).

This fluidity complicates the task of planning in several ways. First the identities of the LGBT community are not fixed, making it difficult for bureaucrats and planners to communicate with, much less actively listen to the needs of, these citizens. Second the uses of space are in some cases also in flux so that queer spaces shift and evolve far more rapidly than cumbersome comprehensive planning documents can comprehend. These challenges to professional planners are not insurmountable, but they do require sensitivity to issues of discrimination and injustice experienced by the LGBT community. Planners must re-examine the ways that zoning, land use regulations, and comprehensive planning documents operate as regulatory regimes at the intersection of sexuality and space. For example, in the late 1990s the City of New York under the leadership of Mayor Giuliani adopted what Smith (1998) called a series of "revanchist urban policies" including changes in the zoning codes to restrict "adult businesses" that were used to eviscerate gay oriented businesses (Warner 1999). Chapters 10 and 11 in this volume illustrate the way that zoning regulations in the United Kingdom and Australia have had similar effects.

Even when urban policies ostensibly aim to encourage the re-use of urban spaces and the creation of cosmopolitan and gay friendly urban villages as entertainment zones, there can be negative impacts. For example the city of Manchester's promotion of its Gay Village as a tourist attraction did result in rapid growth of the area (Binnie and Skeggs, 2006), but at the same time opened the previously "safe space" to large numbers of young heterosexual men and women making many LGBT people (and especially women) feel less safe (Moran et al. 2001). The queer theory approach would be to ask whether such policies promote and preserve diverse understandings of identity and sexual expression or whether they aim to preserve the heteronormative vision of order. Is the goal the creation of a "good city" and if so whose definition of good? Is the goal the promotion of a "just city" and if so then whose sense of justice should be applied? Such re-evaluation is not impossible, but it does require greater openness to change and the ability to undertake reflexive analysis of the inclusive nature of the aims of planning. The authors in this volume recognize that it is time to integrate insights from queer theory into planning theory, and to demonstrate the importance of planning for the needs and perspectives of the LGBT community.

Contents of this Volume

This book seeks to address these concerns directly and demonstrate the legitimacy of the LGBT community within urban spaces and illustrate the ways that LGBT individuals are excluded and at times harmed by planning policies which refuse to recognize their legitimacy. As noted above, planning has at times resisted the incorporation of gay and lesbian concerns, much less other queer orientations and genders into the planning mainstream, leaving it somewhat theoretically outdated. The following chapters seek to address those critics of LGBT inclusion within the profession who continue to be "baffled" as to the relevance and need for LGBT inclusion within planning, as well as those who perhaps unconsciously persist in advocating that "there are no planning issues that face the profession" concerning the LGBT community. This volume incorporates contributions from both planning and geography that examine some of the fundamental assumptions of urban planning as they relate to the LGBT community.

The following chapters interrogate planning practice and pose questions for academic and professional planners about the ways that the queer community and its needs for spaces have shifted. What do those changes mean for the practice of planning 40 years after the North American Stonewall rebellion and looking forward to the next 40 years? To what extent do existing planning procedures constrain the evolution of queer communities or seek to commercialize such spaces to the benefit of large developers and the detriment of marginalized members of the LGBT community? How might planning practice change to provide more direct support to the evolution of the sometimes queer spaces in which LGBT people live, work, and play? How might planning goals and objectives seek to preserve and encourage this marginalized population?

The next section provides the theoretical framework for understanding the relationship between urban planning and the location of non-conformist populations, including sexual minorities and gender variant populations. The chapter by Ann Forsyth is a substantial expansion on her earlier *Journal of Planning Literature* article that makes the case that although LGBT people are marginalized, their concerns are not marginal to planning. The new material draws on the substantial literature from the geography of sexualities to expand the argument to the planning needs of transgendered and other queer populations from within as well beyond the US borders. The chapter by Gail Dubrow reflects and expands on an earlier article that examines the importance of preserving elements of the built environment that are important elements of LGBT history. The chapter by Sue Hendler and Michael Backs fills an important void in planning theory by integrating key concepts from queer theory into the theory and practice of planning. The chapter by Petra L. Doan provides a gendered perspective that heteronormative planning issues constitute a form of tyranny, the tyranny of gendered planning. Planning which is based on a narrowly defined gender dichotomy can have a profound impact on everyone, but falls especially heavily on those individuals who express their gender in ways that fall outside traditional expectations for gendered behavior. Finally the chapter by Katrin Anacker analyzes the growing trend of queer suburbanization across the United States, and provides insights into the needs and experiences of lesbians versus gay men in these areas. Although many early accounts of the evolution of the LGBT population explicitly discuss these populations in terms of the urban areas they inhabit, it is increasingly obvious that there is an LGBT presence in urban enclaves, suburban communities, and towns on the urban fringe.

The next section considers the importance of governance and political issues that affect sexual and gender minority populations. Andrew Gorman-Murray examines the way that multiple scales of urban governance across a metropolitan region can greatly complicate the planning task for LGBT people in the context of Australia. Tom Chapman explores the political economy of anti-discrimination efforts and shows the way local interest groups skewed the urban policy debate, especially with reference to an LGBT inclusive anti-discrimination ordinance in Orlando, Florida. Finally, Tiffany Muller Myrdahl expands on this theme and examines the way that the policy hyperbole that surrounds efforts to promote creative cities complicates the cultural politics of making cities more inclusive. In this chapter she examines the media hype in Canadian cities surrounding "creative city" investment proposals, and considers the consequences for the LGBT community of investments based on this supposedly "gay friendly" strategy.

The last section considers the ways that land use regulations are used to impose "order" on the urban community in ways that have negative effects on the lives of LGBT minorities. Phil Hubbard reviews the use of planning regulations to control "adult businesses" in general and then examines the ways that the sex industry is regulated in the United Kingdom. Jason Prior and Penny Crofts consider another urban policy area with large LGBT planning implications, the regulation of sex-related businesses in Sydney Australia.

Chapter 12 is composed of a brief summation of three landmark articles in planning and queer urban spaces. Each of the original authors has provided current commentary on the climate in which they wrote these articles and the extent to which they feel this has shifted in the intervening years. The first commentary is provided by Mickey Lauria, past president of the Association of Collegiate Schools of Planning and Larry Knopp, past chair of the Sexuality and Space Interest group of the Association of American Geographers. Early in their careers they co-wrote one of the first articles (1985) to articulate the role of the gay community in urban gentrification, and their commentary considers how the situation has changed and how much remains to be done. Sy Adler and Johanna Brenner reflect on their seminal article on gender and space (1992) that helped to expand the discussion about gay men in the city by adding the importance of lesbians in urban spaces. They highlight the continuing dispersal of the gay and lesbian community and wonder how differences in the life course will affect this trend. Finally Michael Frisch revisits his article (2002) which was a challenge to academic planners about the heteronormative nature of much planning practice. He suggests that planning remains a technology of heteronormativity and that the practice of planning has been slow to adjust to wider social changes. Much has changed in the field of urban planning since these key articles were published, but much remains to be accomplished.

The book concludes with a summary chapter by Petra L. Doan that points the way forward to creating a revitalized and reframed planning practice that is truly inclusive of LGBT communities and their concerns. Planning for people whose identities are queer is certainly a challenge for already over-burdened urban planners. Some planning efforts have tried to reinforce the commercialization of the primarily gay space and others have tried to encourage the development of heterogeneous cultural areas where lesbians might feel more welcome. Both approaches have their limitations, and planning for the fluidity of the wider queer community is even more challenging. This chapter provides some basic recommendations for planning officials on how to plan with and for evolving queer communities.

PART I
Planning Theory and Practice

Chapter 2
Queerying Planning Practice: Understanding Non-Conformist Populations

Ann Forsyth[1]

This chapter examines the implications for planning *practice* of the emergence of gay men, lesbians, and related non-conformist groups. Since the mid-1970s, there has been a growing and methodologically sophisticated analysis of this increasingly visible population published in the areas of urban studies, urban sociology, geography, and planning. Very few researchers in these fields specialize exclusively in studying gay, lesbian, or queer populations. However, many researchers have been drawn to work on this issue through more general interests in such issues as gender, gentrification, social movements, social stigma, local politics, economic development, travel and tourism, leisure, public space, social services, and community formation.

A significant body of this work has been chiefly concerned with describing and analyzing the population in sociological or geographical terms. Theoretical writing has also been published around the issue of sexuality and space, but much of this work stems from the literary tradition or from political activism and is quite personal, anecdotal, or polemical. While important it can seem very far from the practice of planning.[2] However, an increasing amount of research and writing is much more clearly oriented toward concrete urban and regional concerns of the type that interest planning *practitioners*. Cities and towns around the US, and in several other countries, have also been developing strategies that are sensitive to these population groups—for example Chicago's gay-themed North Halsted Street streetscape design (Pasternak 1997). The creative class debate of the past

---

1 This chapter represents a considerable revision and expansion of Forsyth (2001).

2 The literature in gay and lesbian, or queer studies, is not always easily applicable to planning. I think this reflects less the character of the subject matter than the interdisciplinary character of the field, where people working from critical and interpretive traditions in literature or from a more contentious activist stance are then read by those more steeped in social science methods. Several interesting collections that contain work with this kind of emphasis also have a geographical or spatial emphasis and thus are more accessible to planners (Ingram et al. 1997; Bell and Valentine 1995a). Frisch (2002) draws connections between such theories and planning. While not easily obtainable, a number of masters theses in planning cover issues like commercial development (Lee 1980) or queer persons of color (Reyes 1993).

decade, for good and for bad, has raised the profile of gay-friendly areas (Florida 2002a, 2005, Florida et al. 2008). Gay and lesbian organizations—from business groups to event organizers—also interact with planners. This chapter aims to make this significant body of research, writing, and practice more accessible to planners. It demonstrates the diversity of the population and the broad range of connections between the gay, lesbian, and queer population and traditional planning issues such as neighborhood formation, economic development, zoning, and housing markets. The chapter's focus is on the situation in the US but it also draws on significant research and practice from all other inhabited continents. While there are certainly many gaps in this literature and practice, it is currently quite extensive.

The chapter first briefly outlines a history of the growth of US gay and lesbian populations, focusing particularly on their characteristics relevant to planning. It is a heterogeneous population with estimates of at least 10 million people in the US, equivalent to the population of Asian and Pacific Islanders in the US in the mid-1990s.[3] While white male owners of beautifully decorated houses are a very visible part of the population, recent census and survey data indicate a more economically and ethnically diverse group. Women in particular are likely to have low incomes.

The rest of the work reviews literature and practice in five areas that have attracted particular attention in planning and urban and regional studies: residential enclaves and neighborhoods, zoning and housing, business development including tourism and the creative city approach, historic preservation, and public space. The extent of these intersections demonstrates the core theme of this paper that although the population has been marginalized in the past, both by the wider society and within planning, their concerns and needs are not marginal to contemporary planning practice. Even when one takes a fairly narrow view of planning practice—as work conducted in mainstream government and non-profit organizations—the intersections are significant. (For those who see planning as a generic human activity, there are obviously more intersection as every person and organization plans. However, a purpose of this chapter is to show the connections between lesbians, gays, queers and even quite traditional planning issues.)

Within these planning areas the literature on enclaves and neighborhoods is most developed and indicates that gay men, and in a different and more complicated way lesbians, have had a significant role in revitalizing urban neighborhoods in North America (and to some extent Europe and Australia).[4] Attention has also recently focused on those not living in "gay ghettos." While in the past these more

---

3 Asian and Pacific Islanders were a fast growing population, going from 3 to 4 percent of the US population between 1990 and 1999 according to the US Current Population Survey. Available at: http://www.census.gov/population/estimates/nation/intfile3-1.txt.

4 Kenney (1998) also reviews this literature but in a chapter that is oriented toward the history of the population. Brouwer (1999), Up Close (1999), and Finucan (2000) contain useful, but brief, discussions of the intersections between gay, lesbian, and queer populations and planning issues.

dispersed groups have suffered from isolation, planners in suburban and exurban areas will increasingly interact with quite "out" populations.

The population still suffers from some forms of discrimination in housing markets and residential zoning, for example in the US being legally excluded from zones allowing only related individuals to live together. On the other hand, planners have also been active in counteracting NIMBY (Not In My BackYard) responses to projects such as group homes for people with HIV and AIDS. Of concern is the situation that gay and lesbian youth unable to live with their families make up a significant proportion of the young homeless, highlighting the housing difficulties caused by discrimination *within* the family. In addition after many decades of gentrification gay, lesbian, and queer populations with lower incomes have found it difficult to find housing options in neighborhoods that have been known as queer spaces (Collins 2004).

Work in economic development planning did not deal much with the business and tourism patterns of the population until work on the creative class developed substantial attention in the past ten years. However, even earlier the GLBT population had been of great interest to marketers and the popular press. Throughout, popular and marketing literature has focused on the more affluent parts of the population. Planners could add a much needed concern with such issues as business opportunities for those who are not as wealthy. In addition, the increasing numbers of cities marketing to gay, lesbian, and queer populations also provide models for economic development and tourism strategies aimed at groups concerned about the potential for discrimination.

Like many marginalized groups, the history of gay men, lesbians, and related non-conformist groups has not been prominent in historic preservation efforts. However, as buildings and sites from the 1950s and beyond are becoming eligible for listing in the US National Register and related state and local lists, planners can play a role in preserving the early history of the contemporary gay and lesbian movements. Other sites that are already listed can be reinterpreted in light of gay, lesbian, and queer history, as part of a wider move by planners to be more inclusive in preservation efforts.

Finally, in the area of public space, while harassment incidents and protests have received the most press attention, the issue of displays of same sex public affection—such as handholding—raises key planning questions about safety in public spaces. More controversial is the issue of public erotic behavior.

The chapter is based on three sources of information: academic and professional literature was supplemented with accounts from major gay and mainstream press, as well as a limited number of primary sources such as original reports and organizations' promotional materials. The press and primary sources were used to fill in the many gaps that still exist in the literature. Given the rapid increase in visibility of the populations in the 1990s and 2000s—due to increasing openness and activism of the population that has been reflected in press coverage—these sources have the advantage of reporting on current developments much more quickly than academic journals. However, the chapter does not draw much from more inaccessible literature such as privately circulated conference papers.

Finally, this chapter requires a note on language and politics. The use of the terms gay men and lesbians is often associated with a particular stance that sees gay and lesbian identity as relatively fixed (see discussion in Smith and Windes 1999). A broader and in some ways more inclusive category, queer, is frequently used by a younger generation more influenced by the flexibility of gender categories (see Chapter 4). "Queer theory" argues that while gender identity is both crystallized and lived as immutable, understanding of the nature of one's identity can be seen to have changed tremendously in the last century and to be relatively flexible within one's own life (Doan 2010 as well as Chapter 5). Drawing on the work of theorists such as Foucault (1978) and Butler (1990) these writers point out that identities are created by performance—so that a very "womanly" person is doing a particular kind of gender performance very well (Butler)—or by language and discourse (Foucault).[5] People living as queer can be unsettling to gay, lesbian, and heterosexual people who regard sexuality as fixed or natural. In addition, other groups claim separate attention including bisexuals, and transsexual and transgendered persons (these latter two groups identifying as a different gender than the sex ascribed at birth). These groups have complicated relationships to gays and lesbians and have not always been welcomed in gay and lesbian organizations. They have also received less attention in writing relating to spatial issues, and are often folded into the other groups or included as "queer" (at least in shorthand). This has led to many acronyms: GLB, GLBQ, LGBT, GLBQT and so on (see also Spain 2001b).

This chapter does not take a position in these debates and uses the terms gay men and lesbians, or queer, in a relatively interchangeable and inclusive way, reflecting usage in the particular cases and research under discussion. Many people actually use different terms to describe themselves in different situations so the division between "gay men and lesbians," or "queers," is not as rigid as it can sometimes seem in academic debates. From time to time the chapter uses the term "gay" to indicate the population as a whole, rather than the specific terms gay men, lesbians, queers, and so on, although as this is not agreed upon by all I have tried to avoid it. The chapter also calls the various groups together the "population" although I am fully aware that it is composed of a large number of sub-groups.

In political actions around gay, lesbian, and queer issues in the public domain Forest points out there have been two basic approaches—a more confrontational group that he labels "liberationist" and a more "assimilationist tradition that tries to work within existing political structures" (1995: 137–8). These positions cut across the queer/gay and lesbian divide; while queers can be seen as more radical, this is often at a personal and not a public level. From time to time planners will face such situations as the "kiss-ins" of Queer Nation in the early 1990s. However, the organizations with which planners will probably have the longest-term interactions

---

5 This can obviously be extended to national and ethnic identities among others.

are likely to be assimilationist. West Hollywood's incorporation, Forest argues, is part of the assimilationist tradition, for example. Groups like gay and lesbian business organizations, those using government funds to develop housing for HIV positive persons, or the American Planning Association division GALIP (Gays and Lesbians in Planning), have all chosen to work within existing structures. The Halsted Street streetscape in Chicago—discussed below—assimilates a gay[6] area into a larger landscape of diverse neighborhoods supported by local government, presumably for reasons of local politics and economic development. The work reviewed in this chapter and dealing directly with queer issues typically takes this assimilationist approach. It is also the main approach of planning itself as a social movement or an approach to social change; even those in the progressive tradition often work inside government, in quasi government organizations, or create parallel institutions that interact with governments, in order to achieve social reform or social transformation.

The Population

There is quite a bit of debate about the emergence of a distinctively gay and lesbian population in the US and elsewhere. Some researchers claim a long tradition, going back for millennia, and others locate the emergence of the contemporary form of the population only at the end of the nineteenth century or even into the twentieth (LeVay and Nonas 1995). Those using earlier dates tend to focus on behavior patterns; those using later dates on contemporary concepts of identity.[7]

Population estimates are difficult to make (Kahan and Mulryan 1995). Black et al. (2000) estimated a range of 2.5 percent of men and 1.4 percent of women in the various queer categories or about 6 million people; this also includes unpartnered people.[8] Estimates based on the Centers for Disease Control's Behavioral Risk Factor Surveillance System (BRFSS) with data from 1996 to 2000 found less than 0.5 percent of households were same sex couples (Carpenter 2004: 81). The 2006–2008 American Community Survey finds approximately 0.3 percent of households are male unmarried partners; another 0.3 percent are female unmarried partners. Gates using the National Survey on Family growth estimated a total of 8.8 million GLB people in the US or 4.1 percent of adults (Gates 2006). For comparison, according to the 2006–2008 American Community survey the number of American Indians in the US is approximately 3.5 million, including children.

---

6 It is largely gay male—another name for the area is Boystown.

7 This is a large and complex literature. Chauncey (1994) and LeVay and Nonas (1995) contain more readable accounts.

8 Earlier estimates of 10 percent of the population were based primarily on interpretations of the Kinsey studies carried out in the 1930s and 1940s and using life history techniques. The Kinsey studies themselves did not make these estimates (Chauncey 1994: 170).

Of course this is not a homogenous population and it is divided by income, ethnicity, location, family status, religion, and a number of more subtle political differences. Marketing studies have been very interested in the buying power of gays and lesbians and have tended to find that the group is young, urban, travel oriented, and with relatively high incomes. These studies have been based on surveys of people in locations such as "gay and lesbian bars, gay pride parades, and other gay-identified events" or of readers of gay magazines (see review in Philipp 1999: 70). However, more recent research has pointed out that the samples used in these studies are unlikely to be representative of the population as a whole. Although there are no really complete sources of data on the gay and lesbian population, researchers have been working with larger and more representative databases to build up more comprehensive pictures of the group.

In 1990 the US Census asked a question about unmarried partner couples and in doing this received replies from a fairly large number of same sex unmarried partner couples—9.2 percent of all unmarried partner couples reporting to the census were same sex (Keene and Stoesen 1994). This was biased in a number of ways. One member of the couple had to be person number one on the census form, it only measured couples and presumably under-reported even this group, and census workers reclassified some couples as different household types (Gates 2001). It nevertheless represented an important first step toward creating a national data set. The 2000 census had an increase of over 300 percent in the number of same sex couples counted, in part due to more such couples identifying themselves and in part due to changes in data collection and cleaning; by the time of the 2005 American Community Survey the number had risen still further (Gates 2001).

Several studies have used Census data and information from other large social surveys to examine household incomes. Klawitter and Flatt (1998) used 1990 census data to examine incomes of gay and lesbian persons. This study, based on Public Use Micro Sample five percent sample data, had two findings related to overall incomes of this population. First, areas with anti-discrimination policies did not have different incomes for same sex couples, although these couples tended to live in higher-earning centers so had relatively higher incomes like everyone else in those centers (Klawitter and Flatt 1998: 658). In addition, and in contrast to the perception of affluent gays, they found that married men earned significantly more than unmarried men in both same and different sex couples, on the order of 26–32 percent. At the household level male-male couples' household incomes were basically the same as married couples even with two male incomes (varying within one or two percentage points depending on different kinds of employment protections in place). While women in both same sex and different sex *unmarried* partner couples earned more than married women—with the same sex couple members earning 17–21 percent more, and the different sex couple members earning 8–4 percent more—in both cases this was explained by these unmarried women working *more hours* (Klawitter and Flatt 1998: 674–5). Same sex couples in the sample were also more highly educated than other couples so it is surprising that they did not earn even more than others of their sex per hour

(Klawitter and Flatt 1998: 660). However, at the *household level*, female-only couples were the worst off, earning 18 to 19 percent less than married couple families because they lacked a high-earning married man. Different sex unmarried partner couples earned 11–16 percent less than married couples. That is, 1990 census data indicated that married couples were as affluent as gay male couples and much more affluent than lesbian couples when controlling for location. This was the case even though married women worked less than lesbians and were more poorly educated, and gay men had two male earners.

These findings were similar to those of Badgett (1995) who used econometric analyses of the General Social Survey from the National Opinion Research Center at the University of Chicago. From 1989 onwards the survey collected data on sexual behavior as well as income, occupation, and employment. This has the advantage of examining a wider range of people than the census unmarried partner couples, but even pooling data from 1989, 1990, and 1991 it only produced a sample of 4426 complete responses, of whom 1680 were employed full time and 4.8 percent had had same sex partners in adult life. Badgett controlled for current full-time work, experience, education, occupation, marital status, and region and found gay and bisexual men earning 11–27 percent less than heterosexual male workers. Lesbians and bisexual women earned slightly less than heterosexual women but in an inconsistent pattern when controlling for all factors. However, as they tended to be disproportionately in lower income occupations their actual incomes were in fact very low, in line with others in those low income occupations (Badgett 1995: 736, 737).

More recently Carpenter (2004) used data from the BRFSS for 1996 to 2000 to examine incomes. This survey identifies unmarried same sex partners living in households with only two adults, coding them as a special household type. Carpenter again confirmed the penalty paid by the same sex unmarried partners in relation to married couples; and in particular the lower incomes of female only couples.

Overall, the popular perception of affluent gays and lesbians has not been borne out by the most systematic research to date. Some readers have commented that the equivalence of gay male and heterosexual married couple incomes may hide differences in disposable income due to the presence or absence of children. However, not all married couples have children, their expense to the household varies greatly and is of a limited duration, and there are a number of economic benefits given by children (from tax deductions to help in old age). Gay men and (particularly) lesbians also do have children. In the 2000 census while 46 percent of married couple households and 43 of different sex unmarried partners had children under 18, so did 34 percent of female and 22 percent of male same sex partner households (Simmons and O'Connnell 2003: 9). While certainly this is an issue, married couples are not necessarily uniformly at a disadvantage because of the costs of having children.

There has also been some reporting of data on ethnicity. Of same sex couples in the 2000 census, 72 percent of householders in same sex couples were white alone (not another race or Latino) compared with 78 percent of married couples (Census 2000 PHC-T-19.) In addition, 11 percent of same sex couples were African American compared with 7 percent of married couples; the figures for Latinos were 12 percent versus 9 percent. Using special tabulations Simmons and O'Connell report that in 2000 while 7.4 percent of married couples were of different races or origins (a category that includes those of Hispanic or Latino background), 15.3 percent of male and 12.6 percent of female same sex couples were of these mixed backgrounds (Simmons and O'Connell 2003: 12). The 1990s census reported that while whites generally dominated the same sex partner census population, in Detroit 65.4 percent of census same sex unmarried partner couples were African Americans compared with 75 percent of all unmarried partner couples.

Overall this highlights the situation that while affluent gay men may be the most obvious in popular culture because of their buying power, the population as a whole is quite diverse with some major sex differences in terms of incomes and the possibility of ethnic differences in male/female distribution (or at least reporting). These income and ethnicity data, although limited in many ways, do start to show a more complex picture of the population which as a whole is less affluent than previously thought.

However, the *visibility* of more wealthy sections of the population may have suppressed interest among planners, especially those interested in social issues who might be uncertain about whether such an affluent population deserves their attention. In contrast, more conservative planners interested in business development and tourism may see the group more positively in economic terms (even if this is to some extent an inaccurate perception) but have moral concerns. The overall result has been a lack of planning attention and even a perception that the concerns of gay, lesbian, and queer people are marginal to the core concerns of planning (whether in its more mainstream or activist dimensions). The one exception has been the creative class debate but that has focused attention on affluent design leaders to the neglect of others. The rest of the chapter examines recent work that in fact makes the connection to the core concerns of planning.

Residential Enclaves and Neighborhoods

In planning practice, neighborhoods are often seen as a basic building block of urban areas, and much attention has been paid to neighborhood growth, revitalization, and stability. In the US neighborhood change has been the most prominent issue in research about the intersections between planning and gay, lesbian, and queer populations, although suburbanization has also attracted attention. In fact it is the only part of the literature that has developed over a number of decades—with studies being replicated in a way that develops a cumulative knowledge base (e.g. Castells 1983 partially replicated by Adler and Brenner 1992 and Forsyth 1997a, 1997b). With a few isolated exceptions, all the other areas dealt with in this chapter have only made it onto the practice and academic radar screen in the 1990s and 2000s and so the work is more exploratory.

Historically, there were some relatively public gay neighborhoods or service concentrations in the early twentieth century in places like Greenwich Village and Harlem in New York (Chauncey 1994). However, significant residential neighborhoods, concentrations of stores and services, and ongoing public events, only really emerged from the 1950s onward, with gay male neighborhoods becoming quite obvious in many major North American cities in the 1970s.

The first significant body of work concerning gays and space was focused on these neighborhoods, their commercial areas, and some more scattered "gay places" such as gay bars (Castells 1983, review in Kenney 1998, Weightman 1980, 1981).[9] Harry's 1974 article on "Urbanization and the Gay Life" used directories of gay male and lesbian bars to correlate bar clientele with city size for over 2,000 bars in the US. This article was a pioneering attempt to bridge from earlier work on the sociology of sexual deviance to a new and more positive interest in the social practices of the emerging gay and lesbian social movements.

Work closer to the core of urban geography and urban sociology followed by the late 1970s. In 1978 Lyod and Rowntree, studying radical feminists as well as gay men, argued that the populations were generally dispersed but did point to some gay male neighborhoods in San Francisco. In the same year Ettorre (1978) published an analysis of a "lesbian feminist ghetto" in London composed of a group of 50 women squatting in a row of semi-detached houses in Lambeth in London. This housing cluster existed over a six-year period from 1971 to 1978 after which most of the buildings were demolished.[10] The residential group formed a core for a wider group of 150 non-resident feminists.

A year later, Wolf's (1979: 98) work on lesbians, while arguing that they were spread across San Francisco, mentioned that they tended to concentrate in specific, low income, inner neighborhoods. In that same year Levine published a study that used gay business directories to create dot maps of "gay ghettos," mostly male, in Boston, New York, Chicago, San Francisco, and Los Angeles. Also in 1979 Murray published related research on Toronto's gay male population arguing that it formed a "community" in a very strict sociological sense. In the environmental design literature that year, Winters published an account of new kinds of revitalizing urban neighborhoods and included gay neighborhoods among these—along with heterogeneous, chic, and artists' neighborhoods.

Since these early studies in the 1970s the literature has expanded as the population became more visible and activist and as researchers discovered more intersections with planning and urban studies. An early model used to analyze this

---

9   There had been some earlier sociological work on gay bars as part of the literature on sexual deviance (Gagnon and Simon 1967).

10 The reason the squat began in the first place was that the buildings had been vacated for redevelopment but this was planned for three to five years in the future (Ettorre 1978: 515).

group was the quasi-ethnic community model where gay enclaves were compared with immigrant ones in terms of residential and commercial structure (see review in Forest 1995: 147–50, popular use in Kahan and Mulryan 1995, De Witt 1994).

The quasi-ethnic model drew on structural similarities between gay and ethnic enclaves. Factors examined included having a concentration of residences of the group, a fairly complete array of commercial enterprises and services, collective action, a sense of history of the group, shared norms, conflict management, and the presence of primary social groups within the population or of isolation from the wider society. These all mimicked the indicators developed to identify and analyze more traditional ethnic neighborhoods (see Murray 1979: 167–73, Levine 1979). As Murray (1979: 175) argued, even following the fairly strict criteria of structural functionalists and Chicago School sociologists who saw community as an entity rather than a process,[11] the "Toronto gay community [in the 1970s] fits the criteria for community as an entity at least as well as Toronto ethnic communities." Even Lyod and Rowntree (1978: 79) who characterized the spatial distribution of radical feminists and gay men as "dispersed," nevertheless claimed that they were a typical form of community, "a community without propinquity." While without concentration in terms of residential areas—with one exception, a neighborhood of gay men—groups did meet at some central places or "nodes" in similar ways to other common interest groups (Lyod and Rowntree 1978: 81).

The comparison of gay/lesbian and ethnic neighborhoods came in for some subsequent criticism. Some see these kinds of studies as ignoring changes in identities and as not taking account of culture (Davis 1995). The character of kinship is another difference. However, the conceptualization was a useful step forward in terms of providing an initial model for the spatial character of these enclaves and showing that on many criteria they shared strong resemblances with other kinds of enclaves that were deemed legitimate. This was interesting more generally in urban studies as it highlighted the growth of a type of urban neighborhood not based strictly on class or ethnic background.

Following this initial analysis, most attention on gay and lesbian neighborhoods has focused on issues of gentrification and urban redevelopment. Many early researchers, influenced by political economic accounts of urban change, used stage models that saw gay men and sometimes lesbians as part of a "pioneer group," looking for cheap rents. In moving to neighborhoods and renovating housing and forming businesses, these pioneers opened the neighborhoods to the more mainstream middle class—and more affluent gays and lesbians—as part of a gentrification process. Godfrey's research on San Francisco was typical of such work, describing a "general life cycle of gentrifying neighborhoods, a successional sequence proceeding through phases of *bohemian influx, middle-class transition, and bourgeois consolidation*" (Godfrey 1988: 177, italics in original). Godfrey

---

11 Sociological approaches emphasizing community formation as a conscious process include symbolic interactionists, ethnomethodologists, and structuralists (Murray 1979: 173).

(1988: 121) identified gays in all three stages of the gentrification of the Eureka Valley area in the 1960s and 1970s, transforming one section of this area into "the Castro." Gay men and lesbians were also part of the bohemian influx in a number of other San Francisco neighborhoods including the Mission District and Haight-Ashbury.

Kerstein, talking more generally about stage models, called the early in-moving, bohemian, group the "risk-oblivious," relocating because of low housing prices and architectural character and because they "value the demographic diversity of the area, and they prefer that the neighborhood substantially retain this characteristic" (Kerstein 1990: 622). This group was quite different to the final stage of gentrifiers, the "risk averse" who wanted more homogeneity, a more stable return on their housing investment, and a "relatively 'suburban' inner city environment" (Kerstein 1990: 622).

Stage models turned out to be only loosely predictive of gentrification processes, however the distinction between the earliest in-movers and later ones seemed to have some continuing salience even if neighborhoods did not "fully" gentrify (DeGiovanni 1983). Other researchers in fact found diverse gentrification processes occurring in different neighborhoods—in different locations relative to jobs, transport, and high status areas; with different histories; and different initial conditions in terms of socio-economic and architectural character (Beauregard 1990, Rose 1984). Generation also mattered. The first period of gentrifiers—in the 1950s and early 1960s—were part of a relatively unknown process and the economic returns were not so obvious. As gentrification has continued over a number of decades, those entering the housing market in the 1980s and 1990s were forced into more and more marginal locations—without some of the excellent locational features of the early gentrifying neighborhoods (Ley 1993).[12] Still more recently new construction and office conversions have been evident, as has gentrification in more varied locations (Visser and Kotze 2008).

Work also highlighted the cultural and social reasons for gay male populations, and to lesser extent lesbians, moving into urban neighborhoods (Castells 1983, Lauria and Knopp 1985). For example, in early research on gay men in San Francisco, Castells (1983) pointed to the variety of incomes in the gay male population, and the fact that community formation was important for social support and identity formation (also Lee 1980: 14–16). The gentrification process was not only an economic phenomenon. As he explained:

> Firstly, it is a fact that gays improved the quality of housing and urban space, mainly through renovations and maintenance. Secondly, it is clear that most neighborhoods that are now residential areas for gays were in a declining condition. Gay location in those neighborhoods … was a decisive element

---

12   In addition displacement does not always occur—Wagner (1995) found that minority residents increased in four gentrifying Baltimore neighborhoods, and the increase was substantial in one neighborhood due to the presence of subsidized housing units.

in improving the housing stock and the neighborhoods' commercial vitality. Thirdly, it is not true that all gays, or even a majority of them, were high income, middle class professionals, particularly in the South of Market and Tenderloin areas (San Francisco's skid row).

Many gays were able to live in their neighborhoods because they organized collective households and they were willing to make enormous economic sacrifices to be able to live autonomously and safely as gays....What the gays had in common with some non-family heterosexual groups is an alternative life style that had close ties with gay culture—a middle class movement that preferred residence in San Francisco, not because they were predominantly middle class, but because they valued personal experience and an active, social street life. In this sense, gays appear to have been a cultural vanguard for these people. (Castells 1983: 160, typographical errors corrected)

Some of the renovation that occurred in San Francisco was in fact the repair of rental properties not owned by the gay men. However it is interesting to note the case of South of Market (SOMA), mentioned in the preceding quote. By the 1990s SOMA became the center of Multimedia Gulch, one of the hottest sites on the globe for multimedia firms in the 1990s. In the 1970s, however, it was a low-income industrial mixed use, multi-ethnic neighborhood with a number of quite marginal populations like street people and drug dealers. It attracted gay men—the "leather" crowd in particular—and some lesbians. By 1978 it was a significant gay and lesbian commercial district (Lyod and Rowntree 1978, Wolfe 1999). The gay and lesbian groups were quickly followed by artists, in a slightly different part of the area, meaning the area became a site for "creatively oriented" firms, eventually leading to the multimedia cluster (Wolfe 1999). As Wolfe explained:

The significance of the emergence of this nonconformist community in SOMA during the 1970s was not that the new residents themselves began converting loft spaces to residential or live-work use. On the contrary, they typically chose to live in the area's numerous Victorian houses. What is important is that they were the group that first bestowed upon SOMA its bohemian, alternative caché, giving rise to a city-wide reputation as a novel, cutting-edge 'frontier' area in which to venture. (Wolfe 1999: 718, citations omitted)

In work on a central neighborhood in Boston, Pattinson (1983) noted similar early renter-initiated changes by gay men along with home purchases of very cheap housing, purchases that involved convincing banks of the viability of the area. As Pattinson (1983: 80) wrote: "one bank made significantly more loans to Bay Village during the entire upgrading process. The loan officer at the bank recalled how some of Bay Village's gay community approached the bank in 1958" impressing the loan officer enough for him to provide finance in spite of urban renewal threats and a negative image of the area due to its large number of rooming houses and bars. While not the only members of the middle class in this central neighborhood—it contained retired people, along with home-owning "lawyers, architects, and school teachers"—the gay population was still a significant group of early renovators (Pattinson 1983: 78).

However, Lauria and Knopp (1985) argued that at least some sections of the gay male population in this period were very affluent, and so their role in gentrification was not always a marginal one. They proposed that gay men had also suffered different oppression to lesbians which may have heightened their perception of the need for territory. They also outlined a more standard set of reasons for gay men wanting to spend their money in creating gentrified enclaves including: work location, proximity to gay cultural institutions, creating an "oasis of tolerance," a sense of belonging, and developing "economic and political clout as a community" (Lauria and Knopp 1985: 158, 161). Certainly, in some enclaves, and in the pages of a number of interior design magazines, the economic clout and territorial expression of some segments of the population has been quite evident.

In the literature on gentrification, the case of gay men and of single and working women was important for planning and urban studies as it was a major spur in rethinking economically-based theories of gentrification to incorporate cultural expression and the positions of those somewhat marginalized in the middle class. These were people who perhaps had mainstream jobs but also complex family responsibilities or social lives not conforming to mainstream norms (Lauria and Knopp 1985, Caulfield 1994).[13] As Castells and Murphy (1982: 237) wrote "Urban researchers and planners should be able to learn, from such rich experience, useful lessons about the interaction between city forms and cultural change." The multiple roles in gentrification of gay men, lesbians, and other non-conformist groups highlighted the complexity of urban redevelopment.

Over the years gay, and more recently lesbian and queer, residential enclaves have become increasingly visible in large North American cities and in parts of Europe and Australasia (Collins 2004). Some smaller towns and cities also have significant concentrations—often part of an academic or artistic population. Concentrations have also been noted in blue-collar areas (Bowman 1993). There has been a change in *popular* perception with gay men, and sometimes lesbians, seen as a potential revitalizing force, even in areas outside the core urban concentrations. For example, in 1996 press coverage, early signs of gay business district formation received positive comment in Ottawa (Boswell 1996, see also Palmer 1999). This attention exploded with the popularization of Florida's work on the creative class dealt with below.

While ethnic populations in enclaves have been frequently mentioned in plans and other planning documents, many of these lesbian and gay enclaves have been ignored or only obliquely referred to. However, by the 1990s some began to receive explicit attention from practicing planners. The most prominent of these projects

---

13 DeGiovanni and Paulson (1984) describe diverse kinds of in-movers to gentrifying neighborhoods, with renters having much lower incomes than owners but still choosing to live in such locations (see also Warde 1991).

in the 1990s was Chicago's Halsted Street streetscape improvements initiated in 1997 (Podmolik 1997, Roeper 1997, Johnson 1997). As part of a city-wide program to create streetscapes reflecting neighborhood social groups—mostly ethnic—the city proposed rainbow gateway elements and street pylons for a six-block stretch in the Halsted Street area, a focus for gay businesses and services. The initial proposal involved 22 steel pylons with rings of rainbow colored neon lights along with the gateway structures. This $3.2 million streetscape improvement program included a range of features in addition to the decorative pylons, including tree planting, lighting, and sidewalk widening. After a number of public meetings the neon was removed from the pylons leaving colored elements (Editorial 1997). The city pylons were complemented by business association rainbow flags. San Francisco's Market Street near the Castro Street area, also the recipient of streetscape improvements in the 1990s, used rainbow flags alone to mark the street. By 2005 the area had formed a special tax district—the Castro/Upper Market Community Benefit District with special taxing powers. With:

> an elected Board of Directors consisting of residents, community activists, business representatives, and property owners, [the board] meets monthly to respond to neighborhood issues such as street safety and cleanliness, and to directly influence land use, economic development, and future planning in their area. (Castro CBD 2010).

City governments have also helped provide focal points for these enclaves and wider communities. Free standing social service centers have been built in some locations, often with at least partial funding from city government. By the end of the 1990s, over 100 centers operated in the US, 19 with annual budgets of $250,000 or more and five with annual budgets of over $1 million (Lesbian and Gay Community Services Center 1999). More have opened. New York's facility provided meeting spaces for over 300 groups (Lesbian and Gay Community Services Center 1999, 2010). This was the center where groups such as ACT-UP, Queer Nation, the Lesbian Avengers first met—groups that subsequently went national in the 1980s and 1990s.

However, not all the environments occupied by gay men and lesbians have had such high visibility. Some studies have showed how the population used the design and location of facilities to reduce such visibility in order to avoid hostility (e.g. Weightman 1980).[14] Even when individuals are relatively "out" many gay populations exist in a countercultural milieu—they coexist as one community layer or are also parts of other populations such as feminist, artists, and single parents, and so are less easily identified. Others live in other kinds of neighborhoods

---

14 There are a number of studies of bars that deal with this issue of keeping low visibility—something that was important for reasons of violence, and also for those in occupations where employment might be threatened by being seen in such a location—for example school teachers (Chamberland 1993, Kennedy and Davis 1993).

defined more by ethnicity, education, or even self-conscious heterogeneity (Adler and Brenner 1992, Castells 1983, Godfrey 1988, Chapter 6, Winters 1979).

This invisibility has been particularly the case for lesbians as a whole, and for persons of color among gay men. In a twist, queer activists are often quite conspicuous, at least when engaged in protest, although the lack of fixity of queer identities presumably means that they can also be less visible. Wolf (1979: 98) in an early study of lesbians, argued that lesbians were dispersed across San Francisco, though she did note some clustering of residences in low-rent areas with good public transport and a capacity for anonymity. A few businesses and services were clustered nearby (see also Lyod and Rowntree 1978: 84–5). However, as much socializing occurred in houses they did not have the equivalent of the obvious clusters of gay male establishments that had emerged in some locations by that time. During the 1980s it was proposed that the spatial pattern of lesbians was in fact essentially dispersed—and less visible than gay men—due to their relatively lower incomes and the character of their politics that was less tied to creating territory and more towards social change (Castells 1983: 140).

In the 1980s and 1990s research appeared that began to describe significant, long-term residential concentrations of lesbians. These concentrations both grew, and grew more open during the 1980s.[15] However, these either lacked commercial establishments or these establishments were not highly visible, for example having ambiguous countercultural or feminist identification (Winchester and White 1988, Adler and Brenner 1992, Valentine 1995, Bouthillette 1997, Forsyth 1997a, 1997b, Krieger 1983, Taylor and Rupp 1993). While a few studies examined the potential for lesbians to be gentrifiers—much as gay men had been—they at most found them acting as "marginal gentrifiers" (Rothenberg 1995). This group unintentionally opened up areas for middle class investment when they sought inexpensive accommodation after having been forced out of other areas by the higher incomes of people with males in the household. At other times they helped create cultural changes in neighborhoods where economic upgrading was in line with state and regional trends (Rothenberg 1995, Adler and Brenner 1992, Forsyth 1997a, 1997b). The only extensive study of the role of lesbians in commercial revitalization focused on the downtown of Northampton, Massachusetts. It examined assessors' records and business directories and found that lesbians were mainly renters and had not profited from the property boom that had occurred with the downtown's redevelopment (Forsyth 1997a). Instead the population had provided a solid market for formerly-vacant upper floor office space in the downtown. While this seemed to be different to the pattern of gay men's activity

---

15 This was part of a larger set of work looking at lesbian social systems or communities in particular locations, although much of this work did not deal with spatial issues (e.g. Franzen 1993, Barnhardt 1975, Ross 1990, Lockhard 1986, Whittier 1995). Ettorre (1978) described a short-running "ghetto;" Peake (1993) a very small cluster of lesbians. In addition some work in urban sociology focusing on marginalized groups also dealt with gay and lesbian populations (Winchester and White 1988).

in commercial space, the lack of studies of gay male property ownership, rather than business ownership, made this comparison impossible.

Adler and Brenner (1992) argued that the different pattern is highly related to women's lower incomes and to their integration into feminist, rather than specifically lesbian, politics. It could also be related to other factors like lesbians' greater propensity to have family responsibilities, something affecting both residential choice and commercial needs. Planning practitioners need to be conscious of the differences between gay men and lesbians, as well as the differences among lesbians, with younger women often more obviously out, and an older generation with more memories of harassment and probably more reticent about public appearances. While it may not be appropriate to intrude on people's privacy, it is also important to make attempts to include these less conspicuous or vocal members of the population.

Further, not all gay and lesbian people live in inner city areas, whether in an enclave or a more dispersed pattern. Mapping research—based on mailing lists, business directories, and more recently US census data—and examining even some of the denser enclaves has consistently found significant populations scattered throughout cities and metropolitan areas. These populations possibly used the enclave as a service center but certainly had a quite dispersed residential structure (Murray 1979, Forsyth 1997b, also Lubrano 1984). The large-scale suburbanization of the "out" gay and lesbian population, that became more obvious in the 1990s, focused renewed attention on these non-enclave populations (Lynch 1987, Kirkey and Forsyth 2001).

This suburbanization is a complicated phenomenon and may be due to different processes for different parts of the population: for example gay men moving to suburban areas in greater numbers and lesbians, who had always tended to be less urban, becoming more visible (Mendelsohn 1995, Forsyth 1997b, also see Anacker Chapter 5). The particular geography of the population also has a complex background—some people are born and stay in an area, others move for work (although this can still cause concentrations such as around universities), and still others are attracted by more diverse or tolerant suburban areas. Popular press in the 1990s focused on such locations as Oak Park (Chicago) that reportedly boasted the first suburban gay and lesbian bookstore, Royal Oak (Detroit), Azalea Park (San Diego), and Tacoma Park (Washington DC) (Hobica 1994, Mendelsohn 1995, Ritter 1993). In fact non-gay residents of Azalea Park actively recruited gay men and lesbians at pride marches hoping they would come to live in this somewhat rundown older suburb of smaller, often two-bedroom, homes—a strategy that had some success. Even in the 1990s, anecdotal evidence indicated that some professional developers used gay and lesbian presence as a positive factor in their investment decisions; this may well have increased with the popularity of the creative class hypothesis.

This work on enclaves and suburbanization was important because of its connection with the core planning issues of neighborhood development and urban growth. However, at the same time other researchers started to examine the "time-space strategies" for managing gay and lesbian identities, pointing out that only a small percentage of gay people lived in places where they were either concentrated in urban neighborhoods, or living "out" in the suburbs, and this was particularly the case outside the US (e.g. Bell 1991, Valentine 1993b, 1993c, Bell and Valentine 1995b). A related development was work about sexuality and the city more generally. Such work argued, for example, that "areas and populations which represent failures of or challenges to aspects of the dominant order (e.g. slums; gentrified areas) tend to be coded in both dominant and alternative cultures as erotic (i.e. as both dangerous and potentially liberatory), while those seen as less problematic either tend to be desexualized or to stress more functional approaches to sexuality" (Knopp 1995: 152–3, Knopp 1992). The suburbanization of the gay and lesbian population makes this coding more difficult.

The interview-based research on relatively dispersed and underground populations, some in rural areas, still found single-sex meeting places, but these were often not clustered and not highly visible (Valentine 1993c, Kramer 1995, Cody and Welch 1997, Kirkey and Forsyth 2001).[16] Of course, there were and are locations with gay and lesbian populations and no such meeting places. Others described fairly isolated small rural separatist communities (Valentine 1997). This more general analysis of urban and rural spaces was interesting for planners in showing groups maintaining identities in dispersed situations, something that seems poised to become more prevalent among a wide variety of social groups as interactions become less localized due to the influence of new forms of digital and interactive media.

In methodological terms this work has also been important due to the difficulty in finding direct measures of the population, and the basic lack of data that describes multiple attributes of the population. For example, one may be able to estimate roughly the number of gay and lesbian persons in a city but not their income, and certainly not their income by ethnicity or political views. Researchers have tended to build up a picture of the population from multiple sources: interviews, mailing lists, business directories, locations of services, data on votes for gay and lesbian candidates or on gay and lesbian issues, addresses for ticket sales for gay-themed plays, demographic indicators including multiple male households and non-family households, local newspaper and newsletter advertisements and stories, and the recent census data on same sex unmarried partner couples (methods most explicitly discussed in Castells and Murphy 1982, Castells 1983, Adder and Brenner 1992, Forsyth 1997a, 1997b, Kahan and Mulryan 1995, Valentine 1993c).

Many of these methods are useful in studying other populations and places where direct measures are not easily available from sources such as the census, and where populations have service cores and a more dispersed residential

---

16 Kramer (1995) studied men in rural North Dakota; Cody and Welch (1997) examined men in northern New England. Both found universities to be a useful meeting place though it is hard to tell if universities are in fact key sites or if this is due to the kind of sampling methods used (i.e. snowball, volunteer).

pattern. Examples include the geography of members of religious groups and the socioeconomic character of recreation and entertainment nodes. The difficulty of defining the population is also not so unusual in planning. From ethnicity to employment categories, there are many blurry boundaries between groups. Planners frequently treat these categories as being much clearer than they are, and the data as more precise than it is. The general sensitivity to this issue in most research on gays, lesbians, queers (and the rest) can give some pointers for how to deal with these issues in a conscious way while still managing to undertake systematic research and policy formulation.

Residential Zoning and Housing

Residential zoning and housing provision are central to planning—whether such planning is carried out in government, nonprofit, and private development settings. The gay, lesbian, and queer populations challenge many of the underpinnings of US practice in these areas. This is particularly the case in terms of the cultural and social values underlying US housing and land use practice, including assumptions about family life (e.g. Perin 1977, Hayden 1984). These marginalized populations also suffer from discrimination in the private housing market, and within the household and family, leading to a number of tragic consequences including homelessness.

In the US, zoning has a preoccupation with families—housing types that in other countries would have such labels as detached housing or apartments, are labeled single family and multi-family in the US with families defined within the local zoning codes. This shows a widespread cultural interest in the social character of the inhabitants rather than the physical character of the buildings. As US households have become more diverse in the post-war period, governments, planners, and the wider public have struggled to deal with this change.

One response, of course, is to give up the focus on the social character of the home and to focus instead on physical issues. This is advocated by the new urbanists who are concerned with building types and sizes, and who also promote different types and sizes on single blocks as an indirect way of accommodating household diversity in single neighborhoods. However, an alternative response has been to define families more stringently to keep some areas more stable in terms of "family" structure even as the world around has changed dramatically. As Ritzdorf explained:

> Municipalities have the right (in all but three states—Michigan, New Jersey, and California) to establish zoning ordinances that determine the number of unrelated individuals who may share a household and whether they are to be considered a family. The typical ordinance defines a family as an *unlimited* number of individuals related by blood, adoption, or marriage, but only a limited

number of unrelated individuals living together in a single housekeeping unit. In some communities, no unrelated individuals are allowed to live together. (Ritzdorf 1997: 83, italics in original)

Ritzdorf conducted surveys of family definitions in the Seattle area in 1984 and 1994. She found over 90 percent of municipalities in this region had family definitions, with a slight increase over the period. In each period, 60 percent used numerical limits rather than merely requiring a single housekeeping unit. Over half the jurisdictions had investigated complaints in each of her surveys; in 1984, 42 percent had enforced the regulations and in 1994, 47 percent had enforced them since 1984.

These family definitions are the subject of quite heated local controversies and affect a number of living arrangements such as group homes for disabled people. They are often present in college towns that try to limit student household size. Household size limitations are used in these cases as an indirect way of limiting noisy households, traffic, and housing market competition (where it is feared student group households can outbid families in the market for large houses). Thus family definitions are frequently a blunt instrument for achieving these aims and have the additional effect of limiting a number of other household types.

DePalma described a typical coalition in University City, Missouri, adjacent to Washington University, that allied group home supporters and gay and lesbian activists against such a family definition (DePalma 1993). The town of Amherst, Massachusetts, home to the University of Massachusetts, Amherst College, and Hampshire College, is typical of many of these college towns concerned about large group households. In the 1990s Amherst defined a family as up to four unrelated individuals. This is quite a broad definition. However, unrelated individuals (apart from a single individual) could not run a bed and breakfast. Presumably this additional restriction on bed and breakfast establishments was to prevent very large households of unrelated people using it as a loophole in the law. However, for some time in the early 1990s one of the local bed and breakfasts was operated very openly by a gay couple—they were interviewed on the front page of the local newspaper talking about their business. The regulation that would have stopped their business was not enforced. Some locations, such as Ithaca, New York, home to Cornell University and Ithaca College, have attempted to get around the discriminatory aspects of family definitions through a variety of measures including counting those in domestic partnerships as being parts of families. However domestic partnership provisions operate in a difficult area legally (Bowman and Cornish 1992, also Berger 1991).

The issue of gay marriage has further complicated this legal situation. While in those areas where gay marriage is legal, queer couples can sidestep these exclusionary zoning provisions, in areas where marriage is not legal, such zoning can pose difficulties to queer couples. The uneven availability of this legal status, however, means that the situation for many is unchanged.

No housing policy or regulatory framework can be value-neutral about social issues—these policies and regulations after all have values about shelter needs, privacy, and space standards. Few people would refuse to place any limits at all on the kinds of relationships within the household—for example abuse and exploitation of children. However, planners can certainly be routinely self-critical about the social values about adult relationships underlying planning regulations and policies, and about whether local planning is the best site for regulating such issues as the structure of the household. US local politics and values do mean it can be extraordinarily difficult to eliminate such regulations as family definitions. However, the US propensity to define social relations within the home has a negative effect on many groups and in particular gay men, lesbians, and queers who—with an increasing number of exceptions—do not currently have the option to marry and thus create a legal family tie. This is likely to remain a difficult issue for planners.

A number of specialized forms of housing are used either totally, or extensively, by gay populations and frequently combine housing with social services.[17] There are many specialized housing developments for people with HIV and AIDS, although few target solely a gay population. One such mixed development, the Marisol Apartments in Oceanside, California, won the 1999 American Planning Association national Paul Davidoff Award. Located in San Diego County, this project involved the city rehabilitating a small courtyard apartment complex to provide housing for low-income people with HIV and AIDS. The city teamed with a non-profit developer to re-house the existing residents (Newman 1999: 14). Such specialized housing may suffer from typical NIMBY reactions. Takahashi and Dear analyzed data from the "first national survey of attitudes toward controversial human services," conducted in 1989 for the Robert Wood Johnson Foundation (Takahashi and Dear 1997: 80). A total of 1,326 persons were interviewed from across the nation. Overall, group homes for people living with AIDS ranked lowest on the national acceptance scale, behind such services as drug treatment centers, mental health outpatient clinics, and homeless shelters (Takahashi and Dear 1997: 83). Certainly this indicates a potential for opposition that has many implications for planners.

Planning is not always a villain, however. In the case of the Marisol Apartments, the City's housing and neighborhood services staff, and its housing commissioners, walked door to door in a 10-block radius of the project in order to speak to neighbors about their concerns (Newman 1999: 14). A research study by Colon and Marston (1999) examined NIMBY responses to a home for low-income HIV-positive persons in the Borough of New Hope in Pennsylvania (population 1,400), a location with a large gay population. They described how in the face of intense opposition the zoning board ruled that this group of

---

17 Those concerned with counseling and social support systems have produced significant literature on the gay and lesbian population's specific needs (e.g. review in D'Augelli and Hart 1987). This literature is not reviewed here.

unrelated persons with HIV did in fact form a family, and this ruling was upheld in higher courts.

The Colon and Marston study itself focused on whether the threat to property values or a more direct anxiety about AIDS and homosexuality was at the base of the opposition to the home. It used a 10 percent probability cluster sample with town blocks being clusters, conducted both face to face interviews and mail-back surveys, and received 106 responses from 150 questionnaires. The sample was mostly wealthy, white married persons with the median home value of $250,000 in the mid-1990s.[18] Over three-quarters of the sample supported the home with support unrelated to distance from the home or home value. Opposition was related to a complicated mix of fear of loss of value and of anxiety about AIDS and homosexuality.[19]

In addition, gay and lesbian youth, particularly homeless persons in their late teens and early 20s, have been the focus for a number of projects that have sparked local controversies. These youth are frequently forced out of housing, including their "family" homes, because of their sexual orientation and thus reportedly are over-represented among homeless youth. However, a significant group targeted for transitional housing projects and drop-in centers are or have been involved in illegal activities such as prostitution and drug dealing making them less than welcome neighbors in some areas. Local press reports in the 1990s emphasized the controversial aspects of such facilities in the Castro area of San Francisco and in West Hollywood. Such facilities in Manhattan—25 places on East 22nd Street and 20 places on East 39th Street—seemed to spark much less controversy (Stamler 1997, Herscher 1999, *Los Angeles Times* 1995).

Other forms of gay specific housing have also received some attention. For instance, a trend in housing for older people is to cluster groups of people with common interests. Small buildings for elderly gay or lesbian individuals have been built or proposed in areas from Toronto to Amsterdam and Los Angeles (Demara 1997, Metz and Russell 1998). For example Gay and Lesbian Elder Housing provides subsidized affordable housing. Its 104-unit Triangle Square project opened in Hollywood in 2007 and is advertised for those earning 60 percent of the area median income or less (GLEH 2010). Most of these facilities are very new, or even still being developed, and have not been studied in the academic literature (Shankle et al. 2003). This is obviously an area where future evaluation would be productive.

An additional literature has examined other forms of housing discrimination in the private market. For example in a study testing social stigma, phone calls were made to 180 people advertising rooms or apartments to rent, with calls

---

18 The questionnaire tested a number of variables including distance from one's home, home value, tenure, fear of losing property value, fear of AIDS (using reactions to 14 statements about AIDS), and homophobia (using a seven-item "Homophobia Scale").

19 An additional literature deals with the design of housing for persons with AIDS—but this generally does not deal with issues of sexuality.

equally divided between three locations: Windsor and London in Ontario and in Detroit in Michigan (Page 1998). Using methods similar to those developed for examining racial discrimination and discrimination against persons with mental illnesses or AIDS, half the calls were "simple enquiries" and half made reference to homosexuality using the form "I guess it's only fair to tell you that I'm a gay person" (Page 1998: 34). In each place calls were equally divided between a male and female caller. The study found that "reference to being homosexual in the telephoned enquiries, for each city and for all combined, significantly decreased the likelihood of a room or flat being described as available" (Page 1998: 36). These findings are similar to those from an earlier study by Page that found landlords in three Canadian cities typically saying rooms were unavailable for rent to persons with AIDS even when they had earlier indicated in a telephone survey that they would be happy to rent to such persons (Page 1989). More recent research using various large US surveys indicated that relatively high proportions of partnered same-sex households were renters, compared with different sex households, meaning rental discrimination has important implications (Black et al. 2000).

Egerton reported on the experiences of a number of housing groups in London as well as research conducted among those groups, claiming that housing was one of the most difficult problems for lesbian feminists in London. This was partly due to the low incomes of single women, although many lesbians also reported specific incidents of violence and harassment (Egerton 1990: 78–80).

Harassment, discrimination, and the low incomes of parts of the queer population mean that housing issues are likely to remain important. Both access to the general housing stock, including single family zones, and to specialized developments raise issues of importance to planners including provision of housing for homeless youth and people with AIDS. These problems are of course related to the formation of gay and lesbian neighborhoods (previous section) in that clustering has been at least partly a response to discrimination.

Business Development and Tourism

Up to the late 1990s economic development planners did not pay much attention to the gay and lesbian populations. In the 2000s, Richard Florida's work made gay populations a more prominent part of the economic development scene. Florida proposed that human capital drives economic development and that certain "creative" occupations (from arts and education to engineering and finance) are better indicators of human capital than education. He then proposed that places with "tolerance and openness to diversity" attract those with high levels of human capital (Florida et al. 2008: 616). Earlier theories had focused on the advantages of locations with universities and high amenity levels, though Florida et al. (2008: 617) point out that the three explanations could be complementary. Areas with large bohemian and gay populations were seen by Florida as indicating areas open to people of high human capital no matter their background, fostering innovative social networks, and "reflect regional values that are open minded, meritocratic, tolerant of risk and oriented to self-expression," factors related to entrepreneurship and economic growth (Florida et al. 2008: 622). Florida initially created a Gay Index (based on census data for male couples) and Bohemian Index (people employed in arts, entertainment, and design occupations) (Florida 2005: 118–19). He combined these to measure tolerance (Florida et al. 2008: 629). Using structural equation models and path analyses showed consistent high and significant associations between tolerance and economic development. Florida and Mellander (2009) also found such associations between a "Bohemian-Gay Index" and regional housing values. Anacker and Morrow-Jones (2005) found some associations between census tracts with high numbers of US census defined same sex couples and high amenity locations.

This work has been critiqued empirically and theoretically—in terms of analyses and in terms of the relationship between people, places, and jobs (Storper and Scott 2009).The gay and tolerance indices are proxies for underlying openness and diversity. Florida's work does not, however, focus specifically on the gay community as consumers or business people but rather as a kind of indicator for a creative regional economy. A different body of work has dealt with these issues. While much of the information on these two groups has been anecdotal or oriented only towards the gay and lesbian population as a potential market, an emerging base of research has indicated a vibrant business scene. As tourists—consumers of urban and rural areas—gay men, lesbians, and queers have been involved in both high-end recreation and more activist events like Gay Pride. As producers, gay and lesbian business people have created guilds and associations that parallel chambers of commerce. While women were initially less visible—probably due to different political ideals and incomes—by the 1990s they formed a growing and conspicuous part of the business environment both as producers and consumers.

Gay-oriented resorts have been around for some time in locations such as Cherry Grove, Fire Island outside of New York, Provincetown on Cape Cod, and Key West in Florida (Newton 1993). However, with the growth of the "out" population, gay and lesbian tourism activities became more extensive. By the 1990s Gay bowling leagues and rodeo associations had annual events from Oklahoma City to San Jose and resulted in the booking of thousands of hotel rooms (De Witt 1994, International Gay Rodeo Association 1999). The week-long 1996 Gay and Lesbian Association of Choruses Festival in Tampa was estimated by the local convention bureau as bringing $6 million into the local economy (Koehn 1996). By the 2000s there were many more such events.

Gay pride marches also bring economic benefits. A city of Toronto-funded study of the 1996 Pride Parade in Toronto estimated direct and indirect benefits of $CAN 42–56 million in an event that reportedly did not receive any public subsidy (Carey 1998, see also Gover 1993). This report was updated in 2006 and 2009 showing substantial positive impacts; with 100,000 nonlocals attending and generating 600 full-year jobs (Enigma 2009). The Sydney Gay and Lesbian Mardi Gras, operated as a company but with strong structures for community representation, had an annual budget of $AUS 4.5 million alone in the late 1990s and was one of the largest international tourist events in Australia (Haire 1999). In 1994, the parade featured 137 floats and "attracted 600,000 spectators out of a greater Sydney population of 3.5 million" (Murphy and Watson 1997: 62). The size of this undertaking led the organization to undertake a strategic planning process with the 1999 plan available on the web in PDF format (Sydney Gay and Lesbian Mardi Gras 1999). The plan aimed to balance political activism, entertainment, diversity, and organizational and financial stability.

Furthermore, this tourism promotion is not only a private or community affair. From Manchester, England, to Montreal, Canada, and St. Maartens in the Caribbean, gay neighborhoods and tourism opportunities have been featured in city- and state-sponsored advertising and gay and lesbian tourists seen as a key niche market (Smith and Richardson 1995, Schwartz 1998, Ravensbergen 1998). Cape Town, South Africa, has emerged as a major gay tourism destination though the emphasis has been on rich white men (Visser 2003, Rogerson and Visser 2005).

The affluent section of the gay and lesbian population has been of interest to researchers in leisure studies and tourism with some of this research focusing on planning-relevant economic and social impacts. Hughes (2004) reviewed the literature on gay tourism and demonstrated that while the affluence of the population was overstated in the tourism literature, there was still a significant affluent subgroup looking for gay-friendly space (Hughes 2004). For instance Philipp (1999) conducted a survey of 1,272 randomly selected tourists near Pensacola Florida on Memorial Day Weekend in 1994.[20] This research was carried out on a five-mile stretch of beach that on summer holiday weekends had become one of the more popular gay and lesbian areas in the US. The survey response rate was 92 percent. This group was dominated by highly educated (64 percent with bachelors or higher degrees), southern, urban, white males in their mid-20s to 30s although women made up 31 percent of respondents. Only 10 percent lived in the area, and 86 percent were visitors intending to spend three or more days in the area. Over 27 percent intended to spend five or more days. The National Parks Service estimate of a total of 27,000 gay and lesbian tourists was combined with spending data gathered by Philipp to calculate the Memorial Day weekend spending of this group for lodging, restaurants, bars, and other expenses in the Pensacola area. The total was $18.7 million or $692 per person. (Travel was an additional cost.) This was the largest tourism event in the area,

---

20 The beach was broken into 100 sections of about 265 feet, and 13 of these were randomly drawn (Philipp 1999: 72–3). The sections could be classed as roughly equal as parking is equally distributed along the sides of the road for the entire length of beach and people stayed near their cars. Between 10 and 2:30—peak beach time—surveys were distributed to beach goers in these sections and then collected using a fairly elaborate process that limited bias in the survey distribution within the sections. The response rate was 92 percent.

dwarfing the World Church of God's 7,000 members who spent $6.0 million that same year.

Philipp pointed out that this huge expenditure was not the only effect but that "the large number of out gay and lesbian tourists suggested the potential for great social impact in small, politically conservative host communities" (Philipp 1999: 81). There were some areas of conflict in Pensacola, where by September 1994 the Tourist Development Council of Pensacola Beach announced that "future advertising will emphasize a theme of 'family vacation fun'" (Philipp 1999: 84). Press reports from other locations have indicated a number of such social conflicts on Caribbean Islands as well as in the US. While some Caribbean islands have aimed to attract gay visitors, a number of protests and harassment incidents have been reported in the Caribbean, most notably Grand Cayman's 1998 refusal of docking permission for a cruise ship carrying 850 gay men (Jackson 1998, DaRosa 1998, Schwartz 1998). The refusal followed a 1987 landing that had offended locals.[21]

However, Philipp also described a growing number of gay and lesbian special events at major leisure areas, such as *Gay Days* at Walt Disney World. This event was started in 1991, by 1994 (the year of Phillip's study) was attended by 20,000 people, and by 2010 had expanded beyond Disney and according to sponsors attracts over 135,000 people annually (Orlando Gaydays 2010, see also Chapman, Chapter 7). As Schwartz reported, the International Gay and Lesbian Travel Association started with 25 members in 1983 and "today [1998] boasts nearly 1400 members, including the Avis and National rental car chains, the Philadelphia Convention and Visitor's Bureau, the Australia Tourism Council, and most of the major US airlines, with the exception of Delta and TWA" (Schwartz 1998). There are a number of subgroups within the population. For example Hughes and Deusch (2010) interviewed gay men in their late 30s through 60s finding their vacation preferences were similar to other older people with the added desire for gay-friendliness. This is obviously a well organized tourist market to which cities have begun to pay attention.

In terms of gays and lesbians as business owners and not merely consumers, the 1990s experienced a relative explosion of gay and lesbian business districts that frequently developed specialist business guilds and associations. Some of these associations and guilds became quite large and it would be difficult for planners in the area to avoid interacting with them and their members. For example, the Key West Business Guild was started in 1978 and by the late 1990s claimed 450 members (Key West Business Guild 1999). The Tampa Bay Business Guild Inc. was formed in 1982 and was still functioning in 2010 with around 150 members (Tampa Bay Business Guild 2010). The largest such association in the US is reportedly the Greater Seattle Business Association with almost 1,000 members (Torres 1996; Greater Seattle Business Association 2010). Not all gay

---

21 A couples-only chain of Caribbean resorts, Sandals, only allows different sex couples (Schwartz 1998).

business concentrations are in the US—others are located in areas from Soho in London, to Manchester, Amsterdam, and Sydney (Binnie 1995, Mort 1998, Quilley 1997).

Many of these business guilds were traditionally dominated by gay men. Many lesbian-oriented businesses emerged in the 1970s as "alternative" types of businesses, women's book stores, coffee houses, women run garages, and these were more interested in providing community services than making money. Others were part of a women's business network rather than a specifically lesbian one. It was only in the 1990s that this group became more up front and entrepreneurial with lesbian dominated guilds emerging in such locations as Northampton, Massachusetts, although this particular guild is no longer in existence (NALGBG 1999). These business groups can be resources for planners particularly in terms of economic development. There are now numerous LGBT business groups with well maintained websites that are fully accessible via Google. Certainly there is an economic impact from such business clusters and the guilds provide an easy way for planners to interact with local business owners.

While the earlier discussion of incomes indicates that the population is not as affluent, as some market research had initially shown, it is still a potentially loyal market that planners can tap into. This can be done directly as in the cases of cities and regions promoting tourism opportunities, or by working with local lesbian and gay businesses.

Historic Preservation

While many of the neighborhoods that have concentrations of gay men, and to a lesser extent lesbians, were notable for their historical architecture, the literature on historic preservation only began to take up the specific issue of gays, lesbians, and historic preservation in the 1990s. Preservation practice also lagged. However, as part of a move to increase the representation of previously marginalized groups in historic preservation strategies, initial steps have been made.

This interest reflected the significant amount of work in the 1990s dealing with spatial aspects of gay and lesbian history. Lesbian and gay bars attracted particular attention as early sites of gay and lesbian organizing, and of the creation of contemporary forms of GLBTQ identity (e.g. Chamberland 1993, Tattleman 2000, Wolfe 1992). For example Chauncey's (1994) *Gay New York* recounted gay male history in New York from the 1890s to the 1940s giving a rich sense of different populations and events in several major neighborhoods such as Greenwich Village and Harlem. Kennedy and Davis' (1993) *Boots of Leather, Slippers of Gold* vividly described, and even mapped, a landscape of lesbian bars and other meeting places in Buffalo, New York, from the 1930s to the early 1960s. While these were very well known examples there were numerous other articles, dissertations, reports, oral-history interviews, and books dealing with local gay and lesbian and queer histories among various social classes and ethnic groups and in a number of countries (e.g. articles in Ingram et al. 1997, Newton 1993).

This history began to attract attention from both activists and professionals seeking to mark or celebrate these historical events in the landscape. Numerous locations created memorials for those who have died of AIDS. Walking tours in a number of cities directed visitors to historical sites (e.g. Drabelle 1997). Some locations went further to mark historical sites. For instance, in 1994 a New York artists collective, REPOhistory, created the Queer Spaces Sign Project, installing triangular street signs in nine locations in lower Manhattan that had significance in gay male, lesbian, and queer history. The signs were pink, and contained text describing each site. Although temporary, under permit from the transportation department, several survived for at least a year (Hertz et al. 1997). This group had also created sign projects on abortion, and on an alternative history of New York's financial district. In the queer sign project they worked with a planner from the city's landmarks commission, with the planner providing research assistance.

From inside the historic preservation and planning field, Dubrow (1998b) proposed a nuanced and multifaceted strategy for preserving gay and lesbian landmarks and districts. The first step was to revise the presentation of existing historic sites and buildings that are associated with gay men and lesbians but where this was not mentioned in current plaques and tours. Dubrow acknowledged the problems of interpreting the private lives of public figures from a different historical period but cited several potential examples already on national or local landmarks registers including Walt Whitman's row house in Camden, New Jersey; Willa Cather's childhood home in Nebraska; and the HH Richardson-designed Boston's Club Baths. Dubrow's second strategy was to nominate key gay and lesbian sites such as the Los Angeles home of Harry Hays, the founding site for the first US homophile political association, the Mattachine Society. As the 50-year cut off mark generally used in the US for defining historical sites and structures moved into the 1950s and 1960s, more of such sites from the early period of homophile organizing and gay liberation had become eligible for listing. Third, some more recent sites such as the Stonewall Inn in New York, or prominent gay and lesbian districts, also warranted special moves for preservation (the inn was placed on the register in 1999, only 30 years after the events that made it famous in LGBT history) (Martinac 2010). Finally, some sites "connected with the history of homophobia" might also be preserved with examples including mental hospitals and activists' homes (Dubrow 1998b: 37).

Planners have perhaps been reticent to designate gay, lesbian, and even queer historic landmarks and districts, fearing public controversy. However, historic preservation has been extended to many different groups with quite different kinds of histories—both positive and negative. Certainly this is likely to be an area of increasing interest in the coming decades.

Public Space

Finally is the issue of public space. Public space remains a planning issue in the context of highly publicized increases in privately owned and monitored "public" spaces such as private streets in subdivisions and the interiors of shopping malls. Some of the claims about privatization have been perhaps overstated; for example malls vary in both regulations and enforcement, and all government-owned spaces are regulated, some highly so.[22] However, the debates about privatization have led to some useful self-reflection about such spaces on the part of planners.

The literature on gays and public space has focused on three main issues: harassment, protest, and the place of public affection or public eroticism. The issue of public space is perhaps the most difficult area for planning and raises questions that have divided the gay, lesbian, and queer population.

Harassment has been a major problem for various gay, lesbians, and queer communities. Incidents have made the news in places as dispersed as Northampton in the early 1980s (Fitzgerald 1983), Manhattan in the 1990s (Howe 1994, Serant 1995, also Geltmaker 1992), and in many places for transgendered people in the 2000s (Doan 2007). This is an issue that debates about public space in general have dealt with quite extensively but in the context of other groups such as the homeless and ethnic minorities (e.g. Davis 1990, Mitchell 1995, Ruddick 1996). There is a dilemma within these debates—while many commentators criticize the increasing regulation of public spaces they also want to protect the marginalized from harassment, through some form of regulation.

In the context of gay, lesbian, and queer populations there have been a number of responses. Houston's community-based police-affiliated Q-patrol focused on ensuring groups of teenagers did not gather in key gay locations for the purpose of harassment (Robinson 1994). The patrol grew out of queer activism. In the 1990s several police departments recruited gay and lesbian officers or created liaisons including Chicago, San Diego, and Brighton (England) (Roberts 1997, Richardson 1997). The situation in Britain was particularly interesting, since this relative openness followed a period of relative suppression (Richardson 1997). Around Oxford Street in Sydney, legal protections were extended through local council decisions and court decisions that ruled against allowing some businesses that were seen as potentially attracting harassers (in this case a video games parlor and café both oriented toward young men). These decisions acknowledged the gay and lesbian population as a major group of local residents (Murphy and Watson 1997: 78–9).

More generally, in the activist and some academic literature there has been an interest in gays and lesbians using public space for protest. In the 1970s and 1980s local governments started to provide permits for such events as gay pride marches allowing the temporary transformation of public spaces. By the 1990s

---

22 Some of the exclusiveness of these environments has to do with location as well—in inaccessible locations in the now highly dispersed US metropolitan areas.

gay, lesbian, and queer groups were pushing boundaries further. For example the Queer Nation "kiss-ins" of the early 1990s and the various attempts for gay and lesbian groups to join St. Patrick's day parades caused some controversy (and the cancellation of the 1994 parade in Boston after courts ruled that gay and lesbian groups must be allowed to participate) (Davis 1995, O'Leary 1994).[23]

While in the late 1990s and 2000s there was some reduction in the more confrontational forms of protest—reflecting some disagreement within the gay, lesbian, and queer populations about the usefulness of such strategies—this issue is still relevant for planners because of its wider implications for the issue of access to public space. Public space is also not just a western phenomenon. Castells (1997: 211) drew on unpublished work by Po (1996) to describe struggles in Taipei over the redevelopment of New Park. A site for both lesbian and gay male gathering, the groups were active in the 1990s both in claiming the space and seeking a voice in its redevelopment.

Planners are relatively used to debates over levels of political action that can occur in locations such as streets and shopping malls—planners generally agree that handing out flyers should be allowed, but argue over whether to push to allow picketing or potentially violent protest in specific locations. However, the issue of public demonstrations of affection has received much less attention, even though it is in fact an important issue for lesbians and gays.

In general, in the US, same sex couples are far less tolerated than different sex couples in such displays, to the extent that same sex couples reportedly feel uncomfortable, and open to the potential for harassment, by holding hands in public (see Kirkey and Forsyth 2001). This is a form of public affection that most people feel is tolerable among different sex couples although there are cultural and personal differences in both directions. Of course, in many other cultures same sex couples can hold hands easily, although this is rarely in the context of a queer relationship. However, it is an issue in the US and Queer Nation protests that used displays of same sex public affection, such as kissing and holding hands, that were meant to highlight this situation.

Gay Mardi Gras and Pride Marches are a continuing example, and their more flamboyant aspects raise a further question about public eroticism (defined as going beyond a hand-holding level of affection). Writing on gay men has dealt extensively with this issue, particularly public eroticism and sex in parks, bath houses, and restrooms (e.g. Chauncey 1994, Tattleman 1997, 2000, Grube 1997). This is a very difficult topic. On one hand some gay, lesbian, and queer people wish to celebrate erotic behavior, and the erotic is certainly a large part of US popular culture—from shopping to movies. It is perhaps a more common use of public space than political activity, given that much political debate occurs in traditionally private spaces like homes and clubs (Staeheli 1996). Many others

---

23 A larger literature looks at the non-spatial public realm and the political effects of gay and lesbians in public office (e.g. Knopp 1987 on Minneapolis, Moos 1989 on West Hollywood, Haeberle 1996, Rosenthal 1996).

within the gay, lesbian, and queer population, however, feel that sex and eroticism have been overemphasized. For this group gay, lesbian, and queer people have been stereotyped as only concerned about sexual behavior (and as a corollary, for example, businesses oriented to this population can then be seen as sexually-oriented in zoning and excluded).

These debates about eroticism represent real disagreements, although the assimilationist groups that planners are likely to interact with are more commonly on the side of playing down the sexual and erotic. There is also a middle ground that allows affection and celebrates some flamboyance, but places other limits on public behavior. Like housing, this is an area where self-reflection and debate may be the best path for planners, recognizing the need for public spaces to be shared by many groups but being open to pushing some boundaries.

Conclusions

The gay, lesbian, and queer population is a marginalized group but its concerns are not marginal to planning. It is a sizeable group, heterogeneous (not least in income), and growing in visibility. The population has already made it onto the radar screen of planning in areas from neighborhood formation to zoning. From homes for the elderly to streetscape improvements and tourism strategies there are now a wide variety of practice examples and this number is likely to grow in the coming decade. Continuing problems relate to housing discrimination, housing costs in long-gentrified queer neighborhoods, and harassment in public space. Emerging opportunities are appearing in business development, tourism, and historic preservation.

While it was common to dismiss or ignore this population in the past century, this is now less possible. Whether they like it or not planners will increasingly interact with this population and it is important to be comfortable with the professional issues raised by gay, lesbian, and queer populations. While initially most obvious in inner city enclaves in the largest US and European cities, gay, lesbian, and queer groups are now visible in smaller cities and suburbs, and a number of international locations—both in terms of residential locations and the locations of festivals and events. They have a number of different household and housing arrangements, different incomes, and different levels of comfort in the public gaze. Understanding the diversity of gay, lesbian, and queer populations is an important first step for planners.

Raising awareness about this population also highlights the situation that planners already reinforce heteronormative sexuality, usually in the form of providing housing for heterosexual families or targeting heterosexual couples in tourism promotion. This population that does not "fit" these categories, that is non-conformist, can lead to useful questioning of core values on the part of planners—particularly ideas about family and community. The groups also raise issues of unusual forms of discrimination—for example rejection by one's own family. Some of the questions and issues don't have easy answers, and there are disagreements within the gay, lesbian, and queer populations about appropriate practices, but planners can still respond. Some sort of dialogue will generally be a useful part of this response.

In the future, while there is a significant scholarly and professional literature and practice already in existence, there is obviously important work to do in tracking developments and extending planning practice.

Chapter 3
Lavender Landmarks Revisited: Advancing an LGBT Preservation Agenda[1]

Gail Dubrow

Introduction

The chapter whih follows originated as a conference presentation at the 1997 annual meeting of the National Trust for Historic Preservation (NTHP). It was the first time in 51 years of annual meetings that the NTHP devoted one of its educational sessions to the topic of "Lavender Landmarks." Nervously anticipated by conference planners on account of its politically charged subject matter, the session actually drew a packed and appreciative audience. Ultimately it shared the honor, with one other session, of receiving the most positive reviews at the Santa Fe meeting.

In a sense, that session was something of a Coming Out party for many LGBT staff and members of that national non-profit advocacy organization. The process of identifying allies, lobbying for the session, and organizing it built collective capacity to advocate for LGBT interests within the Trust and across the broader landscape of the preservation movement nationally. The level of interest and enthusiasm demonstrated by the audience helped to institutionalize LGBT receptions at the Trust's annual meetings, which provide opportunities to recognize local leadership and, where available, offer tours of local lavender landmarks. After Santa Fe, subsequent meetings in gay-friendly cities such as Washington, DC, and the Twin Cities continued to bring new energy and human resources into the fold. Indeed, the Trust's practice of holding its national meeting in a different host city annually has allowed the LGBT preservation advocacy network to grow organically.

Beyond the NTHP, independent efforts continue to make LGBT history visible through projects dedicated to mapping lavender landmarks, often as part of community-based heritage projects that gather oral histories, photographs, artifacts, create exhibits, and develop books and pamphlets focused on local history. While identifying places of significance remains a step removed from

---

1 This chapter draws on a brief discussion of preserving gay and lesbian history contained in Dubrow (1998a). An earlier version of this work was published in Dubrow (1998b). References to properties owned by the National Trust were censored in that version. The author wishes to express gratitude for Coll-Peter Thrush's able research assistance.

preservation action, it is often a first step in making a public case for saving the landmarks of LGBT heritage, and building community support for preservation action when specific properties are in jeopardy.

At the time this piece was first developed and presented, the National Trust for Historic Preservation was in the process of acquiring two historic properties of interest from gay and lesbian perspectives: the architect Philip Johnson's Glass House, in New Caanan, Connecticut; and Georgia O'Keefe's studio in Abiquiu, New Mexico. Indeed, with the NTHP conference held in Santa Fe that year, the studio was one of the most attractive options among the many conference-related tours. Fearing these real estate transactions would be soured by talk about the sexual orientation of the key historic figures associated with them, Trust leadership censored a brief discussion of these properties in the course of publishing a revised version of my conference presentation in a spring 1998 issue of *Historic Preservation Forum* (Dubrow 1998b).

I protested, to no avail, and ultimately decided it was more important to get the bulk of the work into print in a publication that would reach preservation activists and educators nationally. However, I foresaw future possibilities for publishing uncensored versions elsewhere and so pressed to retain copyright in my own name rather than vest all rights in *Forum*. Indeed, subsequent published versions, including this one, incorporate a frank discussion of properties held by the NTHP that were ripe for interpreting LGBT heritage in 1998 and which, more than a decade later, still beg for bolder interpretive approaches than have been presented to date. In my view, it is vital to hold preservation organizations and agencies accountable for developing accurate and complete interpretations of LGBT themes at the relevant historic properties they steward.

The structure of this chapter reflects emerging constructs for framing gay and lesbian history at the time of writing, particularly in its emphasis on the importance of pre-Stonewall forms of forging community and the inclusion of places significant in the oppression of LGBT people, such as psychiatric hospitals and the military. Limited detail about bisexual and transgender heritage, and the overrepresentation of places associated with white gay men, reflect but fail to remedy biases in the underlying scholarship that are now being corrected. A case in point is Compton's Cafeteria, a property in San Francisco that predates the Stonewall as the site of transgender resistance to police harassment which also merits landmark designation. Since most histories of the contemporary LGBT movement center on patron riots at New York City's Stonewall Inn as a watershed moment in political mobilization, the search for previously neglected landmarks has the potential to increase the visibility of the "T" in LGBT history and to find parallel origins of this United States civil rights movement on the East and West coasts. Revisiting an LGBT agenda for the preservation of lavender landmarks will require an ever more mindful approach to the commonalities and differences that have shaped LGBT people and the communities they have forged.

Blazing Trails

In recent years, the leading preservation institutions in the United States have made major commitments to diversity. The preservation movement's search for an expanded constituency and growing awareness of the tangible heritage of Native Americans, ethnic communities of color, and women have resulted in a more inclusive approach to managing the nation's cultural resources.[2] While the issue of preserving gay and lesbian history has arisen from time to time in the context of these initiatives, and at individual historic properties, a movement calling for the protection of sites and buildings associated with gay and lesbian history has lagged behind other cultural diversity initiatives by more than a decade. One can only speculate on the forces that have discouraged gay and lesbian preservationists from organizing to promote the interests of their own communities: a powerful combination of fear, isolation, caution about being pigeonholed, and an alienating ethic of professionalism that shuts its practitioners off from aspects of their own identity at least during working hours, if not for longer periods.

The nation's Culture Wars, played out in the form of conservative attacks on the National Endowment for the Arts' grants to individual artists, National Endowment for the Humanities funding, and the Smithsonian Institution's Enola Gay exhibition,[3] among others, give pause for concern about raising the issue of gay and lesbian history within the preservation programs of the National Trust, the National Park Service, and their state and local equivalents. Even the most vocal advocates for gay rights fear damaging the cause of preservation by stating our grievances. No doubt you've seen Gary Larsen's *Far Side* cartoon with two deer in the woods, standing and talking. One has a bull's eye on its chest; the other offers condolences: "Bummer of a birthmark!"[4] But in spite of the risks, some of us feel a profound need to reconcile our identities as gay people and devoted preservationists. And to be both, in our time, is a troubling experience, since it means rarely (if ever) encountering an acknowledgment of the existence of gays in history, much less a positive depiction of gay identity, at the historic sites and buildings that are our life's work. In the words of Paula Martinac, the author of the first national guide to gay and lesbian historic sites, *The Queerest Places*:

> I can't remember a time when I wasn't attracted to historic places. When I was a child, my parents didn't have to drag me to Civil War battlefields and historic house museums; I went willingly. As an adult, my first professional job was

---

2 See Antoinette Lee's writings on the subject of preserving ethnic cultural diversity (Lee 1987, 1992a, 1992b, Lee and Lyons 1992). Also see Dolores Hayden (1995).

3 Two publications on the Culture Wars are recommended readings for those preservationists who intend to take on the controversial issue of addressing gay and lesbian history in public venues (Harwitt 1996 and Linenthal and Engelhardt 1996).

4 For Gary Larson's collected cartoons, see *The Far Side* and *The Far Side Gallery* (Kansas City, MO: Andrews and McMeel, 1982).

at a restored historic village. I still think a vacation is incomplete unless I've taken in at least one town that time has forgotten. Recently asked about my favorite magazines, I named *Preservation* at the top of the list. But one thing that historic sites and travel guides never taught me was about a most important part of myself – my heritage as a gay person in this country. (Martinac 1997: xi)

Having emerged from a culture of shame to find pride in our identity, many gay and lesbian preservationists are profoundly troubled by the way our heritage is represented at historic properties: the glaring omissions, deafening silences, misleading euphemisms, and outright lies we repeatedly encounter in relation to our gay heritage and our gay lives.

For this reason, gay preservationists, buoyed by a broader movement for social, political and cultural equity, are likely to become the principal advocates for improving the protection and interpretation of their heritage. So too, a number of groups at the periphery of the preservation movement potentially are important allies. A new generation of scholars provides a foundation for documenting places significant in the gay and lesbian past.[5] George Chauncey's prize-winning history, *Gay New York,* reaches back to turn of the century urban institutions, such as bars, bathhouses, cafeterias, and residences that were critical to the development of gay consciousness and culture (Chauncey 1994). Esther Newton's study of Cherry Grove, on Fire Island, suggests the importance of resort destinations where gays and lesbians could "be themselves" long before it was socially acceptable to be open about their sexual orientation in the rest of American society (Newton 1993). Elizabeth Kennedy and Madeline Davis's study of lesbian bars in Buffalo, New York, titled *Boots of Leather, Slippers of Gold*, finds that in the period from the 1930s to 1960s these sites were critical to the emergence of the gay and lesbian liberation movement (Kennedy and Davis 1993). Accounts that more directly chronicle the emergence of the homophile movement in the 1950s, such as John D'Emilio's *Sexual Politics, Sexual Communities*, suggest the importance of groups such as the Mattachine Society and Daughters of Bilitis (D'Emilio 1983). Founded in Los Angeles in 1951, the Mattachine Society was the first American political organization established for the purpose of defending the rights of homosexuals. The Daughters of Bilitis, founded in San Francisco in 1955, was the first lesbian social and political organization in the United States.

There has been an outpouring of work on the physical spaces associated with the gay community, from Alan Berube's history of gay bathhouses (Berube 1996) to the humorously titled collection *Queers in Space*, edited by Gordon Ingram et al. and published by Bay Press.[6] Graduate programs in historic preservation

---

5 Major works on the history of gays and lesbians in the United States include: Faderman (1991), Marcus (1992), Sears (1997), Kaiser (1997), and Miller (1995), among others.

6 Examples of work focusing on the architectural and spatial dimensions of gay lives include: Castells (1983), Ingram et al. (1997), Whittle (1994), Bell and Valentine (1995a), Castells and Murphy (1982), Grosz (1995), Betsky (1997), and Kenney (1998).

are beginning to produce student theses on gay topics (Lustbader 1993, Reyes 1993, Kenney 1994). Works focusing on individual urban communities are being published, such as Susan Stryker and Jim Van Buskirk's (1966) history of San Francisco, *Gay by the Bay*. The rich detail contained in these and other studies raises the prospect of designating particular properties as gay and lesbian landmarks. In addition, recently published works have begun to interrogate the history of urban renewal and the rise of the preservation movement in light of gay and lesbian history. The History Project's *Improper Bostonians* (1998), for example, showed how at least one public official promoted the destruction of gay bars under the guise of urban renewal, claiming "we will be better off without these incubators of homosexuality and indecency and a Bohemian way of life." (The History Project 1998: 190)

Gay and lesbian communities have nurtured their own grassroots history projects for more than a decade (see Duggan 1986 for the United States and Wotherspoon 1992 for Australia) in the form of oral history programs, archives, exhibitions, and, more recently, maps and guides to historic sites and buildings in cities such as Boston, New York, Seattle, and Los Angeles.[7] One project in New York City, by the collective RepoHistory, produced a series of interpretive signs in the form of pink masonite triangles on signposts; however it was only a temporary project.[8] I found this project moving personally, since it happened to include one of the landmarks of my own adolescent coming out, a lesbian bar of the early 1970s named Bonnie and Clyde's. While these projects have increased public awareness of gay and lesbian heritage, to date there have been no efforts to secure landmark status for the historic properties identified on these maps, or to develop on-site interpretive programs. A partnership between community history projects and local preservation organizations might provide the right mix of skills needed to improve the protection of these resources.

In recent years, the preservation movement has taken the first steps toward gaining greater visibility for gay and lesbian heritage. The National Trust's 1996 annual conference featured the first social gathering for gay and lesbian preservationists, followed by the organization's approval of an educational session for the 1997 meeting. Subsequent meetings in Washington, DC and Los Angeles

---

7 See for example: *New York: A Guide to Lesbian and Gay Historical Landmarks* (New York: Organization of Lesbian and Gay Architects and Designers, 1994) [P.O. Box 927, Old Chelsea Station, New York, NY 10113]; Seattle: *Changing Space: A Historical Map of Lesbian and Gay Seattle* (Seattle: Northwest Lesbian and Gay History Museum Project, June 1996); Los Angeles: *Gay and Lesbian History Tour*; Boston: Gay and Lesbian Architects and Designers, and Boston Area Gay and Lesbian History Project (Boston: 1995). More recent compilations include: Beemyn (1997), LeVay and Nonas (1995), and Murphy (1995).

8 RepoHistory designated nine sites as significant in New York City's gay and lesbian history. "Queer Spaces: Places of Struggle, Places of Strength," was commissioned by the Storefront for Art and Architecture (June 18–July 30, 1994).

have featured field sessions that highlighted the cities' gay and lesbian landmarks and neighborhoods. Dennis Drabelle's pathbreaking article in *Preservation* magazine, aptly titled "Out and About in the City," signaled the National Trust's willingness to address this issue in its most public venue (Drabelle 1997). Two regional meetings of the Western Office of National Trust for Historic Preservation[9] forged connections among gay and lesbian preservationists and galvanized plans for a subsequent educational session at the 1997 meeting of the National Trust for Historic Preservation in Santa Fe, New Mexico. Gradually, gays and lesbians within the staff and membership of the Trust have gained space for addressing their concerns. These events have seeded the development of an informal network that is likely to generate future projects aimed at improving the protection and interpretation of so-called "lavender" landmarks.

Martinac's national guide to gay and lesbian historic places, the maps produced by community-based groups, and increasingly rich scholarship suggest several broad themes and a wide array of property types significant in gay and lesbian history. Within each category, public controversy surrounding the protection and interpretation of these sites is likely to crystallize along predictable lines, to which preservationists should be prepared to respond (see for example Herman 1996). Places already designated as landmarks are perhaps the most obvious places to begin remedying omissions and the distortions in the presentation of gay and lesbian history. For the most part, these take the form of historic houses associated with notable individuals,[10] many of which are open to the public and have ongoing interpretive programs, but where little is said about the sexual orientation of the prime subject. M.J. Lowe (1997) in "Outing the National Register," discusses many of these places in greater detail. Examples include:

1. Walt Whitman's row house on Mickle Street in Camden, New Jersey, where he lived with his much younger lover Harry Stafford, who one biographer has called the "central figure of them all."[11] (NR = National Register)
2. "Clear Comfort," the Staten Island, New York family seat of pioneering photographer Alice Austen. Austen lived at Clear Comfort for much of her

---

9 The first of these regional meetings, "Learning within the Castro," held in San Francisco on March 15, 1997, and a follow-up meeting held in Seattle on August 10, 1997 enabled participants to attend Trevor Hailey's lively San Francisco tour, "Cruisin' the Castro" and Jay Gifford's "Victorian Home Walk," which introduced Trust members to places of historical significance in the formation of the San Francisco's gay and lesbian community, as well as contemporary landmarks, from a comfortable distance as armchair tourists.

10 For a list of important gay figures in history, see Russell (1995). The study of gay and lesbian writers is relevant since so many historic houses are associated with major literary figures. For an overview of the subject see Haggerty and Zimmerman (1995), Summers (1995), and Sedgwick (1993).

11 A discussion of the homoerotics of Whitman's poetry and his sexual orientation is pervasive in recent literary criticism and biography. For example see Schmidgall (1997), Erkkila and Grossman (1996), Reynolds (1995), and Fone (1992).

life and shared her life and home there with Gertrude Tate for more than 30 years (Martinac 1997: 124-5).[12] (NHL = National Historic Landmark)
3. Willa Cather's childhood home in Red Cloud, Nebraska, where she created her alter-ego William J. Cather, whose masculine "dress and manner brought her considerable notoriety and made her the subject of much talk about town," prefiguring her unorthodox adult life, both as a lesbian and as a woman writer. In this setting, one biographer claims, Cather "discovered alternative stories for a woman's life."[13] (NR)
4. Gertrude Stein's home on Biddle Street in Baltimore, corresponding to her early days as a medical student at Johns Hopkins University and her first explorations of her lesbian identity. Although Stein's life-long partnership with Alice B. Toklas is well-acknowledged, her early years at Biddle Street mark her involvement in a love-triangle with May Bookstaver and Mabel Haynes that took her "off the academic rails" (Souhami 1991: 52–4). She wrote about it in her posthumously published *QED*, her first book (Wagner-Martin 1995: 28–55).
5. The Durham Street house in Baltimore's Fell's Point neighborhood, from which a young Eleanora Fagen would make her first sexual explorations in the area's street culture before changing her name to Billie Holiday and embarking on a stellar musical career. Holiday was known to have had "many affairs with men and women" (Martinac 1997: 65–7, Clark 1994, Nicholson 1995).
6. Frances Willard's Evanston, Illinois home, which also served as headquarters for the Women's Christian Temperance Union. Willard shared her home there with Anna Gordon for many years. Biographer Ruth Bordin has described them as "almost two sides of a single coin as their years together unfolded and they pursued their common public and private goals."[14] (NHL)
7. Potentially the most controversial site, Eleanor Roosevelt's retreat Val-Kill in Hyde Park, New York, to which she and her longtime companion journalist Lorena Hickok would retire between travels. While many Roosevelt biographers steadfastly have denied the possibility of a lesbian relationship with Hickok, historian Blanche Wiesen Cook's biography (1992) openly explores the possibility of a meaningful love relationship between the two women.[15] (NHS)

---

12 For sources on Austen see Novotny (1976) and Jensen (1987).

13 Several biographies explicitly address Cather's sexual identity (Lee 1989, O'Brien 1987, O'Brien 1995).

14 See Frances Willard's own comments about companionship in her autobiography (Willard 1889) and biographies such as Bordin (1986).

15 Cook (1992) was the first scholarly work to fully address Eleanor Roosevelt's relationship with Lorena Hickok. Cook's view was bolstered by the publication of their correspondence in Streitmatter (1998). Nevertheless, this view remains controversial.

Dealing with gay and lesbian history at these types of properties raises a number of important issues: the relevance of so-called private lives to public accomplishments; the propriety of presenting information about homosexuality to public audiences that include children;[16] the ethics of "outing" historical figures who may have wished to remain "closeted;"[17] the fluidity of people's sexuality over a lifetime; definitions of sexual identity that are themselves historically contingent; and the danger of reading sexuality into close relationships that were otherwise chaste. Nevertheless, enough is known about the sexual and affectional preferences of many major American figures to justify remedial action that honestly addresses the facts at historic places devoted to their lives and accomplishments.

Lest these properties seem too far removed from the mainstream of preservation, a striking example was included on tours offered in conjunction with the 1997 meeting of the National Trust for Historic Preservation, held in Santa Fe, New Mexico, as well as in the Trust's permanent portfolio of historic properties. Tours of Georgia O'Keeffe's Abiquiu home and studio figured prominently in the program of the Trust's 51st annual meeting. Those unable to visit had an opportunity to learn about the property from a movie shown in the conference's closing plenary session, which celebrated the Georgia O'Keeffe Foundation's recent gift of the property to the Trust. Yet the information about O'Keeffe's life presented in both settings would have left most site visitors and film viewers deeply surprised about the inclusion of the property in Paula Martinac's guide to gay and lesbian sites, since existing public interpretation reinforces the common view that her most significant relationship "was with her husband Alfred Stieglitz." Yet, Martinac argues, it was only her most celebrated one, since O'Keeffe "was a bisexual who also enjoyed the company of a number of young women over the years" (Martinac 1997: 296–7).

Recent scholarship has provided evidence to support Martinac's claims. Jeffrey Hogrefe, in his biography *O'Keeffe: The Life of an American Legend*, asserts that:

> The artist, like many married women in this period, maintained secret homosexual alliances. When asked whether O'Keeffe had any beaus, Phoebe Pack – a close friend for many of her later years – stated that the artist had only women lovers when she knew her in New Mexico and that, as she understood it, her union with Stieglitz had been a 'marriage of convenience.' Virginia Christianson told

---

16   For an excellent discussion of the presentation of gay topics and the experience of gay students in the schools, see Debra Chasnoff and Helen Cohen's film, *It's Elementary* (San Francisco: Women's Educational Media, 1996) and Jeff Dupre's *Out of the Past* (New York: Zeitgeist Distributors, 1998).

17   Many individuals who managed same-sex relationships during their lives with an extraordinary degree of candor and discretion, destroyed their personal papers, or directed their families to do so upon their death to avoid exposure. Other flamboyantly gay figures remained adamantly closeted, such as Liberace. On the broader subject of "outing," see Gross (1993).

me that 'All her life, I think, Georgia had been a lesbian.' The son of another friend told me that O'Keeffe was a part of a small and select group of women who lived around Santa Fe in the forties and fifties. He said that although many of the women had relationships with men, it was his understanding that they had sexual relations with one another. (Hogrefe 1992: 26–7)

O'Keeffe's active efforts to hide her lesbian relationships misled some people, although Hogrefe discovered that they were common knowledge in Santa Fe. Those in the know remained silent out of respect for her privacy.

Given O'Keeffe's clear preference for keeping this aspect of her sexual orientation out of public view during her lifetime, the question remains as to whether it is relevant to the public interpretation of her Abiquiu property. The fact that O'Keeffe's home and studio were renovated and managed by her on-again, off-again lover Maria Chabot suggests the relevance of information about her intimate relationships to an understanding of the landmark. In Martinac's words, "the renovation of the Abiquiu house was overseen by Maria Chabot, a writer who began living with O'Keeffe in 1941 in an intimate friendship – 'a tall handsome young woman,' as O'Keeffe described her. Maria planned all the details of the renovation, including the location of the fireplaces, and studied Hopi architecture in order to duplicate its designs." The major biographies of O'Keeffe all acknowledge Chabot's leading role in the renovation, though Benita Eisler's study of O'Keeffe and Stieglitz may be the most emphatic:

> To her function as majordomo, Chabot now added the roles of architect, designer and construction superintendent. She commandeered building materials unseen since the construction of Los Alamos – copper wiring, plumbing, electrical fixtures, even hard-to-find nails. She supervised the fabrication of adobe bricks on site, along with the handwork of the women who traditionally smoothed the sand-and-water mixture into facing, covering perpendicular corners with the famed curves of reddish pink. She saw to the traditional interior features of the two main buildings, both painted white. To these, O'Keeffe contributed her preference for minimal furnishings: built-in cushioned benches around the walls, low shelves for books and phonographs, shells and bones, and a country kitchen that could have belonged to a Wisconsin farm. (Eisler 1991: 482)

A fuller and more candid explanation of O'Keeffe's sexual orientation would help the visitor to understand Chabot's instrumental role in the renovation and help to explain her personal stake in the place.

Also listed in Martinac's guide is Philip Johnson's Glass House in New Canaan, Connecticut, which the architect designed and built in 1949 and recently willed to the National Trust for Historic Preservation. Johnson kept his homosexual orientation a secret for most of his life. As Charles Kaiser wrote in *The Gay Metropolis*, "Johnson was of a class and a generation who were routinely invited to the fanciest dinner parties, but who never brought along a male companion" (Kaiser 1997: 213). Later in life, however, Johnson came out of the closet and spoke openly about his homosexuality in interviews. While some people legitimately might question the relevance of the architect's sexual orientation to the public interpretation of the Glass House, the fact that it served as Johnson's home makes his personal life more relevant than if it were merely one of his vast number of commissioned works.

Architectural critic Aaron Betsky has offered the novel interpretation that Johnson's sexuality actually is expressed in the "queerness" of the design "of many of his buildings:"

> their theatricality, role-playing, licentiousness, twisting of norms and 'passing' as normal – that gives them life. Maybe only a queer could live in a glass house and sleep in a windowless box down the hill on a bed surrounded by domes and floor-to-ceiling curtains. Only a queer, perhaps, would need to push things to the extreme and then sell them and himself as just the right thing. (Betsky 1995: 46–7)[18]

While this interpretation is not entirely persuasive, some facts help to build the case for interpreting the Glass House in light of his intimate relationships. The remarkable collection of art within it was collected by Johnson's lover of over 30 years, David Whitney. The intimacy of their relationship was publicly clarified in Martin Filler's 1996 *New York Times* article:

> The tall, baby-faced Mr Whitney was sitting in a sunny corner of the one-bedroom apartment that he and Mr Johnson, companions now for 36 years, share at the Museum Tower in midtown Manhattan. (Filler 1996: 37, 40)

Though Johnson's willingness to publicly acknowledge his relationship with Whitney came late in life, his eventual candor strengthens the case for incorporating these dimensions of his life into the interpretation of the Glass House and other Johnson landmarks. In years to come, the connection between Johnson's sexual orientation and some of his commissioned works will be difficult to ignore, particularly his design of the 2,000-seat Cathedral of Hope for a gay and lesbian congregation in Dallas, Texas, undertaken at the age of 90 when he finally was living openly as a gay person. The National Trust has its future work cut out for it, as the owner of two and possibly more nationally significant historic properties associated with gay, lesbian, or bisexual people. These holdings provide the organization with an opportunity to assume leadership by bringing new candor to previously suppressed aspects of history.

Beyond the historic houses associated with notable individuals, there is a pressing need to interpret and preserve places associated with the emergence of

---

18 For his interpretation of Johnson's oeuvre also see Betsky (1997: 114–17).

homosexual community and identity,[19] many of which meet the 50 year threshold required to qualify for National Register listing.[20] These properties raise the political stakes even higher, since they are associated with the deeply stigmatized territory of gay men's sexual culture. Landmarks of this period include:

1. Gay bars such as the Doubleheader, in Seattle's Pioneer Square, which reputedly is the oldest continually operating gay bar in the country (Paulsen 1996).[21]
2. Bathhouses, such as New York City's famous Everard, Lafayette, St. Marks and the Mt. Morris (Martinac 1997: 104).[22] Nearly all are gone, many having been closed by local authorities in response to the AIDS epidemic. In New York only the Mt. Morris was operative in 1997 when Martinac published her guidebook.
3. YMCAs such as the Army and Navy Y in Newport, Rhode Island; on G Street in Washington, DC; and the Harlem branch in New York City (Martinac 1997: 41–2; 60–61; 94–5; 226; and 309).[23]
4. Venues in Harlem such as the Hamilton Lodge and the Savoy Ballroom that hosted the colorful Costume Balls of the Jazz Age, thus were an early focus for the culture of Drag (Martinac 1997: 93–4).[24]
5. Various forms of public open space that historically served as cruising places for gay men, such as New York's Washington Square Park and Central Park; Seattle's Volunteer Park; and DC's Lafayette Park, across the street from the White House (Martinac 1997: 53–4).[25]
6. Sections of public beaches and distinctive resort communities, such as Cherry Grove on Fire Island in New York, which began to attract gay people

---

19 Many historical works on the pre-Stonewall period already have been noted. Others include: Noel (1978), Weiss and Schiller (1988), McKay (1993), Nardi et al. (1994), and Gilmartin (1996). Also see several films: *Last Call at Maud's* [Video recording about a San Francisco lesbian bar], by the Maud Project (New York: Water Bearer Films, 1993); *Forbidden Love: The Unashamed Stories of Lesbian Lives* [Video recording of a National Film Board of Canada Studio D Production about Canadian lesbians' experience in the bars of the 1950s and 1960s] (New York: Women Make Movies, 1992).

20 *National Register Bulletin* 16A, "How to Complete a National Register Form," neatly summarizes the qualifications for listing properties on the National Register.

21 Paulson (1996) documented Seattle's gay history and associated bar scene.

22 For a detailed history of gay bathhouses in New York City, including the surviving Mt. Morris Baths, see Chauncey (1994: 207–25, especially 218). Also see Shilts (1992a: 37–9, 1992b: 39).

23 The role of YMCAs in orienting newcomers to the gay urban scene is described in great detail in Chauncey (1994: 151–77).

24 For greater detail see Chauncey (1994: 227–67 and 271–99). Other works that deal with camp sensibility include: Ross (1989), Bergman (1993); and Meyer (1994).

25 Also see Chauncey (1994: 179–205). For a pioneering study of the public sites of gay male sexual encounters see Laud Humphreys (1975).

in the 1920s and 1930s, and has enjoyed a reputation as a gay haven to the present day (Newton 1993). Other resort communities include Provincetown, Massachusetts; Key West, Florida; and Palm Springs, California.
7. Homes, churches, and offices that provided havens for the homophile movement, such as the First Universalist Church in Los Angeles and the homes of movement leaders.[26]

In rare cases, this sort of site has been added to the list of properties on landmark registers for reasons having nothing to do with its queer connections. Boston's Club Baths, for examine, was housed in a building designed by H.H. Richardson, a fact that secured its place on the city's landmarks register. The failure to recognize this and other buildings' historical (as opposed to architectural) significance means that landmark protection powers rarely extend to interior features that may contribute to the property's integrity of feeling and association with respect to gay heritage. But because most historic places significant in gay and lesbian history are completely missing from landmark registers, this broad category of properties needs to be surveyed so that individual properties can be assessed for potential listing in the National Register as well as its state and local equivalents.

Harry Hay's home in Los Angeles,[27] which served as the founding place for the Mattachine Society, is a likely prospect for landmark designation based on its significance in gay and lesbian history. A pre-application has been filed with the California State Historical Resources Commission that will begin the process of evaluating its eligibility for listing on the California State and National Registers.[28] Fortunately, a foundation has been laid for recognizing the significance of this property and others associated with gay and lesbian history in California. Public comments received on a statewide historic preservation plan led gays and lesbians to be added to the list of the state's historically significant communities.[29] This small development in cultural resource management policy probably is a "landmark" in its own right.

Properties such as these are sure to serve as flashpoints for controversy, since a significant portion of the American public still objects to homosexuality on moral and religious grounds. Nevertheless, preservationists and historians have

---

26 Perhaps the best history of male and female homophile organizations is contained in D'Emilio (1983), On the founding of the Daughters of Bilitis also see Martin and Lyon (1972). For oral histories that provide different views of the founding of the Mattachine Society and Daughters of Bilitis, see Eric Marcus (1992).

27 On Hay's historical significance see D'Emilio (1983: 58–70). Also see Timmons (1990), Roscoe (1996), and an interview with Hay in Katz (1976: 406–20).

28 Jeff Samudio and Howard Smith to Gail Dubrow, personal correspondence (October 3, 1997).

29 Office of Historic Preservation, Department of Parks and Recreation, The Resources Agency, *Forging a Future with a Past: A Comprehensive Statewide Historic Preservation Plan for California* (December 1997). Thanks to Jeff Samudio for pointing this out.

a professional responsibility to tell the truth about the past, and to help the public to distinguish between acknowledging historical reality and placing a government stamp of approval on it. If it is even possible to get beyond the political controversy, major issues remain about the relative significance and physical integrity of the surviving historic properties.

A third category of properties, consisting of sites and buildings connected with the gay and lesbian movement from 1969 onward[30] raise the issue of preserving the recent past and promise to draw preservationists directly into alliances with the gay community. These include places such as:

1. The Stonewall Inn, on NYC's Christopher Street, site of the June 28, 1969 police raid where patrons (mostly drag queens and people of color) fought back in response to police harassment (Martinac 1997: 120). Listed on the National Register of Historic Places in June of 1999, this was the first historic property to be listed on the National Register and designated a National Historic Landmark because of its significance in gay and lesbian history.[31]
2. Some gay urban neighborhoods legitimately might be considered historic districts or simply gay-identified districts for the purposes of planning: San Francisco's Castro District, Seattle's Capitol Hill and Pioneer Square, DC's Dupont Circle, Chicago's North Halsted Street, New York's Greenwich Village.
3. Individual historic properties finally are being considered for local landmark status, such as Harvey Milk's Castro Street Camera shop, which served as an ad hoc center for gay political organizing in San Francisco.[32]

Finally, there is another type of property that has not yet found its way into maps and guidebooks, namely places connected with the history of homophobia, ranging from mental hospitals[33] and military bases[34] to Anita Bryant's home in Dade

---

30   On the historical significance of the Stonewall Riot see Duberman (1993). On Stonewall's aftermath see Rutledge (1992).

31   For a report of the path-breaking landmark designation of Stonewall Inn, see Dunlap (1999). Christopher Thompson also provided an insider's account of the NRHP and NHL designation process in an oral presentation at the Third National Conference on Women and Historic Preservation in Washington, DC (May 20, 2000).

32   Harvey Milk's contributions to the rise of gay political power in San Francisco have been chronicled by Shilts (1982) and an Academy Award-winning film released on video, *The Times of Harvey Milk* (Beverly Hills, CA: Pacific Arts Video, 1986).

33   The path-breaking film *Word Is Out* contains a moving account of the institutionalization of homosexuals in the 1950s and 1960s, before the American Psychological Association's 1973 decision to remove homosexuality from its list of mental disorders. See the book based on that film: Nancy and Casey Adair, *Word is Out: Stories of Some of Our Lives* (San Francisco: New Glide Publications, 1978).

34   The history of gays in the military is well-documented in Alan Berube 1990 and in a related film of the same name by Arthur E. Dong, Salome Jens, and Alan Berube (Zeitgeist

County, Florida.³⁵ Efforts to reclaim interpretive space at sites that have harbored deep hostility to gays and lesbians are guaranteed to provoke fevered political battles. Ultimately, gay and lesbian history may have an even broader reach. Similar to women's history, which offers a reminder that the lives of men and women both merit historical interpretation through the lens of gender, the power of gay and lesbian history ultimately may reside in its ability to reveal the ways that heterosexuality is socially enforced and culturally constructed, a perspective that draws attention away from gay and lesbian landmarks and, instead, brings a wide range of locations into focus (Katz 1995).

If a shared fear is that the preservation movement will be drawn into the Culture Wars, and alienate conservative segments of its membership,³⁶ perhaps the best hope is that an honest and direct approach to this subject will lead to new alliances and a broader constituency for preservation that is founded on a genuine appreciation of the diverse heritage of the American people. Advocates for improving the preservation and interpretation of gay and lesbian history are likely to find support in several quarters. First, taking on this issue is likely to release new energy from gay people in the preservation movement, who have been eager for affirming policies and initiatives. Second, willing partners are likely to be found in the ranks of the historical profession and grassroots history groups, where an enormous amount of original work is being done to document gay and lesbian history. Third, gay and lesbian organizations have yet to be approached about the place of preservation in their broader programs, but the need to open a dialogue recently was thrown into high relief when San Francisco's Gay and Lesbian Community Services Center proposed to demolish the historic Fallon Building. Ultimately the building was saved, but the close call with the wrecking ball illuminated the need for focused outreach, not only to preserve gay and lesbian history, but to insure preservation's place in the ethos and on the agenda of gay organizations. One avenue for getting out the word is a thriving gay media, reflected in dozens of national and innumerable local periodicals which have yet to feature many articles on gay leaders and activists in the preservation movement, historic places of interest to gay travelers, or preservation issues relevant to the gay community.

Finally, support for implementing a gay preservation agenda is likely to be found in some segments of the marketplace,³⁷ particularly the real estate and travel industries. The existence of well-defined gay neighborhoods in most American

---

Films; a Deepfocus Production, 1995). On the oppression of homosexuals in the 1950s, see Alan Berube and John D'Emilio (1985), von Hoffman (1988), and Faderman (1991).

35 For her early volley in the emerging Culture Wars see Bryant (1977).

36 Lest we stereotype gays as liberals, a number of publications offer a helpful reminder that gay people can be found at every point in the political spectrum. For example, see Liebman (1992) and Gunderson et al. (1996).

37 The consumer behavior of gays and lesbians has been the subject of several works including: Wardlow (1996) and Lukenbill (1995). For a more critical study see Gluckman

cities, and realtors who explicitly market their services to the gay community, suggest potential alliances. The preservation community has long been aware of the connection between gay people and the revitalization of urban neighborhoods, though for many years this issue was framed exclusively in pejorative terms as "gentrification."[38] The City of Chicago's decision to invest $3.2 million in the renovation of North Halsted Street explicitly recognized the economic and political contributions of a gay neighborhood, while raising questions about the form so-called "gay-themed" street improvements might take (Zavis 1997, Reed 2003).

The emergence of a gay travel market led to the establishment of the International Gay and Lesbian Travel Association over 15 years ago; it now numbers more than 1,300 travel professionals (Holcomb and Luongo 1996, Reynolds 1997). As the National Trust met in 1997 in Santa Fe, the Fourth International Gay and Lesbian Travel Expo held its meeting at the San Francisco Marriott. Perhaps both organizations might be persuaded to find a common meeting site and agenda in the future. Car rental companies, hotels and airlines have begun to recognize the economic value of this market, including American Airlines, which counted "$149 million in ticket sales through primarily gay travel agencies or groups" in 1996. *Seattle's Gay Community Yellow Pages* lists more than a dozen travel agencies that cater to the interests of gay and lesbian clients,[39] including American Express Travel, which actively markets its services to the gay and lesbian community; Travel Solutions, which promotes "Gay and lesbian tour solutions;" Woodside Travel, which features "Gay Ski Weeks;" and Cathay Express, which offers "gay and lesbian travel packages." Perhaps the best is Royalty Travel, whose motto promises "Even if you're not a queen, we'll treat you like one."[40]

The rise of this segment of the travel industry suggests that in their time off, gay people may be seeking a holiday not so much from a heterosexual world, as a homophobic one.[41] This is why the gay travel industry is focused on providing gay-friendly service, carriers, lodging, and tourist destinations. From

---

and Reed (1997). On the broader influences of gay culture in straight America, see Van Leer (1995).

38 On the dynamics of gay involvement in the gentrification of a New Orleans neighborhood, see Knopp (1990b) who found that contrary to expectations, gay developers and speculators actively promoted community development in this neighborhood, whereas gay activists were the most resistant to change. Also see Johnston (1971), Lauria and Knopp (1985), Boyle (1985), DeWitt (1994), Knopp 1997, and also Moss (1997) who explores the role of nontraditional households in urban redevelopment. Fewer works address the presence of gays in the suburbs, however see Lynch (1987).

39 *Seattle's Gay and Lesbian Community Yellow Pages*, 1997/98 Edition (Phoenix: The Community Yellow Pages, 1997–98), 130–33.

40 American Express and Royalty Travel were listed in the *Greater Seattle Business Directory* (Seattle: Emerald City Arts, 1996–97), 237–42.

41 For a discussion of the discomforts of traveling as a gay couple in a homophobic world, see Van Gelder (1991).

the perspective of the preservation movement, however, it still has tremendous untapped potential for promoting tourism connected with gay and lesbian heritage. One tour operator featured a gay history canal tour as part of its travel packages for the August 1998 Gay Games, held in Amsterdam, and for years there has existed a *Pink Plaque Guide to London* (Elliman and Roll 1995). These types of itineraries could be developed for nearly every American city (Hurewitz 1997). Mainstream publishers such as Fodor's finally have begun to tap pent-up demand for gay travel guides,[42] but it is the responsibility of gay preservationists, their allies, and ultimately the larger preservation movement to ensure that something meaningful remains to visit by preserving the tangible resources associated with gay and lesbian history.

Since this issue is such a new one for the preservation movement, an agenda for improving the protection of gay and lesbian heritage is only now in the formative stages, and debate about strategies and tactics looms in the near future. In the interest of sparking a broader discussion, I offer my own tentative list of priorities.

Action Agenda

1. There is a need to write gays and lesbians into the history of the preservation movement, both as individuals and as communities vitally involved in urban revitalization and the development of gay-oriented tourist destinations by documenting their contributions.
2. There is a need to reinterpret existing landmarks to provide more accurate and complete presentations of gay and lesbian history by amending existing landmark nominations[43] and revising the interpretive programs at historic properties.[44]
3. There is a need to identify previously undesignated properties significant in gay and lesbian history by undertaking thematic surveys, both nationally and locally, that generate new nominations to landmark registers and, potentially, by conducting campaigns to protect the most significant properties.
4. There is a need to develop new tools to increase public education and awareness such as maps, tours, guidebooks, and interpretive signage; and

---

42   Gay and lesbian travel guides have been published under the imprint of Fodor, Detour, Out and About, Severe Queer Review, and others. For example, see *Fodor's Gay Guide to the U.S.A.* (New York: Fodor's Travel Publications, 1998).

43   *National Register Bulletin* 16A, "How to Complete National Register Forms," explains the process for amending National Register forms.

44   A recent series of projects aimed at improving the interpretation of women's history at historic properties provides useful models for new initiatives in the area of gay and lesbian history. On this subject see Dubrow et al. (1996), Putnam Miller (1992), as well as the other chapters in this collection.

recruit new sources of financial and political support for our projects by forging partnerships with historians, artists, publishers, architects, planners, social and political organizations, and businesses in and marketing to the gay community.
5. There is a need to develop new mechanisms of communication, mutual support, and activism on behalf of gay and lesbian heritage by establishing informal communication networks and a formal advocacy organization.
6. There is a need to develop strategies for improving the capacity of preservation organizations and agencies to address issues of concern to gays and lesbians by allocating resources, promoting policies and developing projects that commit preservation institutions to making demonstrable progress.

This agenda for change is not merely wishful thinking. While advocates for improving the preservation and interpretation of gay and lesbian history are sure to encounter resistance, more acceptance and support may exist than is commonly imagined, even in places far removed from the gay havens of Greenwich Village, Dupont Circle, North Halsted Street, Capitol Hill, and the Castro District. Chris Reed, an art historian at Lake Forest College, makes this point in telling the story of Pendarvis, a Wisconsin State Historical Landmark in the village of Mineral Point (population 2,400). As it happens:

> [a]lthough it is nominally a monument to the mid-nineteenth century tin miners of the area, the actual guided tour (local gals in nineteenth century costume) dwells at least as substantially on the two men who purchased, restored, and furnished with antiques the collection of cottages, which they ran as a restaurant. Their cottage (one bedroom) is preserved as it was circa 1965, as is the restaurant (very tiny and no longer functioning), complete with souvenir menus autographed by famous travelers such as JFK. These two structures complete the tour, much of which recounts the details of the men's meeting, their respective interests (cooking and antiquing!), their life in the community. No explicit mention is made of their sexuality, but terms such as "lifelong partnership" and "lifelong friendship" are used – and as I said, there is one bedroom. The whole effect is kind of a shrine to this gay couple, maintained by the State of Wisconsin. In addition to finding this curious, I will confess that I also found it rather touching as an example of the way a small town can ultimately come to accept and even celebrate the presence of a gay couple in its midst.[45]

Perhaps gays and lesbians along with other allies in the preservation movement can help to persuade the ladies leading the Pendarvis tour, as well as the institutions that manage major historic properties such as the homes of Willa Cather, Walt Whitman, Eleanor Roosevelt, Georgia O'Keeffe, and Philip Johnson, that it is

---

45 Chris Reed to Gail Dubrow, personal correspondence (October 3, 1997).

acceptable to utter the terrifying words gay, lesbian, bisexual, transgender, or even the newly reclaimed queer in their presentations, if they go on to explain why it is relevant and what it may have meant in a particular time and place.

Chapter 4
Querying Planning (Theory): Alphabet Soup or Paradox City?

Sue Hendler and Michael Backs

Introduction

Since its emergence in the late 1980s queer theory has been deployed in academic and activist circles as a means of problematizing and resisting naturalized Western assumptions about sexuality which are grounded in essentialist thinking that divides subjects into rigid binary divisions such as gay and straight. Queer theory invites interrogation of the fixity of these categories, positing that they are actually culturally and historically constituted. In other words, our modern definitions of sexual identity have been produced through various processes of social, moral, and legal regulation, as well as through an attribution to scientific experts who circulate various truth claims about sexuality. Previous work in the area of gay and lesbian studies sought to uncover the experiences and oppressions of gays and lesbians, who were seen as possessing an innate homosexual identity, through the use of various empirical methods. Instead, queer theory disrupts these understandings of identity, calling into question their discursive origins. With a foundation in poststructural thought, queer theory analyzes "the institutional practices and discourses producing sexual knowledges and the way they organize social life" (Seidman 1996: 13). The utility of queer theory lies in its challenge to a broad range of assumptions about the nature of social life, not simply those that relate in a direct way to sexuality (Green 2007, Stein and Plummer 1994). Over the previous 20 years, scholars of queer theory have provided critical interventions into economic, political, and social spheres. Here we argue that queer theory can help us to unpack normative assumptions about planning, as both a profession and as a process, through identifying the various ways that sexuality has influenced the organizing principles of planning.

We begin this chapter by providing an introductory overview of the origins and central tenets of queer theory, as well as some of the prevailing debates in this area, that have been the subject of much contestation since Michel Foucault first laid its foundations. We offer the caveat that, because of the complexity of queer theory and the vast body of literature, we concentrate on its primary figures and concerns, as well as the social and political contexts that shaped it. Following this introduction, we start to integrate the tenets of queer theory, and its challenges, to the theory and practice of planning. By providing a queer reading of planning as theory and as praxis, we challenge the normative assumptions about sexuality that have played a central, though often implicit, role in the shaping of planning practices. Because the process of queering involves a troubling of norms and an imagining of ways to resist these norms, we conclude by offering suggestions for future work in this area – one which seems to be fraught with more good questions than answers.[1]

Queer Theory: An Overview

The origination of queer theory can be located in the ascendancy of poststructural thought within social theory (Jagose 1996). At its core, poststructuralism encourages consideration of the self within the wider context of a given society, recognizing that individual subjectivities are actually products of multiple and relational forms of power operating at various levels – from institutional practices to social relations in our everyday lives. Namaste observes that, within a poststructural framework, "subjects are not the autonomous creators of themselves or their social worlds", and instead are "precisely constituted in and through specific socio-political arrangements" (1996a: 195). This position challenges essentialist understandings of human identity rooted in structuralist discourse that have long dominated our thinking, which contend that an individual's particular characteristics – one's race, gender, or sexuality, to name a few – are innate, biological properties. The reliance upon essentialist accounts of these characteristics has foreclosed our thinking about how inequality is derived from the construction of these rigid categories (Valocchi 2005: 752). Poststructuralism dismantles essentialist categories by inviting us to think about how individuals are located within culture, history, and space. In so doing, it challenges the pervasive modernist view of an individual's ability to operate as an autonomous agent (Namaste 1996a: 195).

This mode of inquiry is prevalent in the work of the French historian and philosopher Michel Foucault, who is a central figure associated with poststructuralism (though Foucault himself would have likely rejected such a label). Foucault's work seeks to uncover the relations of power that contribute to the discursive production of particular forms of truth and knowledge. This is apparent in the first volume of *The History of Sexuality* (1978), where he employs a genealogical approach to identify the origins of our contemporary naturalized

---

[1] We do not incorporate much work by urban and human geographers in our discussion. Geography, it would seem, is significantly ahead of planning in terms of incorporating considerations of sexuality and queer theory in its literature (especially Bell and Valentine 1995a, Binnie 1997, and Knopp 1994, 1994, 2007, among others). While their work is relevant to, and interesting for, planning academics and planners, we have chosen to focus on planning per se. It is this field that goes beyond analysis to practice and it is this practice that helps shape our physical and social environments in ways that may be more or less conducive to welcoming a variety of both ideas and identities.

knowledge of sexuality by inquiring how it has "been used in the service of the formation of the modern self" (Green 2007: 29). It was through this undertaking that he laid the groundwork for the emergence of queer theory.

Foucault's historical analysis of the contingencies in European society that lead to the establishment of a dominant body of knowledge of sexuality illustrated how competing claims to truth were crucial in the formation of our contemporary categories of sexual identity. He accomplishes this by first describing cultural attitudes towards sexuality prior to the Victorian era, characterizing this as a period when "sexual practices had little need of secrecy" (1978: 3). At the dawn of the seventeenth century, "codes regulating the coarse, the obscene, and the indecent were quite lax compared to those of the nineteenth century" (Foucault 1978: 3). However, "twilight soon fell upon this bright day, followed by the monotonous nights of the Victorian bourgeoisie" (ibid). Victorian values privileged above all others sexual acts whose sole purpose was reproduction, bringing about the normative model of the "procreative couple" (Foucault 1978: 3) which confined such sexual acts to the bedroom. Any consideration of sex that had been present in public discourse faded as heterosexual acts asserted their legitimacy through their utilitarian value, which was to maintain the population. Furthermore, any consideration of sexual acts that deviated from this procreative norm was scrutinized by scientific experts seeking to uncover the "truth" about these forms of sexuality. The lens of science reinforced the view that such acts were "aberrations, perversions, exceptional oddities, pathological abatements, and morbid aggravations" (Foucault 1978: 53). Those forms of sexuality that did not conform to the newly established normative model of the procreative couple were now regarded as an unnatural pathology to be diagnosed, studied, and treated.

Central to the establishment of a body of knowledge focused on these pathologies was a naming process used by scientific and medical experts to render these "peripheral sexualities" knowable. While certain acts between same-sex partners like sodomy[2] had been historically outlawed in a number of societies, these experts began to link such acts to identity. It was this process that resulted in the production of the category of homosexuality. As Foucault explains, while "the sodomite had been a temporary aberration; the homosexual was now a species" (Foucault 1978: 43). The newly identified homosexual "became a personage, a past, a case history, and a childhood in addition to being a type of life, a life form, and a morphology, with an indiscreet anatomy and possibly a mysterious physiology" (Foucault 1978: 43). Observing the rise of homosexuality as a discrete category of identity, Namaste notes that it was "originally a taxonomic device employed within sexology [which] ... subsequently gained currency in judicial and psychiatric fields of knowledge" (1996a: 195). Sedgwick, another central figure in the development of queer theory, calls this categorization, world mapping:

---

2 Sodomy, for example, was "used as an umbrella term to cover a range of practices which did not have procreation as their aim" (Sullivan 2003: 3).

[B]y which every person, just as he or she was necessarily assignable to a male or female gender, was now considered necessarily assignable as well to a homo- or hetero-sexuality, a binarized identity that was full of implications, however confusing, for even the ostensibly least sexual aspects of personal existence. (1990: 2)

This process of world mapping, and indeed Foucault's account of the emergence of homosexuality as a discursively produced identity category, not only reveals the historically specific origins of our normative categories of sexuality. It also reveals the productive relationship between power and knowledge, in that the privilege afforded to scientific discourse and its "experts" allowed for the reconstitution of same-sex attraction into a pathological condition that deviated from acceptable societal norms.[3]

Foucault's writings on the power-knowledge relationship that enabled the identification of the ways that discursive sexual practices were fixed as categories remained prominent in the work of many other scholars in the years following his untimely death in 1984 (see key texts including Butler 1990, Sedgwick 1990, Warner 1990, Fuss 1991). Prominent among these is Judith Butler's deconstruction of gender and sexual identity which began in 1990s *Gender Trouble* and continued in her subsequent work. In reflecting on feminist theory, Butler observes its common tendency to assume "that there is some existing identity, understood through the category of women, who not only initiates feminist interests and goals within discourse, but constitutes the subject for whom political representation is pursued" (1990: 1). Here, Butler recognizes the prevalence of identity politics, whereby universally-defined subjects, assuming themselves deserving of rights and political representation based on their understanding of their identity as being somehow innate, organizes with other similarly defined subjects to seek these rights. Brown (1995: 59) explains that this is necessary within the context of liberal Western democracy because integration into this system of recognition can only be achieved by normalizing – or depathologizing, in the case of sexuality – identities through processes rooted in practices of depoliticization.

This is exactly how the contemporary gay, lesbian, bisexual and transgender rights movement that emerged in the late 1970s has organized itself, with a focus

---

3   While Foucault also examines the role of religion in the regulation of sexual practice, prior to the Enlightenment, "sexual knowledge was primarily concerned with technique and pleasure" (Wilchins 2004: 49). This began to change as the Catholic Church increasingly adopted monastic practices. According to Wilchins, "the Church's approach to sex ... would eventually move sex from the periphery of minor transgressions and place it as the central issue of morality... which demanded of people new forms of vigilance" (2004: 49-50). Sex had, in short, "become something that threatened salvation" (2004: 50). For Wilchins, this marked the first shift in thought about sexuality in the West. Individuals ceased engaging in sexual practices for pleasure for fear of being labeled a sinner, and sex took on a distinctively procreative purpose.

on achieving civil rights for a minority group. While the scientific discourse of the nineteenth century described by Foucault cast homosexual acts as the result of unnatural pathologies, the LGBT movement has deployed essentialist arguments surrounding sexual desire as a means of normalizing homosexuality in an effort to persuade mainstream, heterosexual society of the immutable nature of sexual identity. Essentialist understandings of sexuality have fuelled demands for rights recognition and have played a central role in the recent gains made by this movement, particularly in the granting of same-sex marriage rights in Canada and some US states. In short, homosexuality is presented as a natural disposition – much like heterosexuality. We are either born gay or straight, and to deny equality to individuals on this basis is seen as an affront to civil and human rights.

Queer theorists challenge the conceptually problematic nature of this view. For Butler, sexuality is "culturally constructed within existing power relations" (1990: 30), meaning that there is no innate sexual orientation that we can separate from the various structures and relations of power that surround us. The LGBT movement has made a concentrated effort to present homosexuality as being similar, and therefore equal, to heterosexuality, but Butler asserts that, "gay is to straight *not* as copy is to original, but rather, as copy is to copy" (1990: 31). This suggests that, first, the belief that heterosexuality exists as some kind of default position against which we can define homosexuality is flawed, and second, that even the binary distinction between homosexuality and heterosexuality is inauthentic because of its constructed nature. In this view, heterosexuality is not *more* natural or inherently more acceptable than homosexuality because desire is actually fluid and ever-changing. The deployment of an innate understanding of homosexuality, however, has become necessary – and indeed has proven successful for some – for gaining rights and recognition from the state.

Some queer theorists have attributed the necessity of this tactic to the heteronormative structure that underlies our socio-political relations, as "a set of norms that make heterosexuality seem natural or right and that organize homosexuality as its binary opposite" (Valocchi 2005: 756). Valocchi contends that heteronormativity "works to maintain the dominance of heterosexuality by preventing homosexuality from being a form of sexuality that can be taken for granted ... or seem right in the way heterosexuality can". Again, activists and academics have used queer theory to challenge this approach, on the grounds that it reifies heterosexuality as the dominant binary category, leading LGBT-identified individuals to feel obligated to align themselves with essentialist modes of thought.[4]

---

4 This fact is clear when one considers the reactions to the formation in 1998 of a Gays and Lesbians Division (GALIP) of the American Planning Association (as noted in Chapter 1). Various letter writers made clear that being gay or lesbian was seen as a lifestyle choice. It is little wonder that people having queer identities have felt a need to, basically, essentialize their sexualities in order to address the perceived mutability and hence triviality of the notion of "choice".

Queer theory has evolved remarkably since Foucault laid its foundations in *The History of Sexuality*. It has enabled those who reject the conformist practices associated with identity politics to embody a more fluid form of sexual desire that eschews categorization. The term "queer" has been appropriated and used to challenge normative understandings of sexuality and resist the strategy of assimilation and subjugation used by more "mainstream" gays and lesbians in the quest for tolerance and acceptance from a heterosexual-dominated society. However, queer theory is not without criticism. Some have charged the discipline with elitism and indeed limited relevance outside of academia. Green has associated it with a "theoretical vanguard" in the North American academy, primarily comprised of young scholars (2007: 26). Its highly abstract nature makes it difficult to see its practicality in our everyday lives. As a result, it has been difficult to generate empirically based research from a queer theory perspective (Willis 2007: 186).

Like postmodern feminist theory and other areas of contemporary inquiry, queer theory, in its quest to be inclusive and fluid, has difficulty in defining its own boundaries and subjects. Elder, for example, considers the difficulty in having one "take" on queer theory, stating that by "arguing that it is one thing or another, in fact, betrays its insistence on the fluidity of identity" (1999: 88). In other words, if identities are uncertain, multiple, and partial, how can one base a theory or perspective around these nebulous entities? From an activist perspective, this makes it difficult to build community. Further, and perhaps even more fundamental, is the fact that postmodern and poststructuralist thinking does not allow for absolute truth statements (e.g. only women can be lesbians) but isn't this very statement an absolute truth in and of itself? And does this problem in logic make the whole perspective incoherent? While these challenges to postmodernism are beyond the scope of this chapter, in that their target is not (only) queer theory itself but the much larger realm of postmodern thinking, they are not irrelevant to this sort of endeavor which seeks to "query" a discipline and profession hungry for considerations of diversity and equity.

Some authors and activists have suggested that the appropriation of the queer label has resulted in the establishment of yet another stabilized category of identity. Queer now gets deployed, by many individuals, as shorthand for homosexuality; another box into which we can be placed (Warner 1991: 16). The original intent of the word's deployment has been undermined by its widespread mainstream usage and, when many individuals hear the term, they might automatically think "gay". Expanding on this, Rotello argues that "queer ... function[s], at least at times, as a new, and less wordy, label for an old box" (in Sullivan 2003: 44). By conflating queer with labels like gay and lesbian, we risk glossing over important "differences of class, race, age, and so on" and end up "positing sexuality as a unified and unifying factor" (Rotello quoted in Sullivan 2003: 44). In some respects then, queer is confronted with the same limitations associated with the essentialist categories that get deployed in identity politics, which ultimately weakens the power of the term as a subversive descriptor. However, this challenge can be countered by the usefulness of queer as a category that unites a powerful and multifaceted coalition of outsiders by capturing all "deviant" sexualities and genders under one label, in discursive and pragmatic opposition to hegemonic heterosexuality.

Others have countered the problem of fluidity by highlighting the capacity of queer to exist not as another category of identity – as a way of being – but instead as a mode of *doing*. Butler has suggested that queer is only effective if it exists in a constant state of change:

> If the term 'queer' is to be a site of collective contestation ... it will have to remain that which is, in the present, never fully owned, but always and only redeployed, twisted, queered from a prior usage and in the direction of urgent and expanding political purposes. (1993: 223)

One way of achieving this has been presented by Jakobsen, who argues that the problems associated with queer as an individual subjectivity can be avoided by "complet[ing] the Foucauldian move from human being to human doing" (quoted in Sullivan 2003: 50). In summarizing Jakobsen's argument, Sullivan writes that:

> it may be more productive to think of queer as a verb (a set of actions), rather than as a noun (an identity, or even a nameable positionality formed in and through the practice of particular actions). (Sullivan 2003: 50)

This allows for an understanding of queer as "a deconstructive practice that is not undertaken by an already constituted subject, and does not, in turn, furnish the subject with a nameable identity" (Sullivan 2003: 50). Thus, recent scholarship in the field of queer theory has focused upon the power of the practice of *queering*, which can be regarded as a form of subversion, whereby existing forms of truth and understanding produced through hegemonic power relations are problematized and troubled. It is these subversive and deconstructive elements of queering that are essential to toppling unequal distributions of power.[5]

Thus, queer theory performs two, at times incompatible or even contradictory, functions. First, it highlights those identities that have been omitted or even forcibly eradicated in contemporary discourse and society, more broadly. These identities – the LGBTTIQ alphabet soup as they are somewhat derisively called

---

5   It is also noteworthy that some authors avoid the use of these sorts of nouns and adjectives entirely by, in fact, juxtaposing the objects of their study and language with more acceptable or "normal" sexual preferences. Labels such as "dissident sexualities" (Higgs 1999: 1; our emphasis), "sexual minorities" (Ingram et al. 1997: 3; our emphasis) and "non-conformist populations" (Forsyth 2001: 40; our emphasis) potentially achieve the objective of avoiding the problems associated with more essentialist or rigid language but also fall into the trap of reinforcing dualistic thinking by defining these people and their identities only in contrast to other populations. While we wish to avoid this sort of approach, we also remain unconvinced that "queer" is the best alternative.

– reflect sexuality and gender identities seen to be outside the norm that are often overlooked in fields like planning. Second, however, queer theory also questions or queries those very identities and underscores their constructedness and, hence, fluidity. That this apparent paradox – or paradox city as we like to call it – gives rise to challenges in applying queer theory to disciplines and professions such as planning should be clear. How, after all, can we attempt to incorporate missing identities in our cities and planning processes if such identities are less tangible and questionable than the buildings, parks, and programs that we seek to create?

While we would be the first to acknowledge that this question is vexing, to say the least, we do make several suggestions. In so doing, we have divided our response into three topics or sets of issues. The first, and most traditional, accepts the fact that various bodies and sexualities have been left out of planning discourse or have been actively discouraged. Thus, there is a desire to add these people and their identities, however malleable, into our field. Second are broader analyses of planning as an institution in and of itself that has helped to shape what counts as normal sexuality and what does not. This approach begins to address the fundamental challenges queer theory poses for planning but does not fully encompass. Finally, and most radical perhaps, is the impact queer theory could have on planning and planning theory if one takes the importance it places on construction and deconstruction to its apparently logical conclusions. This third "take" on the integration of queer theory and planning can be seen to take not only sexual identity as uncertain or ambiguous, but other identities as well, as follows.

Queer Thinking (and Theory) and Planning: A Focus on Missing Identities

Contemporary research investigating the relationship between subjectivity and urban space suggests that spaces are not neutral, and instead are shaped by identities – and indeed in turn work to shape identities. In *Postmodern Geographies*, Soja writes that "the organization and meaning of space is a product of social translation, transformation, and experience" (1989: 80). Modernist conceptualizations of identity like sexuality have acted as important organizing structures in urban space, a fact recognized in the recent literature concerned with sexuality and planning that only began to emerge in the 1980s (Frisch 2002: 256). We are thinking here of studies of sexuality and planning per se, not the more or less accidental intrusion of gay men, lesbians and other queer identities into planning discussions, and we attempt in this space to provide an overview of the former body of work.[6] We note that few authors have integrated elements of queer theory into their analysis, likely

---

6 Perhaps most prominent and of current interest in the latter group is Florida's highly contentious work on creative cities and the creative class in which he argues that the presence of gays, along with other groups of "bohemians", is correlated with more vibrant communities in terms of their economic development (2002a, 2005).

due to their consideration of modernist understandings of sexuality, as well as the relatively recent development of that paradigm.

According to Frisch, an example of early work in this area was undertaken by Castells and Murphy who explored differences of gender between gays and lesbians and the various ways these differences affect "the articulation of their communities in space and place" (Frisch 2002: 257). This research prompted further investigation into the roles of gays and lesbians in the city and their use of public space, and scholars from a variety of disciplines began to conduct quantitative and qualitative studies exploring the urban experiences of homosexuals as a discrete population to be studied.[7]

Knopp's "Social Justice, Sexuality, and the City" (1994) was instrumental in connecting urbanization to sexuality, illustrating their complex and mutual histories. Knopp argued that researchers had been primarily preoccupied with the effects of class in mediating one's experiences in the city, and that sexuality had been long ignored despite its importance in affecting conceptualizations of urban justice and socio-spatial change. "The social relations of sexuality (especially homophobia and heterosexism)", he wrote, "are ... important organizing principles in modern life" (Knopp 1994: 644). For Knopp, sexuality had "been implicated" (1994: 644) in processes of urbanization, including gentrification, residential segregation, community development, and in the creation of symbolic landscapes.

Knopp also addressed the hetero/homo binary distinction, noting that it emerged in the nineteenth century at the same time that other binaries, including public/private, home/workplace, and production/reproduction, began to emerge and have a significant impact on the development and growth of cities during the Industrial Revolution (1994: 645). The Industrial Revolution itself, according to Knopp, affected sexuality and urbanization through the creation of a "gender coded spatial division of labor" (1991: 645) where labor, organized on the basis of constructed gender binaries, "created different opportunities and constraints on women's and men's sexual desire and expression" (1994: 645). Heterosexism and homophobia emerged as tools of social control, mechanisms used to "discipline desire in the service of a particular form of capitalist and patriarchal accumulation" (1994: 646). Reproduction was regarded as necessary for the continuation and growth of the workforce – much in the same way that Foucault identified its necessity in maintaining the population – thus reinforcing the privileging of heterosexual reproductive acts. Gendered divisions of labor continued until the 1970s, when, according to Knopp, capital became more mobile.

More specifically "places, as people know them in their daily lives, have become both increasingly differentiated from one another and more ephemeral than in the past" (Knopp 1994: 647). The main contribution of this article was his questioning of the absence of "the role of sexuality in socio-spatial structures and change" in social science and theory, which he believed had been preoccupied with focusing upon the social relation of class above all others (1994: 647). Knopp's

---

7   See, for example, Adler and Brenner 1992.

work has been instrumental in creating an understanding about the increasingly prevalent role of sexuality in city spaces.

Throughout the 1990s, other work on planning and sexuality was published that sought to find or highlight the presence of, especially, gay men and lesbians in cities and in planning. Discussions such as that by Kenney on the inclusion of these groups in planning history (1998), Forsyth on the formation of a particular lesbian community (1997a), and numerous authors speaking of enhancing the role of diversity in planning (and sub-areas such as planning history), where sexuality is one aspect of this diversity (e.g. Bauman 2002, Quinn 2002, Dubrow and Sies 2002), have focused on these missing or ignored identities and asserted their importance.

In the previous chapter Forsyth expands on her earlier article (2001) to provide a more comprehensive overview of the links between urban planning and non-conformist populations. She examined three areas in planning that have affected these populations – which she recognizes as non-homogenous (Forsyth 2001: 341) – namely discrimination against these populations through housing and zoning plans and policies, historical preservation, and incidents of harassment and protest within public spaces. Zoning in the United States, she argued, has been primarily preoccupied with families (2001: 347), which privileges heterosexual familial relations. Forsyth made an important observation in recognizing that housing policies and regulatory frameworks are not value-neutral. She wrote that definitions of families within these frameworks are typically an instrument that serves many functions, such as limiting student household sizes and limiting noise and traffic, but these definitions "have the additional effect of limiting a number of other household types" (2001: 348). Here, Forsyth encouraged planners to be "self-critical with regard to the social values about adult relationships underlying planning regulations and policies" (2001: 349), noting that interactions between planners and gay, lesbian, or queer populations are likely to be increasingly frequent. She concluded by writing that, "the gay, lesbian, and queer population, which does not fit these categories and is nonconformist, can be the focus of useful questioning of core values on the part of planners" (2001: 353).

Another landmark in 2001 was the publication of a special themed issue of *Progressive Planning*, the publication of the Planners Network, with a focus on "Queers and Planning". The objective of this edition was to educate planners on important queer issues directly related to the planning profession. As Cheung and Forsyth wrote in the issue's introduction, "while progressive planners (almost) uniformly agree that queer planners should not be harassed or discriminated against as people, the implications of queer issues for planning practice are seen as much less clear" (2001). They note that queer issues have generally been peripheral to the concerns of planners. The issue included three articles: Doan (2001) explored the experiences of transgendered individuals in the city, Dubrow (2001) examined issues surrounding the preservation of historic queer landmarks, and Urey (2001) analyzed minutes of the Pomona California Planning Commission on zoning regulations that served to exclude queer individuals.

Doan argued that, "transgendered people serve as canaries for the other sexual minorities" (2001). Explaining her use of the canary as a metaphor, she writes:

> Because many trans people visibly challenge gender stereotypes, they often attract the bulk of the hatred and rage reserved for people who are perceived as queer or in any way different from the norm. The hatred serves as a signal and warning to the entire queer community. (Doan 2001)

Doan pointed out that trans issues within planning require greater visibility because of reasons of personal safety. She wrote that the stream of planning research which typically looks at issues of safety surrounding vulnerable populations usually identifies such populations "on the basis of gender, race, ethnic status, or disability" (2001). Particular physical markers amongst transgendered people, "especially during their transitional stage ... raise transgender visibility and make them one of the most vulnerable and least protected communities in social space" (2001). This requires the attention of planners to ensure the physical safety of these populations. Furthermore, Doan noted that "there are no legal protections for trans people" (2001) in the realm of housing and other planning-related services. Because of these realities faced by the trans community, planners must begin to understand these issues and this population.

Dubrow touched on issues surrounding historic preservation of significant sites for queer populations. She argued that:

> Reluctance on the part of historic site administrators to honestly address aspects of sexual identity and orientation that diverge from societal norms parallels problems in telling the truth about slavery in the Great Houses of the South. (Dubrow 2001)

According to Dubrow, "same-sex relationships are often obscured, if they are dealt with at all, at the landmarks of GLBT heritage through asexual euphemisms such as 'special friend' or 'associate'" (2001). By ending this practice, and by awarding landmark designation to historic places for the queer movement such as the Stonewall Inn in New York City, queer identities become part of public space and public record. This is not easily accomplished, since:

> questions of morality ... tend to come into play when the landmarks of GLBT history are proposed for designation, with queer folks claiming we need role models and homophobes arguing against the government legitimizing deviant lifestyles. (Dubrow 2001)

She urges heritage planners to "forge alliances that insure we support one another across lines of difference in making claims to a heritage that resonates" (2001). In doing so, heritage planners can make visible queer populations which, in turn, helps to create a more inclusionary society.

Urey's (2001) paper on the ways that sexuality may be addressed within day-to-day planning practice provides an example in which a zoning regulation may be altered to avoid its application in a discriminatory fashion. Her assessment of a Planning Commission discussion reveals that both ignorance and outright homophobia or discrimination, more broadly, can play a role in making urban environments less habitable for the queer population. Indeed, she asserts that planners, along with queer advocacy groups, can actively "guard the queer interest in planning issues" (2001).

Putting literature aside for a moment, we can cite other indications of the impact of queer theory or, at least, queer thinking in planning circles. As noted in Chapter 1, the development of the American Planning Association's (APA) Gays and Lesbians in Planning Division (GALIP) in 1998 created a focal point for gay and lesbian planners. While its development was not without its drama,[8] it is now a place in which queer planners, as well as queer-positive planners, can meet, get and provide support, and pursue academic and practice-related inquiry into (presumably) a more tolerant and diverse profession. While we do not know of any comparable bodies in other planning institutes, even this single example could be seen as an evolution in our field's broader quest for enhanced diversity, and has in fact been heralded as a "diversity milestone" in the APA (APA 2007).

In sum, this approach to integrating queer thinking/theory and planning completely ignores the constructed nature of identities as discussed previously. Still, it broadens planners' understanding of disenfranchised or marginalized groups from a more traditional focus on class and, more recently, "race", as well as disability. For instance, the mandate of planning is often said to include "a special responsibility to plan for the needs of the disadvantaged" (APA Diversity Task Force 2005), leaving the definition of "disadvantaged" open to interpretation.[9] Certainly, threats of violence or outright discrimination are certainly disadvantageous to individuals and groups, thus bringing them into this normative imperative of planners and the planning profession. Further, the profession is often said to "respect diversity" (e.g. Canadian Institute of Planners 2004) and the inclusion of queer identities can certainly be seen as part of this mandate. Finally, contemporary attention to the "just city" (e.g. Fainstein 2006) and justice as an ethical basis for planning (e.g. Campbell and Marshall 2006,

---

8 Consider these responses; "The recent decision to allow the formation of Gays and Lesbians in Planning (GALIP) as an officially recognized and endorsed division within the APA sets a morally reprehensible precedent" (Fuller 1999: 26, *Planning Magazine*). More generally, it was observed that APA members' "reactions to APA's decision have run the gamut from glee to moral indignation" (Finucan 2000: 13, *Planning Magazine*) and the decision to endorse GALIP "generated more letters to the editor than any other topic in ... [*Planning Magazine's*] ... history" (APA 2000: 15, *Planning Magazine*).

9 While this is accurate in terms of the Institute being silent on a clear definition of "disadvantaged", this particular principle in the code goes on to highlight class and race as issues of identity with which planners should be concerned.

Campbell 2006) highlights the importance of examining justice from the point of view of all persons, not just those who fall into questionable (or at least contestable) views of what counts to some as "normal". The relatively concrete nature of these identities notwithstanding, a focus on gay, lesbian and transgendered people is not inconsistent with broader normative statements of the intent of the profession.

Queer Theory and Planning 2: Institutions of Planning, Institutions of Sexuality

While earlier studies attempted to define and quantify gay and lesbian populations as a homogenous group of individuals within urban settlements, more recent work by Frisch (2002) has shifted the focus away from more sociological or economic forms of analysis toward the planning profession itself, arguing that planning as an institution has posed significant effects upon queer populations within the city. Specifically he explores the widespread failure of the planning profession to recognize and address queer issues. The 2001 issue of *Progressive Planning* further illustrates Frisch's argument that modern planning practice has been heavily influenced by heterosexism. Frisch noted that planning and categories of sexual orientation are both products of the late nineteenth and early twentieth centuries, and argued that planning discourse assumes heterosexuality, thereby excluding homosexuality, leaving it "closeted and coded" (Frisch 2002: 255). His analysis of the planning profession stems from a model of "racial project" by Omi and Winant, which is "simultaneously an interpretation, representation, or explanation of racial dynamics and an effort to reorganize and redistribute resources along particular racial lines" (Frisch 2002: 256). Frisch employs a similar model to analyze planning, identifying it as a heterosexist project. For Frisch, "planning discourse advances heterosexuality and suppresses homosexuality" (Frisch 2002: 258) in a variety of ways. First, its preoccupation with order can help to avoid conditions leading to "abnormal sexuality" (Frisch 2002: 259) by structuring social organization through social and physical forms of planning. Second, single-family zoning tends to be promoted through planning and legal decisions, while "planners suppressed apartments as sites of difference" (Frisch 2002: 261). The distinction between public and private also plays a role, as gay men and some lesbians have used public spaces for private purposes such as cruising, given the invisibility (and lack of acceptance) of potential partners in many of the spaces in which heterosexual people meet their prospective mates. According to Frisch, "planning processes with a strict separation of public and private enforce heterosexist notions of public and private" (Frisch 2002: 263). In short, he concluded that "planning empowers heterosexuality" (Frisch 2002: 263).

To counter the heterosexist effects of planning, Frisch believed that planners need to conceptualize what the inclusive city would look like. He refers to urban sociologist Richard Sennett, who, instead of "building on measures that create exclusion ... wants to create urban areas with a 'multiplicity of contact points'"

(Frisch 2002: 264) where individuals from different communities, including the less rigidly defined queer communities, can interact with one another (see also Sandercock 2003 for a related argument). Frisch argued that inclusive planning "would treat lesbians and gays as full citizens" (Frisch 2002: 264). Achieving this goal of inclusion means finding possibilities for subverting the dominant conception of planning to include and empower those who belong to what Forsyth referred to as non-conformist populations.

Similar to feminist research in planning that has argued that planning often reinforces rather than subverts gender differences in our communities (see, for instance, Ritzdorf 1986, 1993, 2000), planning can be seen to have furthered or even exacerbated the "otherness" of queer identities. If planning attempted to break down the dualism of hetero-/homo-sexuality, its understanding and application of definitions of "family", safety, public space and other sexualized concepts would be very different. Recognizing the "dark side" of "social control" with its concomitant discrimination of "the homosexual community" (see Yiftachel 1998: 397) may well be a first step in achieving this goal. With this recognition may come the dismantling of boundaries within substantive areas of planning that have to do with space and place. Still, this "queering" of planning itself does not engage as fully with queer theory as some might like or advocate.

Queer Theory and Planning 3: Queries, Queries and More Queries

Looking at planning through the lens of queer theory in its purest and most precise form leads to (among other things) our examining planning, not in terms of its inclusion of concrete identities within its purview but, instead, it and its subject matter being scrutinized as an identity itself. As discussed previously, queer theory is about questioning boundaries and making identities broadly understood more fluid and ambiguous. In geography, it has been said to emphasize the deconstruction of categories, the power of space (and ideas of space), the permeability of boundaries, the use of theories of sexuality in realms other than medicine/psychology, the intersection of social boundaries and identities, and challenging truths in the discipline (see, for example, Knopp 1999, Elder 1999).

In planning, this questioning can happen in several ways. First, queer theory challenges planning and planners to consider fluidity and permeability in plans, policies, programs and, more generally, visions and ideas of "the" good city. Thus, a housing development that was clear in its orientation towards heterosexual, "nuclear" families as the norm could be challenged for its refusal to acknowledge the housing needs of people with other identities, however nebulous and ever-changing these identities might be. This is linked to the first category of integration discussed here but has more room for the ambiguous nature of people and the different facets of their lives. Further, the non-static nature of spatial boundaries would need to be recognized and considered in the making of plans.[10] These are a few examples of the ways in which this notion of fluidity may permeate planning given the orientation of the field and a profession that prides itself on making environments more "orderly".

Second, a queer theoretic approach would address the presence and ubiquitous nature of binaries in planning. As with any postmodern project, this has the potential of creating conceptual and practical hardships for planners and planning academics given that our language and thinking is often based on drawing comparisons or at least distinctions between such things as male/female, black/white and even urban/rural. While we might never eradicate these sorts of distinctions from our planning language, we can at least scrutinize them to see whether we implicitly or explicitly privilege any one aspect of a given dualism.

Third, the questioning of boundaries can occur with regard to planning itself. Queer theory, through its emphasis on post-structuralism, forces us to look critically at identities and boundaries of all sorts and this includes planning and planners. What is "the" planning identity and how has this come to be so? What do we mean when we say planning is a "profession"? How has the idea of "profession" been constructed? What counts as expert planning knowledge? Who does, or should, have the right to call him or herself a planner? And so on. The point here is that a full appreciation of queer theory within the bounds of planning cannot leave planning itself unscrutinized.

This approach is consistent with that of authors who have focused their attention on postmodern analyses of the field and profession, and have argued persuasively that such analyses affect most aspects of planning and planning knowledge (e.g. Sandercock 2003).[11] Thus, integrating queer theory with planning forces us to look beyond issues of gender and sexuality; we must take seriously challenges to our expert, even heroic, status and the nature of our endeavor (see Yiftachel 1998 for an example of this sort of pursuit, as well as Sandercock 2003).

Fourth, it is important to remember the importance in queer theory of questioning and problematizing accepted truths. In planning, this approach might question the standards used in the development of plans (e.g. X acres of parkland per Y population) or challenge the faddish use of the term "best practices" in favor of asking "best for whom and under what circumstances and why?". In broader terms, this queering endeavor entails the deconstruction and interrogation of commonplace planning norms with a focus on the underlying power relations and

---

10 This would presumably also have the potential to disrupt the spatiality of gay ghettos and villages that, some might argue, have been a success story for gay men and lesbians.

11 Here, Sandercock (2003: 72) lists: a "deconstructive approach" to modernist traditions, "the disruptive assertion of 'minority' voices in the fact of universalist theorizing", the rejection of "binary constructions", an "historically contingent" and embodied knowledge, an acknowledgement of gendered and power-laden aspects of knowledge production, and the power of language itself.

other factors that have led to their use and widespread acceptance, in planning thought and practice.[12]

Fifth, geographers such as Elder (1999) have said that queer theory may lead us to examine interdisciplinarity as a way of looking at the world that is consistent with the calls of queer theorists for more permeability in boundaries of all sorts. While both planning and geography are both seen as profoundly interdisciplinary in their own right, it may be that a serious consideration of queer theory and its implications would want to deepen this attribute of the field. Planning still is preoccupied with where it "starts and stops" (Sandercock 1998) as part of its continuing search for a defensible and credible and coherent identity. Could it be that the lack of such an identity puts planning in good stead in terms of its being consistent with this objective of queer theorizing? Perhaps, but this flies in the face of most of the planning literature which bemoans this ambiguity.[13]

Finally given queer theory's emphasis on the importance of process, we might focus our attention, not on the products of planning but on planning processes. Queering planning in this sense has to do with examining how planning works, how its practice proceeds, and how these processes reinforce or subvert hegemonic principles. Like the notion of interdisciplinarity, this emphasis on process underscores some recent developments in planning but is counter-current to many others that have regretted the focus on process that is apparent in approaches such as collaborative or consensus-based planning theory.

This list is similar to those of other writers who discuss postmodernism and planning (see, for example, Sandercock 2003, Harper and Stein 2006, and Allmendinger 2001). These authors and others highlight both the potentialities and paradoxes of applying or integrating postmodern thinking with planning. Queer theory shares these challenges as well as the benefits. Most importantly, for the purpose of this chapter, is the fact that it can highlight inclusionary aspects of planning, albeit in a rather ambiguous and sometimes counter-intuitive manner.[14]

---

12 Again, this sort of scrutiny seems to be difficult for planning and planners as we think about the criticism it has endured for its quick acceptance of ideas such as new urbanism within its practice (especially).

13 The notion of planning being a space-based profession seemed to be the most common defining attribute of planning as we wrote this chapter; while the importance of space and place in the field is clear, we are interested in how this became so heavily privileged in planning discourse – especially (at least partially) as a response to social planners whose work was seen by some as evolving too closely towards that by other professionals such as social workers.

14 While we were writing this chapter, email messages flew back and forth as we tried to think through issues such as queer space that are typically based on identifiable and non-ambiguous identities. Was this a good thing or bad, according to the tenets of queer theory as discussed here and explored more fully in its literature? We left many of these questions unanswered as we endeavored to simply survey the territory and identify challenges as well as opportunities in melding the two fields. However, the questions remain …

Conclusion

In this chapter we have staked out several intersecting territories between queer theory and various aspects of planning and planning theory. We have argued that these territories are three-fold: conventional, mid-range and radical in terms of the depth of their impact on planning theory and practice. Most of the work on sexuality that has been done in planning appears to fall into the first category and even this work pales in comparison to that in cognate fields such as geography. The third category has much in common with other critical discussions of planning that question its status as a profession, its knowledges, its methods and its very nature or intent.

We contend that much in the way of opportunity exists in terms of gaps in planning literature in all three aspects of the integration of queer theory and planning. There continue to be publics (including students and faculty) who feel invisible in a theory and practice that affects most aspects of their lives. This means that the sometimes discredited "identity politics" might still have a role in rendering these individuals, their lives and their ideas more visible. While academics might continue to wonder whether this is appropriate, people on the street might well prefer to be noticed and respected than not.

With regard to the second category we identified, we feel that the heterosexist (and sexist) nature of planning has only begun to be explored. Accordingly further study of the ways that the planning field as an institution reinforces or challenges heterosexism remains a fruitful area of research in this area.

Finally, there is also much work that remains in making the language-oriented and academic aspects of queer theory practicable in the sense of making a difference to planners who make decisions about how our environments look and work. That queer theory is fraught with inherent (apparent) contradictions and challenges is clear. However, the possible contributions of queer theory to the transformation of planning into a more inclusive discipline and profession are also clear. It remains the task of others working in this field to reconcile the identity politics of alphabet soup with the non-essentialist, yet perplexing, paradox city.

Chapter 5
Queerying Identity: Planning and the Tyranny of Gender

Petra L. Doan

> [In] the tyranny of the majority ... society is itself the tyrant ... Society can and does execute its own mandates; and if it issues wrong mandates instead of right, or any mandates at all in things with which it ought not to meddle, it practices a social tyranny more formidable than many kinds of political oppression, since, though not usually upheld by such extreme penalties, it leaves fewer means of escape, penetrating much more deeply into the details of life, and enslaving the soul itself. (J.S. Mill 1869: 5)

Introduction

Chapter 1 argued that the integration of gender and diversity issues into planning theory and practice has been a slow and rather cumbersome process for a variety of reasons. Others have argued that planning is a heterosexist project (Frisch 2002), and that planning does not adequately consider non-normative populations, especially lesbian, gay, and bisexual populations (Forsyth 2001). This chapter expands the argument by suggesting that the gender variant and transgendered populations are also harmed by planning practices that fail to consider gender as a continuum. This lack of consideration is linked to the patriarchal tendency to see the world as a man's world where gender effectively becomes a simple dichotomy of male and not-male, i.e. everyone else. The problem with seeing the world from such a narrowly gendered perspective is that people are infinitely more complex than this binary division, and those whose gender does not conform are often constrained and sometimes harmed by municipal regulations that rely on patriarchal assumptions about gendered behavior. This chapter will explore in greater depth the consequences of these assumptions for the gender variant and make suggestions for how planners might intervene to ensure equal access to urban spaces and facilities regardless of a person's gender expression or identity.

Tyranny refers to an exercise of power which is cruelly or harshly administered; it usually involves some form of oppression by those wielding power over the less powerful. Mill (1869) warned about the tyranny of the majority and argued that the sheer weight of numbers could never be sufficient to make an unjust act any more just. Those who claim victories get to write the history, and likewise those who wield the most economic and social power get to establish the frameworks for administrative decision-making. When those histories and administrative frameworks routinely exclude minority groups, tyranny flourishes.

The tyranny of gender is a special kind of tyranny that is derived from the perspective that the world is neatly divided into two clearly demarcated gender categories, based on the essentialist understanding that sex equals gender. Although everyone must deal with gender in some form, most people never really question the fact of their gender. Gender is often used as a more polite word for sex. As a result the majority never consider the fact that their gender could be other than the sex they were born as. The idea of questioning one's gender is like questioning whether the sky is really blue – an interesting question for some, but ultimately self evident and therefore not worth pursuing. From this perspective sex and gender are synonymous and dichotomous – a person is either male or female – and any variations are aberrations from the societal norm. However there is considerable recent theoretical work that challenges this perspective, arguing that this simplifying schema is deeply flawed.

In an effort to simplify complexity, many people use a variety of dichotomies including white or black, straight or gay, but one of the most pervasive is masculine or feminine. In each of these dichotomies, one category is dominant and thereby privileged, and the other is subordinated. In addition everything which falls outside of these acceptable boundaries is subject to extreme social sanctions, and in some cases state-sanctioned punishment. This chapter argues that the subordination of non-normative genders is a form of gender tyranny which is often reinforced by the social construction of space and concretized in the built environment. As a result planning theory and practice have incorporated these pervasively dichotomous gender categories in critical areas of planning practice, including the design of safe public spaces for all citizens, the development of affordable housing policies, and the promotion of local economic development. After reviewing the theoretical arguments which challenge the idea of a binary gender category and how this dichotomy constrains urban theory, the chapter then considers the nature and size of the population harmed by these narrow conceptions. This description is followed by an explicit consideration of specific consequences of these narrow conceptualizations for the most vulnerable gender variant people, transgendered individuals, given the limited consideration of this population in most planning literature as cited by Forsyth (Chapter 2). Finally the chapter considers how planners and urban policy-makers might intervene to make cities more inclusive of people expressing genders that challenge heteronormative and dichotomo-normative expectations.

Moving Beyond Dichotomous Gender Theories

For centuries women were considered a faulty reflection of the male ideal, as far back as the Genesis story of creation. Beauvoir (1949) suggests that influential philosophers and theologians perpetuated this approach. For instance she notes that Aristotle argued that women are women by virtue of a lack of useful qualities, and St. Thomas Aquinas declared that woman is an imperfect man. At the beginning of the modern era these definitions were enshrined in two fundamental conceptualizations: the inferiority of women and reification of the sex/gender dichotomy. First wave feminist suffragettes effectively contested the notion that the inferior status of women should restrict them from voting. It took longer to challenge the second conceptualization, that of a constructed dichotomy (man/woman vs. male/female), because such polar opposites provide a regulatory frame within which expectations for appropriate behavior can be established. Second wave feminism began with Beauvoir's (1949) rejection of the "not male" residual category by her assertion that women are made, not born. Mead's contemporaneous contention (1949) that sex and gender are not synonymous also provided a critical enabling step for the women's movement that allowed people to express a wider range of possible identities (Tarrant 2006). This shift created an opening in which not all males are expected to be narrowly masculine, not all females are expected to be narrowly feminine, and all persons are permitted to express some combination of masculinity and femininity.

Further exploration of the process of "making" a woman subsequently developed with more complex arguments that gender is a social construction heavily influenced by patriarchal and hegemonic powers (Connell 1987, Lorber 1994). The social construction of womanliness was followed by the deconstruction of gender categories and queer theoretic arguments for the dismantling of dichotomous thinking (see Hendler and Backs, Chapter 4). Rather than sex being wholly defined by bodies, some contemporary theorists have suggested that the body should be seen as a specific situation that serves to mediate one's understanding of the outside world (Moi 1999). The concept of embodiment is widely used in the feminist literature to describe the way in which we all must live in our bodies. Sex and gender are not just abstract concepts but are embodied constantly as we go about the business of our daily lives.

One scholar has suggested that gender might be most usefully explained as a lived social relation (McNay 2004) and argued that gendered behaviors are linked to the habitus, i.e. a "system of durable, transposable dispositions, structured structures predisposed to function as structuring structures, that is, as principles which generate and organize practices and representations" (Bourdieu 1990: 53). Each habitus operates within a particular field, where the field is analogous to the rules of a particular type of game and the habitus is the sense of how best to play that game (Hillier and Rooksby 2002).

Gender variations result from "a lack of fit between habitus and the field" (Adkins, 2004: 196) and explain how masculine and feminine behaviors can be expressed by both men and women. However, Bourdieu (2001) called attention to this "symbolic violence" of the patriarchy that imposes behavioral expectations on individuals. Women (and men) who refuse to act in a gender appropriate manner are subjected to vicious tormenting (McRobbie 2004).

Sometimes, gender variations act to destabilize traditional and heteronormative conceptions of gender roles. For instance, when a femme lesbian exerts a different kind of power within her relationship, she helps to undermine traditional masculine/feminine power dynamics (Skeggs 2004). Butler (1990: 6) argued that this situation poses a conundrum since "taken to its logical limit, the sex/gender distinction suggests a radical discontinuity between sexed bodies and culturally constructed genders." This lack of fit has caused some theorists to suggest a more fluid understanding of gender which exists in a state of flux (Jagose 1996). Other queer theorists urge the adoption of a non-dichotomous vision of gender (Wilchins 2004) with greater fluidity in subject positions that "recognizes no borders or rules of gender" (Bornstein 1994: 52).

The Tyranny of Gendered Planning

This chapter uses the term tyranny of gendered planning to describe the ways that planning practice effectively sanctions those who do not fit into the neat dichotomous boxes of the hetero-patriarchy. This tyranny is felt especially keenly by transgendered people (Doan 2007) and is made manifest in a variety of public and private spaces with urban areas (Doan 2010). The field of planning has begun to recognize the need to incorporate gender more centrally into planning theory and practice (Sandercock and Forsyth 1992), but the conceptualization of gender commonly used is usually dichotomous, and seemingly unaware of the tyranny of gender. Spain (1992) has argued that spaces are inherently gendered by the social and cultural practices that determine the ways that men and women are permitted to use that space. Although women have played key roles in the development of urban spaces (Spain 2001a), they have been often left out of more formal theories of cities and the urbanization process (Spain 2002). Greed (2005) expands this argument and argues that gender is a topic that is not well integrated into planning practice.

> Gender mainstreaming presents a major challenge to current planning practice: as yet under-estimated. The integration of gender into spatial-policy-making would result in a more sustainable, equal and accessible built environment for all members of society. (Greed 2005: 244)

Jarvis (2009) concurs that urban theory remains limited in the first decade of the twenty-first century because of the unfinished business of integrating gender into the field of urban studies. Chapter 1 highlighted this failure to incorporate gender in meaningful ways into the theory and practice of urban planning by both the profession as well as the academy. Certainly raising gender issues challenges the entrenched practices of hegemonic masculinity embedded within the patriarchy. But it is compounded by the common expediency of simplifying complex problems into neat descriptions that are easily reduced to simple two by two contingency tables. This chapter does not contest the usefulness of such

Table 5.1   Dichotomous Sex/Gender and Space

	Public	Private
Male	Productive	"His castle"
Female	"loose women"	Reproductive

reductions, but argues that planners must be aware of the human costs of such strategies for those populations who are excluded or rendered invisible by the adoption of binary solutions.

Consider, for example, the dualistic conceptualization of space as public and private, which some scholars have attributed to nineteenth century Victorian social divisions (Duncan 1996). These divisions are based on the traditional premise that "the built form of modern Western cities is characterized by a gendered separation of 'productive' and 'reproductive' spheres" (McDowell 1993) where the productive realm was reserved for men and the reproductive for women. When a man entered the private sphere of the home, it was frequently as the owner of "his castle." When a woman entered the "public realm" unaccompanied by a male protector, she was considered a "loose woman." Table 5.1 illustrates the result of such simplistic conceptualization.

Twentieth century feminist scholars have critiqued the binary conception of space into public and private areas by deconstructing this artificial division and highlighting the importance of semi-public, public-private, semi-private, and other gradations in between. While much feminist research has focused on tearing down the Victorian public/private divide, many cities are struggling with the realities of a post-modern world. Not only is the spatial dichotomy crumbling, but there is also a more challenging discourse that suggests that genders are much more diverse than simply men and women. Planning practice needs to adjust for these changing conceptualizations.

Consequences of Gender Tyranny for the Gender Variant

> In some ways transgendered people serve as [mine-shaft] canaries for the other sexual minorities. Because many trans people visibly challenge gender stereotypes, they often attract the bulk of the hatred and rage reserved for people who are perceived as queer or in any way different from the norm. The hatred serves as a signal and warning to the entire queer community. (Doan 2001)

Prior to this volume, there has been little research on the subject of planning for non-normative populations with several notable exceptions. Forsyth (2001) provided the most comprehensive perspective on the implications for planning and the LGBT community. Frisch (2002) also noted that planning is often little better than a "heterosexist project." Both authors concluded that much work remains to be done in order for planning issues to consider the needs of the gay and lesbian community, but neither spent much time considering the needs of the transgendered population. The following section examines the consequences of the tyranny of gender for gender variant people in specific areas of the city and in particular situations. Furthermore, the chapter also highlights issues related to some of the most vulnerable gender variant people, the transgendered population. This section will argue that although the transgendered community has been marginalized and rendered virtually invisible to most mainstream communities, planners can mitigate and find ways to make this population and other gender variant individuals more visible and included (Sandercock 1998).

Sanctions resulting from the tyranny of gender fall most heavily on gender variant people as they move through public spaces. Social retribution is imposed on anyone who is perceived as a gender outlaw (Bornstein 1994), resulting in swift and unforgiving punishment for those who violate gender norms in public spaces and facilities that are essential for ensuring full public access to a variety of public and private locations (Doan 2010). The consequences for transgressing the gender binary may include various forms of harassment and violence that are increasingly understood as hate crimes. The tyranny of gender also influences the possibilities for gainful employment of the gender variant, and especially for the transgendered. In addition, there may be consequences for the gender variant in terms of their ability to obtain affordable housing and to live in neighborhoods of their choosing.

The tyranny of gender oppresses those whose behavior fundamentally challenges socially accepted gender categories. Some gender variant individuals regularly transgress gender norms but may not identify as transgendered. Others may identify as genderqueer and challenge gender norms wherever they go. Furthermore, many transgender individuals struggle to present an outward gender that matches their own understanding of their gender identity, and this can be expressed in a range of displays from the hyper normal to the outright transgressive.

Prior to the 1969 Stonewall rebellion gender variance was a common way to signify queerness. Gay bars frequently had drag shows and lesbian bars were frequented by "butches" and "femmes." The gay liberation movement of the 1970s persuaded parts of mainstream America "to debate some degree of rights for gays, but they were actively hostile to anything that smacked of genderqueerness" (Wilchins 2004: 16). Within the lesbian community gender became more overtly political, and radical feminists among them adopted a standard attire of jeans and a flannel shirt (Faderman 1991). There were distinct class and race based elements to this shift, since middle class gays and lesbians were less comfortable with any overtly non-normative gender presentations (Minter 2006). Gendered expectations occurred in the gay community as well since men who continued to act "too gay" or as "flaming queens" were often marginalized (Taywaditep 2001) or kept at a distance (Berkowitz et al. 2007). In reality many gender variant people are not necessarily transgendered, but they are also likely to be victimized by the tyranny of gender.

The media contains powerful images of the consequences of transgressing gender. The movie *Boys Don't Cry* and the novel *Stone Butch Blues* (Feinberg 1993) both provide graphic detail (rape, murder, loss of employment) about the consequences for butch women who display masculinity and trans men whose transgender status is discovered. Men who appear too feminine are equally victimized. In short, actual gender transgressors remain vulnerable and highly marginalized in both queer and other public spaces (Namaste 1996b, Doan 2006, Doan 2007).

Intersexed people should also be included among the gender variant, since some of this population may exhibit gender variance, and certainly most can be considered victims of dichotomous gender categorization. This type of gendered embodiment challenges the notion that all gender is socially constructed (Kessler 1998). Intersex activist Cheryl Chase (1998: 189) argued that the "insistence on two clearly distinguished sexes has calamitous personal consequences for the many individuals who arrive in the world with sexual anatomy which fails to be easily distinguishable as male or female." In the United States prior to a shift in pediatric practice[1], approximately 1–2 babies in every 1,000 live births were recommended for corrective surgery shortly after birth. The total number of intersex people is surprisingly high. Fausto-Sterling (2000) argues that if one includes all possible inter-sex conditions, including chromosomal and other irregularities, then approximately 1.7 of every 100 babies is born inter-sexed in some way. Such a high percentage of anomalies (2 percent) undermines the narrow dichotomous world view. These statistics provide tangible evidence that anatomical sex is not always dimorphic.

Transgendered individuals must also be considered clear victims of binary gender tyranny since many such individuals experience an embodiment of gender which does not match their biological sex. This chapter uses "transgendered" or "trans" as umbrella terms to refer to a wide range of people who share to some degree this lack of fit between their sense of their gender (gender identity) and their anatomical sex at birth.[2] Exact numbers for the transgendered population are difficult to estimate because there is no census category for transgender or transsexual. There are somewhat better estimates of the number of transgendered people who have presented themselves to the medical community and requested sexual reassignment surgery, but there are large variations in these numbers across countries.[3] There are also such high levels of social stigma that many trans

---

1   The American Academy of Pediatrics set new policy in 2006. See P.A. Lee, C.P. Houk, S.F. Ahmed, and I.A. Hughes. 2006. "Consensus Statement on Management of Intersex Disorders," *Pediatrics* 118: e488–e500.

2   This terminology is widely accepted in the literature and among the transgendered community (Bornstein 1994, Feinberg 1996, Stryker 1998).

3   The American Psychological Association (2000) suggests that 1 per 30,000 adult males and 1 per 100,000 adult females seek sex-reassignment surgery and are therefore considered transsexual. These statistics have been called into question by results in other

people never come forward to be identified, and the costs associated with gender reassignment surgery discourage many others.

The intolerant responses faced by transgender people have led some transgender activists to describe the dichotomy of sex as a form of apartheid (Rothblatt 1995). Others have described it as a kind of legally sanctioned caste system.

> [T]he American gender classification system, no less than the historical caste system of India, also creates 'untouchables' who exist in a netherworld of discrimination outside the order established by 'heredity' and 'biology.' (Weiss 2001: 125)

Although gender variance is prevalent in non-western cultures (Herdt 1994), only in the latter part of the twentieth century has the transgendered population dared to risk public exposure in the United States. The social stigma of a gender orientation at variance with one's birth sex marks transgendered people profoundly. Although feminist and queer activists have opened the door to a much wider range of gender expression and allowed females to express a much greater degree of masculinity than ever before, the dichotomy of gender still persists. Indeed the tyranny of gender remains strongly entrenched in the ways that urban spaces are planned and developed.

Ensuring Safety in Public Accommodations for the Gender Variant

Ensuring public health and safety is a fundamental task of planning. Planners who are concerned with health and safety issues for all members of the urban community should take careful note of the vulnerability of gender variant and transgendered community members. At present individuals whose gender expression is not consistent with the dichotomy of gender are uniquely vulnerable as they move through public spaces. Prior to Congressional passage of the Matthew Shepard and James Byrd Hate Crimes Prevention Act in October 2009, statistics on hate crimes against transgendered individuals were not collected by the FBI. However, the Human Rights Campaign has estimated that approximately one in every 1,000 murders is committed against a transgendered person (HRC 2010).

In 2007 The National Coalition of Anti-Violence Programs (NCAVP) collected data on 2,430 victims of hate related violence against lesbian, gay, bisexual and transgendered people (NCAVP 2007). Planners should note that this study found that most of these hate crimes occurred in public spaces and facilities. While it is not clear what proportion of these crimes are a result of gender tyranny, it is likely that many of these lesbian and gay individuals were victimized because their

---

countries. In the Netherlands the prevalence is 1 per 11,900 males and 1 per 30,400 females (Bakker et al. 1993) and in Singapore the rates are 1 per 9,000 males and 1 per 27,000 females (Tsoi 1988).

identity was highly visible, often linked to non-normative gender presentations. The NCAVP study found that public streets and transportation facilities accounted for 19 percent of the crimes, another 5 percent happened in a school and 13 percent in the workplace. In addition public accommodations accounted for 7 percent, and an additional 8 percent of the incidents occurred at gay bars, LGBT organizations or public LGBT rallies. Approximately 13 percent of these LGBT victims identified as transgender, which is substantially higher than the prevalence of this community in the population at large. Furthermore, since many trans people are fearful of public exposure the actual rate of anti-trans violence may be even higher.

This kind of anti-trans discrimination and violence reinforces a dichotomous social order and punishes the display of alternate genders in public places (Felsenthal 2004). Gender-bashing is a particularly brutal form of violence used against the transgendered population (Namaste 1996b). Feinberg (1996) distinguished between gender-phobia that targets the expression of non-normative genders by, for instance gay men and lesbians, and trans-phobia that causes disgust and revulsion of people who actually take steps to change their sex. Witten and Eyler (1999) have suggested that these acts of gender terrorism help to ensure that the patriarchal system is maintained.

The likelihood of such violent attacks has led to a powerful silencing of transgendered individuals, rendering them invisible for the most part to North American society. One study of transgendered people in the United States found that one third of all respondents were the victims of aggressive staring or the hetero-normative gaze, 22 percent received verbal harassment and 17 percent experienced violent confrontations (Doan 2007). Another study found higher levels of violence where over half of the transgendered respondents indicated they had been harassed and nearly one quarter reported they had been a victim of a violent assault (Lombardi et al. 2001). A third study in Philadelphia (Kenagy 2005) found roughly half of this population had suffered physical abuse and violence within the home.

The National Center for Transgender Equality (Grant et al. 2011) conducted a study of over 6,450 transgender individuals in the United States and found that 63 percent of the respondents had experienced some form of serious discrimination. The types of discrimination included in this study include the following:

1. Loss of job due to bias
2. Eviction due to bias
3. School bullying/harassment so severe the respondent had to drop out
4. Teacher bullying
5. Physical assault due to bias
6. Sexual assault due to bias
7. Homelessness because of gender identity/expression
8. Loss of relationship with partner or children due to gender identity/expression

9. Denial of medical service due to bias
10. Incarceration due to gender identity/expression

Furthermore 23 percent of the respondents experienced what the authors of the study refer to as "catastrophic discrimination" which is a combination of three or more of the above life-altering events. In total this nationwide study suggests a very broad pattern of harassment, discrimination, and violence against transgendered individuals.

Because of this epidemic of discrimination and violence, planning for safe public spaces, parks, streets, and shopping areas is critically important for trans people since these are often the places hate crimes occur. It is likely that such locations are associated with a broader range of intolerant behaviors that affect a much wider population. However, most efforts to make public spaces safer involve Newman's (1972) "defensible space" measures including: changes to the physical design and lay-out of parks, limiting the number of through streets, and creating neighborhood watch programs that may not protect non-normative individuals. These steps may be effective in reducing some crime, but the "eyes on the street" strategy which is a part of making space defensible, often assumes a heteronormative perspective interested in preserving the status quo. Accordingly, such surveillance may, in fact, increase the risks to transgendered and gender variant people since attention from nosy neighbors may be the last thing that they wish to endure. The search for anonymity may drive the gender variant away from safer and more heteronormatively defensible neighborhoods into less safe neighborhoods or to existing queer spaces, such as gayborhoods.

With respect to public facilities, planners should be concerned with ensuring equal rights and universal design access so that everyone is able to access services and facilities provided to the public. One of the pernicious effects of the above-mentioned violence is that gender variant and transgendered people feel significantly constrained in their ability to move through public spaces and conduct basic activities without harassment. The list of public and semi-public facilities in which transgendered and gender variant people are at risk includes: train stations, bus terminals,[4] shopping centers,[5] downtown streets, public parks, schools, community centers, and other gathering places. Grant et al. (2011: 124) report that 53 percent of transgendered respondents indicated that they were verbally harassed or disrespected in a place of public accommodation, and 8 percent were physically assaulted in such places. While some of these locations are private spaces run by businesses, others fall clearly within the purview of public agencies, including transit facilities, government offices (including police, the courts, and

---

4 Moulton and Seton (n.d.) cite the case of Amanda Milan who was waiting outside the Port Authority Bus Terminal in New York City and was brutally murdered.

5 Moulton and Seaton (n.d.) cite the case of three transgendered women who were driven out of a Toys R Us store in Brooklyn by store employees wielding baseball bats and calling them "homos" and "fags."

Table 5.2 Percent of Transgender Respondents Who Experienced Discrimination in Public Accommodations (N = 6450)

	Denial of equal treatment	Harassment or disrespect	Physical assault	Any problem
Retail store	32%	37%	3%	46%
Police officer	20%	29%	6%	35%
Doctor's office or hospital	24%	25%	2%	35%
Hotel or restaurant	19%	25%	2%	33%
Government agency/official	22%	22%	1%	32%
Bus, train, taxis	9%	22%	4%	26%
Emergency rooms	13%	16%	1%	22%
Airline or airport staff/TSA	11%	17%	1%	21%
Judge or court official	12%	12%	1%	19%
Mental health clinic	11%	12%	1%	18%
Legal services clinic	8%	6%	1%	12%
Ambulance/EMT	5%	7%	1%	10%
Domestic violence shelter	6%	4%	1%	9%
Rape crisis center	5%	4%	1%	7%
Drug treatment center	3%	4%	1%	6%

Source: Table constructed by the author from data.

various social service centers). These figures are a strong indication that there remain large barriers to the full inclusion of transgendered people.

Ensuring Equal Access to Public Toilets

If the threat of violence has been contained through measures to ensure public safety for all citizens, then a key constraint that limits access to most public facilities is the ability to use gender appropriate or gender neutral public toilets (restrooms). One of the most significant constraints to nineteenth century women moving through public spaces was the lack of public toilets for women. During this time the only public toilets available were for men, and it was only after prolonged campaigning by groups like the Ladies Sanitary Association that cities began providing some form of public accommodation for women (Greed 2003). Gershenson and Penner (2009) suggest that the sex-segregated bathroom is an "invention" of the modernist era. The first public toilets for women were strongly resisted by male shopkeepers in the vicinity because the very idea of women using a public restroom for what had been considered very private functions was nearly unthinkable. Of course the implicit assumption was that only a certain kind of woman would use such a place, increasing the likelihood of toilets being used for illicit sexual encounters. As public toilets became more widely available, codes of etiquette were constructed to prevent public licentiousness and later to ensure compliance with compulsory heterosexuality. Contemporary public restrooms for women are commonplace: the battles are over "potty parity" or the equal provision of facilities.

However, gender non-conforming individuals' lack of access to safe restrooms that is reminiscent of the constraints faced by women in the nineteenth century. For some people the idea that a transgendered woman might use a women's restroom is deeply abhorrent and raises deep-seated fears about public order and safety. Some gender non-conforming women who are not transgendered also experience harassment in women's restrooms (Browne 2004, Lucal 1999). The fact that gender variant and transgendered people are not able to access appropriate public bathrooms is a serious constraint to their ability to move freely through public spaces. The fear of verbal harassment, physical confrontation, and acts of violence can cause members of this population to curtail a range of everyday activities (shopping, errands, business meetings, etc.) that might result in a prolonged absence from home and the safety of an anonymous toilet.

The threat of imminent unisex bathrooms was used as a sort of shibboleth by the conservative movement to torpedo the Equal Rights Amendment and still echoes in city and county commission chambers. In addition, possibly because of a fear of public sexual encounters, facilities in public parks rarely include single access facilities. However, planners should balance these political concerns with the fact that people whose gender is non-normative frequently suffer from harassment and physical threats in single sex facilities. Language requiring separate bathroom facilities for males and females is integral to most building codes for public and commercial facilities, and exacerbates the problem of the tyranny of gender for trans and gender variant individuals. Alternatives that allow establishments to offer single access multi-gendered bathrooms should be permitted and encouraged.

One example of useful flexibility in interpreting planning and building codes occurred when a religious congregation (Quakers) in Tallahassee, Florida purchased a house in a residential neighborhood to convert into a Meetinghouse. The existing residence had two single use bathrooms, but the city code for a small religious assembly called for two bathrooms (one for each gender) with a minimum of two stalls in each and all had to be handicapped accessible. Because the Quakers wished to be fully inclusive, they resolved the requirements by dividing the larger bathroom into two separate facilities with separate entrances. A third new handicapped accessible bathroom was created out of a hallway, and the fourth bathroom was left as is. The city code enforcement officials asked that in the submitted plan two bathrooms be "labeled" for men and two for women. However the Quakers argued that all bathrooms would be unisex which dropped the issue of "potty parity" and had the added advantage of only requiring one handicapped accessible facility, which resulted in some savings. More inclusive and permissive language should be incorporated into codes so that organizations can seek creative solutions to this issue.

Planners should make every effort to ensure that public spaces and public accommodations are more gender friendly. The provision of more single access bathroom facilities would go a long way to ensuring that trans people, as well as handicapped individuals, the elderly, and parents with children are able to use bathroom facilities with dignity. While some might argue that the purview of planning does not extend to toilets, Greed (1995, 2003, 2009) has consistently argued that public toilets are in fact critical to ensuring access for women and other "disenabled" groups (Greed 1996). The bathroom issue is a particularly sensitive one, which still generates derision when it is raised as an important planning issue. The public response described by Gershenson and Penner (2009) as a result of their call for papers for their volume on public toilets and gender suggests that the "need to pee" is still undervalued by the mainstream media as well as by many in the design professions.

Creating Safe Spaces for the Gender Variant

For the transgendered population, issues related to public access in cities need special attention. However, many gay and lesbian neighborhoods that have been in existence since the 1970s are shrinking because of a resurgent gentrification by upper class, formerly suburban couples who have grown tired of long commutes. As a result many lesbians and gay men are moving further away from the city center into white suburban areas or other low income, often minority-dominated areas. This disappearance of queer enclaves poses a significant problem for trans people because the public presentation of non-normative gender is so problematic. Many young trans men and women first experiment with gender variance by visiting queer safe zones, walking on public streets, going to restaurants, and hanging out in the omnipresent bars. Without such spaces, queer youth and newly emerging trans people will be forced into other spaces, malls and suburban shopping areas that are not nearly as queer-friendly.

Constraints on movement through public spaces also make it very difficult for gender variant and transgendered people to connect with others and establish the kinds of connections and social capital that would enable them to press for changes. In addition, given the huge social stigma imposed on this population, there is a significant need to establish peer networks to provide critical social support systems to alleviate the frequent depression, anxiety, and suicidal tendencies that are all too common in this community.

One possible alternative could involve making internet connections more widely available. The internet has opened doors and enabled a wide range of connections between isolated trans people. Extending the wireless canopy at a reasonable cost within urban areas could be enormously helpful in enabling trans people to gain access to information and support groups. Many transgendered individuals live close to the edge, with not much room in a meager budget to support the purchase of a computer, much less a subscription to an internet server. Additionally, since many transgendered people experience overt employment discrimination resulting in stagnant salaries or actual firings, their limited income may further restrict their ability to pay for internet services. Policies to ensure widespread, free access (or low cost) would be enormously beneficial to this community as well as other low income communities within the city.

Ensuring Affordable and Appropriate Housing

Another area which is traditionally of concern to urban planners is the provision of safe and affordable housing for all urban residents. Because of the high levels of vitriol directed at transgender and gender variant people they are uniquely vulnerable in residential spaces. While many local governments have enacted protections for housing discrimination on the usual grounds of race, ethnicity, and religion, only a small subset of municipalities also include gender identity and expression as a protected class.

All too frequently if a person comes out as transgendered and begins to transition, he or she can be denied a renewal of their lease with no questions asked. The NCTE study (Grant et al. 2011: 106) found that 19 percent of transgender respondents in their survey had been denied housing and another 11 percent had been evicted because of their transgender status. Furthermore, if an individual has been kicked out of the family home (for trans youth living with parents) or from the marital home (in the case of a trans person whose spouse or partner is not supportive), it may be very difficult to find a landlord willing to rent to someone who is visibly transgendered. Recent changes in the availability of public housing have imposed a burden on the poor and indigent, and some researchers have suggested that this burden falls especially hard on women, leaving them "embounded" or caught in place by social and spatial restrictions (Miranne 2000). These shifts are likely to have adverse effects on the transgendered and gender variant. Welfare policy which assumes that recipients can find work at the end of a fixed period of time or risk losing benefits does not take into account the added employment difficulties of the transgendered discussed above. As a result transgendered and gender variant people may find it difficult to access public support available to others.

The challenges of transgendered people are compounded by the pressures of gentrification in many LGBT residential areas within cities that are experiencing increasing rents. Policy measures to protect LGBT enclaves are likely to have positive effects on transgendered people as well. Doan and Higgins (2011) suggest planners consider enclave protection measures such as: cultural overlay districts used to preserve Chinatowns and other ethnic enclaves, limits on the demolition of existing housing for new commercial development, and limits on the size of businesses to reduce chain store buy-outs. In addition re-gentrification efforts driven by investors with seemingly unlimited capital often benefit from special development districts that avoid or undermine neighborhood input in the development process and provide fast-tracking for the largest projects. Such initiatives are destructive to the fabric of the LGBT community, often dividing the community along class lines, leaving by the wayside the more marginal including retirees, other fixed income residents, low income residents, and the transgendered population.

Because the trans community faces a kind of "double whammy" consisting of lower incomes resulting from employment discrimination combined with overt discrimination in the housing market, planners' efforts to preserve affordable and non-discriminatory housing stock are likely to have significant benefits for the trans population as well as other low income populations. In an era of rapidly commodifying queer space (Nast 2002), condominium conversion of rental properties is a frequent by-product. Efforts to limit conversions which result in high numbers of evictions would be beneficial for many in the LGBT community, but especially for the most marginalized. Other alternatives including community land trusts might be considered as an alternative to single family housing. Finally zoning codes designed to protect the single heterosexual family by limiting the number of non-family members living under a roof (Frisch 2002) can be especially difficult for low income trans people, since many in this community share housing with others like themselves in order to save money for therapy, hormones, and surgery, all of which are rarely covered by insurance.

If a transgendered individual becomes homeless, there are likely to be significant issues in accessing shelter (Moulton and Seaton n.d.). Grant et al. (2011: 106) found that for transgender respondents who attempted to access a homeless shelter "29 percent were turned away altogether, 42 percent were forced to stay in facilities designated for the wrong gender, and others encountered a hostile environment." The hostile actions encountered in shelters included: harassment (52 percent), physical assault (29 percent), and sexual assault (22 percent).

Efforts to protect women who are homeless have resulted in sex segregated separate facilities for men and women. Transgendered individuals may not be permitted to reside even temporarily in gender appropriate facilities, once more putting them at risk of great harm. Moreover, it is unlikely that a transgendered person would seek out a shelter, leaving them to sleep on the streets at the mercy of the elements and at even greater risk of violent crime. If a transgendered person is then arrested and incarcerated, the same issue is even more difficult and dangerous. A transgendered person who has transitioned but has not yet been able to afford the expensive surgery required in most states for a legal sex change is in most cases considered by the authorities as their birth gender so a male to female transgendered person would be housed with men. A transgendered person in these circumstances is extremely vulnerable to sexual abuse, rape, and other violence by both the prison guards and other inmates (Moulton and Seaton n.d.).

There is only limited scope for planning practitioners to address issues for the gender variant and transgendered in congregate housing such as homeless shelters and prisons. However, ensuring the safety of all residents should be a primary objective, even if that means establishing separate facilities. Planners should consider adopting planning standards for group housing that are fully inclusive of gender identity and expression.

Providing Protection from Economic Discrimination

Planners seeking to ensure that cities are tolerant and welcoming to a diverse population base should note that while economic discrimination against people whose gender expression falls outside the dichotomo-normative is difficult to measure, it appears to be quite common. Broadus (2006) cites several studies (see in particular, Daley and Minter 2003) that indicate that nearly half of all transgendered individuals report workplace discrimination. Researchers at the Williams Institute at UCLA reviewed a number of studies done between 1996 and 2006 and found a distressing pattern of discrimination (Badgett et al. 2007). A nationwide convenience survey found that 37 percent of transgendered people experienced employment discrimination (Lombardi et al. 2001). Another study conducted in Los Angeles reported that 28 percent of the transgendered respondents had been fired based on their gender identity, and a third study noted that 47 percent reported difficulty in finding a job (Reback et al. 2001). In a broad cross section survey done in San Francisco there was evidence that 57 percent of transgendered people experienced employment discrimination because of their transgender status (Bay Guardian and Transgender Law Center 2006). Finally the National Center for Transgender Equality (NCTE) survey found that 47 percent of respondents had suffered an adverse employment result (such as not being hired or not receiving a promotion) because of their transgender status and 26 percent had been fired. For transgender employees of color these rates were two to three times higher (Grant et al. 2011: 51).

Unfortunately, the United States Supreme Court found in the infamous *Ulane v. Eastern Airlines* case in 1984 that discrimination based on transgender identity is not constitutionally protected. While some jurisdictions have passed anti-discrimination legislation that does protect people who transgress gender norms and challenge the tyranny of gender, many courts continue to use the Ulane decision to find against transgender plaintiffs claiming discrimination (Currah 2006).

The importance of employment non-discrimination ordinances that are inclusive of gender identity and expression cannot be over-stressed. The harsh consequences in terms of outright discrimination, firing, and refusal to hire gender variant individuals have been discussed above. If non-discrimination ordinances are not feasible, then planners need to be aware that some members of the transgendered population are likely to be among the most indigent citizens in the community. Any existing gender bias against women and women-headed households (McDowell 1999) is likely to be magnified for the trans and gender variant population.

One manifestation of the effect of discrimination is that some less affluent trans people may be only able to find employment through what Grant et al. (2011) refer to as the underground economy (16 percent), including selling drugs and engaging in sex work (11 percent). Other studies have examined the ways cities and planning administrators regulate adult and sex-related businesses (Hubbard 1999, Prior 2008), but an additional area of concern is whether these regulations will have an adverse effect on the transgendered community. Unfortunately people who have experienced profound social stigma and marginalization may feel that sex work is the only viable employment option. Municipal efforts to clean up and eradicate sex districts often focus on areas like the Tenderloin in San Francisco which are a locus for transgendered prostitutes (Weinberg et al. 1999). Accordingly efforts to clean up these areas can have a detrimental effect on trans individuals, forcing them to work in more remote districts which may in turn make them even more vulnerable to hate crimes, as well as further reducing their incomes.

Conclusions

Overcoming the dichotomy of gender is not a simple process; however opening the minds of planners to the possibility of alternative gender presentations is an important first step. Creating policy that does not exclude or render invisible people who identify as gender variant or transgendered may be complex but is essential in making urban spaces welcoming to all citizens. Planners concerned with making cities truly inclusive should work to include the transgendered and gender variant population in their efforts to address issues of public safety. In doing so planners may also create urban spaces that are safer for other lesbian, gay, bisexual, and intersex people to express a broader range of gendered identities. Using models for neighborhood planning that assume a "traditional" (and heteronormative) household does not promote safety for all, but further marginalizes vulnerable populations.

Similarly, planners should seek to be inclusive in their expectations of who will use public facilities, and work to change existing codes and regulations that limit creative solutions to the problem posed to the gender variant and transgendered of rigidly sex segregated toilets. Ensuring that single access toilets are widely available would be another significant step forward and would have the additional benefit of providing spaces for families and the elderly who might need assistance. A similar issue arises with respect to sex-segregated housing in shelters and jails. These specialized facilities are not strictly within the purview of urban planning, but planners can promote plans for capital improvements and infrastructure that are more broadly inclusive.

Finally, planning practitioners need to recognize the essential diversity of genders and orientations that exist within the city. Populations that do not fit the traditional family model should have equal rights to be protected against discrimination in housing and employment. When planners are asked to review or actively promote economic development initiatives, they should be careful to consider how existing populations that use the spaces in question will be affected. Too often planners assume a more "family-oriented" neighborhood is the most desirable alternative, even if that means driving out LGBT oriented businesses and institutions that often are welcoming of a broad range of genders and gender expressions. Efforts to reduce the tyranny of gender, and empower people of whatever gender persuasion to become full participants in the life of the city will enrich the cultural diversity and create a true urban mosaic in our cities.

Chapter 6
Queering the Suburbs: Analyzing Property Values in Male and Female Same-Sex Suburbs in the United States

Katrin B. Anacker

Introduction

The majority of Americans live in suburbs (Orfield 2002). Up until about a decade ago, the vast majority of suburbs were perceived as primarily homogeneous (i.e., non-Hispanic White, middle- and upper-income, and heterosexual communities as suggested by Désert 1997, Harris 1999, Lynch 1992). However, recently some authors have realized that there is diversity when it comes to suburbs.[1] Whereas suburban diversity has been discussed and analyzed in terms of race (Anacker 2009, Logan, Alba and Leung 1996), ethnicity (Ponce 1993), nativity (Friedman and Rosenbaum 2007), and class (Nicolaides 2002), not much has been published on queer households in suburbs (for exceptions see Doan and Higgins 2011, Gates and Ost 2004, Lynch 1987, Hodge 1995, Mendelsohn 1995, and Parker 2009). Suburbs are often perceived as places where two-parent, nuclear, heterosexual families live in single-family, owner-occupied homes and where queer identify formation is inhibited (Altman 1982, Knopp 1992). Black et al. (2002) believe, consistent with the Tiebout hypothesis, that queer couples are avoiding suburban areas. Alternatively, others conclude that "suburban homosexuals, like many other Americans, are finding suburban life increasingly attractive and that the lure of large cities and gay ghettos has faded." (Lynch 1987: 13) This study will shed more light on same-sex households in select metropolitan areas in the United States, differentiating between central cities and suburbs and focusing on property values.

Despite the current national crisis triggered by the house price crash, the tsunami of foreclosures, the credit crunch, and the ailing economy, owning housing is still considered to be a good strategy to build equity *in the long run*. Nationwide, the homeownership rate is almost 70 percent, although it has declined slightly over the past several months, most likely due to the wave of foreclosures

---

1 In October 2009, the National Center for Suburban Studies hosted the conference "The Diverse Suburb." Available at: http://www.hofstra.edu/Community/culctr/culctr_events_suburb.html [accessed: September 25, 2009].

(US Census Bureau 2009). Some argue that home ownership by homosexuals "is the best way to preserve secrecy and privacy. Nosy neighbors cannot spy, and watchful landlords cannot evict" (Warren 1974: 30; see also Ingram et al. 1997), and it facilitates home socialization, which is considered important by many gays (Betsky 1997, Warren 1974). For the majority of homeowners, a home represents the biggest investment in their lives. While much research has been conducted on property values in central city communities that are characterized by high proportions of residents in terms of race, ethnicity, and nativity, not much research has been undertaken on property values in communities that are characterized by relatively high proportions of same-sex households (see Lauria and Knopp 1985, and Knopp 1990a, 1990b as exceptions). Even less research has been conducted on property values in *suburban* communities with high proportions of same-sex households. This study takes a closer look at suburban communities characterized by high proportions of male and female same-sex households in terms of their housing and neighborhood characteristics, as well as their property values, and compares these communities to similar communities in central cities.

This chapter examines housing and neighborhood characteristics and property values in census tracts with high proportions of male and female same-sex households. The unit of analysis is the census tract. The geography of this study is the 50 counties of major metropolitan areas in the United States that ranked highest in terms of the proportion of male and female same-sex households out of all couples. These rankings, which were provided by Gaydemographics.org, are based on data from the US Bureau of the Census. The data source for this study is the National Change Data Base (NCDB) by Geolytics, Inc., which is also based on the US Census. Most studies that focus on queer topics are case studies of a neighborhood or a single city; not many have focused on the entire nation (see Anacker and Morrow-Jones 2005 as an exception).

This chapter focuses on the census-tract scale instead of the individual level. To the author's knowledge, there are currently no representative data available at the individual level. This is an analysis of the local scale within selected counties—it is not about the individuals who live in those census tracts. Thus, the author will use the terms "neighborhood" and "census tract" to describe these local areas.

Because Census data are used, the author uses same-sex households as a proxy for queer households. People use the term "queer" to express the full range of human possibility, disrupting dichotomies such as heterosexual/homosexual and gender/sex (Bem, 1993, Butler 1993, Désert 1997, Doan 2007). In this chapter, the terms "male same-sex households" and "female same-sex households" will be used to describe the cases under study based on Census data. When the terms "queer," "homosexual," "gay," or "lesbian" are used, they are referring to specific items in other literatures.

The following research questions are asked, differentiating between central city versus suburban census tracts:

1. Are there differences in demographic, socioeconomic, housing, and neighborhood characteristics as well as property values?
2. Are there differences in property value appreciation rates?
3. Are there differences in factors that influence property values?

The chapter is structured as follows. The introduction is followed by a literature review that focuses on queer clusters, differentiating between the metropolitan level and the neighborhood level. The third section deals with data and the data set used in this research. In this section, the author focuses on neighborhoods of those counties that rank highest in terms of male householders with male partners and in terms of female householders with female partners. The fourth section presents results of a Weighted Least Squared (WLS) regression to explain the factors that influenced property values and a discussion of those results. This is followed by a conclusion and suggestions for future research.

Literature Review: Locations of Queer Household Clusters

With respect to the location of queer household clusters at the metropolitan level, the literature finds that some regions, such as the North Central United States (LeVay and Nonas 1995) and some metropolitan areas, have a higher density of queer households than others (Black et al. 2000 and 2002). Some authors point out that roughly 45 percent of same-sex householders live in 15 major metro areas (Witeck-Combs Communications 2002), among them Los Angeles (Castells 1983), New York (Chauncey 1994, Weightman 1981), and San Francisco (Black et al. 2002, D'Emilio 1992, Weightman 1981). Some employ rankings of metropolitan areas in terms of relative numbers of same-sex households to focus on those metropolitan areas that have high densities (Anacker and Morrow-Jones 2005, Black et al. 2000), whereas others focus on the visibility, community activity, and neighborhood organization of gays (Castells 1983) and lesbians (Adler and Brenner 1992, and for an alternative opinion see Castells 1983), as well as on amenities (Black et al. 2002).

Reasons for the high density of queer households in some metropolitan areas could be the perceived appreciation of diversity (Moss 1997), the presence of tolerance (Black et al. 2002; Doan and Higgins 2011, Forsyth 1997b, Godfrey 1988, Ingram et al. 1997), the anonymity that, in the case of lesbians, makes it "easier to manage and control others' images of their sexual identity in such an environment" (Valentine 1993a: 398; see also Elwood 2000), or, possibly, for defense against those who disapprove of their lifestyle (Ingram et al. 1997, Lyod and Rowntree 1978), among other factors. Some argue that the presence of gay household clusters at the metropolitan level contributes to the competitiveness of the area, pointing out a high correlation between a large gay presence and a large presence of the high-tech industry and its growth (Florida and Gates 2001, see also Bell and Binnie 2004), although the high correlation does not necessarily imply causation. Others argue that the presence of bohemians and queers has a substantial effect on house prices, introducing the terms "aesthetic-amenity premium" and "tolerance" or "open culture premium" (Florida and Mellander 2007).

Research on the location of queer household clusters has been undertaken in urban, rural, and suburban areas, although the majority of studies have concentrated on urban areas where many suspect that the highest densities of queer households exist (Bell 1991, Lyod and Rowntree 1978, LeVay and Nonas 1995). Many urban studies have focused on housing and neighborhood characteristics typically found in neighborhoods with a high density of male and female same-sex households.

In the case of gay male neighborhoods, gays seem to concentrate in gay-friendly downtown neighborhoods and urban cores (LeVay and Nonas 1995, Witeck-Combs Communications 2002, although see Cody and Welch 1997 as an exception). These areas are often characterized by gay bars and restaurants (Weightman 1981, Winters 1979) and sometimes by alternative bookstores, travel agencies, historical societies, charities, or savings-and-loan associations (Murray 1992, Dubrow 1998b, see also Chesnut and Gable 1997 on lesbian-feminist bookstores). Often there is gentrification, which typically increases property values (Castells 1983, Godfrey 1988, Knopp 1990a, 1990b, 1992 and 1995, Moss 1997, Visser 2003). Examples of these gay neighborhoods can be found in San Francisco (Black et al. 2002, Castells 1983, D'Emilio 1992, Levine 1979, Sides 2006), West Hollywood (Forest 1995, Godfrey 1988), New York (Chauncey 1994), New Orleans (Knopp 1990a, 1990b, 1992 and 1995), Toronto (Nash 2006), Vancouver (Bouthillette 1997), Washington, DC (Myslik 1996), and Mexico City (Sanchez-Crispin and Lopez-Lopez 1997), among others.

While gay male households seem to concentrate in gay-friendly, downtown, mixed-use neighborhoods and urban cores, lesbian households appear to cluster in lesbian-friendly, residential neighborhoods in urban cores of metropolitan areas, in both smaller metro areas and suburbs (Chamberland 1993, Dubrow 1998b, LeVay and Nonas 1995, Lockard 1985, Retter 1997, Witeck-Combs Communications 2002). Examples of neighborhoods in urban cores of large metropolitan areas studied in the United States include Park Slope in Brooklyn, New York (Rothenberg 1995) and select neighborhoods in San Francisco, such as Bernal Heights, the Mission district, the Castro, and the Haight-Ashbury, all of which are connected to public transportation; are ethnically mixed, working class, and/or low-income; and are characterized by an old, small-space, low-rent housing stock, lesbian bars, and community projects (see Wolf 1979). Examples of urban neighborhoods studied in Canada include Montreal's Boulevard St.-Laurent (Podmore 2001) and the Grandview-Woodland neighborhood in Vancouver (Bouthillette 1998). Other examples are the urban and suburban neighborhoods studied in connection with gentrification in Atlanta (Doan and Higgins 2011). Winchester and White (1988) argue that the Parisian lesbian community is socially yet not economically marginal, contrary to Rothenberg's (1995) insights for Park Slope in Brooklyn, New York (see also McNee 1984).

Only a few studies have focused on small cities in rural areas in the United States and in Europe, and most of these studies are about female same-sex households (see also Bonfitto 1997, Kirkey and Forsyth 2001, McCarthy 2000, Bell and Valentine 1995b). With respect to the US, the downtown area of Northhampton, Massachusetts has experienced revitalization and gentrification over the past two decades. Forsyth (1997b, see also Hemmings 2002) focuses on Northampton's downtown area, where lesbian businesses and services are located, pointing out building renovations, increased rents, displacement, and the "Massachusetts miracle," in which Northampton experienced an increase of housing values of 123 percent in real terms between 1980 and 1990 (Massachusetts experienced an increase of 112 percent during the same time). Nevertheless, Forsyth points out that despite the fact that lesbians became culturally visible, they did not economically benefit from the increase in property values, as building ownership by unmarried women remained low between 1975 and 1995. Forsyth also compares 32 lesbian census tracts to non-lesbian census tracts in the Connecticut River Valley, where Northampton is located, finding that lesbian census tracts have significantly higher values in terms of several characteristics, among them the proportion of non-Hispanic Asian and Pacific Islanders; the proportion of people with college, graduate, professional, and doctoral degrees; the proportion of females with graduate, professional, and doctoral degrees; and median non-family household income for females (see also LeVay and Nonas 1995).

An example of a provincial urban area studied in the United Kingdom is Melchester, which is a pseudonym assigned by Valentine (1995). Melchester's lesbian neighborhood, called Hightown by the author, is characterized by two-bedroom, Victorian, terraced housing units and low-cost rental housing and a social mix with a high proportion of students and ethnic minorities. Thus, Valentine argues that Hightown is not a gentrifying neighborhood.

Fewer studies of queer households have focused on the suburbs, such as in Western Sydney (Australia) (Hodge 1995) and Atlanta (Doan and Higgins 2011). This study fills gaps in terms of both the suburbs and a nationwide scope, both of which have been understudied.

Data and Methods

As mentioned above, there is an abundance of case studies on same-sex male and female households yet a dearth of national studies on the same populations, let alone queer households. There is also a lack of national studies on same-sex male and female households that are located in the suburbs. The reason for this shortage is the lack of good national data on same-sex households. Although there are several data sets available that have information on same-sex households, such as the General Social Survey (GSS), the National Health and Social Life Survey (NHSLS), and the Behavioral Risk Factor Surveillance System (BRFSS) (Black et al. 2000), none are representative of the entire nation and/or they do not have information on the locations of same-sex households. The best currently available source for the purposes of this study is the 2000 US Census, which is representative of the nation and which provides information on the locations of the surveyed householders.

The US Census Bureau asks each householder to fill out a questionnaire. One of the questions of interest for this study asks about the existence of other member(s) in the household and his/her/their relationship to the householder.[2] One of the possible answers is "unmarried partner" (variable PCT1: Unmarried Partner Households by Sex of Partners). However, there is a possibility of a potential undercount when it comes to this question. Based on polls and studies, Smith and Gates (2001, see also Bowes 1996) estimate the gay and lesbian undercount to be 62 percent, which makes using data from the 2000 US Census a very conservative approach. The undercount might range higher in suburbs because of suburban residents' perceived middle-class orientation and socio-cultural environment, which might inhibit queer identify formation. Future Censuses may have less of an undercount, since an improvement in the societal climate is likely in the long run to encourage gays and lesbians to gradually come out of the closet.

The following breakdown is provided by the US Census for PCT 1:

1. Unmarried-partner Households
    a. Male householder and male partner
    b. Male householder and female partner
    c. Female householder and female partner
    d. Female householder and male partner.

Although the US Census Bureau provides the number of *unmarried* (same-sex) partner households, this number also contains married (same-sex) partner households. During the writing of the editing program used for the 2000 US Census, the legality of same-sex marriages was challenged in some courts. Despite these legal challenges, same-sex spouse responses were recorded in the Census questionnaires. Thus, the Census decided to assign the responses of same-sex married couples to the same-sex unmarried couples category (US Census Bureau 2000, see also Smith and Gates 2001, Gates and Ost 2004).

In order to avoid extremely small observation numbers, only the 50 counties with the highest proportion of unmarried male and female same-sex couples, respectively, were chosen for this analysis. Therefore, only those counties that had 100 or more same-sex couples were selected. As mentioned above, the unit of observation is the census tract within counties, not cities, metropolitan areas, or Census regions. Same-sex households tend to cluster in urban as well as suburban areas, although they also reside in rural areas—just in smaller numbers per census

---

2 Available at: http://www.gaydemographics.org/USA/USA.htm [accessed: May 25, 2009].

tract (typically below the chosen threshold of 100 same-sex couples) (see also Forsyth 1997b).

The male and female same-sex household variables were used in order to select the 50 counties with the highest proportion of unmarried male and female same-sex couples, respectively. Since the US Census's edit and allocation process in 2000 was different from its edit and allocation process in 1990, same-sex households cannot be compared between the two points in time (US Bureau of the Census 2000). Nevertheless, all other variables used in this study are comparable, as the NCDB data base provides data based on normalized census tract boundaries that often change between two centennial Censuses, making the 1990 and 2000 data comparable. Thus, many variables used in this analysis are either taken from 1990 or 2000 (depending on multicollinearity).

The research questions of this study differentiate between central city and suburban census tracts. Thus, a list of cities with populations of 100,000 or more (according to 2000 US Census data) in the 50 counties with the highest proportion of unmarried male and female same-sex couples, respectively, was compiled. Census tracts that are partially or fully located in cities with populations of 100,000 or more will be called "central city census tracts"[3] in this study. All other Census tracts will be called "suburban census tracts" (for alternative approaches see Lucy and Phillips 2006, Mikelbank 2004, Puentes and Warren 2006, and Hanlon 2008). The analysis will compare and contrast both clusters of census tracts.

Since one of the foci of this contribution is on home equity, it is important not to give too much consideration to those census tracts that have a low proportion of homeowners. Therefore, only census tracts that have a homeownership rate above 50 percent were included in the analysis.

Results

The following research questions were asked, differentiating between central city and suburban census tracts:

1. Are there differences in demographic, socioeconomic, housing, and neighborhood characteristics as well as property values?
2. Are there differences in property value appreciation rates?
3. Are there differences in factors that influence property values?

Of the 10,183 census tracts in the top 50 male same-sex household counties that had a home ownership rate of 50 percent and more, 66.11 percent (6,732 census tracts) did not report any male same-sex households at all. Of these 6,732 census

---

3 The City of Boulder, Colorado, had a population of 94,673 in 2000. Since its population is very close to the suggested threshold of 100,000 people, it was considered as the central city of Boulder County, Colorado.

tracts, 2,543 (37.77 percent) were located in central cities, 4,189 (62.23 percent) were located in the suburbs, and 3,451 (33.89 percent) reported at least one male same-sex household. Of these 3,451 census tracts, 1,357 (39.32 percent) were located in central cities and 2,094 (60.68 percent), surprisingly, were located in the suburbs. This finding is consistent with Lynch (1987) but inconsistent with Black et al. (2002), as discussed above, for the counties analyzed in this chapter. Many male same-sex households visibly cluster in gentrified central city neighborhoods (Castells 1983, Florida and Mellander 2007, Gates and Ost 2004, Godfrey 1988, Knopp 1990a, 1990b, 1992, 1995, Moss, 1997, Visser 2003, among others). Therefore, one would expect a higher proportion of Census tracts with male same-sex households in central cities than in the suburbs. However, this is not the case for the analyzed counties. So far, the literature seems to have focused on visible clusters of male same-sex households in central city neighborhoods. These findings suggest, however, that there are many male same-sex households who live in the suburbs, possibly in a scattered residential pattern.

Of the 10,340 census tracts in the top 50 female same-sex housing counties that had a home ownership rate of 50 percent and more, 65.10 percent (6,731 census tracts) did not report any female same-sex households at all. Of these 6,731 census tracts, 2,543 (37.78 percent) were located in central cities, 4,188 (62.22 percent) were located in the suburbs, and 3,609 (34.90 percent) reported at least one female same-sex household. Of these 3,609 census tracts, 1,377 (38.15 percent) were located in central cities and 2,232 (61.85 percent, taking 3,609 as 100 percent) were located in the suburbs, opposing the myth about primarily straight suburbs in those counties analyzed in this chapter. These proportions illustrate that female same-sex households disproportionately live in suburbs, a finding that has been understudied in the literature (Chamberland 1993, Dubrow 1998b, LeVay and Nonas 1995, Lockard 1985, Retter 1997, Witeck-Combs Communications 2002).

Table 6.1 shows the regional distribution of census tracts of all selected counties. Census Region West has the highest proportion (about 40 percent, depending on the group) of census tracts of each analyzed group, followed by Census Region South, Census Region Midwest, and Census Region Northeast (ranging from about 5 percent to about 12 percent).

The descriptive statistics in Table 6.2 reveal that the differences between the 50 male same-sex household counties and the entire nation and the top 50 female same-sex household counties and the entire nation are always significant at the 5 percent level. In terms of diversity of race, ethnicity, and nativity, the results indicate that all four analyzed subgroups have a lower proportion of non-Hispanic Whites and a higher proportion of foreign-borns than the nation as a whole, confirming hypotheses about the perceived appreciation of diversity (Moss 1997) or tolerance (Black et al. 2002, Doan and Higgins 2011, Forsyth 1997b, Godfrey 1988, Ingram et al. 1997). These findings are not surprising, since only the 50 counties with the highest proportion of unmarried male and female same-sex couples based on a threshold population of more than 100,000 are the basis for

Table 6.1 Regional Distribution of Census Tracts with at least One Reported Male or Female Same-Sex Household by Census Region with Home Ownership Above 50 percent

	Male Same Sex HHs		Female Same Sex HHs	
Census Region	Number of Central City Census Tracts	Number of Suburban Census Tracts	Number of Central City Census Tracts	Number of Suburban Census Tracts
Northeast	140	103	150	127
	-10.32%	-4.92%	(10,89%)	-5.69%
Midwest	221	476	238	540
	-16.29%	-22.73%	-17.28%	-24.19%
South	416	684	395	672
	-30.66%	-32.66%	-28.69%	-30.11%
West	580	831	594	893
	-42.74%	-39.68%	-43.14%	-40.01%
Total	1,357	2,094	1,377	2,232
	-100%	-100%	-100%	-100%

the analysis, as discussed above. These counties are urbanized and, thus, expected to be diverse in terms of race, ethnicity, nativity, and other factors (see Frey 2001, Gates and Ost 2004, Rothenberg 1995, and Simmons and O'Connell 2003, among others). Comparing the four subsets, the urban subsets have a lower proportion of non-Hispanic Whites but a higher proportion of foreign-borns than the suburban subsets, as expected. Furthermore, queer households seem to appreciate diversity, the presence of tolerance, and anonymity, which are most likely appreciated by foreign-borns as well. It might be that both groups co-exist in particular neighborhoods in select metropolitan immigrant gateways. More research should be undertaken on this aspect.

In regards to education and income, the proportion of the population 25 years and over with a Bachelors or higher degree is higher in the four analyzed subsets than in the nation as a whole, confirming Badgett (2001) and Black et al. (2000), among others. Similarly, median household incomes in 1989 and 1999 were higher in the four analyzed subsets than in the nation as a whole, confirming Gates and Ost (2004). These findings are no surprise, as metropolitan areas are typically characterized by higher levels of education and salaries than rural areas. Also, higher levels of education typically result not only in higher salaries but also higher labor force participation rates, which in turn result in higher household incomes. Comparing the four subsets, Census tracts with male same-sex households in central cities have the highest proportion of residents with advanced degrees (Bachelors and higher; 31.64 percent), followed by Census tracts with female same-sex households in suburbs (30.63 percent), Census tracts with male same-sex households in suburbs (30.51 percent), and Census tracts with female same-sex

Table 6.2 Descriptive Statistics for Census Tracts with Home Ownership Rate Above 50 percent

Mean (Standard deviation)	Male Same Sex HHs Census Tracts in Central Cities (N=1,357)	Male Same Sex HHs Census Tracts in Suburbs (N=2,094)	Female Same Sex HHs Census Tracts in Central Cities (N=1,377)	Female Same Sex HHs Census Tracts in Suburbs (N=2,232)	Total United States
Percent Non-Hispanic Whites (2000)	**0.5621** (0.3146)	**0.6757** (0.2796)	**0.5685** (0.3069)	**0.6901** (0.2735)	0.7701
Percent 25 Years and Over with Bachelors or Higher Degree (2000)	**0.3164** (0.2151)	**0.3051** (0.1839)	**0.305** (0.2089)	**0.3063** (0.1796)	0.2606
Percent Foreign-Born (2000)	**0.1692** (0.1433)	**0.1448** (0.1334)	**0.1668** (0.1411)	**0.1363** (0.131)	0.1105
Median Household Income (1989 dollars)	$36,307 ($21,005)	**$33,700** ($19,129)	**$34,976** ($17,621)	**$33,603** ($18,415)	$30,056
Median Household Income (1999 dollars)	**$55,156** ($24,408)	**$57,060** ($21,526)	**$53,255** ($22,054)	**$56,873** ($20,880)	$41,994
Median Year Housing Unit Built (2000)	1954 (15.9569)	1970 (14.1755)	1954 (16.0311)	1970 (14.0276)	1971
Percent Housing Units Vacant (2000)	**0.0454** (0.0349)	**0.0568** (0.0588)	**0.0447** (0.0332)	**0.0538** (0.056)	0.0899
Median Value for Owner-Occupied Housing Units (1990)	**$136,997** ($121,531)	**$117,694** ($94,310)	**$129,315** ($110,426)	**$115,353** ($92,949)	$79,100
Median Value for Owner-Occupied Housing Units (2000)	**$201,041** ($161,128)	**$192,329** ($123,513)	**$189,179** ($145,295)	**$189,613** ($121,133)	$119,600

Table 6.2 Continued

Mean (Standard deviation)	Male Same Sex HHs Census Tracts in Central Cities (N=1,357)	Male Same Sex HHs Census Tracts in Suburbs (N=2,094)	Female Same Sex HHs Census Tracts in Central Cities (N=1,377)	Female Same Sex HHs Census Tracts in Suburbs (N=2,232)	Total United States
Cost of Living Index (2000)	22.34 (22.14)	26.97 (23.14)	22.78 (22.44)	26.44 (22.66)	N/A
Transportation Index (2000)	91.64 (7.65)	84.14 (20.92)	91.29 (8.31)	82.8 (22.59)	N/A
Number of New Jobs Index (2000)	81.04 (18.53)	79.87 (20.07)	80.84 (18.57)	79.1 (20.81)	N/A
Educational Institutions Index (2000)	86.2 (10.69)	78.44 (17.63)	86.06 (10.8)	78.8 (17.9)	N/A
Health Care Facilities Index (2000)	75.71 (16.4)	72.48 (17.74)	75.48 (16.19)	72.66 (17.68)	N/A
Recreational Facilities Index (2000)	88 (8.2)	85.05 (16.69)	87.86 (8.67)	83.97 (17.23)	N/A

Note: **Bold** = significant at <.000; *Italic* = significant at <0.05 for one-sampled T-test against the entire United States.

households in central cities (30.50 percent). Nevertheless, the differences between the subsets are small. In terms of median household incomes, they were highest in 1989 in Census tracts with male householders in central cities and lowest in Census tracts with female householders in suburbs. In 1999, median household incomes were highest in Census tracts with male householders in suburbs and lowest in Census tracts with female householders in central cities. These findings, which are inconsistent throughout the years and areas, could be addressed with a study based on a national data set that provides information on salaries of male and female same-sex households. To the author's current knowledge, such a data set does not exist.

In terms of the housing stock, the findings indicate that the housing stock for all four subgroups, when compared to that of the entire nation, is older but of higher value and is also characterized by a relatively low proportion of vacancies. These factors are typically found in urban or urbanized areas. Comparing the four subgroups, the two urban subsets have an older housing stock than the two suburban subsets, which is not surprising.

In regards to the age of the housing stock, the median year housing units were built in urban Census tracts was 1954, whereas in suburban Census tracts it was 1970. Many suburbs developed rapidly in the 1950s, 1960s, and 1970s, a time characterized by an architectural style that some might describe as boring and a construction style that many would characterize as shoddy. In terms of gays, some authors have focused on the correlations between gays and aesthetics (Florida and Mellander 2010) and gays and urban gentrification (Castells 1983, Godfrey 1988, Knopp 1990a, 1990b, 1992, 1995, Moss 1997, Visser 2003). Thus, one would not expect to find many male same-sex households in the suburbs. However, results discussed above show that there are a disproportionate percentage of male same-sex households located in the suburbs, a finding that deserves to be explored further in future research efforts (Doan and Higgins 2011, Hodge 1995). In terms of lesbians, the literature finds that there are lesbian residential neighborhoods in urban cores of metropolitan areas, in smaller metro areas and suburbs (Chamberland 1993, Dubrow 1998b, LeVay and Nonas 1995, Lockard 1985, Retter 1997, Witeck-Combs Communications 2002). Results presented above corroborate this literature.

With regards to median values for owner-occupied housing units in 1989, the two urban subsets had a higher median value than the suburban ones, consistent with the literature in land economics (Burgess 1925, Hoyt 1933, Harris and Ullman 1945, Alonso 1964, Muth 1969, and Mills 1972). However, in regards to median values in 1999, Census tracts with male same-sex households in both central cities and suburbs had higher absolute values than Census tracts with female same-sex households in both central cities and suburbs, implicitly confirming Forsyth (2001). However, appreciation rates were highest in Census tracts with female same-sex households in suburbs (64.38 percent), surprisingly, and lowest in Census tracts with female same-sex households in central cities (46.29 percent). More research is needed to investigate these surprising findings.

What cannot be answered based on the data set analyzed for this study is the question of whether male and female same-sex households who reside in the (mature) suburbs are homeowners and whether they rehabilitate their homes, similar to what gays have done in many urban gentrifying neighborhoods. Anecdotal evidence suggests that some male same-sex households do (Thomas Bier, expert interview, 9 October 2003) although this aspect has not been discussed in the literature for either male or female same-sex households. Related to this aspect, the question also remains whether male and female same-sex households who invest in the housing stock in the (mature) suburbs will receive a decent return on investment—however "decent" may be defined. Prior to the national house price crash, some authors pointed out that many home owners in the mature suburbs did not receive a good return on their investment (Bier 2001). While this insight is currently true for many neighborhoods in many areas, it needs to be seen whether returns on investment will increase in general and in the (mature) suburbs in particular in the near and distant future. If male and female same-sex households cluster and invest in the (mature) suburbs, similar to what gays in gentrifying urban neighborhoods have done, then a decent return on investment might happen, especially when there is a critical mass of investing homeowners. While property values and their appreciation have been covered to some degree in the literature (Anacker 2009), not much has been written on the return on investment in general, in the suburbs, and in the (mature) suburbs where male and female same-sex households cluster. More research is needed.

In regards to vacancy rates, the two suburban subsets have higher rates than the two urban subsets, surprisingly, although the differences are small. These findings might indicate that some suburbs have a housing stock that is less appealing to some, due to undesirable aesthetics and poor construction quality, and that there is an unacceptable return on investment, as already discussed above. These findings might also indicate that some suburbs are in a location that lacks amenities such as vibrant neighborhoods with many amenities, preferred by many, including gays and lesbians. Future research efforts should focus on housing and neighborhood preferences of suburban gay and lesbians, similar to efforts undertaken by Doan (2007). With regards to Savageau and D'Agostino's (2000) quality of life variables, when differentiating between the two central city subsets and the two suburban subsets,[4] we find that the two central city subsets are characterized by a higher cost of living (the higher the score, the less expensive); better access to transportation and educational, health, and recreational facilities; and a higher number of jobs created, as expected (see Florida 2002).

The second research question asks whether there are differences in property value appreciation rates between 1990 and 2000 based on the variable Median Value for Specified Owner-Occupied Housing Units in 1990 and 2000. Table 6.2 displays the absolute values for the four subgroups. In regards to *nominal* appreciation rates, Census tracts with female same-sex households in suburbs

---

4 Savageau and D'Agostino (2000) do not provide data at the national level.

Table 6.3 Regression Analyses for Census Tracts with Home Ownership Rate Above 50 percent

Coefficient (Standard Error)	Male Same Sex HHs Central City Census Tracts (N=1,357)	Male Same Sex HHs Suburban Census Tracts (N=2,094)	Female Same Sex HHs Central City Census Tracts (N=1,377)	Female Same Sex HHs Suburban Census Tracts (N=2,232)
Constant	**10.3663** (0.0845)	**11.389** (0.766)	**6.7331** (0.833)	**10.9352** (0.7175)
Census Region Midwest	NS	NS	NS	NS
Census Region South	*0.0778* (0.0357)	*0.1204* (0.0321)	NS	*0.0849* (0.0269)
Census Region West	0.4019 (0.0295)	0.3837 (0.0271)	0.3683 (0.0262)	0.3461 (0.0228)
Commute Time <=20 Minutes (2000)	NS	NS	*0* (0.00)	*-0.089* (0.0346)
Total Population (2000)	NS	NS	NS	NS
Proportion of Non-Hispanic Whites (2000)	**0.2035** (0.0251)	**0.3594** (0.0198)	**0.1857** (0.0229)	**0.3623** (0.0198)
Proportion 25 Years and Over with Bachelors or Higher Degree (2000)	**1.0109** (0.0548)	**0.9877** (0.0425)	**0.9549** (0.0523)	**1.0377** (0.0388)
Proportion Foreign-Born (2000)	**0.6332** (0.0471)	**0.5374** (0.0424)	**0.3977** (0.0453)	**0.582** (0.0422)
Median Household Income (1989 dollars)	*0* (0.00)	**0** (0.00)	*0* (0.00)	**0** (0.00)
Median Household Income (1999 dollars)	**0** (0.00)	**0** (0.00)	**0** (0.00)	**0** (0.00)

Table 6.3   Continued

Coefficient (Standard Error)	Male Same Sex HHs Central City Census Tracts (N=1,357)	Male Same Sex HHs Suburban Census Tracts (N=2,094)	Female Same Sex HHs Central City Census Tracts (N=1,377)	Female Same Sex HHs Suburban Census Tracts (N=2,232)
Median Year Housing Unit Built (2000)	**0.0022** (0.0004)	NS	**0.0021** (0.0004)	NS
Proportion of Housing Units Vacant (2000)	*-0.8735* (0.2354)	*0.3133* (0.1004)	**-0.8932** (0.2137)	*0.2084* (0.0989)
Cost of Living Index (2000)	**-0.0036** (0.0005)	**-0.0063** (0.0003)	**-0.0047** (0.0005)	**-0.0065** (0.0003)
Transportation Index (2000)	**-0.0138** (0.0008)	NS	**-0.0143** (0.0009)	NS
Number of New Jobs Index (2000)	**-0.0037** (0.0004)	*-0.0006* (0.0003)	**-0.0042** (0.0004)	NS
Educational Institutions Index (2000)	**0.0069** (0.0007)	**-0.0038** (0.0005)	**0.004** (0.0007)	**-0.0031** (0.0005)
Health Care Facilities Index (2000)	**0.0049** (0.0004)	**0.0016** (0.0003)	**0.0046** (0.0004)	**0.0011** (0.0003)
Recreational Facilities Index (2000)	**0.0131** (0.0009)	NS	**0.0117** (0.0008)	NS
F Value	1,004.10	811.72	998.66	897.12
Pr > F	<.0001	<.0001	<.0001	<.0001
Adjusted R Squared	0.9319	0.8813	0.9307	0.8858

Note: **Bold** = significant at <.0001; *Italic* = significant at .05; NS = variable not significant.

had the highest appreciation rate (64.38 percent), followed by census tracts with male same-sex households in suburbs (63.41 percent), census tracts with male same-sex households in central cities (46.75 percent), and Census tracts with female same-sex households in central cities (46.29 percent). Nationwide, the *nominal* appreciation rate was 51.20 percent between 1990 and 2000. The higher appreciation rate in the suburbs, regardless of the subgroup, confirms the expectation that property values in suburbs appreciate faster than property values in central cities (with the exception of gentrified areas).

The third research question asks whether there are differences in factors that influence property values. These questions are examined in the Weighted Least Squared (WLS) regressions in Table 6.3. In the following discussion, only coefficients significant at the 5 percent level will be mentioned.

Census Region Northeast was taken as the base case for the Census region dummies, as this region has the lowest number of Census tracts with at least one household that had a male householder and male partner or a female householder and a female partner, respectively. In the cases where the Census region variables were significant, the coefficients were positive. For Census Region West, the coefficient was expected to be positive, consistent with the fact that housing is more expensive on the east and west coasts. For Census Region South, the coefficient was expected to be negative, confirming lower property values in this Census region. The coefficients may have been positive because only urbanized counties were included in the analysis, and these counties are often characterized by high house prices.

With respect to demographics, the total population, when taken as a proxy for demand for housing, was only significant and positive in the case of Census tracts with female same-sex households in central cities. This is consistent with expectations, as demand for housing typically has a positive effect on property values.

In terms of diversity of race, ethnicity, and nativity, the variable Proportion of Non-Hispanic Whites (2000) was significant and positive in all four subsets. The two suburban subsets had a higher coefficient than the two urban ones, possibly indicating a lower appreciation of diversity (Moss 1997). The proportion of foreign-borns was also significant and positive in all four subsets. Not surprisingly, the coefficient was highest in Census tracts with male same-sex households in central cities (Florida 2002), but the coefficient was second highest in Census tracts with female same-sex households in suburbs. Surprisingly, the coefficient was lowest in Census tracts with female same-sex households in central cities. To the author's knowledge, not much literature has been published on the effect of foreign-borns on property values (see Saiz and Wachter 2006 as an exception).

With respect to socioeconomics, all variables are consistent with the expectations. Variable Proportion of Population 25 Years and Over with Bachelors or Higher Degree was positive and significant, and the coefficient of this variable, compared to all other variables, is large. Surprisingly, among all four subsets, the coefficient is largest in Census tracts with female same-sex households in suburbs and smallest in Census tracts with female same-sex households in cities, where the coefficient is still quite large. Similarly, the variable Median Household Income (1989 and 1999) had a positive (albeit small) coefficient, consistent with the housing literature (Manning 1986, 1989).

The housing stock variables provided more mixed results. The variable Median Year Housing Unit Built was expected to be positive, and this was the case for the two subsets in the central cities, confirming the literature (Colton 2003), but the variable was insignificant for the two subsets in the suburbs. The variable Proportion of Housing Units Vacant was expected to be negative, and this was the case for the two subsets in central cities, also confirming the literature (Colton 2003). However, the two subsets in the suburbs had a positive coefficient, which is surprising since vacancy rates in these two subsets were slightly higher than in the two subsets in central cities.

The results for the quality of life variables were more mixed. The variable Cost of Living Index was negative, as expected (the higher the index, the higher the cost of living). This is consistent with the hypothesis that the proportion of same-sex households is higher in those metropolitan areas that are thriving and rich in opportunities (Florida 2002).

The variable Transportation Index was only significant for the two urban subsets, where it was negative, indicating that access to transportation has a negative influence on property values. This implies that transportation is considered a negative amenity (associated with noise and air pollution, among other factors), not a positive one (potentially associated with access to opportunities). This finding is confirmed by the negative coefficient of the variable Commute Time 20 Minutes and Under. In 2000, the year taken for this analysis, more people might have associated transportation with something negative rather than something positive than they would in 2009, and this assumption might explain the negative coefficient.

The variable Number of New Jobs Index had a negative coefficient but was insignificant for Census tracts with female same-sex households in suburbs. This is inconsistent with expectations, possibly reflecting the construction of the index (see Roback 1982, among others). Newly created jobs are assumed to at least partially attract new in-movers to areas, thus increasing demand for housing, which in turn results in increased property values. Other indices for newly created jobs should be analyzed to see whether they generate similar findings that are inconsistent with the literature.

The variables Educational Institutions Index, Health Care Facilities Index, and Recreational Facilities Index are considered amenities, so their coefficients were expected to be positive. This is the case for all subgroups with the exception of the variable Recreational Facilities Index for the suburban subsets.

Values of the Adjusted R Squared were calculated as a measure of goodness of fit for the WLS regressions. They ranged from 0.9319 for the subset Census Tracts with Male Same-Sex Households in Central Cities to 0.8813 for the subset Census Tracts with Male Same-Sex Households in Suburbs, indicating a good fit.

The number of significant variables ranges from 15 (in the case of the central city subsets) to 12 (in the case of the suburban subsets), indicating a sufficient number of variables.

Conclusion

Suburbs are often perceived as places for two-parent, nuclear, heterosexual families who live in single-family, owner-occupied homes and where queer identify formation is inhibited (Altman 1982, Knopp 1992). The results of this study indicate that among those neighborhoods included in this analysis, suburban neighborhoods have a higher proportion of male same-sex households and female same-sex households, respectively, than urban neighborhoods, confirming that there is suburban diversity in terms of queers. The findings reveal demographic and socioeconomic differences among the four subgroups that are expected and consistent with the literature. In terms of differences in housing, however, vacancy rates in the two urban subsets were lower than in the two suburban subsets, possibly indicating issues with the suburban housing stock. More research is needed in order to investigate this rather surprising finding. Similarly surprising, median values for specified owner-occupied housing units in 1999 were very similar for Census tracts with female same-sex householders in central cities versus female same-sex householders in the suburbs. The latter finding may indicate potential housing affordability issues among female same-sex households, as discussed in the literature (see Forsyth 1997b, among others). Results also indicate differences in property value appreciation rates between 1990 and 2000, which are much higher in the two suburban subsets than in the two urban subsets, and are consistent with the housing literature (Anacker 2009).

Furthermore, the results indicate differences in factors that influence property values. The variable that influences property values the most is Proportion of Population 25 Years and Over with Bachelors or Higher Degree (2000), followed by the variable Proportion Foreign-Born. These findings imply foreign-born in-movers have positive impacts on property values. Whereas much research has been undertaken on the effect of well-educated residents on property values, much less research has focused on the effects of foreign-borns on property values (see Saiz and Wachter 2006, as an exception), be it in neighborhoods that are characterized by high proportions of male and female same-sex households or any other neighborhoods.

On a broader level, and in the grand scheme of things, suburban decline in select mature communities is fundamentally a problem of housing as well as income. On the one hand, if incomes of homeowners in the mature suburbs are too low in the medium to long term, many will not be able to make sufficient investments in their aging homes. On the other hand, if returns on investments are undesirable, most will not be willing to make investments. Thus, in the medium to long term there might be decay in select mature suburbs similar to the decay experienced in central cities.

Unlike central cities, mature suburbs are not supported by many federal public policies with the exception of the Community Development Block Grant (CDBG) Program for municipalities with populations of 50,000 and more. Thus, local planners need to create policies that support sustainable home ownership opportunities in the mature suburbs. An example of such a program is Cuyahoga County's (Ohio) Housing Enhancement Loan Program (HELP). HELP allows homeowners in eligible communities to borrow money to alter, repair, or improve a property to protect or improve its basic livability and enhance the property's value for a reduced interest rate. While this program facilitates access to credit, it does not guarantee a decent return on investment.

Homeowners bear an enormous risk yet there are a few local policies in place that address the insurance of homeowner equity. The City of Syracuse, for example, administers the Home Equity Protection (HEP) program, which is implemented by Equity Headquarters, Inc. This program provides financial protection to homeowners or homebuyers in the event that home prices decline. Decline is determined by a repeat sales house price index in the zip code in which the house is located between the time of the purchase and the time of the sale in exchange for a one-time fee. Another example is the Southwest Home Equity Assurance program, which insures property values for an extended time and is administered by nine (unpaid) volunteer commissioners who are appointed by the Mayor of the City of Chicago. This program is financed by an annual levy on all single- through six-unit residential properties within the Home Equity District and is capped at 0.12 percent of the equalized assessed valuation of these properties. Furthermore these programs do not document the participation of same sex partner households so it is difficult to assess whether they are "equally" available irrespective of sexual orientation.

In conclusion, this contribution finds that there is suburban diversity in terms of queers, that many findings need further investigation as they are complex, and that some suburbs face challenges in terms of housing and income. Federal, state, regional, and local public policies will be needed to provide place-based investments and to prevent, stop, or reverse (mature) suburban decline, especially in neighborhoods inhabited by often marginalized queer populations.

PART II
Governance and Political Issues

Chapter 7
Queerying Planning in Australia: The Problems and Possibilities of Multiscalar Governance for LGBT Sexual Minorities

Andrew Gorman-Murray

Introduction

Despite the progressive legal recognition of LGBT sexual minorities – lesbian, gay, bisexual, trans[1] and other non-heteronormative subjects – across the West since the 1970s, they remain only partially integrated into planning discourses, policies and practices. Over the last decade, planners and geographers have critiqued ongoing exclusions and called for inclusive planning processes. Frisch (2002: 255) contends that planning is 'a heterosexist project', which 'fundamentally promotes heterosexuality and represses homosexuality' in Western societies via mechanisms that control sexuality and create order for heterosexual nuclear families. In the face of this heterosexism, Forsyth (2001) argues that the emergence of LGBT populations in the late twentieth century has significant implications for planning practice, and documents how their claims impact on a range of planning concerns: enclaves and neighborhoods, residential zoning and housing, business development and tourism, historic preservation, and public space. Fincher and Iveson (2008) thus encourage urban governance forms that accommodate diverse sexualities, promote inter-group interaction, and ultimately foster a politics of recognition and inclusion. Frisch (2002) similarly seeks to reconstruct planning as a 'queer inclusive project' where LGBT minorities are recognized as families, but where extra-familial interaction is also encouraged. Advancing such calls for inclusivity, this chapter discusses some ways in which the needs of LGBT minorities might be better accommodated in planning processes.

One major issue that affects the inclusion of LGBT minorities in planning processes is the multiscalarity of legislative and planning responsibilities, where decision-making is distributed in a complex and overlapping manner between national, state and local levels of governance. This has been largely overlooked in extant queer critiques of planning, but recent calls to consider the different

---

1 Following Felsenthal (2004), I use trans as an umbrella term for those who self-identify as gender-variant, transgender, transsexual (pre-, post- or non-operative), androgynous, intersexed or hermaphrodite.

scales of sexual citizenship (Grundy and Smith 2005, Bell and Binnie 2006) – that is, the governance of social inclusion/exclusion based on sexual subjectivity – suggest greater attention must be given to the multiscalarity of planning with regard to LGBT minorities. This chapter investigates the multiple scales of governance within which planning for LGBT minorities occurs in the specific context of Australia. The political and legal geography of Australia provides an important case for exploring how multiple, interrelated scales of planning affect the inclusion of LGBT minorities in planning processes. Australia is a federation, with a tripartite hierarchy of political, jurisdictional and legislative power divided between national, state/territory and local tiers. Each tier is responsible for different aspects of planning, with various legislation, regulation and responsibilities attached to different scaled arenas. This can lead to jurisdictional conflicts over planning powers, on the one hand, or shirking responsibility for planning, on the other. Both are evident when it comes to planning for LGBT sexual minorities, at times hindering social inclusion. But simultaneously, these multiscalar horizons paradoxically present possibilities for the recognition of LGBT minorities in planning policies and practices.

My contention, then, is that the effective inclusion of LGBT minorities requires consideration of the multiscalarity of planning and the relationships between scales of governance. I argue that recognition of LGBT minorities in planning is both complicated and enabled by Australia's multiscalar governance. This chapter will explore some of these multiscalar complications and potentials, focusing on two particular attempts to recognize and incorporate LGBT minorities at the local scale: first, the Australian Capital Territory's (ACT) efforts to introduce legislation recognizing same-sex partnerships; second, inclusion by some New South Wales (NSW) local governments of LGBT minorities as a targeted group in compulsory social plans. First, though, I set the conceptual and empirical context for these case studies, discussing governance and planning for social diversity and LGBT minorities in Australia, and suggesting how attention to scale adds to this work. I then interrogate the multiscalarity of social planning in Australia, focusing on the two case studies noted. While these examples highlight the problems and possibilities posed by multiscalar governance for LGBT minorities in the context of Australia, the underlying principles contribute to the wider project of 'queerying' planning and recognizing sexual diversity.

Governance, Planning Scales, and LGBT Sexual Minorities: The Australian Context

Before we can consider how (and where) planning can accommodate LGBT minorities, we first need to understand something about what planning is. But as Thompson (2007a: 11) asserts in a recent (and excellent) Australian text: 'It is not easy task to define planning precisely'. One reason it is not easy to define planning is its broad-ranging remit which encompasses place, people, conservation and development. This holistic reach is shown in the definition provided by the Planning Institute of Australia:

> Planners develop strategies and design the communities in which we live, work and play. Balancing the built and natural environment, community needs, cultural significance, and economic sustainability, planners aim to improve our quality of life and create vibrant communities. ('About Planning'. Available at: www.planning.org.au)

Thus, planning includes various domains – urban, regional, environmental, economic, transport, heritage, *inter alia*. Within this inventory, consideration of LGBT minorities in Australia falls under the responsibility of *social planning*, which is concerned with understanding the needs and aspirations of different social and cultural groups within a community, and accommodating this diversity as equitably as possible (Thompson 2007b).

Thompson (2007b: 199–200) argues that 'social planning ... is at the core of all good contemporary planning, which should aim to integrate physical land use with socio-cultural factors in the quest to build sustainable environments for us all'. The increasingly central importance of social planning reflects the shifting aims and scope of planning in Australian society over the last century – a move from modernist utopian concerns with public health, slum clearance and garden suburbs in the early twentieth century, to a postmodernist appreciation of plurality and the need to sensitively account for social and cultural diversity in the twenty-first century (Sandercock 2003). Accordingly, the figure of the professional planner has moved from a rationalist expert who advocated what was best for communities, to a democratic collaborator who facilitates dialogue between parties in planning issues. This has given rise to the so-called 'communicative turn', where planning is recognized as an ongoing process of interaction between stakeholders, not a top-down process of technical design. In facilitating communication, planners have to be socially-conscious and politically-aware in order to ensure maximum participation of interest groups, the marginal as well as the powerful. These principles lie at the center of social planning.

In this way, social planning entails much more than simply the application of regulations about local land-use zoning, which is often construed as the main work of planners. Instead, the notion of *governance* underpins the practice of social planning. Indeed, several Australian planning scholars have recently considered planning in terms of governance. Williams (2007: 32) denotes governance as the long-term decision-making structures and mechanisms that incorporate democratic stakeholder participation in order to shape planning goals. For Gleeson and Low (2000), governance puts people at the heart of planning processes, since it is about ensuring that all the services people need in a place (city, region, neighborhood) are provided when and where the need occurs. Fincher and Iveson (2008) explicitly link urban governance to social planning, arguing that the principles of planning should recognize social and cultural diversity, encourage encounter between different groups, and redistribute wealth and services to alleviate social disadvantage and inequality. Across all these discussions, governance describes the way different levels of government – local, state and national – come together with community interest groups and (sometimes) private enterprises to facilitate the principles of redistribution, recognition and encounter.

But where and how are LGBT minorities accounted for amidst the scope of social planning and governance? On the surface, they should be well incorporated in the visions of social planning, since this specifically aims to implement non-discriminatory practices, protect the interests of marginalized groups, and foster respect for differences across gender, age, socioeconomic means, ethnicity, culture, religion, physical disability *and sexual orientation* (Thompson 2007b). But despite these goals, LGBT minorities are only partially integrated into social planning in Australia. There are several possible reasons for this. On the one hand, legal and social acceptance of LGBT minorities has been relatively recent, and their accommodation in planning policy and practices has been hindered by inertia around the centrality of the heterosexual nuclear family household in 'traditional' Australian society (Johnson 2000, Thompson 2007b) – the Australian example of Frisch's (2002) charge that planning remains a heterosexist project. On the other hand, in a settler nation-state like Australia, with high per capita migration intake, there is arguably a perception for social planning practices to prioritize culturally and linguistically diverse immigrant groups (Gorman-Murray and Waitt 2009). However, the lack of explicit planning for LGBT minorities is also complicated by scales of governance.

As Williams (2007: 33) asserts, '[t]he structure of urban governance in Australia is closely related to the division of political power among the tiers of government'. As I noted in the introduction, there are three basic tiers of government: national, state and local. At the national level, no specific statutory requirements for social planning have been made. Instead, social planning has been left as one of the legislative responsibilities of each separate state or territory to take up as they (or rather, as their political cultures and systems) see fit. In turn, most states (but not territories) have devolved strategic social planning to authorities in local government areas. Thompson (2007b: 209) points out that these requirements are uneven across Australia, with the most powerful found 'in New South Wales where the *Local Government Act 1993* stipulates that all councils must prepare a social plan, under the provision of the *Local Government (General) Amendment (Community Social Plans) Regulation 1998* (NSW)'.

Articulation and governance of social planning is therefore most comprehensive at the local scale over much of Australia. But local strategies are also bounded and influenced by decisions made at other scales of government (Fincher and Iveson 2008; Young 2008). While the functions of local government are extensive, these authorities are not Constitutionally-recognized; they were created by states and derive most of their 'powers solely from state legislation, such as Local Government Acts' (Williams 2007: 34). Local authorities are thus mediated by states, and tensions have arisen in recent times regarding state 'interference' and changes to local governance. In New South Wales this has included local government amalgamations as well as the centralization (under the state Minister of Planning) of some planning responsibilities (although these generally relate to 'development proposals' rather than social planning) (Williams 2007). Likewise, both local and state strategies and policies are affected by statutes and decisions at the national scale from the federal government. For instance, immigration, which heavily bears on social planning and presents differentiated local impacts, is a matter of federal powers. In this sense, authorities at local scales have to plan how to accommodate the social outcomes of decisions made at the national scale.

But simultaneously, the complications of different scales of governance can also *enable* the inclusion of socially diverse groups. Social and cultural mix differs widely between neighborhoods, and local authorities have a reasonable degree of autonomy and flexibility when it comes to planning for social inclusion. Local governance of inclusion therefore allows strategic planning to be molded to the particular social and cultural patterns of localized areas, and there is perhaps greater opportunity for authorities to be responsive to the diversity of the community and accountable to a range of socially and culturally differentiated needs. For instance, the local scale is foregrounded in Fincher and Iveson's (2008) *Planning and Diversity in the City* not because it is a privileged political scale, but because its containment makes it a pragmatic scale for the inclusive governance of social difference. Their analysis focuses on three social logics of planning – redistribution of resources, recognition of diversity, and everyday encounter between individuals – and suggests that these might be most readily achieved by planning at the local scale. Certainly, it seems that defining the attributes and needs of different social groups (recognition) and providing opportunities for interaction and sociality between them (encounter), in order to facilitate social cohesion, are best enabled in localities. They argue that these locally-situated strategies and actions simultaneously negotiate (and transform) wider trans-local processes at regional, state, national and transnational scales.

These complications and potentials of multiscalar governance significantly affect social planning for the inclusion of LGBT minorities. Since the 1970s, LGBT minorities have been recognized in legislation and policy. But many of the legal rights underpinning sexual citizenship are matters for federal or state legislation, including decriminalization, anti-discrimination, public anti-vilification, and partnership recognition. Moreover, equality with normative heterosexual citizens has not been universally achieved, with LGBT minorities still marginalized from many statutory claims, such as the full suite of partnership rights available to opposite-sex couples (Johnson 2003, Baird 2006), and with evidence of ongoing workplace discrimination and fear of harassment and violence in public spaces despite legislative prohibitions (Flood and Hamilton 2008). However, multiscalar governance provides an opportunity to challenge these social and legal limitations. For instance, the social planning processes of local governments can be used to counter the shortcomings of LGBT inclusion instituted at the national and state scales. This ability is, of course, also constrained by the limits on local regulatory powers within a multiscalar system of governance. Nevertheless, some local (and territorial) authorities in Australia have initiated plans and protocols which aim to include LGBT minorities as full citizens in local neighborhoods and communities, simultaneously contesting the national and state limits of sexual citizenship. To illustrate these multiscalar complications and possibilities, I outline two examples where authorities have sought to extend LGBT inclusion through localized governance, social planning and legislation.

Same-sex Partnership Recognition in the ACT

The first example of the challenges and constraints of multiscalar governance I wish to present is the Australian Capital Territory (ACT) Legislative Assembly's efforts to recognize same-sex partnerships in legislation. The ACT is the region around the national capital, Canberra, and was created by the *Australian Capital Territory (Self-Government) Act 1988* (Commonwealth). Along with the Northern Territory, the ACT is one of two self-governing territories on the Australian mainland, and offers an important case study for the nuanced complexity of multiscalar governance and planning in a federal nation-state. These two territories fit awkwardly into, and complicate, the tripartite hierarchy of federal, state and local governance. On the one hand, the territories are equivalent to states in that they do not overlap with state boundaries and jurisdictions. On the other hand, they are not Federation signatories and lack the full legislative powers of a state *vis-à-vis* the federal government: territorial legislation can be overruled by the Commonwealth Parliament or the Governor-General. Moreover, unlike the Northern Territory, the ACT has not created internal local council areas. In effect, its government is *both* territorial legislature *and* local council – a highly localized territorial parliament. The ACT therefore exhibits an especially complex scalarity, which is also affected by Canberra's status as national capital. This multiscalarity affects the ACT's endeavors to account for LGBT minorities, illustrating the impacts of the contingent relationships between different, intersecting scales of governance.

I want to use one example to highlight this scalar dissonance: the legal recognition of same-sex relationship rights through such mechanisms as civil partnerships and civil unions. Fincher and Iveson (2008: 132) argue that '[r]ecognizing the significance of same-sex relationships is rare in urban planning'. Yet, such partnership rights are an important part of the inclusive governance and planning for LGBT minorities. The right to have intimate relationships with same-sex partners is one of the foundations of LGBT rights activism across the West, and increasing numbers of same-sex partners are 'coming out' in contemporary Australia. Same-sex *de facto* couples have been able to voluntarily declare their relationship status in the last three Censuses (1996, 2001 and 2006) and the number of persons in same-sex couples has increased significantly over this decade, from 19,594 in 1996 to 49,364 in 2006. This equates to a 152 percent increase, and the

Australian Bureau of Statistics (2005) attributes this to growing awareness that same-sex couples can now be counted in the Census, combined with wider public acknowledgement of same-sex relationships. It is time, then, for governments and planners to better recognize the needs of same-sex couples across the life-course. This includes legislation, plans and protocols that ensure safety in public space, protect residential property, provide for partnered taxation and succession claims, and encourage interaction between diverse sexualities in local neighborhoods.

Before assessing the ACT case, I first want to acknowledge that there is contention *within* LGBT politics about same-sex civil unions and marriage, where some commentators see such partnership rights as problematically assimilative, defining equality through existing legislation which reference heterosexual relationships as the norm (Duggan 2002a). Some, instead, seek a transformative politics where laws are amended to reflect a denaturalization of heterosexuality – for instance, a critique of the normalization of 'coupling' as the 'acceptable' form of intimate sexual relationship in Western society, sanctioned through a range of options (marriage, civil union and *de facto* partnerships). I want to move beside these arguments, and consider the 'grounded' push for same-sex partnership recognition in Australia. Same-sex marriage is probably the most significant current claim asserted by LGBT populations and civil rights activists in Australia, regardless of their view of marriage. For instance, NSW Gay and Lesbian Rights Lobby's 2007 consultation with 1,313 self-identifying LGBT people found that 74 percent thought marriage should be extended to same-sex partners, even if they opposed the institution in theory (Bavinton et al. 2007). This push is partly due to the scalar framing of relationship rights in Australia, where marriage is a federal power, and other legal partnerships (such as civil unions and *de facto* relationships) can be legislated – supposedly – at the discretion of states and territories.

In this multiscalar Australian context, one of the highest-profile battles for LGBT rights is the ACT Legislative Assembly's endeavors to recognize same-sex partnerships in legislation, culminating in ongoing attempts to allow civil unions. This has been a fight across – and about – scales of governance and planning. According to data from the 2006 census, Canberra has one of the highest per capita concentrations of same-sex couples in Australia (Gorman-Murray et al. 2010).[2] Moreover, the ACT has a history of responding positively and inclusively to LGBT rights claims, particularly for same-sex couples. For instance, it was the first Australian jurisdiction to legally recognize same-sex partnerships, through the *Domestic Relationships Act 1994* (ACT), which provided for the distribution of property and finances in the event of separation, and inheritance in the event of death. In 2006, the ACT sought to further enhance the recognition and rights of same-sex couples in legislation, with flow-on effects

---

2   Our analysis found the Statistical Sub-Division of North Canberra, in particular, had the fourth highest per capita concentration of same-sex couple family households across Australia, and moreover, the second highest concentration of female same-sex couples specifically (see Gorman-Murray and Brennan-Horley 2010).

for social planning: the Legislative Assembly, headed by a Labor government, passed the *Civil Unions Bill 2006* (ACT), which provided for civil unions for both same-sex and opposite-sex couples resident in the ACT. The ACT Chief Minister, Labor leader John Stanthorpe, made it clear in press statements that the Bill responded to the Commonwealth's proposal that states and territories could enact same-sex civil union (e.g. anon 2006; Humphries 2006a, 2006b). This suggestion was made by the Coalition government after the Commonwealth parliament passed the *Marriage Amendment Act 2004* (Commonwealth) which altered the *Marriage Act 1961* (Commonwealth) to define marriage as 'the union of a man and a woman to the exclusion of all others'.

In drafting and passing the *Civil Unions Bill 2006* (ACT), the ACT illuminated how inclusive governance of LGBT minorities is a multi-scalar process. The Commonwealth had 'banned' same-sex marriage at the national scale through its amendment; the ACT government consequently tried to recognize same-sex partnerships through other legal mechanisms instituted at a different scale of governance – through civil unions at the localized territorial scale. On the one hand, this was an attempt to *rescale* the legislative recognition of same-sex relationships, and thus foster inclusive social planning for LGBT minorities within the ACT's jurisdiction. On the other hand, widespread interest in the Bill brought attention to the continued refusal to account and plan for the inclusion of LGBT minorities at the national scale. The *Civil Unions Bill 2006* (ACT) passed the ACT Legislative Assembly on 11 May 2006, and was enacted on 9 June 2006. There was considerable national interest in the scalar conflict it sparked between the Territory and the Commonwealth. On 13 June 2006 the Federal Executive instructed the Governor-General to disallow the Act on the basis that the legislation equated civil unions with marriage, thus challenging the amendments to the *Marriage Act*, while attempting to usurp the Commonwealth's exclusive constitutional power to legislate for marriage. This move was criticized by civil rights advocates, minor parties and even some Liberal parliamentarians. Moreover, effective planning for the needs of same-sex couples was inhibited by the complications of multiscalar governance and inherent power relationships.

But the ACT did not give up its push for social inclusion of same-sex couples. The shifting political relations between scales of governance also provide opportunities to recover jurisdictional power. Such an opening was presented in October 2007 when a federal election yielded a change in the federal government from Coalition to Labor, which was now in government in both arenas. Prime Minister Kevin Rudd said he would not override new legislation passed in the ACT since he believed the recognition of same-sex relationships was a matter for states *and territories* to decide. This altered the shape of multiscalar governance between the national and territorial parliaments, allowing the ACT to begin to chip away at national exclusions. A new *Civil Partnerships Bill* went before the ACT Legislative Assembly in December 2007, but was stalled by lack of support from the Federal Attorney-General, who found the ceremonial components of the new legislation inappropriate since they 'mimicked' marriage, and preferred sub-national relationship registers to civil unions. Thus, when the *Civil Partnerships Act 2008* (ACT) finally passed the ACT Legislative Assembly on 8 May 2008, there were successes and concessions. On the one hand, civil unions had been left aside for registered partnerships. On the other hand, an enhanced level of legal recognition was achieved: the Act permitted administrative ceremonies performed by a representative of the ACT Register-General, and gave same-sex couples improved taxation, superannuation and social security access.

These concessions also offered the opportunity for further amendments to the Act, and the ACT continued to challenge national governance limitations to same-sex partnerships. In December 2009 the ACT Legislative Assembly passed the *Civil Partnerships Amendment Bill 2009 (No. 2)* (ACT), which amended the *Civil Partnerships Act 2008* (ACT) by re-introducing the ceremonial component of civil partnerships, allowing ceremonies to both be performed by a civil celebrant and carry legal effect – that is, the ceremony, rather than the registration, marking the date when the relationship is legalized. This amendment had effect for same-sex couples only, not opposite-sex couples seeking civil partnerships – for that would usurp the power of the *Marriage Act 1961* (Commonwealth) – and with its passing the ACT became the first jurisdiction to legalize civil partnership ceremonies for same-sex couples. Given tensions between the Territory and federal governments over this issue, it was not surprising that the Commonwealth threatened to overturn the amended legislation again. This time, however, after discussions, the Federal Attorney-General was satisfied that the legislation did not interfere with the *Marriage Act 1961* (Commonwealth), noting that same-sex civil partnership ceremonies would not mimic marriage if same-sex partners were required to also register their intention to hold a ceremony with the ACT Register-General. With this, the ACT finally rescaled the recognition of rights for its LGBT constituencies, enabling better opportunities for inclusive social planning of LGBT minorities in a localized arena.

Local Government Social Planning in NSW

The second example of the limits and potentials of multiscalar governance of LGBT minorities I consider is the regulation of social planning by local governments in New South Wales (NSW). This builds on the previous example from the ACT in three ways. First, it draws attention to the critical role of local authorities in extending social justice to LGBT minorities, complementing and augmenting claims for sexual citizenship at the national and state arenas. Relatedly, it explores the scalar relationship between the local and state levels, showing how LGBT inclusion at the local scale is promoted and enabled, but also bounded, by state governance. Third, social planning at the local scale in NSW takes in the diversity of LGBT populations, not just same-sex couples.

New South Wales is the most populous state, with over 7 million residents in 2010, and it has the most comprehensive and powerful social planning regulations of the states (Thompson 2007b). The provisions of the *Local Government (General) Amendment (Community Social Plans) Regulation 1998* (NSW) confer planning powers to the local level, requiring all local governments – there are 152 in NSW – to prepare social/community plans for their jurisdictions. The *Social/Community Planning and Reporting Guidelines* from the Department of Local Government – the state authority that regulates planning – stipulate that local authorities should prepare their social/community plans in consultation with various social groups identified in their communities (NSW DLG 1998a). These *Guidelines* argue that 'local government is increasingly the key interface between people and government' with augmented responsibility for including communities in the activities of building a collective future (NSW DLG 1998a: 1). The aim of the planning process is thus to identify community needs and develop ameliorative strategies. This aim is guided by the NSW government's Social Justice Direction Statement to ensure equitable access for all to community resources, services, facilities and spaces in order to meet basic needs and improve quality of life. To meet these goals democratically, local authorities are encouraged to 'acknowledge that there are no homogenous views within a community', 'take particular care to involve and protect the interests of people in vulnerable positions', 'avoid discriminatory practices and promote positive opportunities for participation by discriminated groups' (NSW DLG 1998a: 9).

To narrow these broad social justice aims to practical activities, the Department of Local Government provides specific parameters for achieving democratic and non-discriminatory participation in community consultation, needs and strategies. Apart from addressing general community needs, local councils must include data and information about the needs of seven mandatory target groups:

1. children (0–11 years)
2. young people (12–24 years)
3. women
4. older people
5. people with disabilities (with the specific inclusion of people living with HIV/AIDS)
6. Aboriginal and Torres Strait Islander people
7. people from culturally and linguistically diverse backgrounds (racial, ethnic and ethno-religious minority groups)

In addition, the *Guidelines* offer a range of optional target groups that councils might also discretely include if 'relevant'. The optional groups specifically suggested are:

8. low income earners
9. gay, lesbian, bisexual and transgender people
10. families

11. new residents
12. unemployed people

The inclusion of LGBT minorities in this list is important, and elsewhere the Department encourages local governments to carefully consider including sexual minorities in social/community plans. Drawing attention to the state and Commonwealth anti-discrimination legislation – particularly the *Anti-Discrimination Act 1977* (NSW) which prohibits discrimination on the grounds of homosexuality and transgenderism – the Department's *Social/Community Planning and Reporting Manual* asserts:

> Although gays and lesbians are not one of the seven mandatory target groups, councils should make sure that their planning takes their needs into account and council does not inadvertently discriminate against these groups. (NSW DLG 1998b: 5)

The *Manual* consequently provides a page of specific instructions on how to assess barriers inhibiting the participation of LGBT people, and strategies for their inclusion in planning processes (NSW DLG 1998b: 17).

These regulations and official guidelines reveal a critical and complicated multiscalar dimension to the governance of LGBT minorities in NSW. State regulations are empowering councils to practice inclusive planning at the local scale. However, while these directives encourage social/community planning to account for the needs of LGBT minorities in local government areas, this is not mandatory. Empowering councils means giving them the authority to decide *if* LGBT people are a significant minority in their jurisdictions or not. It could thus be argued that in giving such decision-making power to local councils, the state government is shirking the responsibility to mandate social planning practices which account for LGBT minorities, placing the onus on local government instead. Yet, in a populous and geographically-expansive state like NSW (especially compared with the constrained geography and population of the ACT), the local is perhaps the most appropriate scale for effective planning, providing the primary interface between communities and government. State level anti-discrimination legislation should impel local councils to be inclusive. But the complications of guiding effective planning at the juncture between the state and local scales provide the possibility that some groups – like LGBT minorities – might fall through the cracks.

Indeed, there are significant variations in the levels of pro-activity from local governments regarding the inclusion of LGBT minorities. Using data collated on the Department of Local Government website (www.dlg.nsw.gov.au) and site-specific advanced internet searches of the NSW government domain (nsw.gov.au), I looked for social/community plans implemented by local councils which included strategies for meeting the needs of LGBT minorities (as of early-2010). I searched using the terms 'gay', 'lesbian', 'bisexual', 'transgender', 'homosexual' and 'same-sex'. While not an exhaustive survey, the basic findings are telling. Only 22 percent of NSW's 152 local government social/community plans specifically mention LGBT people. Less than half of these – less than 10 percent of all councils – have included LGBT people as a separate target group. The other 12–13 percent have rolled LGBT needs into those of other target groups, notably youth (referring to LGBT youth organizations), but also women (for lesbians), men (for gay men), children and families (for same-sex couples, especially with children), and people with disabilities (equating LGBT minority needs with HIV/AIDS health services).[3] There are also significant divergences between urban and rural localities. All the councils which include LGBT minorities as a separate target group are designated 'urban' (either metropolitan or regional centers) by the Department of Local Government (NSWDLG 2007). Overall, over 35 percent of 'urban' councils make some mention of LGBT minorities in their social/community plans, but less than 10 percent of 'rural' councils do, perpetuating the occlusion of rural LGBT populations.

Local inclusion of LGBT people in social planning is thus uneven, with omission from many localities. Nevertheless, there is great potential for advancing the needs of LGBT minorities through the process of local social/community plans. Where they are included as a discrete target group, there is significant acknowledgement of LGBT needs and empowerment at the local scale. These pro-active councils are concerned with developing what they call 'active citizenship', that is, in initiating consultative mechanisms to include LGBT individuals and communities in councils' decision-making processes. Interestingly, these pro-active councils fall into geographical clusters, with active citizenship for LGBT people spanning several adjoining local government areas. There are three clusters in NSW where LGBT people have special status in local social/community plans:

1. Inner Sydney: including City of Sydney, Marrickville, Leichhardt, North Sydney and Manly councils
2. North Coast: including Newcastle, Port Macquarie-Hastings, Lismore, Byron and Tweed councils
3. South Coast: including Shellharbour, Eurobodalla and Bega Valley councils

Other local councils, such as Hornsby, on Sydney's metropolitan fringe, have also designated LGBT minorities as a target group, but these three clusters underpin 'extended' zones of recognition, inclusion and citizenship which reach across neighboring localities.

For these councils, the objective raised by addressing LGBT minorities as a separate target group is to *directly* incorporate their needs into social/community plans. On the one hand, this means providing specialized services

---

3 Recognizing the multifaceted identities of LGBT people – the intersection of sexuality with gender, age, ethnicity, disability, etc – is also crucial for effective planning for inclusion. I return to this point later.

required by LGBT residents, and on the other hand, developing anti-homophobia/ transphobia initiatives to facilitate social integration between heterosexuals and LGBT minorities at the local scale. It also means extending legal rights to LGBT residents to the extent local regulatory powers allow. These councils thus deploy a range of mechanisms to encompass LGBT minorities in social/community planning:

1. Dedicated council staff[4]
2. Anti-homophobia/transphobia training for council staff
3. Anti-homophobia/transphobia education for residents, businesses and schools
4. Regular liaison with LGBT residents through advisory meetings
5. Regular liaison with LGBT and relevant state organizations through advisory meetings (state bodies include NSW Police and the Attorney General's Department)
6. Meeting harassment and violence concerns through providing 'safe spaces'
7. Provision of funding and space for LGBT community groups
8. Support for LGBT events, such as festivals
9. Including LGBT groups in planning and running community festivals
10. Including LGBT communities in public art and memorials (e.g. queer dedications at Newtown Square in Marrickville local government area)
11. Including LGBT couples and families in sponsored family events and child care
12. Same-sex relationship registers (e.g. City of Sydney Relationship Declaration Program)
13. Lobbying state and federal governments for LGBT-inclusive legislation

Pro-active councils are also aware that LGBT people are 'more than' their sexual identities, and that accounting for *only* their requirements as LGBT people runs the risk of essentializing their inclusion and maintaining ideational boundaries between 'special' LGBT needs and general community needs. Instead, LGBT identities intersect with gender, age and ethnicity: LGBT people are women, men, young, elderly, disabled, and culturally, linguistically and religiously diverse, and these intersections must be included in effective social planning. Consequently, these local governments often attempt to integrate LGBT minorities into the full range of council planning, including strategies for aging, youth and multicultural difference. Recognizing and responding to the multifaceted intersections of LGBT identities is another way of fostering cohesion across local social groups, emphasizing the knotted web of needs that bring various residents together in different ways around common claims.

---

4 For example: City of Sydney Council has a full-time GLBT Project Coordinator; Marrickville Council has a full-time Gay and Lesbian Liaison Officer; Tweed Council has a part-time Gay and Lesbian Advocacy Worker.

Governance at the local scale thus carries great potential for extending social justice to LGBT minorities. State regulations offer authority to local governments to plan for the inclusion of sexual minorities, and where these powers are deployed, LGBT people are conferred 'active citizenship' in decision-making and planning. Simultaneously, local extensions of LGBT rights are limited by multiscalar governance – by the constraints of state and federal legislation. The recognition of same-sex couples at the local scale is a case in point. Local governments have no power to legislate for relationship recognition. The best they can do is relationship registers, as the City of Sydney Council has done, which provide a symbolic documentation of same-sex partnerships in the local area. While they do provide an official record of same-sex relationships, no legal rights are attached to such registers. However, I contend that local initiatives do offer possibilities for broader social change. The multiple scales of governance are interconnected: as well as being informed by state and federal legislation, local actions also generate feedback through this multiscalar loop, informing processes and beliefs at wider scales. Thus, social/community plans are not confined to local contexts: they negotiate and seek to transform attitudes and policies in state and federal arenas (Fincher and Iveson 2008). By extension, I suggest that local policies which encourage recognition, encounter and understanding across sexual difference – for example, in community meetings, public plazas, safe spaces, schools and at festivals – are means for fostering a transformative politics which reaches beyond the local arena.

Conclusion

My aim in this chapter has been to consider how multiscalar governance affects planning decisions and outcomes for LGBT minorities. This has been both an empirical and conceptual project. Planning has an empirical goal to improve people's quality of everyday life, but improving planning's own operations requires conceptual scrutiny of its foundational assumptions and frameworks. My discussion has therefore woven conceptual analysis through grounded case studies in order to enhance our understanding of the theory and practice of planning for LGBT minorities. My specific intervention concerns scales of governance: I argue that enhanced accommodation of the needs of LGBT minorities in planning requires researchers and practitioners to give more consideration to the multiscalar framework of planning and its impact upon the inclusion of LGBT minorities in planning processes. To elucidate this contention – and how multiscalar governance works in practice – I focused on Australian examples. I argue that Australia, with its intersecting tiers of government, is a telling case for interrogating the effects of multiscalar governance on planning for LGBT minorities.

I drew out two significant examples to highlight how *different* multiscalar relationships both constrain and enable the social and legal inclusion of LGBT minorities. First, I interrogated the ACT government's attempts to recognize same-sex partnerships in legislation. Such legal recognition is a critical step in LGBT social justice claims in the ACT, with important flow-on effects for inclusive planning. Through this discussion I elicited how same-sex relationship recognition was constrained by federal power *vis-à-vis* the ACT, but also how the Territory government nevertheless negotiated these power relationships and restraints to rescale some LGBT rights. The second example delved further into the problems and possibilities of multiscalar governance, focusing on social planning regulations in NSW, which confer planning powers to the local scale in that state. This discussion explored the power relationship between state legislation and local authority. State regulations stipulate localized social planning, encourage the inclusion of LGBT minorities in social/community plans, but render this inclusion a discretionary decision of local councils. While less than 10 percent of councils have fully embraced LGBT communities in planning, those which have show the important role local authorities play in social justice. Local actions flow through a 'feedback loop' which encourages social transformation at wider scales.

Planning and social change are deeply entangled – planning is arguably about 'change management'. It should not be surprising, then, that it is impossible to 'fix' the relationship between planning and social change in a given example. At the time of writing – early-2010 – a shift is already underway in local government social planning in NSW. The *Local Government Amendment (Planning and Reporting) Act 2009* (NSW) came into operation on 9 October 2009. This Act changes the planning requirements of NSW's local governments, integrating social plans into wider community strategic plans by 2012. In the new regulations there are no mandatory target groups, but it is still recommended that particular groups' needs be considered in the formulation of new strategic plans – and one of these is 'people of diverse sexualities' (NSWDLG 2009: 29). Will planning for LGBT minorities be enhanced or diminished by these legislative and regulatory changes? Regardless, the continuing modulation between the scales of governance in NSW (and the ACT) should prompt us, as researchers and practitioners, to be ever-aware of how multiscalar frameworks impinge on how planning can best accommodate the needs of LGBT people.

Chapter 8
Queering the Political-Economy: Anti-discrimination Law and the Urban Regime in Orlando, Florida

Thomas Chapman

> Economic space subordinates time to itself; political space expels it as threatening and dangerous (to power).
>
> Henri Lefebvre, *The Production of Space* (1991: 95)

In today's postmodern global city, notions of queer citizenship are becoming more and more coupled to various processes of urban transformation and governance, mostly through various city "branding" strategies that incorporate sexual others into a "tournament of entrepreneurialism" (Bell 2004: 1808). Tied to these global processes are various urban policy decisions made by key actors at the regional and local scale that not only impact the local citizenship agenda, but also have implications for the politics of urban planning. When it comes to various debates on granting legal and social rights for sexual minorities, urban development policy and planning strategies are sometimes framed within a curious paradox: "are queer civil rights 'good for business', or 'bad for business?'" The queer citizen, therefore, becomes a commodity of sorts, where "rights" become tied to an intrinsic (and ill defined) economic value, sometimes reducing aspects of citizenship to nothing more than pawns of economic development. This chapter explores these connections between the sexual citizen and urban politics by examining the 2002 debate in Orlando, Florida, on whether to incorporate sexual orientation as a protected minority class into the city's existing human rights ordinance.

Of course one cannot imagine Orlando's urban landscape without making direct connections to the familiar global entertainment empires of *Disney-MGM* and *Universal Studios* (and others), where urban policy at the local scale is tightly bound to global cultural commodification processes, writ large through the promotion of "spectacle" (Gotham 2002, Swyngedouw and Kaika 2003). Complicating the mix are the various pro-growth "scripts" that are inexorably bound within multiple narratives of the tourism experience in Orlando. As tourism studies have suggested, this "experience" embodies complex webs of power, where both residents and tourists alike assign different meanings and define normative behaviors for specific places (Morgan and Pritchard 1998). The vociferous debate surrounding the proposed change to Orlando's human rights ordinance invites a critical examination about these ways in which identity and a sense of belonging are articulated through a discourse of the sexual citizen's "place" in setting urban policy related to economic development.

The Queer Citizen in Orlando: A Tale of Three Paradigms

McCann (2002) argues that the integration of cultural politics with economic development strategies can sometimes become rhetorical containers for debates and strategies on how particular social values become "naturalized," centering around struggles on place-making and the future of local and regional economies. Cultural politics becomes the medium in which larger economic forces operate (Bailey 1999). Indeed, in this globalized, hyper-capitalist world, any issue involving the cultural politics of identity is unavoidably bound within the dominant theme of economic development in urban policy decision making. These urban policy games differ from place to place because they are driven by changes in each locale's social and economic ecology. In one sense, a premium is placed on economic development strategies that assume that places, like firms, compete with others in the marketplace, while avoiding other non-economic sources of urban transformation. This is a notion that situates people and capital (especially investment capital) as mobile, motivating local decision makers to pursue a pro-growth urban policy. Human identities, however, are not parcels of land, nor are they specific locations whose economic value is tied to value-added capacity. But in today's post-industrial society, there is indeed an undeniable synergistic relationship between the political economy of a place, local culture, and identity politics (Harvey 1989a, Mitchell 2000). Debates over "rights" for the queer citizen (including the push for non-discrimination policy and law), are certainly no exception to this melding of economic and cultural discourse (Bailey 1999, Deleon 1999, Forest 1995). With this paradox in mind, three economic development paradigms are discussed in the context of the 2002 debate in Orlando, Florida, where various overlapping arguments were invoked by an array of community actors in order to justify or oppose the proposed amendment to the non-discrimination ordinance. These three perspectives include: *Traditional Growth Coalitions* (Logan and Molotch 1987), Richard Florida's thesis on the *Creative Class* (2002a, 2002b, 2005), and the *City as "Entertainment Machine"* (McCann 2002).

The Body Politic and the Queer Citizen

Though greater Orlando has a sizable gay and lesbian population, when it comes to promoting social change, local activists generally concede that prior to 2000 Orlando's queer community had been largely invisible. Indeed, many might acknowledge that queers in Orlando were less likely to be active in political causes than communities in other cities about the same size. For example, one newly arrived transplant from Des Moines, Iowa was expecting to find a progressive body politic with an activist queer community. Instead, "it was like stepping back in time when it came to gay issues. Des Moines made Orlando look downright backward" (quoted in Schlueb 2002a). Central Florida is also home to one of the strongholds of the Religious Right. About 18 percent of Orange County's population (where Orlando is located) belongs to an evangelical fundamentalist protestant church, compared to about 10 percent for the United States as a whole (GlenMary Research Center 2000). Winter Park, a suburban city just outside Orlando, is home to the North American headquarters of Exodus International, the umbrella organization of 140 "ex-gay" ministries across the country that embraces prayer and therapy to "convert" gay people to heterosexuality. According to executive director Alan Chambers, "Orlando is a haven for Christian organizations. The body of Christ here is a lot more accepting of our redemptive message" (Billman 2003). Indeed, Exodus International spokespeople were among the several religious groups that were the most vocal, forming a group called "People for a United Orlando" in order to fight proposed changes in the ordinance. Justifying Exodus International's very public opposition to the Orlando ordinance, Chambers said "because we're citizens of the community, we had a real opinion to air [about the ordinance]. We're called [by God] to use our story in a political way" (quoted in Billman 2003).

When it comes to Orlando's overall labor force, the local queer community is not immune from the low wage service occupations associated with a regional tourist economy (Judd and Fainstein 1999). There are a number of Orlando LGBT residents that are well-paid professionals, but there are also many more who are low-paid theme-park workers – generally not the type who gravitate to political causes. And like many in Central Florida, residents are transient; they move to Orlando for a year or two and then move on. One local activist in Orlando summed it up this way: "This is such a transient community. People do not see that greater need for involvement in this area because so many people will be moving on in three years, five years" (quoted in Schlueb 2002a).

Until 2000, official city policy in Orlando did not directly address queer anti-discrimination issues. But the two largest regional employers of queer workers, *Disney-MGM* and *Universal Studios*, had long ago banned employee discrimination based upon sexual orientation, even providing health care and other benefits to their workers' same-sex partners. As one Disney employee said, "If you work at one of the theme parks, it's a relatively supportive atmosphere. You feel comfortable being out, and therefore you don't feel a need to be active." Indeed, many LGBT activists in and around central Florida felt that "the time never seemed right to risk cracking the region's veneer of tolerance by bringing their cause out of the shadows" (quoted in Schlueb 2002a).

But all of that began to change in 2000, when openly lesbian community activist Patty Sheehan launched a successful campaign for Orlando City Council. Sheehan initially ran for a seat on the Orlando City Council in 1996, but lost after her sexual orientation became a campaign issue. But by 2000, Sheehan's campaign had gained support from many outside the queer community. Sheehan's win seemed to embolden the community to become more aggressive in petitioning for legal and social rights, first by lobbying the mayor and city council members to incorporate a policy prohibiting LGBT discrimination for city employees. The measure easily passed the city council with little fanfare (Tracy 2000). Shortly thereafter, a handful of local activists formed an anti-discrimination ordinance committee, hoping to bring the same anti-discrimination protections to all of Orlando's queer citizens. In April of 2002, after two years of behind the scenes lobbying, the city council finally approved opening up the issue for public comment at the next regularly scheduled council meeting.

To the surprise of many, a standing-room-only crowd packed City Hall chambers, most of whom were opposed to amending the local human rights ordinance that would add the words "sexual orientation" to the list of classes protected from discrimination in the workplace, housing and public accommodations within the Orlando city limits. The Reverend Jim Perry, an Orlando minister and former member of the citizen coalition responsible for the original anti-discrimination ordinance in 1973, was one of the most vocal opponents. Perry pointed out that "adding sexual orientation to the list would be legalizing sin. There is a large Christian community in this city and this county. Orlando has always been a community with a reverence to God ... I don't want us to cross a line and bring his anger" (quoted in Schlueb 2002b). Other groups also spoke out against the proposal, including the Orange County Christian Coalition, the Florida Family Association and the Liberty Counsel, a national Christian Evangelical fundamentalist legal group, based in Orlando, whose mission is to "restore the culture one case at a time" (Liberty Counsel 2007). Subsequently, council members instructed the city's human relations board to research the issue and come back with a recommendation. In June, the board made a recommendation to amend the city code to include protections for LGBT residents. Such recommendations from the city's advisory boards are typically placed on the next council meeting agenda for an official vote as a routine matter. But in this case, a "workshop" for city council members was scheduled instead of a public hearing, seen by many as a way to avoid the circus-like atmosphere of the previous hearing, giving council members a more private forum to lobby each other.

After much debate in the local media over several months, a deeply divided Orlando City Council gave preliminary approval to the local ordinance that would protect LGBT citizens from discrimination in private sector business and public accommodation. The 4-3 vote followed a marathon eight-hour public hearing filled with impassioned speeches by dozens of supporters and opponents. The measure would have just one more hurdle – a final public hearing, scheduled two weeks later for a final vote (Schlueb 2002c). On December 2, for the third time, hundreds jammed council chambers for a chance to address the council during a five hour debate. The council vote remained the same, 4 voting for approval and 3 voting against (Schlueb 2002d). Orlando residents now had a city ordinance that incorporated a non-discrimination clause based on sexual orientation.

The Queer Citizen and Traditional Growth Coalitions

During the debate, urban elites in Orlando constructed narratives of economic development in a variety of ways. One such narrative falls within the realm of traditional growth machine theory. This notion suggests it is urban elites (i.e., coalitions of businessmen, real estate developers, bankers, politicians, etc.) who work together to transform their city (Cox and Mair 1988, Logan and Molotch 1987). The growth ethic pervades all aspects of local life, including the political system, agendas for economic development, and the social relations that contribute to local culture. The role of government is strictly limited to making use of the "rational planning sciences" in order to protect capital investment and the interests of the wealthy elite. Though growth coalition elites emphasize a libertarian (hence "value-free") economic development strategy, evidence has shown that their rhetoric is laden with social and political metaphors and narratives that work to marginalize minorities (Chapman 2007, Wilson 1996). Growth coalition elites are not necessarily a diverse cross section of an urban population. They tend to give a fiscally and socially conservative flavor to local government, for which cultural issues are chosen only for their benefit to those with the most capital investment to gain or lose (Logan and Molotch 1987). Orlando's growth machine elite mirrors a particular value system that is politically and socially conservative, and decidedly heteronormative.

With growth machine strategies, it is often the "appearance" of affluence that "gives geography the Midas touch" (Logan and Molotch 1987: 120). Not only does this notion provide a strategy to help "sell" the area to outside wealthy investors, but it also serves to advertise places as showpieces, intended to symbolize a locality that welcomes those from other places, but only those with the proper social pedigrees. Hence, a growth machine elite's sense-of-place is not only about protecting capital exchange values, but also about the maintenance of a cultural system that guides the pursuit of continued growth for those with similar cultural, social and political ideologies, while excluding those with a different set of cultural values and political identities. Challenges to these established "norms" in the form of demanding "rights" for the queer citizen are seen as being "out-of-place," and they are almost always not part of the "story" narrated by urban elites about their city. In other words, growth coalition elites link parochial settings with cosmopolitan interests that reflect a "norm" of neo-liberal economic principles and a social conservatism, in an attempt to make places "safe" for the business climate.

During the debate about the rights of Orlando's queer citizens, these heteronormative constructions of citizenship were used to argue over whether certain social or civil rights are "good for business" or "bad for business." For example, city council member Vicki Vargo, an early opponent of the proposed anti-discrimination measure, expressed a concern that "before the city interferes with private business, there should be proof that there is a need" (quoted in Schlueb 2002c). Others voiced similar concerns, arguing that inclusion of anti-discrimination protections for its queer residents would hurt the economic climate, because it would cost the taxpayer by forcing the city to investigate baseless discrimination complaints (Schlueb 2002c). One speaker at December's public hearing stated:

> This ordinance will have an adverse impact on small business in Orlando, and ultimately economic development within our city ... small businesses will close, small business will leave the city. And for those that stay will be forced to pass on the additional costs [of this legislation] to the citizens of Orlando. (Orlando City Council Public Hearing 2002)

In their eyes, any government intervention that threatens to affect negatively the growth process itself, particularly government-imposed social regulation, is seen as a threat to increased rents. In other words, the growth ethic is what brings jobs and expands the tax base, and any deviation from attracting investors (including various actions taken by local government unrelated to this goal) is undesirable and should be avoided. Worse yet is the fear that queer citizenship rights will "cost the taxpayer."

The Queer Citizen and the "Creative Class"

Richard Florida's economic thesis situates racial, ethnic, gender and sexual diversity as a crucial and integral part of business innovation, economic development, and human talent, thus necessitating a critical need to establish full citizenship rights that reconcile and value the politics of difference. This notion privileges creativity and economic talent, for which human diversity is the fundamental engine of economic growth, particularly in today's knowledge-based economies. Arguments for sexual minority rights are placed within the context of "new" urban-economic geographies that are tightly linked to highly valued employment sectors such as computer technology, higher education, and the arts and entertainment business. The most skilled and educated workers become a highly prized commodity of sorts, for which diversity and tolerance of racial, ethnic, and sexual identity is very much implicated with the desirability of a place. Recognition of this new economic geography by some business and political elites in many regions across the country has provided a basis for supporting anti-discrimination law that places racial, ethnic, gender, and sexual diversity as a valued commodity, and to many represents the key to economic growth. This sort of diversity, according to Richard Florida, plays a key role in the attraction and retention of the kinds of economic talent required to regional growth. In particular, it is diversity that contributes to low entry barriers for economic talent, enhancing a region's ability to compete globally. Several of Orlando's residents clearly saw passage of the amendment as an economic advantage of inclusion in a global sense. Incensed by a flyer placed at his door urging residents to "vote No for special rights for homosexuals," one Orlando resident summed up these feelings by stating "this is not the kind of stuff we need if Orlando wants to be a global city"

(Orlando City Council 2002). Indeed, others favoring passage of the human rights ordinance amendment argued that sexual minority inclusion of this sort would do wonders to help Orlando compete with other cities in Florida that already have such anti-discriminations in place:

> We want to attract better-paying jobs. One of the things Miami or Tampa-St. Pete has that we do not have – and one of the things that Fortune 500 companies look at when they're considering whether to relocate – is [anti-discrimination] protections for gays and lesbians. (quoted in Schlueb 2002d)

Indeed, Richard Florida employs a unique measure of openness or diversity, the diversity index, also known as the gay index.[1] The gay index is a good proxy for diversity, mainly because:

> As a group, gays have been subject to a particularly high level of discrimination. Attempts by gays to integrate into the mainstream of society have met substantial opposition. To some extent, homosexuality represents the last frontier of diversity in our society, and thus a place that welcomes the gay community welcomes all kinds of people ... gays can be said to be the canaries of the Creative Age. (Florida 2002b: 256)

The presence of a relatively large gay population thus functions as a signal cultural indicator of a region that is open to various other cultural groups. When compared to all 268 regions nationwide, Orlando ranks 9th in the Gay Index. While Miami-Dade County ranks second (losing only to San Francisco), and Tampa Bay 26th (Florida 2002b).

The key to overall economic growth lies not just within measures of diversity, of course, but in the ability to translate competitive advantage into creative economic outcomes in the form of new ideas, new knowledge intensive businesses, and real regional growth. To better gauge these capabilities, Florida (2002a) develops a measure called the Creativity Index. The diversity, or gay index, is equally weighted with three other measures: percentage of knowledge-intensive occupations in a place (labeled by Florida as *creative class* occupations); innovation, as measured in patents per capita; and the number of high-technology firms in an area. Florida argues that this composite indicator is a better measure of a region's underlying creative capabilities than just measuring diversity, because "it reflects the joint effects of its concentration and of innovative economic outcomes" (Florida 2002a: 245). The creativity index is thus offered as an overall barometer of a region's longer run economic potential, where Orlando ranks 77 out of 268 metro areas nationwide.

---

1   Richard Florida incorporated this index early on into his research after discovering a strong statistical correlation between the location of knowledge intensive industry, and a graduate student's demographic model on spatial distribution of the gay and lesbian population. See Black et al. (2000).

The Queer Citizen and the City as "Entertainment Machine"

Another rhetorical framework of economic development is built around the idea that goals of urban policy and development are inseparable from notions of consumption and entertainment, the city as an "Entertainment Machine" (Nichols 2004). Closely related to Richard Florida's premise of the creative class, the city as entertainment machine places emphasis on how consumption, amenities, and culture drive urban development policy. Nowhere is this phenomenon more pronounced than in the Orlando area, where mythical and utopian notions of geography and history are mass produced on such a scale that "Walt Disney World is like a mouse on steroids" (Fjellman 1992: 394). Indeed, where else can one spend the morning sitting pool-side watching the palm trees sway; the afternoon cocooned within a special climate controlled building kept at 9 degrees (winter parkas are provided), meandering through 100 acres of scenes carved by Chinese artisans from over two million pounds of ice; and the evening strolling along the back lot of Disney's MGM Studios, wearing special holographic glasses that let one view over five million lights draped over the neighborhood facades from *The Golden Girls* television series? Orlando has become the world's fourth largest tourist destination in the world, behind Mecca, Kyoto, and (just barely) the Vatican (Fjellman 1992). But what was traditionally seen as a "family oriented" destination, and where entertainment empires such as Disney dominate Orlando's urban politics and social history (Fogelsong 2001), the heteronormative cultural spaces of Orlando have recently been called into question. And for a time, sexual politics became the center-piece of this expansion.

Nichols (2004) makes the argument that urban policy decisions at the local or regional scale associated with the city as entertainment machine often come up against acts of politicized consumption that become community based "morality plays," where moral concerns (such as rights for the sexual citizen) are raised by some residents, yet actively opposed by others. Urban regime actors are then presented with dueling interpretations of the "moral landscape" that reveal somewhat of a cultural divide. The community debate surrounding Orlando's anti-discrimination measure is one such example, particularly when some members of the public raised concerns about imagining Orlando as a "family oriented" entertainment playground. A case in point is this statement made at the November 2002 public hearing:

> Orlando's reputation as the king of family vacations will be replaced by one on par with those of Sodom and Gomorrah. Are we going to say to America that this is what Orlando stands for? Is it fair that when family comes to visit, we have to warn them about this? (Orlando City Council Public Hearing 2002)

The subtext at play is of course the "type" of tourists Orlando citizens envision, and ultimately hope to attract. Indeed, when the Disney Corporation extended health coverage to the live-in partners of queer employees in 1995, company officials stated that the action simply "brought health benefits in line with a corporate policy of non-discrimination" (Navarro 1995). But the "Religious Right," a dominant presence in Central Florida, saw things quite differently. With over half a million members nationwide, and over 35,000 members in Florida alone, the American Family Association continues to be a major force in efforts to repeal anti-discrimination ordinances across the nation. Soon after the Disney announcement, the head of the Florida chapter accused the company of losing its "moral compass" as it grew, allowing itself "to be a vehicle to influence American society regarding homosexuality being mainstream or normal" (Navarro 1995). A coalition of Florida legislators quickly followed suit, writing an "open letter to Michael Eisner and the Disney Corporation:"

> For more than 50 years Walt Disney Company has represented all that is good and pure and wholesome in our nation. Families flocked to Walt Disney World and Disneyland because they knew that Walt Disney respected and nurtured the traditional American family and its strong moral values ... we strongly disapprove of a lifestyle that should not be given the same status as heterosexual marriage. (quoted in Griffin 2000)

In terms of law and policy set forth by the state, the dominant ideology of family remains a privileged realm defined as a heterosexual nuclear family unit. But to queer citizens, "family" is a deeply embedded historical and social archetype that conveys a strong sense of queer community cohesiveness. It is also a code word long used by queers to denote the presence of other queers. Indeed, among Disney World's large contingent of gay and lesbian employees, "the Disney Family" is a commonly used appropriation that means all of the theme park's queer employees (Griffin 2000). These competing visions of "family" in Orlando's tourist economy are deeply implicated within a "culture war" rhetoric that mirrors the changing realities of the political economy. But *Disney-MGM, Universal Studios*, and other entertainment empires in Orlando have a significant financial stake in how these competing sense-of-place imaginings are interpreted, and then acted upon. These global corporations are the major contributors to capital investment in the area, and by default the dominant members of the area's urban elite. The economic stakes are high, holding a precedent over any "moral concerns" of the community, including taking sides on debates about sexual politics.

The most dramatic example of dueling visions of Orlando as a "traditional family playground" is the annual *Gay Days* celebration. This event is arguably the largest appropriation of traditional family space in history, replete with a series of parties, performances and gatherings throughout the city during the first week in June. The trips en masse to the local theme parks are the event's highlight, where thousands wear red T-shirts to set themselves apart from other tourists. In spite of a string of protests from fundamentalist religious groups, the event has soared in popularity. What began as a single-day visit to Disney World in 1991 has now expanded to a weeklong event, attracting more than

135,000 attendees from across the nation and around the globe, and infusing over $100 million into the local economy in 2008 (Gay Days 2009). Though Disney does not officially sponsor *Gay Days*, it also does not make any attempt to discourage *Gay Days* participants. Disney officials have stated that from their point of view, *Gays Days* are "real good days inside the Magic Kingdom. We feel no impact except handling media calls" (United Press International 2001).

The bottom line on the cultural commodification of such large scale spectacles is, of course, the need to accommodate the queer tourist for purposes of capital accumulation. Disney, along with the other entertainment giants in the area, are well versed in making sure that the area's world renowned reputation as a tourist haven and a "welcoming place" (and thus its potential to make money) holds precedence over any local moral concerns. This notion is particularly important in a place such as Orlando, since the economic stakes are so high. International tourism plays such a prominent role in setting the local political agenda that anything that might affect the economic payoff is immediately suspect, however benign or malignant the "cultural threat" might be. To borrow Fogelsong's (2001) term, the "Disney-Orlando" bond is a "marriage." And marriage, as has been so often stated by religious fundamentalists and other traditionalists, is "under assault" by those who wish to redefine it. Thus the only solution, it seems, is to either restrict both partners to an established norm, or make the necessary adjustments to expand that norm. The major theme parks seem to have chosen the latter. The choice to welcome *Gay Days* with a wink and a nod rather than an official proclamation is not about any moral imperative (far from it), but simply because it makes a great deal of economic sense. During the community debate on Orlando's anti-discrimination ordinance, some residents did indeed invoke the huge economic payoff for the area because of *Gay Days*, arguing that failure to pass the amendment would send the wrong message that would ultimately result in a big economic "hit."

Conclusion

The debate rhetoric in Orlando is strikingly similar to other debates on rights for the sexual citizens in other places, invoking the typical culture war narratives involving moral concerns expressed through religiosity, "special rights" arguments based upon bodily attribution, discourses of othering, and so on. But the debate in Orlando also was very much about battles over a redefinition and expansion of the "Disneyesque" image, and how this might affect the cultural domain – primarily for economic development reasons. Orlando is also geographically situated in central Florida, where concentrations of Evangelical fundamentalist populations are much greater than in other parts of the country. These groups were more politically savvy and organized here, and until one member of the queer community became part of the city's urban elite in 2000, activist politics was not high on the agenda for most queer citizens. The majority of Orlando residents that participated in the public debates gave eloquent arguments for amending the human rights ordinance, particularly by imagining Orlando as a progressive and inclusive place. These arguments were highly personal, passionate, and they arguably helped to sway the urban elite to incorporate the two words "sexual orientation" into the city's human rights anti-discrimination law. Control over ownership of the economic and social space was certainly divisive, but in the end it was a geography of inclusion that ultimately won out.

As with any conceptual distinction between "culture" and "economy," it is often helpful to look at how groups involved in local social struggles construct sense-of-place strategies that frequently make reference to the political economy. No matter what theory, model, or thesis one chooses as the basis for sexual politics and capitalist social relations, these sorts of community narratives are a significant driving force behind different interpretations of the social history and geography of a place. The internal dynamics of capitalism, though not deterministic of outcomes of queer rights, nevertheless are increasingly likely to be interrupted and changed by the increasing complexities of postmodern identity politics in general, and the socio-cultural identities of the sexual citizen in particular. The diversity of forms that capitalism has taken in recent years parallels these changes in social relations, and many local actors now place this line of thinking as advantageous to a strict interpretation of labor and capital value (Amin and Thrift 2007). Issues involving social and civil rights for the queer citizen (including anti-discrimination protections) are inseparable elements in any of the economic development themes, and help to reveal some lessons on how diverse forms and structures of capital are spatially organized in a place.

It would be naïve to suggest that simply arguing for (or against) passage of LGBT anti-discrimination ordinances is a means to an end in terms of economic development planning and policy. Indeed, incorporating LGBT social rights discourse into these narratives adds yet another layer to the already "fuzzy causal logic" already inherent to these non-material and relational economic development paradigms (Russo and van der Borg 2010, Markusen 2006). However, adding the human rights element to the various arguments does bring these meta-narratives down from the clouds by linking citizenship rights to those planning practices that emphasize both economic *and* social sustainability of cities. The goal is to find creative ways to implement the sorts of policy decisions and strategies that ultimately take shape as material outcomes of urban development. Connecting these dots also presents planners with the greatest of challenges.

Chapter 9
Queerying Creative Cities

Tiffany Muller Myrdahl

Introduction

In her discussion of the application of creative city policy in Singapore, Yue (2007: 368) writes, "Cultural policy critique has to encompass wider issues than can be explained by the top-down approach to creative economy studies, economics, and social significance. More than simply policy analysis on cultural and media institutions, it is also about questioning the cultural right to participate in social life, and how access and equity are integral to the politics of resources and allocation." Yue's call for a critical analysis of so-called creative policy initiatives – one that extends beyond an institutional focus to attend to the logics at work in creative policy initiatives, as well as the potential impacts of these logics – is one of many within geography and planning (see, for example, Bell and Binnie 2004, Bontje and Musterd 2009, Catungal and Leslie 2009, Kong 2000, Leslie 2005, Markusen 2006, McCann 2007, Peck 2005, Thomas and Darnton 2006, Zimmerman 2008, and the articles published in *Urban Studies*, 46 2009). A central feature of these calls is a concern for the assumptions employed within the creative city thesis, as well as an interest in the explicitly uneven effects of its application (see Lewis and Donald 2010: 33, McCann 2007).

Even so, the creative city model retains a high profile among administrators of Canadian cities and the planners who put such models into practice. As Sands and Reese (2008: 9) note, "The appeal of economic development strategies based on creative city principles is obvious and understandable"; the desire to grow and retain a creative class, and thus compete in the knowledge economy, is "politically seductive" (Peck 2005: 766). Thus, it may be unsurprising that creative city modeling is driven and funded at a variety of scales in Canada (Smith and Warfield 2008, compare Walks 2009). In London, Ontario, the "Creative City Task Force" is an example of an urban governance strategy that propels local public policy development. Likewise, the Vancouver, British Columbia "Creative City Initiative" seeks to "align resources with strategic directions for the City's ongoing and future role in the creative sector" (see: http://vancouver.ca/creativecity/). At the scale of the provincial government, the Ontario Ministry of Culture has earmarked $9 million (CDN) for municipal cultural planning via the "Creative Communities Prosperity Fund." In short, the creative city model has had a direct effect on the praxis of Canadian urban governance and planning (compare Leslie 2005).

Starting from this premise – that despite its many critics Florida's (2002a, 2005) creativity thesis for regional economic development (not to be confused with Landry and Bianchini's similarly titled 1995 book) has been widely pursued – I interrogate one problematic implicit in Florida's creative city thesis: the reliance on, and consequences of, a politics of *visible* difference. The idea that the presence of heterogeneous groups *in and of itself*, regardless of the enfranchisement of groups who are located on the margins of dominant society, should translate to "tolerant" or inclusive urban centers is a flawed assumption (Lewis and Donald 2010: 31, cf. Catungal and Leslie 2009, Hoyman and Faricy 2009, Rushbrook 2002). The subtext of this assumption, that embodied difference is necessarily visible, is equally troublesome. Florida and the adherents to his creative city thesis, however, employ "diversity of population" as a taken-for-granted indicator of economic productivity: diverse populations signal that a region is "open to diversity," and this "makes local resources more productive and efficient" (Florida et al. 2010: 282). Used in this way, "diversity" retains an unexamined logic that segregates and reifies embodied, visible difference to support a theory of supply-side regional economic development.

In this chapter, I examine the implications of this logic; specifically, I contend that creative city policies reify and reward certain forms of visible difference. To do so, I review scholarly responses to the creative city thesis, focusing specifically on the forms of diversity that are legitimized in Florida's (2002a, 2005) arguments. I then contrast the way that diversity functions in the creative city thesis with the way that Fincher and Iveson (2008) conceptualize diversity within a framework of recognition. Finally, I discuss the politics of visibility, which I situate as a contemporary iteration of debates about the function of identity, difference, and claims to citizenship and access to urban space (Fincher and Jacobs 1998, compare the important tradition within planning theory of scholarship that discusses difference and social equity, e.g., Fainstein 2000, Fenster 1999, Greed 1994, Listerborn 2007, Rankin 2009, Sandercock 2000, Snyder 1995). These discussions, which include reflections on *how* and *whose* identity/ies are understood to be "authentic" (see, for example, Duggan 2002b, Halberstam 2005, Oswin 2005), have theoretical significance but must also be understood to hold material consequences: in particular, they reflect inequities in access to the resources allotted within planning strategies. Following Rankin (2009), I maintain that the implicit assumptions about visible difference contained within creative city policies have specific material effects for both the populations subsumed under the umbrella of "diversity" and for the communities in which these populations live.

Diverse Identities in the Creative City

Florida's creative city thesis received widespread attention in the popular media for casting urban diversity and tolerance as a central feature of urban and regional economic growth. Diversity is a driver of creativity, as Chapman et al. (2007: 29) write: "tolerance of racial, ethnic, and sexual identity is now very much implicated with the desirability of a place, rather than being a hindrance to economic growth." Florida's focus on diversity, however, extends only insofar as diversity's usefulness for economic development. Moreover, Florida's definition of diversity has an implicit class and race bias. Bradford (2004: 4) describes this as inattention "to the reality of racialized urban labor markets and the fact that some of his creative hot spots are also socially polarized places" (cf. Hoyman and Faricy 2009: 315). Yet, the uptake of his work has implications for marginalized communities. Bedore and Donald (2010: 22), for example, find that the municipal efforts of Kingston, Ontario to adopt creative city planning strategies have resulted in the development of exclusive spaces that reflect the needs and desires of some (wealthy urban dwellers) at the expense of others.

To a certain extent, Florida's creative city thesis can be read as an opportunity to revisit the benefits of heterogeneity in urban centers. As Thomas and Darnton (2006: 156) note, "Florida has succeeded in helping to reshape the conversation about diversity in the metropolis ... Florida's model forces a reconsideration of the dynamics of race, ethnicity, and other forms of diversity." Yet, the critiques of Florida's model have illustrated its flaws both in theory and in practice, especially with regard to its consequences for diverse communities. Many critics, for instance, speak to the "fuzzy" theoretical and methodological underpinnings of the creative city thesis (see, for example, Bell and Binnie 2004, Clark 2004, Markusen 2006, Peck 2005, Thomas and Darnton 2006, Lewis and Donald 2010). Many others take aim at the repercussions of creative policies in their place-specific applications (see, for instance, Barnes and Hutton 2009, Bedore and Donald 2010, Catungal and Leslie 2009, Catungal et al. 2009, Long 2009, Luckman et al. 2009, Zimmerman 2008). Catungal and Leslie (2009), for example, discuss the consequences of commodifying racialized identities: while many people of color (and others) are displaced by the application of creative city policy (through the creation of creative districts, for instance), city marketers capitalize on "difference" to brand and sell the city (compare Silk 2004, Silk and Amis 2005, Silk and Andrews 2006). Likewise, as Yue (2007: 366) argues, sexuality becomes "a technology for cultural policy in the creative city": it is a policy from which the city is intended to benefit economically under the guise of an embrace of diversity. Thus, a revamped urban image is produced in part through a seemingly inclusive promotion of a "brand identity," which obfuscates existing inequalities that are arguably exacerbated through public investment and subsidy of consumption-driven urban redevelopment. Silk and Amis (2005: 285) aptly point out that "key questions emerge within the practices of urban regeneration with respect to *whose* aesthetics really count, *who* benefits, *whose* collective memory is being performed, and *whose* interests are being furthered" (emphasis in original; see also Harvey 1989b).

Critiques of creative city theory and praxis dovetail with critiques of cosmopolitanism (see Binnie and Skeggs 2004, Binnie et al. 2006), which have focused on, among other things, how difference is sanitized, rationalized, and consumed (see also Rose 2000). Germain and Radice (2006: 113) describe this approach to cosmopolitanism and its urban spaces as "cosmopolitan only in that [these spaces are] apprehended through knowing and consuming the 'Other'." The discourse of cosmopolitanism may thus be deployed to connote the safe, sanitized leisure and tourist activities that cities use to attract capital. Indeed, the discursive expression of "safety" in the city serves to incorporate *some* identity markers into the folds of the creative city in a gesture toward cosmopolitan difference while simultaneously counteracting perceptions of fear associated with marginalized others (see especially Smith 1996, Mitchell 2003, compare Barnes and Hutton 2009: 1265). In short, discourses that emphasize safe entertainment do so by distinguishing between (often literally) palatable difference and non-normative others for an implicitly non-urban audience.

At the root of urban strategies that seek to capitalize on difference is an expectation that diverse identities must be categorizable, stable, and visible: the groups who are the targets of such policies must be simplified into essential, legible categories that are static, knowable, and not too troubling to the "mainstream" consumer. It follows that in order to be "consumable," difference must be perceived as legitimate and it must be recognizable. These problematic requirements, as I discuss below, have particular consequences for the ways in which marginalized communities are implicated in the theory and praxis of creative city policy.

Recognition: Alternative Models for Approaching Diversity in Planning

The adoption of creative city policies has implications for planners on a variety of fronts. Lewis and Donald (2010: 34) note, for instance, that the population (size)-based hierarchy implicit in Florida's creative cities model "result[s] in misguided conclusions about economic growth and creativity, poor policy applications and general inapplicability in small cities." Planners must thus be wary of the utility of this model outside of large population centers. By comparison, in cities like Toronto, where creative city policies are already in place, planners must be cognizant of the ways that such policies generate exclusionary outcomes. Bedore and Donald's (2010) findings about Kingston, Ontario suggest that this is a well-founded concern: they argue that the adoption of creative class tactics, employed in conjunction with a particular style of political leadership and "growth machine politics," have exacerbated existing class inequalities and divisions among urban populations. Referring to Montreal, Leslie (2005: 404) echoes this point: "the city becomes an increasingly exclusionary space for those deprived of economic and cultural capital." It is possible to imagine a similar outcome for Toronto simply based on recent strategic planning documents. The following quote, for example, comes from the *Creative City Planning Framework* (2008: 18) prepared by the marketing firm AuthentiCity for the city of Toronto: "Returns from creative policies, partnerships or projects can be calculated in greater asset and property value, higher revenues, stronger quality of place, ... and more inclusive social practices and outcomes." The lip service to inclusivity, while perhaps well-intentioned, is drowned out by the focus on increased property values and higher revenues, which often are joined by an increase in the sanitization and privatization of public spaces (see Barnes and Hutton 2009: 1265).

By comparison, "just cities" models offer a far more nuanced conceptualization of diversity and difference (e.g., Fainstein 2010, see also Healy 1997). Fincher and Iveson (2008), for example, argue that planners need to critically engage the policies they enact. These authors claim that:

> to create more just cities, planners need a framework for *making judgments between* different claims in the planning process, as well as for *facilitating* them. That is to say, planning frameworks must enable planners to make calculations about 'what should be done', not just about 'how it is done'. (Fincher and Iveson 2008: 5, emphasis in original)

For Fincher and Iveson then, the function of planning is, in part, to redress material inequalities and to enable full access to and participation in urban life (2008: 9). To that end, the authors detail one of the central lingering debates about identity politics: drawing from political philosophers Nancy Fraser and Iris Marion Young, they discuss whether (and how) recognition of difference serves to segregate marginalized communities, and whether segregation is advantageous or detrimental to these communities and to society as a whole. While the authors suggest that recognition of a singular, essentialized identity is a problematic undertaking (2008: 91), they demonstrate that two dominant models of recognition, affirmative and relational, remain important strategies for planners to create just cities.

Fincher and Iveson (2008: 91) define the affirmative strategy as follows:

> Where different identities are considered to be the product of pre-existing differences between those who belong to distinct groups, then recognition becomes a matter of defining, acknowledging, and/or protecting group distinctiveness. Recognition, in this form, establishes and maintains boundaries between groups in order to protect their members from any social norms or institutional arrangements which prevent them from 'being themselves.'

Thus, affirmative recognition may take the spatial form of a separate district, like a gay village, and it may be accomplished with the use of a "group checklist" approach (2008: 96), in which representatives from different interest groups comment on and participate in the planning process. As the authors point out, both of these tactics have the potential to celebrate and "normalize" marginalized groups. In their discussion of the Manchester Gay Village, the authors write, "The recognition of gay and lesbian attachment to this part of the city has helped to construct a concentration of community and commercial facilities which sustain, rather than repress, the formation of communities which seek to explore alternative forms of affection and desire" (2008: 139). Still, the authors *also* recognize that these tactics run the risk of reifying the status of sexual and transgender minorities as victims, while also serving to exclude some who identify as members of LGBT communities. Other planning theorists have echoed this critique: as Rankin (2009: 226) contends, for example, affirmative strategies do little to disrupt existing structural norms and policies that perpetuate enduring inequalities.

The contrasting model of recognition, the relational strategy, differs with the affirmative strategy in two important ways. First, the relational strategy does not rely on an essential identity for recognition. Fincher and Iveson comment, "Those who believe that cultural differences are not total or essential argue that claims for recognition of cultural difference should not be made with reference to a fixed or stable conception of group identity based on some vision of an 'authentic' self" (Fincher and Iveson 2008: 96). Indeed, this strategy is informed by the logic that status, rather than identity, should be the basis on which a political claim is made (see Fraser 2003). As a consequence, the authors state, "claims for recognition should instead be based on appeals to justice which are open to public discussion and debate among all members of a polity" (Fincher and Iveson 2008: 96). There are innumerable benefits associated with this strategy, the most significant of which is its independence from the essentialized identity. The authors use Podmore's (2001, 2006) study of lesbian visibility in Montreal to illustrate the usefulness of relational recognition; Podmore's discussions illustrate that the diversity of street life enables lesbians to *not* foreground their sexual identity in order to participate in public space. However, relational recognition is not a magic bullet that ensures equitable and just planning. Fincher and Iveson conclude their discussion of Podmore's case studies by pointing out, "the integration of lesbians into heterogeneous spaces does not necessarily facilitate the 'critical mass' of commercial and community facilities that are possible in more territorialized community formations, thus potentially reducing lesbian visibility in the city" (Fincher and Iveson 2008: 142). In other words, the risks associated with the lack of visibility – loss of community space, for instance – are precisely the benefits provided by the affirmative strategy of recognition.

Taken together, these recognition strategies offer a counterpoint to the ways in which marginalized identities are positioned in the creative city: under recognition strategies, and particularly a *relational* strategy, marginalized groups are not used as a source of capital but instead are equal actors who strive to participate fully in the city. Further, the recognition framework actively engages with the problematics of visibility and the legible subject, which, by contrast, the creative city model takes for granted. Such distinctions throw into relief the significance of interrogating dominant models for approaching diversity in planning. This point comes to the fore again in the following section.

The Creative City and the Problematic of Visibility

Seen through Fincher and Iveson's framework of recognition, creative city policies are grounded in two key assumptions. First, queer and other diverse identities *can and should* be commodified. Second, the affirmative strategy – a strategy that relies on visibility and legibility of identifiable categories – is the appropriate method of recognition in creative city policies. These assumptions are troublesome for a variety of reasons. Let us look at each in turn.

The first assumption, that diverse identities can and should be commodified, ignores the process by which commodification of one segment of a marginalized population has the effect of pushing other segments further into the margins. As Catungal and Leslie (2009: 702) argue, for instance, the inclusion of certain commodified forms of race into local policies "serves to normalize some performances of identity and community in the public realm, while leaving little room for other forms" (see also Amin 2002). Indeed, the same could be said for queer communities: while *certain* recognizable forms of same-sex desire or gender-troubling practices may become acceptable through the commodifying practices of the creative city, many other forms are further marginalized in their inability or unwillingness to constitute cultural capital. As a result, many claims to public spaces are rendered illegible. As Yue (2007: 366) notes, creative city policies "[expose] social stratification and competing claims to cultural citizenship and civic identity." Indeed, stratification may become *more* apparent in cities that appear, from certain scales of analysis, to have achieved economic growth via creative policy strategies (Atkinson and Easthope 2009, Bedore and Donald 2010, Lewis and Donald 2009, McCann 2007).

Likewise, commodification and the affirmative strategy of recognition as employed by the creative city thesis are based in an ideology of tolerance that idealizes the (homophobic, transphobic, white, middle class) norm. Commenting on the phenomenon of tolerance, Brown (2006: 14) maintains, "Almost all objects of tolerance are marked as deviant, marginal or undesirable by virtue of being tolerated" (see also Liu 1991). In other words, tolerance encourages a limited acceptance of difference that neither considers nor displaces relations of power. Rankin (2009) argues that this ideology underscores postmodern planning theory. She asserts, "What emerges in practice is little more than mainstream multiculturalism:" difference is depoliticized and presented as accessible and available for consumption (Rankin 2009: 266).

Thus, applications of creative city policy that promote a tolerance of difference succeed primarily in setting up "Others" to be compared to and consumed by the normative center. Moreover, these applications ignore the power relations that are exacerbated by creative city policies. Zimmerman (2008: 240), for example, argues that the growth coalition who adopted Florida's model in Milwaukee, Wisconsin endorsed the desires and cultural practices of one group of citizen-consumers, which also had the effect of turning political attention away from large, significant portions of the city's population, including African Americans, the immigrant working class, and the poor.

Additionally, these assumptions produce and perpetuate an ambiguous form of sexual citizenship (see Bell and Binnie 2000, 2004). Sexual citizenship is informed by the combination of social and economic forces like urban entrepreneurial strategies that seek to capitalize on sanitized forms of difference (Binnie et al. 2006, G. Brown 2006). Yet, these forces also serve to legitimize rather than trouble particular social arrangements and relations. This limited (and limiting) form of citizenship, and the logic upon which it is based, assumes a particular essentialized, fixed articulation of gay or lesbian identity: namely, one that is legible to the dominant mainstream. In short, this form of citizenship is ambiguous at best, as it is conditioned upon fitting within the narrow parameters of an acceptable if different citizen-consumer.

The visible, knowable subject is a key component to the creative city; visibility is an unreliable tool upon which the creative city appears to depend. Yet, the visibility of identity is intrinsically tied to identity performance: the ways we read and understand identity are tied to recognizable codes that (we assume) make particular identity categories knowable (compare King 2009, Peace 2001, Podmore 2001, Skeggs 1999). Thus, the visibility of any given marginalized group depends on particular enactments of legible identity codes, which themselves are gleaned from essentialized notions of identity. Queer visibility, then, is grounded in the culturally accepted meanings that dominant, gender- and sexual-conforming society assign to readings of particular bodies and performances.

For queer people and other marginalized groups, being marked and thus clearly readable is understood to be both a necessary evil and a trap (Barnhurst 2007, Clarkson 2008, Munt 1998, Phelan 1993, Samuels 2003, Walters 2001). To a certain extent, setting oneself up as different is encouraged within the identity politics paradigm of civil rights, and there is an implied reward for those who are recognized as legitimate within the boundaries of a particular group (Skeggs 1999). As such, visibility has been a key strategy for the Canadian and US lesbian and gay civil rights movements: it is understood to play a central role in the increased acceptance of (certain) sexual minorities and a concomitant surge in political and economic empowerment (King 2009, Reed 2009). At the same time, the legibility of some always comes at the expense of others: the normal/deviant binary is continuously reproduced through a regime that relies on visuality and expects a coherent, bounded subject (Amin 2010). As King (2009: 281) asserts, "a singular focus on one form of visibility (be it sexual, racial, or gender) will inevitably exclude or erase those other facets of politicized identity that it cannot contain." Therefore, the success of visibility will always be limited by that which is legible.

Taken as a whole, the assumptions of difference and visibility in which creative city policies are grounded have a particular effect when they are adopted by commentators who expound the virtues of the creative city for (exclusively) gay and lesbian people. Journalist Richard Gorelick (2004) provides one such example. Writing for "The Queer Issue" of the *Baltimore City Paper*, his column,

"Baltimore Needs a Visible Gay and Lesbian Community to Thrive – and the Gay and Lesbian Community Needs to Get with It," argues:

> Tolerance laws and domestic-partner benefits will remain important issues for the gay and lesbian community, but what's at stake now is the kind of diverse, beautiful, and soul-affirming everyday life that brought us to the city in the first place ... The point of comparison, as often as not, is Washington's upscale Dupont Circle neighborhood, which not only provides abundant and diverse dining, entertainment, and retail sites catering to gays and lesbians but, more urgently, is an environment where gays feel comfortable, and where – and this trope was offered repeatedly – gay couples can walk hand-in-hand.

Gorelick offers his readers a binary between legal protections and an urban-centered "soul-affirming everyday life," as if these are mutually exclusive entities. This binary is telling: legal protections remain important because they are not guaranteed for sexual and transgender minorities. That they are often fleeting demonstrates that sexual minorities (specifically, in this case) are tolerated rather than accepted. Gorelick's commentary is steeped in this ambiguous positioning: Baltimore *needs* its gay and lesbian citizens, gay and lesbian citizens desperately seek an environment where they can feel comfortable showing minimal public displays of affection, but the two realities do not inevitably match. Furthermore, who will be served by gays and lesbians "getting with it"? Visibility appears to be required for gays and lesbians to "serve" the city, but at what cost? And who will then be excluded?

These questions are especially resonant in urban centers where planners and policy makers seek to implement, or have implemented, creative city strategies. However, just as practitioners have been inattentive to the questions of causality that emerge from Florida's findings, there is an inattention to the logics of identity difference and visibility that sustain the creative city thesis. Instead, the affirmative strategy of recognition and the discourse of tolerance operate as common sense and above questioning while simultaneously concealing unequal power relations (see Duggan 2002b). Within this context, queer visibility in the creative city takes on a decidedly un-queer look. What becomes visible is an "authentic" gay persona: a *Queer Eye for the Straight Guy* or *Will and Grace* set of identity markers with all of its attendant cultural capital. Anything outside of these parameters is lost, excluded, or illegible. As a result, the resources earmarked for "diversity" efforts will be narrowly allotted to those who are contained within recognizable, exclusive categories.

Conclusion

The implicit assumptions about visible difference contained within creative city policies have specific material effects for both the populations subsumed under the umbrella of "diversity" and for the communities in which these populations live. Accordingly planners considering adopting a "creative cities" approach should do so with considerable caution. In a practical sense, planners must be mindful of the ways that creative city policies rely on a logic of aestheticization of non-normative identities (see Goonewardena and Kipfer 2006), which has the implicit effect of "othering" some LGBT people while excluding others altogether. Furthermore, planners must consider the effect that creative city and similar policies for regional economic development have on the planning context. Listerborn (2007: 70), for example, comments, "It is therefore not only a question of 'who speaks' but also the institutional conditions in which the speech acts takes place." In other words, it is insufficient for participatory planning efforts to recognize a range of diverse identities within the city and subsequently seek out contributions from marginalized groups. Instead, participatory planning efforts must *also* account for the ways that the creative city paradigm shapes how these contributions are heard. Thus, when marginalized groups engage with policies that have the power to both highlight their visibility and vulnerability and to shape the neighborhoods in which they live, work, and play, planners must carefully consider how the dominant creative cities model informs the ways that such community engagement is read. Doing so would enact a rethinking of how diverse bodies and identities are incorporated into planning praxis.

PART III
Regulating Sex in the City

Chapter 10

Planning for Sex/Work

Phil Hubbard

Introduction

Whilst the sexual topographies of the city are constantly in flux, with spaces of transgression occasionally threatening to 'queer' the city, there is now a substantial body of work demonstrating that the heterosexual order of the city is maintained by a plethora of legal and administrative instruments enacted by state agents such as the police, the judiciary, medical officials, planners and licensing officers (Houlbrook 2005, Knopp 1995, Sanders and Scoular 2010). Collectively, such instruments seek to define the boundaries between the polite and the obscene, layering these distinctions with understandings of when and where sexual acts are permissible (Hubbard 1999). The actions and decisions of individuals, groups, and organizations are hence construed and regulated within the overlapping complexity of such *moral geographies*, with the striation of the city into legally-distinct realms (e.g. the home, the street, the neighborhood) attaching legal and moral values to particular sexual practices and identities.

Though planning and environmental laws are framed dispassionately in terms of amenity and rights to property, it is evident that planning plays a significant role in this process of socio-spatial ordering. Indeed, numerous studies have shown that the interpretation and enactment of planning laws through the work of enforcement officers, businesses and government produces a 'patchwork' of local norms, marking conduct as either appropriate or transgressive depending on where it occurs (see Catungal and McCann 2010, Collins 2004, Forsyth 2001, Frisch 2002, Prior 2008). The consequences of this for LGBT businesses can be far-reaching, with pubs, clubs, saunas and shops targeting 'gay' consumers deemed inappropriate in many residential spaces: for example, Doan and Higgins (2011) provide plentiful evidence that planners seek to promote neighborhood renewal by displacing LGBT businesses to make areas more appealing to heterosexual families. Irrespective of their function, many LGBT facilities are classified as 'adult' businesses, and hence subject to the same zoning ordinances that seek to locate sexually-oriented businesses and sex premises away from 'family' areas, educational facilities and other 'sensitive' land uses (Papayanis 2000).

The power of planning to heterosexualize space is thus considerable. Yet in this chapter I wish to underline that planning needs to be understood not merely as a heterosexist project (Frisch 2002), but as a *heteronormative* one. To these ends, this chapter explores how spaces of commercial sex – whether targeting LGBT or 'straight' consumers – are regulated by the state and law to normalize a specific notion of heterosexuality. By reducing sex to a commercial transaction, rather than one based on notions of 'love', commercial sex has historically been regarded as a disturbing sign of the city's potential to harbor sexual and moral disorder (Houlbrook 2005). Such concerns have coalesced to encourage the state to adopt different forms of regulation designed to keep these moral threats in check, repressing forms of commercial sex (e.g. prostitution, pornographic display, sex shows and striptease) primarily through police enforcement of obscenity and decency laws. This given, planning has historically had little formal role in determining the place and space of sex consumption: sex premises have not been recognized as legal land use and hence have not fallen within the remit of planning and environmental law. However, in recent decades this has begun to change, with a moderate opening in the space allowed for commercial sex evident in many nations since the 1960s. For example, in Australia the activities of pro-sex campaigners arguing for the right to buy and sell sex has resulted in varied forms of decriminalization and legalization across different states (see Chapter 11, this volume), generating the increasing possibility that planning – and related bodies of licensing and environmental law – can have a say in where (and how) commercial sex occurs (Sullivan 2010). In the City of Sydney, for instance, the Adult Entertainment and Sex Industry Premises Development Control Plan (2006) has produced a very comprehensive set of guidelines recognizing and appropriately regulating the location, design and operation of adult entertainment and sex industry premises (Boydell et al. 2011). While this *de facto* acknowledgement of commercial sex as a fully legal land use is somewhat unique, throughout the urban West planners are now tasked in various ways with identifying suitable sites for commercial sex whilst protecting the rights of those who do not want to buy or sell sex. Given the lack of precedents here, a key question hence emerges: how can we possibly decide where is appropriate for a sex business – and where is not?

In this chapter, I want to consider the ways in which planning acts to resolve the seemingly intractable conflicts between sex businesses and those who object to their presence in their streets and neighborhoods. But rather than focus on NSW or Australian cities, I want to talk about the situation in the UK, where there have in fact been recent moves away from decriminalization towards a more punitive stance for certain forms of sex working, yet where other forms of commercial sex are becoming more obviously and widely accepted. As such, I want to focus on four different sites of commercial sex: spaces of street sex work, off-street sex premises, sex shops and sites of adult entertainment, each of which raises particular quandaries for planning. Before examining each in turn, I begin by considering why such businesses have traditionally co-located in specific areas of cities that have become notorious as 'red light districts'.

Locating Commercial Sex

While the buying and selling of sex has never been a solely urban phenomenon, it is in specific areas of towns and cities that it has been most visible, creating the phenomenon of well-known 'red light' districts, often skid row areas in semi-industrial and transitional areas. Such areas have principally been associated with female prostitution, though in many instances, they have also been home to commercial sex in the form of other 'adult-oriented' businesses including sex clubs, strip shows, and sex shops. Though most are spaces of heterosexual consumption, many of these cater for a broader range of sexual predilections and tastes, and include LGBT consumers among their clientele: in some instances, businesses explicitly target the LGBT population, with some areas of 'gay gentrification', such as Soho (London), contiguous with areas of street and off-street sex working. Historically, the most infamous and widely-noted red light districts evolved in those cities experiencing high rates of in-migration, particularly of young, single men. Indeed, prostitution and commercial sex has historically tended to thrive in ports, garrison towns, railroad communities, gold-rush and mining towns:

> If one were to summarize the characteristics of a traditional red-light district, they would include centrality – as close to the business core as possible. They are often alongside the central business district, frequently between it and major gateways or transport terminals serving that district. They might seem to be peripheral to the social and economic life of the city, but they are often characterized by a high throughput of people, high anonymity, and in many cases a large number of single-occupancy rooms. They may be located in areas with a relatively low permanent residential population but with a high population of transients. (Ryder 2009: np)

However, such clustering of sexual services in red light districts cannot be considered a simple response to patterns of supply and demand; rather it is the outcome of a complex interaction of moral codes, legal strictures and police strategies (Hubbard 1999). As noted above, there have been few societies – past or present – where premises offering sexual services have been legalized, with brothels, 'bawdy houses' and nude dancing venues having been subject to varied forms of control and censorship enforced through criminal law. These forms of control have often been highly pragmatic, recognizing that prostitution and pornography will simply move elsewhere if a premise is prohibited in a particular neighborhood. As such, the state and law have enacted explicit strategies of containment – principally through police surveillance and the threat of arrest – seeking to limit commercial sex to areas where it can be controlled and regulated. Significantly, these areas have usually been in the central or inner city, away from the whiter, wealthier suburban populations most likely to protest about the presence of commercial sex (Symanski 1981).

Yet in contexts where the criminalization of sex work has been brought into question, and where police have often found it hard to devote significant resources to the policing of 'vice', civic leaders and urban governments have developed 'command-and-control' techniques, including planning powers, to organize and even micro-manage spaces of commercial sex (Ryder 2004). In the US, for example, zoning ordinances have been widely used since the 1970s to prevent adult businesses opening in particular locales, typically prohibiting sex-related land uses near homes, schools and religious facilities, effectively restricting businesses to industrial districts (Kelly and Cooper 2001).

Though such attempts at control have been contested, not least by those who argue that zoning restricts rights to free expression (Liepe Levinson 2000, Hanna 2005), the US Supreme Court confirmed the legality of adult use zoning restrictions in 1976 when Detroit's 'Anti-Skid Row Ordinance' was upheld in *Young v. American Mini Theaters, Inc* on the basis it served a substantial governmental interest (namely, reducing the 'negative secondary effects' surrounding adult businesses) (Edwards 2010). Municipalities wishing to prohibit adult businesses from operating in certain areas have thus cited a need to protect communities from secondary effects such as increases in crime, decreased property values, and neighborhood deterioration, drawing on a number of (possibly flawed) studies from the 1970s which indicated that, compared with other land uses, there are increased crime rates and lower property values near sex-related businesses (Paul et al. 2001). On this basis, federal courts have accepted that high concentrations of adult businesses damage 'the value and integrity of a neighborhood', further stipulating that a city 'does not need to wait for deterioration to occur before setting out to remedy it' (*15192 Thirteen Mile Road v City of Warren*, cited in Tucker 1997: 420).

Alongside zoning, however, is licensing. Governmental licensing involves the stipulation of particular controls over a defined area of activity, and usually relies on systems of monitoring, inspection and policing to ensure compliance with rules. The consequences of non-compliance usually involve licence revocation, fines or, rarely, imprisonment. The forms of licensing evident in the US vary from state to state, with the type of control that can be exercised over sexually-oriented businesses dependant on whether the business serves alcohol or not. Licenses may accordingly be granted subject to certain conditions which, in the case of a sex business, can relate to the character of the owner, the operating hours of the establishment, the levels of nudity permitted, the form of interactions between workers and customers, appropriate forms of tipping, as well as security measures enacted on premise (Hanna 2005). Though zoning conditions may seek to control some of these operational issues, once a zoning has been granted there is little discretion to adapt the zoning or impose more stringent conditions. Licenses, in contrast, are generally renewed annually, and may be revoked for failure to uphold the conditions (Kelly and Cooper 2001). As such, licensing provides a flexible means by which the state can ensure that those who make their living selling 'risky' pleasures take responsibility for managing and running their business in accordance with the stipulations of the local state. Licensing also absolves the state from subjecting individual premises to constant surveillance, as secondary evidence of licensing infractions can be given material weight in any application for a license renewal (Hubbard et al. 2008).

While restricting commercial sex to red light districts via licensing and zoning powers has some advantages for both customers and non-customers (who can avoid such areas if they are offended by the sight and sounds of the sex industry), in some instances such areas had become something of an embarrassment to city governors as they represented a concentration of sleaze and sex at odds with the image that the city wanted to project. A much discussed example here is Boston, Massachusetts, which used zoning powers in the 1970s to bring commercial sex together in a well-known 'combat zone' between Boylston and Kneeland Street. Rising rates of crime in the area, and the highly-publicized murder of Harvard footballer Andrew Puopolo in 1976, led to a rethink, with the reversal of zoning ordinances and an attempt to disperse sex businesses to the city fringes (Tucker 1997). Similar strategies were pursued in the Times Square area of New York in the 1980s, which by that time had become a 'no-go' area for many women (and some men) because of the concentration of (poorly-managed) sex cinemas and 'girlie' shows. In the context of attempts to 'clean up' Manhattan, local police were encouraged by mayor Rudy Giuliani to arrest and charge street prostitutes in the area, while radical zoning laws were introduced to drive sex businesses out of Manhattan (something that had a profound effect on the LGBT community as well as the 'straight' sexual tourists who thronged around Times Square's adult bookstores and theaters) (Warner 1999). In this instance, zoning laws forbade sexually-oriented businesses within 1,000 feet of one another on the basis that clusters of such businesses are associated with nuisance and criminality (Lasker 2000). Such ordinances have since become widespread in the US, with the 'success' of New York in cleaning-up its sex businesses mirrored in similar efforts to make city centers safer and prostitute-free elsewhere in North America, Europe and Australasia (for example, see Kunkel, 2008 on Hamburg, Kerkin 2003 on Melbourne, Ross 2010 on Vancouver, and Doan and Higgins 2011 on Atlanta). Yet it is a moot point whether planning powers of zoning and licensing respond to community or public anxieties about commercial sex or whether they serve the interests of property developers seeking to profit from areas 'blighted' by sex businesses: the zoning laws adopted in New York, for example, have been widely interpreted as working in the interests of corporate developers (Papayanis 2000), while Ross (2010) contends that the 'cleansing' of Vancouver's red light areas was a thinly-veiled attempt to make it safe for 'bourgeois (queer) capitalism'.

These recent efforts to clean up vice areas, when coupled with the tendency for clients to contact sex workers via mobile phone or download pornography from the Internet means that red-light districts are becoming less numerous in Western cities, and are now very rare in North America. But, as Sanchez (2004) notes in the context of Portland, Oregon, such efforts at zoning out commercial sex are highly contradictory, for at the same moment that some forms of sex work are being represented as profoundly anti-social, and becoming less visible in the urban landscape, others are seemingly becoming more significant in the urban entertainment economy. Indeed, the demand for pornography, strip clubs, lap-dancing, escorts, and sex tours seemingly draws affluent consumers towards cities, particularly in the form of business and group tourism. Imbued with a new-found respectability, such sex-related businesses have been re-dubbed sites of 'adult entertainment', and have often been deemed central to the production of vibrant 24-hour city centers that appeal to the creative and gentrifying classes (Bernstein 2007). Hausbeck and Brents (2002: 102) thus identify the proliferation of 'upscale' adult entertainment venues at the heart of Western cities as one of the clearest manifestations of the transformation of the sex industries from a 'small, privately-owned, illegitimate and almost feudal set of businesses dependent on local sheriffs looking the other way' to a 'multi-billion dollar business dominated by corporations'. Liepe-Levinson (2002: 22) likewise argues 'the sleazy nudie bar, hidden away in a municipal district of-ill repute' no longer epitomizes the 'cultural and geographical location' of adult entertainment, with commercial sex being increasingly centralized, both socially and spatially.

These contradictory spatial tendencies – marginalization and centralization – point to the fraught context in which planners are deliberating over the appropriate location for sex work in contemporary cities. It can therefore be hypothesized that the proactive regulation of commercial sex involves a complex spatial politics in which various constituencies attempt to order urban space according to their particular interests. Consequently, whether a sex-related business is permitted to open in a given circumstance may be dependent on the decisions made by the planners who have jurisdiction within a given territory, but this always involves the consideration of admissible knowledges, whether these emanate from 'experts' such as planners, solicitors and the judiciary (who advise as to which planning laws can be invoked in particular contexts), sex workers and their advocates or the community groups who may raise concerns relating to nuisance, anti-sociality or the decline of the public realm (Hadfield 2006). In this regard, we need to remain mindful of the different types of sex-related businesses that characterize the contemporary city, and recognize these are subject to different forms of regulation dependant on their perceived suitability in different communities. For instance, planners may regard 'adult cabarets' acceptable in some residential neighborhoods, but not an X-rated bookstore. The suggestion here is that the acceptability of sex-related businesses in particular locales is adjudged by regulators who consider the nature of both the business and its location: examination of these contested legal knowledges is hence vital if we are to understand why commercial sex flourishes in some spaces, but not others.

Planning for Commercial Sex in the UK

Whilst the UK shares much in common with other Western nations where technological changes have made commercial sex more visible, and arguably more democratic (see Smith 2007), the 'sexualization of culture' has been challenged in a number of ways. Most notable, perhaps, were the efforts of the New Labor administration between 1997 and 2010 to check the 'unbridled ethic' of sex consumption via attempts to limit the supply and demand for commercial sex through adaptations of the criminal law. At times, this meant a diverse and inchoate range of sexual materials and practices were grouped together within 'panic' legislation such as the Criminal Justice and Immigration Act 2008 – which criminalized the distribution of 'extreme' pornographic images (Wilkinson 2009) – and the Sexual Offences Act 2003, which introduced new powers relating to incest, trafficking, brothel keeping and paedophilia (Mcalinden 2006). However, these sometimes punitive laws were pushed through on the basis that commercial sex is rarely consensual, and is a key site of gendered exploitation: tellingly it was often women MPs who pushed for these new laws, contrary to other feminist campaigners fighting for recognition of 'sex work' as legitimate work (Scoular and Sanders 2010). In this sense, it is not easy to characterize the UK as drifting towards a more punitive stance towards commercial sex: rather, it makes more sense to speak of variegated responses to the different forms of sex consumption emerging in different spaces.

Planning for Street Sex Work

Traditionally, street sex working has been an accepted part of the metropolitan street scene, accepted by urban governors because of its seeming inevitability but simultaneously condemned as a source of disease and immorality. Though the majority of street workers are thought to be women, it is increasing acknowledged that significant proportions of those working on the street are young men (Scott et al. 2004, Whowell 2010), with some street sex markets also host to large numbers of transgendered individuals (see, for example, Browne et al. 2010 on Brighton and Hove, UK). In the UK soliciting and kerb crawling laws were used from the 1950s to effect a containment strategy which pushed street soliciting to certain, notorious inner city districts. Such enclosure fulfilled dual purposes, allowing the vice police to monitor and survey sex markets whilst placing them away from neighborhoods where the presence of sex work would have generated most controversy and opposition (see Hubbard 1999).

By its very nature, street sex work can be highly visible, and once established can have substantial deleterious effects on communities (Pitcher et al. 2006). These include late night noise and disturbance, discarded condoms or drug paraphernalia in local alleys and gardens and general exposure to the sights and sounds of vice.

In some areas, street prostitution is thought to attract other forms of criminality – notably drug dealing – whilst in many neighborhoods it appears clients have caused annoyance by approaching non-prostitute women (and sometimes men) for sex. This means street sex work has only been tolerated in marginal inner city areas, reproducing what Lowman (1992) terms a 'discourse of disposability' in which the placement of the prostitute in marginal, nocturnal spaces reproduces myths of their 'deviant' status.

Given the marginal nature of many street working environments, questions arise as to whether these are safe working environments, and it was here that multi-agency working was often important for ensuring these were not only spaces of punitive surveillance by the police but of supportive surveillance by outreach and medical services. Indeed, in some cases relative stability in the location of female street soliciting did allow for good relationship to be developed between outreach services, workers and the wider community, as was the case in Edinburgh or Bolton in the 1990s. In practical terms, this involved local authorities designating a safe soliciting zone away from residential populations, ensuring there was adequate lighting and support on site, and allowing kerb crawlers to evade prosecution on the basis that their actions were not causing any annoyance. However, in the UK such spaces enjoyed only quasi-legal status, being tolerated rather than encouraged, essentially allowed in the interests of maintaining the social and economic value of particular land uses which might be adversely effected by the secondary impacts and negative externalities of sex work.

This given, while local planners have played a role in identifying suitable areas for street soliciting and kerb crawling, the planning system in the UK has never recognized commercial sex as a legitimate land use, meaning that sex work has never been equated to the 'best and highest use of land'. This means street sex work has often been displaced by redevelopment (Hubbard and Whowell 2008), with planned programmes of urban regeneration often being predicated on the destruction of existing street beats. For example, in Leith Docks, Edinburgh, an established tolerance area with an on-site drop-in center for women was ultimately shut down following the development of new rental flats in what was previously an industrial area, with the movement of working women to adjacent streets prompting concerted community pickets that ultimately dispersed street working across a wide area of Edinburgh (see Bondi 1998 on the gentrification of Leith).

In many other communities, residents have also claimed that the effects of street prostitution have reached intolerable levels and canvassed the police, politicians and local authorities to take measures. In some, residents have taken action themselves and have organized street patrols or pickets to remove visible, female sex work from their neighborhood (most notably in Birmingham, Bradford and Cardiff – see Sagar 2005). Justifying their campaigns, protestors often stress they are concerned about the *visibility* of sex work on the street, declaring that it undermines the 'family' character of the neighborhood. Specific concerns may be voiced about children witnessing street sex work, and the fears of non-sex working women and young people who feel intimidated and 'unsafe' in streets where sex workers solicit. Overall, there is much evidence to suggest that vociferous campaigns of opposition to street prostitution are led by sections of the community who have a moral or religious objection to sex work, and do not always enjoy the support of other sections of the community. Pitcher et al. (2006) hence report a wide variety of views towards sex workers and their clients, and actually surprisingly few instances of non-sex working women (or men) reporting being solicited by kerb crawling men. However, such 'quieter' voices have been lost in debates about sex work, meaning those more tolerant or accepting of street prostitution have their opinions subsumed within the oppositional rhetoric that dominates the local media.

The conclusions drawn by Pitcher et al. (2006) that street sex working and residential land use might co-exist were, however, at complete odds with the dominant ethos of the Home Office that, under New Labor, pushed a line which stresses street sex work is a form of anti-social behavior. Following a period of widespread consultation, the Home Office's Coordinated Prostitution Strategy 2006 rejected any notion of legalizing toleration zones despite considerable support in some quarters for planning for street working in this way (following the example of the Dutch tippelzones). For example, in January 2005, Liverpool City Council had requested approval from the Home Office to establish (on a three year pilot basis) a managed zone for street soliciting in the city, based on consultation with residents' groups and sex worker outreach projects that had identified a suitable zone (Bellis et al. 2007). Far from decriminalizing street working in all or some areas, as was suggested by Liverpool City Council (among others), Section 72 of the Criminal Justice and Immigration Act (2009) introduced new powers allowing a court to make an order for a person convicted of loitering or soliciting (for purpose of prostitution), requiring them to attend three meetings with a specified supervisor to promote the 'offender's' rehabilitation. Failure to attend any sessions can result in a further summons and a possible 72 hours' imprisonment. Sanders (2009: 572) refers to this as 'regulatory therapy': a form of surveillance, exclusion and control masquerading as support.

Despite being a 'victimless crime', street sex work is hence figured by the UK government, alongside other behaviors such as begging and soliciting, loitering, vagrancy and sleeping rough, as profoundly anti-social. As urban public space becomes increasingly structured according to 'a territorial division between the excluded and the included, between the spaces of consumption and civility and the savage spaces on the margins' (Sanders 2009: 573), the public display of sex for sale has thus become viewed as 'out of place', despite the fact that the sexual act itself is negotiated between adults and usually transacted in private space. Despite this, anyone, whether male or female, on the street (or on a balcony or in a window) can be found guilty of soliciting for the purpose of prostitution. An important shift in this drift towards Zero Tolerance for sex work in public space has been a discourse of gendered exploitation: the (women) worker is seen as not merely antisocial but responsible for putting herself at risk of exploitation by men. In dominant representations of street work, the kerb-crawler is assumed male and depicted as a sexual threat. The increase in laws against 'the kerbcrawler' is testament to this – for example, the 2001 Criminal Justice and Police Act made kerb-crawling an arrestable offense; in 2003 the Criminal Justice Act allowed for on the spot fining, driving license and high profile naming and shaming. In this sense, the idea that areas might be set aside for street working has been rejected, and the idea of planning for male sex work dismissed entirely given it is only female rather than male or transgendered workers who are assumed to be vulnerable to male violence and coercion (Browne et al. 2010).

Planning for Off-street Sex Work

Given the UK government has repeatedly insisted that street sex working has no place in a 'civilized' society, with more punitive approaches adopted to street soliciting and kerb-crawling, it might be anticipated that off street work would be facilitated to allow for the displacement of street workers. To the contrary, the UK government has repeatedly backed away from the idea of legalizing off-street sex work, founded on the idea that prostitution could take place in brothels which would need to acquire licenses and observe select conditions of operation, such as requirements that the owners follow particular health and safety guidelines. Such licensing, as pioneered in the Netherlands since 2000, Nevada (US) since 1978, Germany since 2002, and New South Wales since 2002, delegates control over prostitution to local councils who handle planning procedures and are expected to identify and close down illegal brothels. This approach is somewhat different than outright decriminalization (as passed in New Zealand in 2003) which removes all laws applying solely to sex work and simply makes sex workers and clients liable to the laws that affect all citizens (such as those around nuisance). For its proponents, the advantages of licensing over decriminalization are thought to allow for taxation of businesses (and workers) whilst allowing the state to exercise some control over businesses that might be deemed as problematic when located in specific locales.

Despite pressures from sex worker groups (such as the English Collective of Prostitutes) for decriminalization or legalization, off-street work remains in a legally indistinct void in the UK. As prostitution itself is not illegal in the UK, home-based work is not illegal where one individual works from a private premise, but such premises do not exist in business or planning terms (despite tentative efforts in the 1980s to classify a house used by a single home worker as a non-residential land use). As such, these premises are 'out of sight and out of mind' and the women (and men) who choose to work in this way may well escape taxation. But if more than one woman or man consents to non-marital sex on a premise, under the 2003 Sexual Offences Act, the owner of this premise can be prosecuted for running a brothel or 'disorderly house' and accused of living off immoral earnings. This said, 'massage parlors' do exist as legal businesses in most UK towns and cities, and in the majority of these workers provide sexual services that are negotiated between the client and the worker. Such premises require planning permission as a retail use, and the owner must seek a license for massage or 'special treatments' from the local authority.

Whilst it is widely known that massage parlors in the UK are effectively brothels (with web sites and guides providing the uninitiated with a guide to prices and services), they are not licensed as brothels per se, and can actually be closed if it is proved that the owner is knowingly allowing sex on premise (their defence being that any sexual services negotiated are between the client and worker and not with their encouragement). This means that while the local state can exercise some control on the location of massage parlors, they are not planned for or regulated as sex premises per se and no attempt is made to place them 'where they are least likely to offend' (cf. NSW, *Hornsby v Martyn* 2010 – see Boydell et al. 2011).

In 2009 the Crime and Policing Act was passed, introducing a new offense – 'Paying for sexual services of a prostitute where a third person has engaged in exploitative conduct which encouraged that prostitute to sell that sex'. As a result police can enforce brothel closure if an officer has reasonable grounds for believing that the making of a closure order is necessary to prevent the premises being used for prostitution or pornography. Quite why these powers have been ushered in at a time when there is increased recognition of prostitution as sex work (Sullivan 2010), and sex itself is widely depicted as recreational (Bernstein 2007), can perhaps only be explained with reference to the emerging discourse that sex work involves and encourages trafficking: there has been a real conflation in the public imagination of sex work and sex exploitation, with all migrant work assumed to be the result of enslavement and trafficking (Jeffreys 2008). Those working with sex workers dispute this to posit a more subtle distinction between forced and voluntary sex work (Mai 2009); moreover, the UK police's Operation Pentameter conducted 822 premise raids over six months, many of them choreographed for the media, but ultimately only 22 people were prosecuted for trafficking.

In dismissing the possibility of licensing brothels, and responding to political pressures around trafficking and sexual exploitation, the UK government sent out a symbolic message that it will not tolerate trafficking or sexual exploitation, at the same time perhaps assuming that in reality off-street work may actually be safer (and more lucrative) than street work. While this is generally the case, the government's failure to bring brothels into the ambit of state surveillance or to enforce licensing has meant that it has been impossible to enforce minimum standards of working. Moreover, by placing off-street prostitution into a zone of legal indistinction where is it neither fully legal nor illegal, the state performs a contrary set of moves where sex workers are excluded from the law's protection yet remain subject to its disciplinary power (see Hubbard et al. 2008). Furthermore, by failing to legitimate prostitution as legal land use, the government has not allowed planners to exercise any control over the location of businesses that some clearly identify as unsuitable in 'family' areas or in the proximity of religious or educational facilities. Continual concern about the spread of home-based sex working into suburban areas, and the continued visibility of massage parlors in some inner city areas, suggests that acknowledgement of brothels as a legal land use may be overdue.

Planning for Sex Retailing

While prostitution currently enjoys only a semi-legal position within UK cities, and is not planned for despite the evidential demand and supply of sex for sale, other forms of commercial sex have become arguably more visible and mainstream in the early years of the twenty-first century. An example is the increased prominence of 'sex shops' selling goods restricted to over-18 year olds. Such shops have been licensed in the UK since 1982 if they sell 'a significant degree of selling things provided for the purpose of stimulating or encouraging sexual activities'. Though the 1982 Act allowed local authorities little discretion over the nature of materials sold in sex-shops, it permitted the imposition of conditions prohibiting display of products in shop windows (by insisting windows were blacked-out), refusing access to under-18s and restricting opening hours from 9am to 6pm (or rarely 7pm or 8pm). The 1982 Act also allowed refusal of a license on a number of grounds, such as the 'character of the applicant' or the unsuitability of the location. Backed up with threats of fine and imprisonment for running a sex-shop without a license, and, latterly, the enforced closure of unlicensed premises, while the 1982 Act did not go far enough for some, it certainly gave considerable powers to local authorities. Controversially, it also opened up the possibility of local authorities making considerable revenue through variable fees for sex-shop licenses (e.g. in 2008 an annual license cost £1,500 in Peterborough, £4,500 in Salford, £5,000 in Liverpool and £20,000 in Westminster).

Given sex shops require planning permission as retail land use rather than sex land use per se, it is licensing, not planning, that has been used to reduce their visibility in areas where 'vulnerable' populations might be, and away from children in particular (Coulmont and Hubbard 2010). Indeed, in the UK it is possible for local authority to refuse a sex shop license if it judges that a new license would exceed the appropriate number in the relevant locality (where an appropriate number might be zero). Grounds for refusing sex shop seem to be if in locality of facilities used by children and 'families' (a seeming shorthand for 'heterosexual families'), places of worship, and schools. This still leaves the vexed question of how extensive a 'locality' might be, and while it has been established that there may be many localities within a local authority boundary (so that a locality cannot be defined as being an entire town), localities have been defined variously as approximately 'one quarter of a mile' and 'one-third of a mile' around a sex-shop.

For all of this, selling Restricted 18 pornographic videos or DVDs has been the traditional distinction between a shop requiring license and one that does not – not the fact that the shop is blatantly selling sexually-oriented goods. In an increasing number of cases when owners have been refused a sex shop license, owners have opened anyway and merely ensured that they have no DVDs certified as Restricted 18, simultaneously insisting that the majority of their stock is not encouraging sexual behavior (claiming that, for example, underwear and leather goods are adult-oriented rather than sexually-oriented per se). As such, licensing has effectively encouraged a move away from stores focusing on R18 videos and DVDs and inadvertently led to an increased visibility of stores selling sex-related goods on the UK High Street, such as the Ann Summers chain which boasts upwards of 130 shops in the UK selling sex toys and lingerie. While Ann Summers is marketed as a store for women and heterosexual couples, effectively sold as a 'love shop' as opposed to a sex shop (Smith 2007), others (like *Sh!* women's emporium in London) cater more explicitly for members of the LGBT community. Because these outlets are not legally understood to be sex shops, there is no way for them to be controlled through the licensing process, even if they might appear to have 'a significant degree' of sexual goods for sale (including sex toys, lubricants and erotic books). Openly trading on British high streets, such shops have both normalized and gentrified sex retailing: in turn, by allowing them to trade as 'normal' retail outlets the state and law effectively leaves decisions about the display of sex-related goods – and the way these can be viewed or accessed – to the store operators (Coulmont and Hubbard 2010).

Planning for Adult Entertainment

'Adult entertainment' is a term now widely used in the UK to describe a variety of sex-oriented entertainment where the undressed body is presented as object of pleasure and titillation. The range of businesses that conform to such a definition is incredibly diverse, including pole-dancing and table-dancing clubs, striptease parlors, exotic dance clubs, and topless bars, though lap dancing is the most common synonym. Although striptease has a long if hidden history in Britain, dedicated clubs emerged mainly in the late 1990s and early 2000s, initially described as 'US-style' given they included forms of straddle and pole dancing which were associated with North American chains (Hubbard et al. 2008). While most of these venues target male consumers by hosting female dancers, some clubs also promote male striptease. The fact that any such entertainment could be put on in a venue with a relatively straightforward waiver on the public entertainment license, in much the same way that a pub or club might become licensed for music, was seen to be a factor encouraging a rash of new venues in the early 2000s, with lap dancing clubs opening across the length and breadth of the UK, including towns with little obvious history of commercial sex. These clubs appear to have aroused much controversy at a local level, prompting residents and local business groups to mobilize against clubs that they see to be 'lowering the tone' and encouraging the 'wrong type' of nightlife to visit their towns (Hubbard 2009).

The idea that such venues are inappropriate in areas near to facilities used by children has been emphasized in many campaigns of opposition, which have made objections on the basis of the four goals of licensing system, namely reducing crime and disorder, promoting public safety, preventing public nuisance and protecting children from harm (see Hadfield 2006). The latter was found to be particularly effective given there is little evidence from the UK that premises with adult entertainment cause increases in crime in the local area (but see McLeary and Weinstein 2009 on the US context). Fears about the moral corruption of children and young people have indeed convinced licensing officers that a waiver for lap dancing would not be appropriate in the vicinity of schools or colleges, albeit that in some cases licensing conditions have simply suggested that clubs can be in the proximity of such facilities so long as their opening hours do not coincide with times when young people would be around (Hubbard 2009).

The case for tightening control on such venues gained considerable momentum in 2007 when the feminist anti-pornography campaign group *Object* launched a campaign, 'Stripping the Illusion', which argued for increased control of adult entertainment on the basis that it is of a different nature than, for example, live music or karaoke. The subsequent inclusion of clause 27 of the 2009 Crime and Policing Act, which created a new licensing category of Sexual Entertainment Venue, was hence a victory for campaigners and provided a tool for local authorities to refuse a license for lap dance venues on moral grounds, and not just concerns of public order or safety. In effect, adult entertainment venues in the UK are now licensed in the same manner as sex shops, meaning local authorities will be able to refuse a license for a lap-dancing venue if it is regarded inappropriate in the locality, providing a basis for a strict exclusion of striptease venues from specific localities. It will also allow stringent conditions to be imposed on clubs, with the possibility of no-nudity and no-touching clauses constraining the entertainment offered, shielding further the already 'hermetic' body of the striptease performer and curtailing what Uebel (2004) terms the 'lure and power of erotic dancing'.

Rather than being viewed merely as a mechanism for reducing negative externalities, licensing in the UK is being explicitly recast as a means to control the form and content of adult entertainment, and is becoming an arena where questions of sexual morality, taste and censorship are blatantly to the fore. Whether or not planning or licensing law should be used to intervene in this way is a moot point. Although the new powers have been contested by female burlesque dancers as well as others who feel the new law will not genuinely differentiate between well-run spaces of entertainment and exploitative or inappropriately located venues, local authorities are allowed to deploy stereotyped assumptions about the nature and impact of such clubs without due consideration of their actual effects on local land uses and amenity values (Hubbard 2009).

Conclusion

Commercial sex, whether in the form of prostitution, sex retailing or adult entertainment, remains a highly contested realm, with places and spaces of sex consumption often caught up in the politics of NIMBYism ('Not in my backyard').

In theory, planning offers an effective basis for mediating such disputes, weighing up varied claims to urban space to decide where commercial sex ought to be allowed. Yet on the basis of this brief review of the regulation of commercial sex in the UK, it is apparent that the idea of planning for sex work remains something of an oxymoron. In short, given that there is no recognition of sex-related businesses as a distinct category of land use, there is no possibility of identifying areas suitable for sex consumption. However, at the same time that criminal laws and the police power continue to be used to remove specific forms of prostitution from the city, it is apparent that other forms of sex consumption are becoming accepted and normalized within certain legitimate businesses and adult-oriented premises over which planning and licensing has some control. For the state, planning thus provides the basis for 'governance through use', making a space for some adult businesses, but not others.

As a technique of governance, there hence remains much that might be said of planning as a distinct set of practices that work alongside policing and social work to construct appropriate sexual orders, setting out the boundaries between legitimate and illegitimate sex consumption and, by implication, reaffirming the limits of the state's interest in the sexual lives of its citizenry. Whether or not planning can ever act in a more socially and sexually liberatory manner is a moot point given that the planning system tends to reinforce dominant, largely heterosexual, moralities. Yet for socially-just decisions to be made it is important that the views of those who are offended by sex work are balanced with those who benefit from these legal land uses. Most importantly, perhaps, it is important that the voices and rights of sex workers and those in the industry are heard in the planning process; this is perhaps the main failing of the UK system of regulation, which, by effectively criminalizing many forms of sex work, fails to acknowledge the fundamental right of adults to buy and sell sex, and hence forecloses opportunities for sex workers, business owners and advocates to make effective claims to space. In this sense, I would make the more general argument that where it is used to influence the place of sex work, planning and licensing tends to privilege the rights of residential property owners over the rights of sex workers, placing commercial sex in areas where it is neither safe or profitable. In such ways, commercial sex is marginalized within social and spatial hierarchies, deemed inferior to domesticated, 'loving', and assumed heteronormal sex.

To conclude that the planning of sex work reinforces dominant ideologies that connect property, propriety and coupledom is to underline that urban space reproduces a specific version of heterosexuality, namely, heteronormativity. As Oswin (2009) notes, the actions of the state and the law serve not just to marginalize gays and lesbians, but also 'queer' a range of other groups and practices. Commercial sex is not necessarily 'queer' (though many venues and premises clearly promote polymorphous perversity, and cater for LGBT individuals), but clearly a queer theoretical approach is useful for considering why the state seeks to marginalize various forms of 'perverse' sex consumption so as to maintain the heteronormative, moving other forms to the center only if they can be accommodated within the plenary geographies of capitalist accumulation. In the final analysis, it is therefore essential to consider commercial sex not simply as heteronormativity's Other but as a variegated set of commercial and social transactions which constantly demand new forms of planning and spatial governance so that their 'moral threat' is co-opted, transformed or contained according to the imperatives of consumer culture.

Chapter 11
Queerying Urban Governance: The Emergence of Sex Industry Premises into the Planned City

Jason Prior and Penny Crofts

Introduction

This chapter analyzes the emergence of sex industry premises, in particular gay bathhouses, into formal land-use processes in Sydney, Australia in the late twentieth century. The chapter traces a shift in regulatory mechanisms in the last decades of the twentieth century away from explicitly moral and criminal discourses to planning policies to regulate and organize sex industry premises. This chapter details the regulatory transition of gay bathhouses from a catch-all category of *disorderly premises* that included other businesses such as brothels, to an official definition that differentiated bathhouses from other sex industry premises.

Throughout, we highlight the centrality of planning to organizing and regulating sex in the city, both historically and in the present. Planning expresses and organizes an idea(l) of urban order, and those sexualities which breach this order are regarded as disorderly, contaminated and polluted. These ideas of order vary across time *and* place, and an analysis of the organization of sexualities through the prism of planning places emphasis on *place*. We also explore the ways in which planning was utilized not only to regulate from above, but also was utilized by proprietors of gay bathhouses to assist with their survival, whether formally or informally.

In this chapter we analyze the relevance of planning processes to gay bathhouse developments in Sydney, Australia from the 1960s until the early 2000s. We have drawn upon the archives of local councils in Sydney to examine the development application processes.[1] Some applications were denied consent by the local councils and were appealed to the New South Wales

---

1 Documents were sourced from the archives of these five different councils – 300 files were retrieved from The City of Sydney, 150 files from South Sydney City Council, 30 files from Randwick Municipal Council, 20 from Waverley Municipal Council and 6 files from Parramatta City Council. Out of the documents viewed, about 156 proved to be useful. They contained development applications, building applications and special files relating to BAs and DAs that related to the gay boathouses explored within this study.

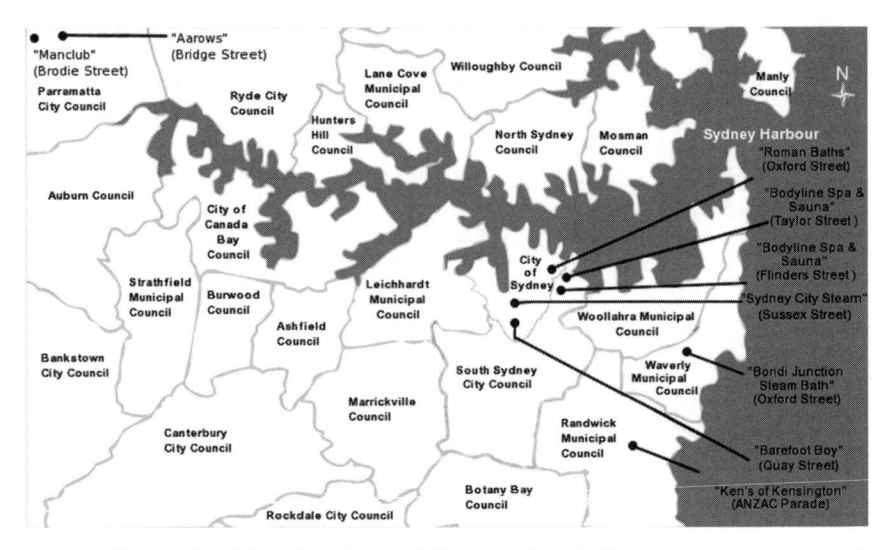

Figure 11.1 Map Showing Central Sydney Local Government Areas, and Location of the Bathhouses Discussed in the Study
Source: Map constructed by the author.

Land and Environment Court (NSWLEC) a state government judicial body created to review planning matters. The study presented here focuses on seven consecutive development application processes (1960, 1972b, 1973b, 1976c, 1986b, 1992c, 1996b, Williamson 1999) (see Figure 11.1). The findings from the documentary research are supported and developed through 11 semi-structured, highly conversational interviews with gay bathhouse proprietors, councillors and council officers/planners conducted in Sydney between August 2000 and November 2002.[2] Quotations from these unpublished interviews are indicated by the interviewees' names (pseudonymous or real) and the year of the interview.

We begin the chapter by providing a theoretical framework for our analysis, emphasizing the extent to which planning organizes and expresses sexuality. We then present our analysis in four successive snap shots, each reflecting a shift in the placement of gay bathhouses in Sydney through planning processes during the past 50 years. In the first, we analyze gay bathhouses in the 1960s and 1970s,

---

2 The interviews were carried out in Sydney. The list of interviews classified by the dominant role played in the development application processes is as follows: Proprietors – Dawn O'Donnel, 12 October 2000; Denise Coussens, owner King Steam, 13 October 2000; Len Stone, 11 August 2000; Peter Russell (Pseudo.), 5 August 2000. Local Councillors – Craig Johnston, Sydney, 17 August 2000; James Malone (Pseudo.), 17 January 2001. Local and State Government Employees – Julie Bates, Sex Liaison Officer for South Sydney City Council, 20 November 2000; Fred Parkinson (Pseudo.), 17 January 2001; Mark Stirling (Pseudo.), 18 January 2001; George Thomas (Pseudo.), 24 October 2001.

and their operation, regulation and placement strategies for survival during a time when homosexuality and brothels were illegal, and the city was understood as being divided between a disorderly, dangerous inner-city and an orderly, pure suburbia. In the second, we consider the place of gay bathhouses in the disorderly inner city in the 1980s, when homosexuality was no longer criminal, but brothels were, resulting in approval for the *social* aspects of the bathhouse, but not the *sexual*. In the third, we explore narratives of decline of the pristine suburb, and arguments about the appropriate locale for the bathhouse in the disorderly inner city in the 1990s, based on both its *social* and *sexual* functions, at a time when brothels and other sex industry premises were no longer considered illegal. We investigate how the place of the bathhouses in the inner-city during the 1980s and 1990s were inextricably linked with processes of gay territorialization. We conclude by considering the city and suburb divide, through consideration of the place of gay bathhouses in outer Sydney in the late 1990s and 2000s.

Planning Order

Sexuality is one area of conduct that is organized and expressed through a range of complex and conflicting discourses which include religious, psychiatric and psychological, legal, popular, economic and political. These discourses provide guidance on which sexualities are considered good, healthy, normal, virtuous, efficient or profitable for the city and its communities and which are considered otherwise (see for example, Foucault 1990, Knopp 1995, Knopp 1998, Hubbard 2004a, Hubbard 2000, Frisch 2002). These discourses inevitably privilege some at the expense of others and 'signify which ... [sexualities] are virtuous and useful and ... [which sexualities are] dangerous and inadequate, [and] which ... will be rewarded and which penalized through governance' (Kerkin 2004: 185). Since the 1970s, research has argued that these discourses have tended to privilege a very small portion of human sexuality that is seen as sanctified, natural, safe, normal, healthy, mature, profitable, legal or politically correct – heterosexual, monogamous relationships (Rubin 1993, Foucault 1990, Warner 1995).

Discourses of sexuality are not stable, and have been subject to change across time and place. This instability has meant that in recent decades some sexualities at the border of acceptability – such as prostitution and some forms of (monogamous coupled) homosexuality – have edged across the line of acceptability and been rewarded for that shift with greater levels of support from governments (Rubin 1993, Duggan 2002b).

Whilst these discourses provide rationales for the governance of sexuality within urban space, the ability of authorities to deploy these rationales depends on the complex assemblage of diverse mechanisms – legal, architectural, policing, planning, administrative, financial, judgmental – such that aspects of the decisions and actions of individuals, groups, organizations and populations come to be understood and regulated in relation to these mechanisms (Foucault 1991, 1992).

The way in which these mechanisms are used to deploy governance over sexuality includes attempts to weave mechanisms together to create an all-pervasive web of 'social control' by which to eliminate particular sexualities from urban communities and urban space, through to assorted attempts to manage sexualities and sexual institutions through countless, often competing, local tactics of persuasion, inducement, management, incitement, motivation and encouragement. Over the last few decades scholarship has begun to foreground the way in which mechanisms such as health regulation (Foucault 1990, Blotcher 1996), policing (Bailey 1999, Chauncey 1994, Colter et al. 1996, Hubbard 2004a, Wotherspoon 1991, Prior 2009), legislation and law (Crofts 2006, Crofts 2003, Gerstmann 1999, Hubbard et al. 2009), and politics (Knopp 1998) have been used to govern sexuality within urban communities and urban space in the later twentieth century.

Whilst mechanisms such as policing have received significant attention, historically less attention has been given by researchers to the role that planning has and continues to play in governing the presence of sexualities within later twentieth century urban space (Bauman 2002). An emerging body of work has begun to highlight how formal urban planning processes and regulations are increasingly used as a mechanism to govern sexuality within contemporary western cities, particularly through the placement of sex industry premises (see e.g. Papayanis 2000, Ryder 2004, Bell and Binnie 2004, Hubbard 2004a, Hubbard 2001, Crofts 2006, Crofts 2003, Prior 2009, Prior 2008, Cusack and Prior 2010, Hubbard et al. 2009). This chapter contributes to this literature through an analysis of the regulation of gay bathhouses through planning processes in Sydney, Australia, in the later twentieth century.

A theme of this chapter is the continued reliance upon and relevance of a rhetoric of contamination and pollution of gay bathhouses. We draw upon Mary Douglas' ideas about disorder in *Purity and Danger* (Douglas 2002). Douglas assumed a predilection in humans to create clear-cut classifications of the objects in their world. According to this theory, anomalous items such as those that instantiate properties of different classes or are unique are disturbing and become objects of pollution or taboo. Things that are acceptable or even attractive when in their proper place can be polluting or dangerous when out of place. For example, we may admire someone's beautiful head of hair, but if their hair is in our food, it is disgusting. The construction of systems of order is necessarily contingent. However, the central point is that dirt, literally matter out of place, offends.

Our ideas about dirt protect our visions of the good community, particularly at the margins and vulnerable points. The main function of dirt is to protect distinctive categories of the universe, shoring up uncertainty and reducing disorder. Dirt, or matter out of place, offends against order. The elimination of dirt is not a negative movement, but an attempt to organize the environment and make it conform to an idea. Douglas transposes these responses to dirt to people, things and ideas that are anomalous or ambiguous. Persons, things or ideas that cross boundaries or margins of structures are polluted and polluting – they are disorderly and threaten disorder. Our responses to disorder may be negative or positive. We may seek to eliminate, expunge, punish or condemn the offending substance, or we can change our systems of order to incorporate and accept the anomalous or ambiguous. This potential for instigating change is one of the reasons why we find 'matter out of place' so dangerous.

These ideas about disorder are particularly relevant to planning (Sibley 1996, Hubbard 2000). Planning can be seen as a technique that allows society to arrange and rearrange the environment, to make the world conform to ideas (Foucault 1991, see also Philo April 1992). Throughout its history zoning has often been considered 'the heaven-sent nostrum for sick cities, the wonder drug of the planners, the balm sought by lending institutions and householders alike' (Scott 1969: 192). Planning offers the fantasy that we can control the worst aspects of industrialization and urbanization within cities by identifying potential nuisances and segregating them from other uses. The ultimate aim of the planning framework is to order and regulate the use of land to secure physical, economic and social efficiency, health and well-being of the population.

Pollution and contamination belief systems have both a visual and spatial component (Douglas 2002) and are always discussed in terms of borders and boundaries, and threats to those borders and boundaries. In eliminating pollutants we are involved in a perpetual spatial and visual process of arranging and rearranging the environment, 'making the world conform to an idea' (Douglas 2002: 2, also see Chapter 10). Land-use planning has a long history as a governance mechanism aimed at curing the pathogenic and disorderly city through interventions such as zoning and other regulations aimed at making the city more orderly, regular, disciplined and healthy (Corburn 2007). The governing legislation for planning in NSW is the *Environmental Planning and Assessment Act* (1979). We already associate the regulation of the environment with the protection of order, whether an ideal of nature, or the suburbs or the city, and attempts to control, exclude, or expel contamination and pollution. These ideals of order are extended in planning from the explicitly physical environment, to land uses, people, and things. Planners are required to take into account potential 'amenity' impacts of proposed developments. 'Amenity' is a broad, ambiguous concept, that is 'wide and flexible', including practical and tangible environmental aspects such as traffic generation, noise, nuisance, appearance, and more elusive social concepts, such as the standard or class of a particular neighborhood, and the reasonable expectations of a neighborhood. Planning aims to protect a broad concept of the ordered environment.

The planning process is one discourse that expresses order. The process of ordering sexuality within urban space can be understand as part of a broader process of spatial purification operating within urban governance processes. Historically, discourses of crime and morality were particularly important with regard to gay bathhouses. These discourses regarded gay bathhouses as inherently disorderly, as they breached the moral, social, and legal codes. More recently, concerns about gay bathhouses have been articulated through the rhetoric of planning. As we argue at the conclusion of this chapter, the language of disorder and contamination has been sustained, but the rhetoric has shifted from moral disorder to planning disorder.

Excluding Disorderly (Bath)houses and the Inner-city/Suburban Divide

In the 1960s and 1970s proprietors sought to develop the first gay bathhouses within Sydney. These proprietors drew upon the gay bathhouses that they experienced or understood to exist in both the United States and European Union (see for example Prior 2009), and to cater to the emergent gay subculture within the city which was also being influenced by counter-cultural processes emergent within such cities as New York and San Francisco within the northern hemisphere. Like the USA and Europe gay bathhouses on which they were modeled, the interiors of the gay bathhouses that emerged in Sydney during the twentieth century had two distinct regions that radiated out from the entrance foyer. The furthest region from the entrance, and the largest part of the built domain, was the playspace – a series of spaces such as labyrinths, cubicles and darkened rooms – that were designed to facilitate consensual sexual exploration between patrons. Closest to the entrance were areas designed for transition in and out of the bath, casual socialization, and rest from the sexual explorations that occurred within the playspace (Prior 2009).

During this time, homosexuality and brothels were illegal. We highlight the use of planning to contribute to the policing of gay bathhouses, but also demonstrate the way in which this policing was locationally specific.

Gay bathhouses were associated with both homosexuality and prostitution. The association with prostitution came about in part because of sex on premises, but also due to a unitary category of undesirable and disorderly sex. Proprietors of gay bathhouses in the 1960s and 1970s offered a service that was associated with disorder. Homosexuality and prostitution breached morality, health and the law. During this period concern for homosexuality developed into a vast public discourse within Sydney. It extended far beyond the judicial and medical professions where the discussion of homosexuality had until then often been confined (1955d: 3238) and was given detailed coverage in newspapers, parliament (new legislation), medical journals (curative and behavioral modification), police (control to protect the community) and government enquiries (the establishment of a New South Wales Committee to look into the Causes and Cures of Homosexuality) (see e.g. French 1986). Driven by a broad range of beliefs from the religious – sinful, sacrilegious – to the psychological – abnormal – homosexuality was identified as inherently disorderly and dangerous.

In the post-World War Two period the presence of homosexuality and prostitution within Sydney were seen as a 'growing cancer' (*Sunday Telegraph* 1953), a super and sub human force with the ability to be ubiquitous but invisible within the populous, as 'animal', as 'predator' (see for example, 1955a), that had the potential to contaminate and pollute the city, and to corrupt the more vulnerable of its citizenry, as one media report of the time noted:

> [The vice squad's] hardest task is to trace the men who induce youths to join a homosexual group through a series of tactful introductions. Often such youths spend weeks with male groups drinking in hotels and coffee 'clubs' without any hint of unnatural behavior. They join in discussions on matters ranging from art and ballet to philosophy and literature. But when the homosexual reveals the real reason for them seeking his company the youth is so closely connected with the group that he finds it difficult to break away. He then often joins the group 'sex' parties and slips more and more away from normal society. (1968a: 1643)

The government's approach to homosexuality was steeped in a constellation of emotional expression of disgust, fear of contagion, and pollution avoidance, and manifested in a legislative concern about boundary vulnerabilities between the broader population and the ubiquitous danger of homosexuality, and provided authorities including police and local government authorities with the power to eliminate homosexuality from the city. New crimes associated with homosexuality were created (1900: see parts 79–81), (1955b, 1955c). As the Attorney General, Mr Sheadan, stated when he introduced the 1955 amendment:

> The government has acted because it considers that the homosexual wave that unfortunately has struck this country – though not to the extent of continental countries – must be eradicated ... [as he went on to say] ... it is the government's duty to protect the community, and especially its young members, who might become victims of the dirty behavior of homosexuals. (1955d: 3230 and 3296)

Homosexuality is framed in the language of disorder, the behavior by homosexuals is 'dirty', and there is a fear that it will contaminate the rest of the community.

Regulation focused not only upon the body of those who had succumbed to the contagion, but to the perceived growing and organized networks of places – 'hotel bars', 'cafes', 'parks', 'theaters', 'public lavatories' and 'private residentials and flats' – that were being habitually used to support homosexuality. Police relied upon the *Disorderly Houses Act 1943* (1943a),[3] which gave police powers to close

---

3   The main purpose of the *Disorderly Houses (Amendment) Act, 1943, Assented to 15 December 1943* (The Statutes of NSW), in its first few years, as Mr Whelan asserted in Second Reading of *Disorderly Houses Amendment Bill* in Legislative Assembly, 20 September and 18 October 1995, NSW Parliamentary Debates (Hansard), 1187–1189 and 1935–1941 and 1951–1954 and 1958–1963 at 1187, was: 'to keep American servicemen out of sly grog shops and unlicensed nightclubs, by closing the venues. The government of the day was concerned that nearby residents may be disturbed by drunken and or indecent behavior by servicemen visiting such premises'. It was in the 1950s that it began to lose

premises upon which '... disorderly or indecent conduct or any entertainment of a demoralizing character takes place in the premises, or has taken place or is likely to take place again on the premises ...' (1943a: section 3(1)(a)). This general legislation was relied upon by police to regulate undesirable and disorderly expressions of sexuality, including homosexuality and prostitution. The Act continued to be relied upon by the NSW police and local government authorities to close sex on venues such as gay bathhouses and brothels until the 1990s (1943b, 1995, 1968b).

The discovery by the police and planning authorities that sauna baths and massage parlors were being used as a front for 'immoral purposes' within Sydney in the late 1960s led to the strengthening of the *Disorderly House Act* in 1968 (1968a: 1630). As the Honorable F.M. Hewitt noted when introducing the amended legislation to parliament:

> The past few years have seen the development in Sydney ... of a type of business which is established ostensibly to provide massage, sauna baths, and similar services to customers, but is in reality a mask for prostitution and other objectionable and indecent conduct [my emphasis]. This type of activity has posed a problem for the police, having in mind that the [disorderly house] act itself, as well as the soliciting of the customer, does not occur in a public street or place. It is a most insidious form of vice and is particularly distressing to those people who carry on legitimate and reputable businesses of this kind. (1968a: 1630)

This demonstrated the tendency to combine all aberrant sexualities into the one undesirable category.

Of particular concern was the perception of a growing cluster of vice and sex industry venues; within older inner-city suburbs such as East Sydney and Kings Cross, it was argued that the cumulative impact of these venues was causing 'decent' and 'normal' people to retreat to the safer suburbs further out from the city's center (1968a: 1643). As the Honorable Edna S. Roper proposed:

> The economic effects of the current plague of crime and vice in the Kings Cross area are not without significance. As we can remember, back in the late fifties in this city, suave continentals lent a touch of European elegance and sophistication to the coffee shops in Kings Cross, but they have now retreated to Double Bay where they are not yet pestered by deviants and drug addicts. (1968a: 1643)

Despite the simplistic nature and weak empirical veracity of this claim, it articulated a particularly powerful belief within Sydney in the post war years where the disorderly older inner city was routinely juxtaposed with the emergence of orderly new suburbs. This juxtaposition can be traced back to the processes which constituted suburbia from the late nineteenth century as an aspirational space that

---

this connection and was refocused on controlling sexual deviants such as prostitutes and homosexuals.

allowed the predominately middle class to move up and out of overcrowded older inner city areas whose poor environmental conditions were believed to generate social pathologies of urban life and acted as a breeding ground for vice, violence, crime, poor morals and bad habits (Prior 2011).

This juxtaposition was deeply entrenched in Sydney's planning rationale throughout the twentieth century. For example, the Honorable J.J. Cahill, State Minister for Local Government in New South Wales, noted when discussing the reasoning behind the introduction of new legislation that gave local government greater control over land use planning in the mid-1940s (1945b):

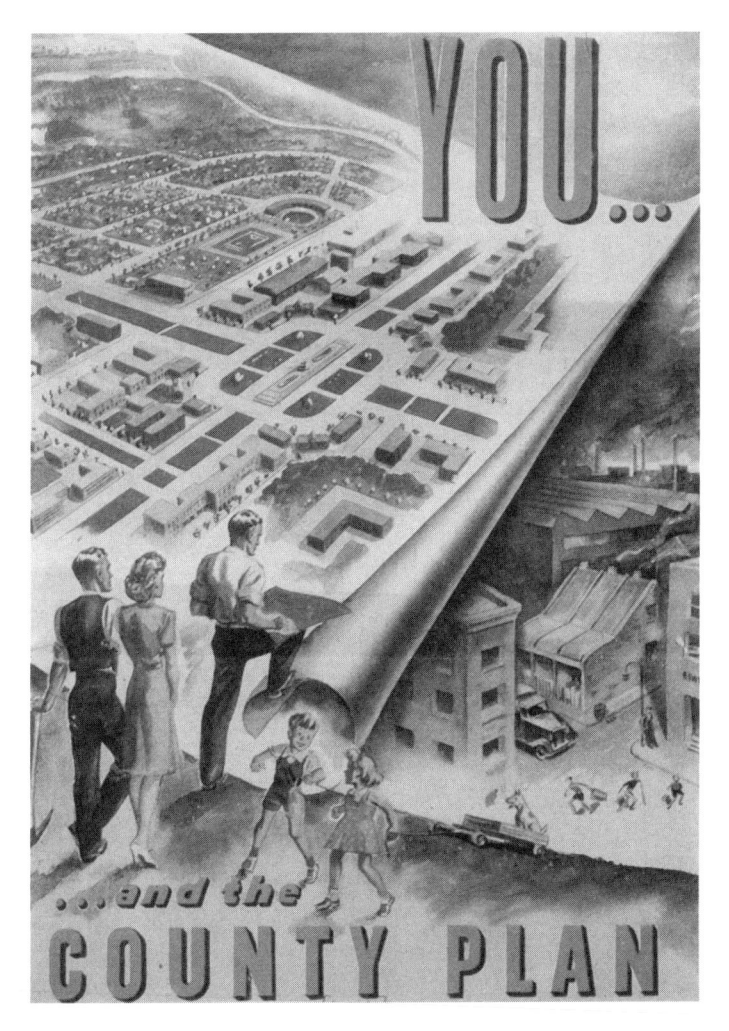

Figure 11.2   Cover of the Cumberland County Council Pamphlet
Source: Planning document from the 1940s in the public domain.

> The need for adequate town and country planning machinery is now so insistent, having regard to the need for the orderly regulation of post-war development [of new suburbs] and for the correction of evils of the largely haphazard and uncontrolled development of our [older inner] cities ... in the past, ... satisfaction of these needs can no longer be denied. (1945a: 1720)

A key image within a government publication detailing the impact of this new land-use planning legislation depicts the vision of the planned reconstruction (Spearritt and Marco 1988: 70). It presents a bleak picture of the existing older inner city suburbs – overcrowded, polluted and unhealthy inner-city suburbs where factories exist alongside terrace houses. These are to be replaced by the new orderly planned suburbs that unroll over the existing disorderly city. The heteronormative dimensions of this planned future is evident in the picture; a Planner overlooks the unraveling of these new suburbs, behind him stand the occupants for whom this reconstruction is being designed: the nuclear family of hard-working husband ready with pick in hand, diligent wife posing beside him and two children – one boy, one girl – playing (see Figure 11.2).

It was into this 'hostile' (Prior 2000: 12 October, Prior 2000: 11 August) context of homosexual policing and restrictive land-use management in the latter 1960s and early 1970s that proprietors sought to develop the first gay bathhouses in Sydney. Various survival strategies were adopted by proprietors with different and inconstant levels of success. In the 1960s, when these bathhouses were at their most clandestine, their interiors were protected by complex threshold mechanisms, which included vestibules, bolted doors and check points to thwart intrusion and detection by authorities (Prior 2009).

Sydney's first gay bathhouse – the Bondi Junction Steam Bath (BJSB) was located in a rundown gymnasium. Like other gay bathhouses such as Ken's Karate Club in Kensington and the Barefoot Boy in Haymarket, the BJSB used pseudonym development applications applying as 'health clubs and gymnasiums (1960, 1972b, 1973b, 1971, 1974, 1976a, 1976c) saunas baths, massage parlors, sports clubs among others (1960, 1972b, 1972a, 1974).

The BJSB was located in Bondi Junction which is part of the inner city, but outside the 'disorderly' older inner-suburbs of East Sydney and Kings Cross. Much of the policing and regulation of gay bathhouses was focused upon the older inner suburbs of Sydney. Those gay bathhouses that chose to locate in inner city areas of East Sydney and Darlinghurst (1976b, see also Dora 1980) or other inner city suburbs such as Haymarket drew a greater level of attention from both the local council and NSW police (1977b). For example The Barefoot Boy closed in 1977 following a series of inspections by council building inspectors following up on their own suspicions and formal complaints. The police and inspectors found evidence that the enterprise was operating as a gay bathhouse which was non-compliant with the land use consent granted for the premises (1977c). A 'Notice to Comply' was issued, legal proceedings to have the premises declared a disorderly house were initiated, resulting in the closure of the bathhouse (1977b).

Thus ironically, those gay bathhouses that were located in suburbs further out from the inner city drew little or no attention. Gay bathhouses survived through low visibility and limited policing in the 'orderly' suburbs, taking advantage of assumptions about the orderly suburbs to survive.

The majority of the attention of popular discourse during this time was focused upon the use of police to enforce criminal sanctions against homosexuality. An example of this attention can be seen in the closure campaigns that were initiated against a sex club called Club 80 from the late 1970s through to the early 1980s just prior to the decriminalization of homosexuality in 1984. The broad reportage and coverage of these events focus predominantly upon the police and its war on gay institutions (*The Star*, 1983a). As one newspaper reported:

> The vice squad seems to be going to great lengths to prosecute gay men. This is part of a systematic and very deliberate homophobic campaign. Inspector Shepard is 'against' any sort of homosexual activity and is committed to enforcing the anti-homosexual provisions of the Crimes Act. (*The Star*, 1983a)

No attention was paid to the role the local government and its building inspector played in collecting evidence, supporting police raids and taking legal action against the proprietors of Club 80, leading to its eventual closure as a Disorderly House (O'Malley 1978, O'Malley 1979, O'Malley 1983, Rendall 1983, Miller 1981, *The Star* 1983b, 6 May 1983a, 22 April 1983, also see Cusack and Prior 2010).

An analysis of the development applications, and building records within council for gay bathhouse and other sex industry premises during this period suggest that local council planning and building units and their building inspectors played a proactive and ever present role in working with police in securing evidence that could be used to close establishments (see 1976d, 1977a, 1977b, Kelly, 1975, O'Malley, 1978, O'Malley 1979, O'Malley 1983, Rendall 1983). Whilst homosexuality was illegal, gay bathhouses could not receive consent to operate as a premises used for homosexual activities. Consequently, planning powers could be, and were, used to shut down gay bathhouses for non-compliant use.

Planning powers were used during this time period to contribute to the regulation of deviant sexualities. Gay bathhouses were by definition disorderly. They breached the criminal law and planning powers. Proprietors utilized various strategies to survive, including pseudonymous applications and drawing upon assumptions about the orderly suburb to exist. As Cusack and Prior have noted, within the popular discourse of the time there was a general lack of awareness of council's involvement in the closure of sex industry premises (Cusack and Prior 2010).

Locating Homo(sexual)-sociality in the (Dis)orderly Inner-city

From the 1980s until the 1990s the legal regulation of homosexuality changed greatly. This was brought about through the implementation of anti-discrimination laws (1982e, 1982a) combined with the decriminalization of homosexuality (1984d, 1984c, 1984b, 1984a). This resulted in the dismantling of proactive policing techniques to exclude homosexuality from the city, including the cessation of 'blanket' and maintained surveillance of homosexual men and 'places frequented by [them]' (1982e: 359), and a cessation of the practice of keeping dossier files on homosexuals (1982e: 359). In place of these proactive campaigns police were only to approach premises habitually used by homosexuals on two grounds: firstly, that a 'substantial complaint had been received' (1982e: 379), and secondly, that such an approach would only go ahead if it would also have been applied to heterosexuals (1982e: 368). These changes reflected a broader liberalization of policing approaches to street sex work in the late 1970s (1979) and brothels in 1995 (1968b, Crofts 2003).

In late 1986 the proprietor of the Roman Baths chose to 'openly' submit a development application to the Council of the City of Sydney seeking permission to locate a 'Gay Recreation Center and Bathhouse', (1986b) within the visibly gay precinct that was emerging at the time around Oxford St, Darlinghurst. This was the first time that a gay bathhouse was brought openly into a local council's view. The council was required to formally consider the development application for the 'gay bathhouse and recreation center' (1986b) through its development approval processes.

In determining the impact of a development application, as is normal process, the local councils sought comment from members of the community and public authorities it thought may be affected by the application. These comments were primarily negative, but some letters of support were received. Letters of support were based upon specifically localized arguments that the social order in that particular area of the city had changed. Homosexuality was not disorderly, but rather part of the norm. Prior to the decriminalization of homosexuality, gay bathhouses could not refer to the large gay population to support development applications. For example in the case of Club 80 discussed earlier, just prior to the decriminalization of homosexuality the owners of Club 80, in attempting to fight a 'disorderly houses order', were precluded from arguing that the premises provided a service and fulfilled a need for the men of the emergent visible gay community within the Oxford Street area (Cusack and Prior 2010: 365). However, with decriminalization, supporters argued that the proposed 'gay bathhouse' would provide an important service and fulfilled a need for the gay men who used the then visible 'gay environ' that had established itself around Oxford Street (1986b) and consequently have a positive impact on the surrounding area. In the next section we argue that these arguments of gay territories have grown in strength, with arguments framed in terms of the needs and constitution of the local community.

The objections to the Roman Baths can be divided into two categories. The majority of these objections were informed by the perception that gay bathhouses were inherently disorderly – they were immoral, illegal and unnatural. Drawing on religion, particularly Christo-centric religions, objections described the proposed gay bathhouse as sinful and sacrilegious, arguing that the fact that the gay bathhouse caters to 'homosexual' men 'and prostitutes' made it intrinsically 'immoral'. Other objections made more secular value judgments, on the basis that the gay bathhouse was 'just revolting', 'vile', 'gross', and 'dirty'; and unacceptable because 'citizens of its surrounding community deem it to be unacceptable'(1986b).

The second category utilized the rhetoric of planning to object to gay bathhouses as inherently disorderly. The arguments against gay bathhouses focused on the supposedly immoral, criminal or unnaturalness of the gay bathhouse itself and alluded to the potential negative consequences on the surrounding area. Perceived adverse social, economic and environmental consequences included the way in which the gay bathhouse development would led to increased levels of crime, illegal parking, disorderly behavior, harm of local children and young people, reduced economic activity for nearby businesses, drug use, pedophilia, prostitution, violence, or decreased local property values. Whilst some of these objections were based purely on concerns about the practical impacts that the venue may have on such things as 'an already constrained customer parking capacity' (see 1986b) in the local area, the majority of these objections alluded to the belief that the inherent immorality, illegality and unnaturalness of the gay bathhouse would pollute and contaminate the local area. Despite decriminalization, homosexuality continued to be perceived as immoral and disorderly, and likely to attract immorality and illegality. In this sense, premises that offered services to gay men retained the historical taint of illegality and immorality, with a potential to pollute any area in which they were situated. As a local council planner and councillor explained; 'Residents and business owners believed that the premises would lure undesirable elements ... encourage violence ... [and] muggers and druggies to hang around' (Prior 2001: 17 January). The fear of illegal parking particularly captures the sense in which the gay bathhouse is perceived to be contagious. The assumption is that people who go to (or work in) gay bathhouses are immoral and thus likely to break other moral and legal codes, such as parking regulations. Objections also cited fears that the bathhouse's presence would have a negative economic impact on the Oxford St commercial zone – 'Business owners believed [the proposed bathhouse would] lead to a rise in the level of crime, lead to the development of a red light district and halve their property values' (Prior 2001: 17 January), thus undermining the viability of what are perceived as more orthodox commercial businesses, such as news agencies, pen shops, grocery stores and restaurants.

Building on these fears of contamination and contagion, the fear that a gay bathhouse could also 'cause the spread of AIDS' was raised within the objections (1986b). The emergence of AIDS (initially called Gay Related Immune Disease) within Sydney in the 1980s added a level of complexity to the tolerance and acceptance of gay sex industry premises within the city (*The Star* 1983c: 3), as a result of the emergence of 'environmental' aetiological theories which sought to find the origin for the disease within gay lifestyle and institutions, giving new life to long standing fears that homosexuality would pollute and contaminate the city (Monaghan 1987, Anderson 1981, see also Alexander 1996).

Whilst concerns about the inherent disorder of gay bathhouses were less explicitly stated, they continued to inform the development and application of highly restrictive planning principles. The underlying concern about disorder remained, but it was reframed in planning terms. For example, in the Roman Bath development application process council officers and general citizens argued in favor of highly restrictive requirements such as the unsuitability of the building structure, extensive sound insulation, limits on signage, excessive parking requirements and overly complicated ventilation systems. These requirements were used to make the proposed development economically unviable or impossible within the land constraints (Johnston 1986a). During the process this practice was brought to the attention of Councillor Craig Johnston, who attempted to expose such surreptitious actions through an open letter to the public:

> A sauna is a permissible use on Oxford Street ... the only relevant factors in the application therefore are any environmental impacts. These are assessed by the council as a matter of course, under planning law. ... It would be a travesty of the proper planning processes for environmental factors to be used as an excuse to refuse a development application for other than environmental reasons. (Johnston 1986b: 22 August)

The planning department recommended that the development application should be refused partly due to the large number of objections, but primarily because of the planning department's classification of the gay bathhouse as a brothel (1986d). At this time, the brothel was the only sex industry premises classification within the city's planning instruments, and brothels were illegal under the Disorderly House Act. This categorization of gay bathhouses as 'brothel' was based on evidence collected during a series of inspections of the Roman Baths existing establishment at Pitt Street in the City which suggested that sex took place in a series of 'private cubicles' (1986a, 1986c). The planning department thus relegated bathhouses to the only existing category for undesirable sex on premises activities – the brothel. As one bathhouse proprietor explained:

> The [Sydney city] council [through the 1980s and 1990s kept] on confusing gay [bathhouses] with brothels, and we [kept] on saying no – they're not the same ... I don't really know what we are in terms of council classifications, but we're not a brothel. Sex does go on, so certain rules and regulations should apply, but not the same ones that apply to brothels. (Prior 2000: 13 October)

Council aldermen ignored the Planning Department's recommendation and granted consent for the 'gay recreation center and bathhouse' with the exclusion of the 'cubicles'(1986d), so as to avoid any sense of discrimination against 'homosexuals' whilst at the same time as not being seen to approve what might be a brothel. As Alderman Morka explained:

It would be discriminatory to refuse the development – footballers have their clubs – but we wanted to guard against promoting [illicit sexual activities by deleting the cubicles which were seen to harbor] those sorts of activities. (Aubin 1987)

The aldermen had provided a partial consent for the gay bathhouse, acknowledging the role that the institution played in providing a place for semi-public homosociality within the emerging 'gay environ' within Oxford Street Sydney. In denying the cubicles the approval had explicitly not recognized or understood the sexual element of the institution. As Alderman Johnston noted: 'The Roman Bath approval was a significant turning point for [the council of the City of Sydney] ... It wasn't only about overcoming prejudice, it was about understanding a new world' (Prior 2000: 17 August).

The legalization of homosexuality started a shift in discourse away from the inherent disorder of gay bathhouses to a rhetoric framed in planning concerns. However, these concerns about disorder continued to underlie and inform the construction and application of planning provisions. The legality of homosexuality and the illegality of brothels resulted in approval of the *social* aspect of the club, but not of its *sexual* aspect.

Placing Homosexuality in the (Dis)orderly Inner-city and the Decline of Pristine Suburbia

It was not until the 1990s that the first gay bathhouse received planning approval based on both its social and sexual function. The development application process demonstrated an increasing reliance upon a rhetoric of planning by both objectors and supporters of the gay bathhouse. The process resulted in a debate about the order of the city, and whether or not gay bathhouses were a part of this order.

The proprietors of the Bodyline Spa and Sauna submitted two development applications to SSCC for a gay bathhouse called Bodyline Spa and Sauna: the first in 1992, to establish the bathhouse in the city, and the second for its relocation in 1996 (1992c, 1996a). Bodyline Spa and Sauna was the first new bathhouse to be established within the city since the relocation of the Roman Baths in 1986.

Like the Roman Baths development application process, there were many more letters of objection than letters of support. Some objectors continued to frame their concerns in terms of the inherently disorderly nature of gay bathhouses and homosexuality. This was supported by an overtly moralistic protest campaign that operated outside of the formal planning process through letter drops and community meetings to rally more objectors. For example, one flyer for a rally meeting in the first Bodyline application read:

LIFELine to BECOME DeathLine? At 58a Flinders Do WE WANT IN OUR AREA: – POOFTERS, FAGGOTS, HOMOS, QUEERS, DRUGS, SEX, NEEDLES, NOISE, AIDS, AND HIV. LETS TELL OUR COUNCIL NO. (1991a)

In the Bodyline Spa and Sauna planning processes there were fewer objections received than in the Roman Bathhouse process that spoke solely of the inherent immorality, illegality and unnaturalness of the gay bathhouse. However, there were an increased number of objections that sought to couch such beliefs in their concern for the impacts that were perceived to result from the bathhouse. This shift reflected the fact that objections in planning processes against gay bathhouses (as with other sex industry premises) were far more likely to succeed if they framed their arguments in the planning vocabulary of impacts. The Land and Environment Court (LEC) has been clear that morality is not relevant to planning decisions. As a consequence, objectors have frequently retained their belief as to the inherently disorderly nature of gay bathhouses, but have attempted to shift to the rhetoric of planning disorder to support this. Thus, in making these arguments several objectors explicitly sought to claim that their underlying intentions were utilitarian rather than moral. For example one objector went as far as to clarify that their objection was 'not tied to a moral issue, but to practical concerns about zoning and property values, noise and crime' (1991b). Another objector who argued against the gay bathhouse used a rhetoric about its tendency to promote crime and drugs in the area, and indicated that their concerns were for 'public nuisance, not from some angle of upholding morality' (1992c). These shifts in rhetoric, strategies and style of objections indicate that individuals and organizations were aware of the utility of their specific argumentative modes for affecting planning processes.

The council rejected both applications by the proprietor of the Bathhouse, resulting in appeals to the Land and Environment Court. In the first case in 1992, a central issue was whether or not a bathhouse was a brothel. This was because brothels could not operate legally until reforms to the Disorderly Houses Act (1995). The council argued that the Bathhouse could not be approved because it enabled sexual activity to occur in a way that was an 'outrage to public decency' and was thus a 'disorderly house'(1992b). The Land and Environment Court held that gay bathhouses were not brothels:

> The sexual acts which occur on the premises [were] between consenting adult males. Such acts do not constitute criminal offences. They take place in the privacy of the cubicles with locked doors. They are not public exhibitions or performances, but rather consensual private sexual activity ... In the circumstances it may be argued that an outrage to public decency could not be established. (1992b: 436)

This meant that the council could not refuse a bathhouse on the grounds that it was a disorderly house, that is, a brothel. This was the first time in planning law that a distinction was made between brothels and bathhouses, rather than placing them in the single category of disorderly houses.

As a result, the primary issue in both Land and Environment Court cases was whether or not the bathhouse would have a positive or detrimental impact upon the amenity of the locality. The Bodyline Spa and Sauna received many more community objections than the similar Roman Baths application, primarily because it was not to be located in the main commercial strip of Oxford Street as the Roman Baths had been, but in locations close to mixed residential zones. As a result of this close proximity to residential usages we saw the emergence of a complex mix of narratives about neighborhood decline that had various temporal and spatial dimensions. These narratives of decline occurred in their most intense state in the attempts to relocate Bodyline Spa and Sauna to little Taylor Street – a small side street with uses which transitioned from a commercial strip at one end through to a primarily residential area. Intermingled with this notion of neighborhood decline was the notion of the broader breakdown of 'community' of the past which was manifest through stories of increased social conflict; the decline of common values and goals, with shared morality and codes of behavior; and a decline in social order, including cooperation.

These narratives drew a picture of a once 'pristine' residential neighborhood, through remembered images and nostalgic yearnings for times gone, that was being increasingly besieged and polluted by 'the worst aspects of city life' (1992a). Whilst the gay bathhouse was the focus of the objections, it was identified as only the most recent addition to the many existing sources of pollution that exist in the 'messy' adjoining commercial strip and public thoroughfare which generated illegal parking, drug use, prostitution, and violence in the vicinity. The ability to save this 'residential neighborhood' was based on an urgent need to shore up the increasingly porous and precarious nature of its boundary by staving off any further polluting sources, such as the gay bathhouse, from establishing within or near its borders, sources which would make the neighborhood 'dirtier' (Prior 2001: 18 January). These narratives of adverse impact and decline of the neighborhood were supported by the assertion that the proposed gay bathhouse and its patrons were inherently polluting. Patrons were commonly described as dangerous, immoral, undesirable, and lurking. A broad cross section of the objections argued that the patrons would engage in anti-social behavior, such as urination and vomiting as they entered or left the premises and 'that they would attract gay bashers to the area' (Prior 2001: 18 January). This demonstrates the association of gay bathhouses with breaches of order – whether as victims or perpetrators; a bathhouse was criminogenic and would result in disorder. As with the earlier Roman Bath application, some went as far as to proclaim that the gay bathhouse would attract persons with a criminal record, and would increase crime in the area, affecting both commercial and residential properties. As one bathhouse proprietor recalled:

> There is a perception that the people who used bathhouses are dangerous – criminals, drunks or disturbed; that encounter with them will lead to the corruption of local residents and children in particular, that they can taint local communities. The irony is that many of the people who use bathhouses are local people. (Prior 2000: 12 October)

These narratives of decline were revived and debated in the Land and Environment Court cases. Whilst there was some attempt to refer to statistical data, the evidence presented was largely anecdotal. For example, crime statistics indicated merely that a greater proportion of certain crimes had occurred in the area but did not link them to the gay bathhouse. In both cases no cause-and-effect relationship could be conclusively proven and that, moreover, in an area as dense and diverse as Darlinghurst and Surrey Hills, it would be nearly impossible to attribute a specific cause to any given effect. As a consequence the Land and Environment Court relied upon the opinions of planners, police, and local residents about the potential impact of the bathhouse.

In both cases, the Land and Environment Court paid serious attention to the proposed location of the Bathhouse. In the first case, the Court noted that the Local Environmental Plan required consideration of the impact of the development on 'residents', but did not define who a 'resident' was. As a consequence, the Court accepted that 'residents' did not just come from the people who lived in the street of the proposed development, but embraced those living in reasonable proximity to the proposal, which included the substantive gay community of 18,000–30,000 gay men known to live in the area (1992b: 437–8). Based on this different notion of resident, it was successfully argued that Bodyline Spa and Sauna was an important 'social' and 'sexual' amenity for the 'significant' 'gay resident community' in Darlinghurst given that it provided safe opportunities for socializing out of the reach of gay bashers and an environment for the practice of and education about safe sex. As an expert witness from the AIDS Council of NSW noted, gay bathhouses had become key sites for the dissemination of information on safe sex practices. The final judgment asserted that the gay bathhouse was not only important, but 'crucial for the establishment and maintenance of the gay community and [that it fulfilled] a legitimate social function' (1992b: 437–8).

Accordingly, the Court accepted a different notion of community order in that specific locale. In the terms of Mary Douglas, the conceptual order had changed, so that gay bathhouses were no longer regarded as inherently disorderly, but instead, were integral to the order of the community. Far from generating crime, ill health and immorality, gay bathhouses provided an essential service and promoted health and order. The Court thus reframed the narrative of decline and replaced it with the development of a vibrant, alternative community.

In the second Bodyline case, the issue of community was again considered by the Land and Environment Court (1997a). In this case it was argued that Bodyline would contribute to the decline of the neighborhood. The Land and Environment Court rejected this argument stating:

> Taylor Street is *not a pristine, untainted residential area*. The majority of the street is occupied as residences, but there is considerable commercial activity at the Flinders end where the site is located. Furthermore, *the street is located within* ... the Oxford Street, Flinders Street and South Dowling Street area which is notable for its venues for entertainment of the gay and lesbian community. ... A factor which must also be taken in the context of public interest is that the site is intended to provide a safe sex venue. The applicant asserts, and I accept ... that it is committed to disseminating information about the spread of HIV-AIDS ... Looking at it from a planning perspective I see no reason why development consent should be refused in the public interest. (1997a: 14–15)

This assertion by the Court was locationally specific, noting that the gay and lesbian community was prevalent in that particular area. An interesting subtext is the note that this was not a 'pristine, untainted residential area'. The Court thus retained the oppositional notions between suburbs and the disorderly city, importing notions of the suburbs as a place of domesticity where presumably gay bathhouses would not be permitted.

In response to these cases, the City of Sydney developed standards specific to bathhouses and other sex on premises venues (1993). Planners visited sex industry premises and reviewed formal planning documentation (2000: 4 October). Rather than placing all sex on premises venues into the same category, the council accepted the need to create a distinct classification for venues that were based on membership and included consensual sex. Both South Sydney City Council and the City of Sydney consequently adopted the category of 'sex on premises venue' which included establishments such as gay [bathhouses], backrooms, SM clubs and swingers clubs which were based on consensual sexual acts, and differentiated from brothels where the sexual acts were contractual and involved sex workers (2000: 4 October).

The development process demonstrated a debate about the order of the environment, and whether homosexuality and gay bathhouses were inherently disorderly or had a place within the community. By approving the Bathhouse for its social *and* sexual function, the Land and Environment Court accorded a place to bathhouses within the community. This was then taken up by the City of Sydney, developing a category in planning that was specific to bathhouses. The LEC cases placed much emphasis on *place*, drawing upon notions of the older, disorderly city and asserting the greater presence of gays and lesbians in the area.

Protecting Suburbia from Disorderly (Bath)houses and the Assumed Planning (Dis)order

In this section we consider the development applications for a gay bathhouse to Parramatta City Council in 1999 and again in 2004. Aarows Sauna (often called Arrows) was proposed in one of Sydney's western suburbs – Rydalmere – far from the 'visibly gay' environs of Darlinghurst and Surrey Hills (Williamson 1999, see also Prior 2000: 14 December, 2004).

As a consequence of amendments to the Disorderly Houses Act (NSW) in 1995, councils were required to regulate sex industry premises through their plan making powers, governed by the Environmental Planning and Assessment Act 1979 (NSW) (Crofts 2006: 87, Ratcliff 1999: 152–3). Like the majority of councils in New South Wales, Parramatta City Council had not developed planning policies that were specific to gay bathhouses; instead, all sex services premises were regulated under the catch-all category of 'brothel'. Parramatta City Council restricted all 'brothels' to industrial areas. Clause 24 of the *Parramatta Local Environmental Plan 2001* further limits the areas within the industrial zones where brothels are permissible, by not allowing brothels where they are located within 200 meters of residences or land zoned residential; or near or within view of a range of sensitive uses such as schools, churches, community facilities, open space or other places frequented by children; or within 50 meters of various public transport facilities.

The 1999 and 2004 development applications by Aarrows complied with the planning instruments for placement of sex industry premises developed by Parramatta City Council (1997b). The bathhouse was to be located in existing warehouse style buildings in an industrial estate to the east of Rydalmere station. They complied with anti-cluster planning guidelines in that they were not located in proximity of another sex industry premises, nor were they in proximity of any sensitive land use such as a school, church, etc.

The development applications resulted in a barrage of objections based on the perceived inherent 'immorality' or 'danger' of the premises and its ability to pollute the local area and vulnerable residents. Within these objections some reiterated the distinction between the 'dirty' urban and the 'pristine' suburbia, presenting the image of suburban communities, besieged (from the outside) by sex industry premises and deviant sexualities (Prior 2000: 14 December). In the 1999 development application process some argued that the industrial estate itself was an inappropriate location for the proposed premises given that it would have potential adverse impacts on a nearby 'sheltered workshop' – a place that provides day work for people living with a disability (Prior 2000: 14 December). The objectors argued that the sheltered workshop represented a 'sensitive use'.

In contrast to the above objections, supportive discourses within these development applications sought to argue that the placement of the premise in Rydalmere was essential to cater for those members of Sydney's queer communities that lived in outer western Sydney. It was argued that the bathhouse would 'provide a safe, secure site for the gay male rate-payers of Parramatta to meet and socialize ...' and 'reduce public nuisance to rate-payers of Parramatta of gay men meeting in parks and other public places by the provision of a clean, safe, comfortable alternative site in which gay men can meet and socialize' (Williamson 1999). These arguments thus supported the provision of a gay bathhouse with order, with a reduction of nuisance.

The Aarrows Bathhouse applications proffered an opportunity for debate about what constituted Sydney's 'gay community' and the appropriate location of institutions to service it (Hodge 1995, David McInnes 2001). As one writer on the subject proposed: There are a variety of 'gay communities' and Oxford Street (the main street passing through the environs of Darlinghurst), whilst the most public and publicized of these, is not the only one to promote a strong sense of identity (Carrigan 1988: 35). The Aarrows Bathhouse thus shifted the argument away from a gay territory or ghetto in the inner city, and asserted the presence of homosexuality in the pristine suburbs.

The 1999 application was refused by the Council on the grounds that the existing premises were unsuitable due to a lack of parking places. The Council also asserted that the development was not in the interest of the public. This decision was not appealed. However, the 2004 application was later approved on the basis that the existing premises were suitable for the proposed use, both in terms of built form and in terms of providing 23 car spaces for both employees and visitors (2004). Reflecting the shift towards the assessment of sex industry premises applications on the basis of numerical compliance with relevant planning instruments, the final determination was presented in a formulaic fashion with little if any emotive language (2004). The approval stated that the consent was not for a brothel, nor for prostitution, but it noted that consensual sex would take place within the premises and that the AIDS Council of NSW was to be allowed to provide regular updates of safe sex information and posters were to be placed on the walls throughout the premises (2004). The period of consent was limited to five years (2004). This practice of limited timeframes for consent has become a common practice for sex industry premises within many councils in Sydney including the City of Sydney (2001a, 2001b, 2002, 2009, 2003). As a consequence, sex-on-premises venues like gay bathhouses receive only temporary and contingent approval. The 2004 development consent for Aarows in Rydalmere represented the first gay bathhouse to be approved on the basis of its sexual use, without the necessity of an appeal to the LEC.

The Aarows application provides an insight into the development of complex and elaborate planning instruments which prescribe restrictive zoning, numerical distances between sex industry premises 'sensitive' uses, and notification requirements. The rationale informing the instruments is based on a history of discourses which have brought to the fore a belief that sex industry premises are in some way inherently disorderly and polluting. In the absence of complete exclusion, planning instruments aim to provide a mechanism to protect the community from the complex and diffuse array of presumed polluting effects of disorderly sexualities such as increased levels of crime, illegal parking, disorderly behavior, harm to local children and young people, reduced economic activity for nearby businesses, drug use, pedophilia, prostitution, violence, or decreased local property values. Planning instruments are an integral part of the planned city which seems to promise safety, unhindered commerce, prosperity and unproblematic connections by managing the dirty and dangerous to which we are exposed in the gregarious proximity of the urban space. Planning processes and instruments not only specialize these threats but also seek to contain the filthy and disgusting, by guarding against the violation of bodily and social boundaries, and in so doing divide the city into zones of purity and zones of danger. Sex industry premises, like the polluting garbage to which they are so often compared, if left uncontained by planning instruments, are liable to be placed anywhere. Through planning instruments, zones of purity, associated with the figure of a child and other vulnerable persons and places, can be sealed off.

A key consequence of the development of such formulaic planning instruments within planning law and council policy is the loss of need for express reasoning and justification within development application processes to support perceived adverse secondary and cumulative impacts stemming from social contamination beliefs. These contamination beliefs remain largely unsubstantiated by any evidence, despite a broad range of international research that has sought to establish causal-links between sex industry premises and perceived adverse 'secondary effects' such as crime and loss of property values associated with such premises and their concentration (see for example Papayanis 2000). Moreover, there has been a lack of formal complaints against many well established gay bathhouses that have operated within highly pedestrianized and populated areas of Sydney. For example, the recent determination of the continuation of the use of Sydney City Steam in Sussex Street, Sydney noted that 'the use has been established since 2001 without formal complaint to council' (2009). Similarly a review of the council records of Ken's, located in the southern Sydney suburb of Kensington since 1972, has no record of a formal complaint (see e.g., 1972b, 1973b, 1973a, 1975a, 1975b, 1982b, 1982c, 1982d).

The reification into planning law and policy has meant that adverse arguments surrounding the perceived polluting effects of sex industry premises remain tacit in planning documents at the same time as being automatically operationalized within the planning process. As one local planner astutely pointed out: '[these new planning laws and guidelines] helped to partially conceal a broad range of negative beliefs that had existed for [decades] around the placement of sex industry premises within the city' (Prior 2007: 7 October).

The new planning laws and instruments associated with the restrictive placement of sex industry premises that emerged in the late 1990s and early 2000s provide a spatial metaphor for safety and protection, against a use that is perceived by the heteronormative majority to be polluting, but which unfortunately can no longer be expunged from the city. The fact that their locations are mapped and controlled offers the fantasy of the city whose dangers can be made entirely legible and controllable, and are not liable to pop up anywhere. A planned city that is divided up through zoning and regulation offers the promise that the city can be separated into zones of purity and zones of danger. In this way the mapping and zoning of sex industry premises through planning laws and policy locates the threat and offers the fantasy that their mobility can be contained, and the zones of purity, associated with the figure of the vulnerable child and residential neighborhood, can be sealed off. The underlying fantasy is that land-use planning through its processes of segregation and separation can foster social interactions and reduce the motivations and opportunities for antisocial, deviant or other undesirable behaviors (Bannister et al. 2006: 926, Hubbard 2004a).

Concluding Remarks

By concentrating on an analysis of a series of successive development application processes for gay bathhouses in Sydney over a period of a half century, this chapter has contributed to a developed understanding of the role that urban planning plays in the governance of sex industry premises. Our focus on gay bathhouses provides an alternative viewpoint to the existing research which focuses largely on sex shops/restricted premises (e.g., Papayanis 2000) and brothels (e.g., Crofts 2006, Ratcliff 1999). The period of the study extends far beyond that of other existing research in the field which is focused predominantly on the 1990s (see for example Papayanis 2000, Kerkin 2004, Crofts 2006, Ratcliff 1999).

Supporting the established research into sex industry premises, our analysis provides insight into how sex industry establishments, are perceived as contributing to or manifesting the disorder of cities (see for example Papayanis 2000, Kerkin 2004, Crofts 2006). Moving beyond the established research, the analysis illuminates emergent discourses which outline the ways in which sex industry premises, in particular gay bathhouses, may positively contribute to urban ordering. Our research revealed how these assumed (dis)ordering effects were inextricably connected with assumed sexual geographies within the city, such as: the historic perception of suburbia as a heteronormative utopia that is increasingly subject to threat; processes of visible gay territorialization within the inner-city; and recent attempts to posit the need for a greater distribution of institutions throughout the city to cater for the variety of queer communities beyond the environs of Darlinghurst.

The broader historical context of the study allowed us to identify the shifting role that planning, as one technique of urban governance, plays in imposing and regulating order within cities. The analysis reveals how historically, homosexuality and gay bathhouses were explicitly associated with disorder – offending against sexual mores, morality, and the law. Like other forms of sex industry premises gay bathhouses were placed in the same catch all category as other undesirable sexualities by law and planning, i.e. disorderly houses. The 1960s and 1970s pseudonym development applications revealed how planning officials contributed to policing efforts to expel these disorderly (bath)houses from the city, and conversely how during this period proprietors of gay bathhouses utilized various strategies that took advantage of the cities assumed sexual geography to operate clandestinely in suburbia.

Our analysis revealed the rapid shift to planning in the later twentieth century, accompanied by a shift in rhetoric away from gay bathhouses as offending against moral and legal order, to offending against planning order. The gay bathhouse development applications in the 1980s and 1990s and its acceptance into the planned city based firstly on its social functions, then later in terms of its sexual function, provides insight into the crossover point in the shift of sex industry premise from criminal legal order to planning order. This shift had a unique spatial dimension, given that criminal law operates at the macro-level of the state, and planning order operates at the more micro-level of local government areas and environs within them. Through the development applications in the 1990s and 2000s we see the consequences of this shift to local planning order as the means of regulating sex industry premises within Sydney's urban context. This resulted in distinctly different approaches to planning applications for gay bathhouses in the City of Sydney and Parramatta City Council in Sydney's west. In South Sydney City Council consent was driven by arguments that the order of particular inner city environs had changed as a result of processes of gay territorialization, and gay bathhouses contributed to their order. In contrast, in Parramatta City Council, placement within an industrial estate was driven by a need to protect suburbia against a use that continues to be perceived by many to be disorderly, with grudging consent granted based on the understanding that the use can no longer be expunged from the local area but must be located and restricted within. Our analysis demonstrated the ways in which the shift towards planning order in recent decades has incorporated assumptions about the disorder of sex industry premises into planning instruments without debate.

PART IV
Reflections and Conclusions

Chapter 12
Reflections on Classic Articles on Planning and LGBT Communities

Sy Adler, Johanna Brenner, Michael Frisch, Larry Knopp and Mickey Lauria

The following chapter is divided into sections that provide commentary on three classic articles that laid the groundwork for much of our current understanding of the way that queer communities have evolved in cities and the role of planning in this process. Each sub-section begins with a brief editorial summary of the relevant article, followed by commentary from the authors of that article. The editor asked each of the authors to reflect on the original context in which they wrote these articles, the reactions of their peers to this ground-breaking work, and whether they think the climate for such research has improved in the intervening time frame.

The earlier articles provide seminal contributions and established the theoretical groundwork for much of the subsequent planning applications. These articles are very well cited in the literature which marks them as foundational work in the field of LGBT studies and planning. The third article broke new ground in the field of planning theory. The publication of Frisch's article in the *Journal of Planning Education and Research* represents one of the earliest treatments of LGBT issues in a major planning journal (Ann Forsyth's literature review in the *Journal of Planning Literature* was published just before Frisch's article. An updated version of this article appears in this volume as Chapter 2).

The intent of including these commentaries in this volume is to re-connect with some of the pioneers in the field of planning and LGBT communities and give them voice in answering the editorial questions about how the research and practice climate has changed. The resulting short essays provide a rich overview of the changing context of planning and queer communities. They also help to set the stage for the concluding chapter in which the editor synthesizes the various contributions and provides a direction for where and how to reframe the heteronormative nature of planning.

Editor

****

Reflections on "Toward an Analysis of the Role of Gay Communities in the Urban Renaissance"[1] by Larry Knopp and Mickey Lauria

The field of planning has lagged behind other social sciences where there is a rich literature on LGBT issues. This classic article by Mickey Lauria and Larry Knopp provided a "social constructionist" framework for analyzing the role of gay communities in the urban renaissance and is still widely cited in a broad spectrum of journals. This piece set the stage for a great deal of subsequent work by urban planners seeking to make sense of the ways that LGBT people and particularly gay men participated in urban redevelopment. The authors suggested that the marked neglect of gay urban communities may have been due to "a certain squeamishness regarding sexual issues" (152) among planners and academics working in this area. Furthermore, they argued that the involvement of gay communities in urban redevelopment must be understood in terms of the sexist social structure that serves to oppress the gay-identified minority. They highlighted the vital role of gay neighborhoods as a territorial basis for political mobilization, and a locus for neighborhood capital formation (gentrification) that is critical in establishing this political power base.

Editor

****

Much has changed in the academic, intellectual, political, economic, policy, and cultural environments since this article was first conceived and written in the early 1980s. And much has not. Gentrification, which as a complex class and cultural phenomenon in many ways inspired our article, has fallen somewhat out of fashion as a subject of academic inquiry. Yet it has accelerated and broadened its reach in the "real world", with dramatic and contradictory consequences for a variety of populations, including during periods of significant recession. Sexuality and space studies, meanwhile, have developed as a surprisingly robust and arguably much less marginalized subfield within several of the social sciences and humanities, most notably Geography, Urban Studies, LGBT Studies, and Queer Studies. Theoretical synergies and tensions with feminisims, critical theories of race and racism, queer theory, postmodernism, and poststructuralism (among others) have infused and catalyzed this development. At the same time, the politics of sex and sexuality have become even more central to the North American (and to a degree global) culture wars, with certain segments of sexual minority populations having gained new visibility, protections from discrimination, and a "place at the table" in policy-making circles. Middle class, largely (but not exclusively) white gays and lesbians in particular now hold positions of influence in many North American

---

1   M. Lauria and L. Knopp. 1985. Toward an analysis of the role of gay communities in the urban renaissance. *Urban Geography*, 6, 152–69.

cities' and regions' Planning Commissions, elected Councils, advisory bodies, and administrative infrastructures.

By contrast, and despite a large network of gay, lesbian, bisexual, transgendered, and queer-identified professional planners (which existed, albeit in a more closeted and informal way, even back when we wrote the original article), planning-specific journals and theory still feature very little scholarship, or even simple empirical investigations, of sexuality and sexual minority issues. Geography, Urban Studies, LGBT Studies, and Queer Studies, meanwhile, engage with planning theory and practice only peripherally, and usually in the context of fairly abstract discussions of space and spatiality. What accounts for this?

As geographers who have worked with (in Larry's case) or in (in Mickey's case) the planning field for most if not all of our careers, we think we may be in a position to at least do some educated speculation about this question. When we first conceived "Toward an Analysis of the Role of Gay Communities in the Urban Renaissance", the only previously available academic work that addressed the roles of sexual minority populations and politics in urbanization were by the sociologist Manuel Castells, two of his students, and a few scattered geographers who had presented at conferences but not published their work. A larger group of social scientists and humanists, concerned with broader but related issues such as urbanization (including gentrification), sexuality (especially sexual identity constructions), general social theory (including organizational theory and attempts to reconcile structural vs. behavioral perspectives), and methods in social science, of course also informed our project. But we were largely on our own in developing a theoretical and methodological framework appropriate to investigating the particular intersections of economic, political, cultural, and historical events that at the time we called "the role of gay communities in the urban renaissance".

While we are proud of what we produced, it was, like all scholarship, a product of a particular agenda at a particular time and place, which was in turn situated within a particular set of social and spatial hierarchies. In that time and place, our intervention was inescapably (and intentionally) political as well as intellectual, and involved negotiating a set of cultural and political parameters that were at the local scale contingently supportive, but at higher spatial scales much more reactionary. In short, it was a risky paper to write. Mickey had been solicited by a senior colleague involved with *Urban Geography* to contribute an article to a special issue on "the urban renaissance", and he in turn proposed collaborating with Larry (a second year graduate student at the time) on a topic about which Larry was passionate and that he was developing for his dissertation. This speaks to the important role of mentoring, patronage, and networking in shaping intellectual trajectories and academic cultures. Couching our project in terms of fashionable theoretical and empirical preoccupations, while honest in terms of how we had each been socialized within academia at the time, was also very strategic. Clearly the article opened up a space for subsequent work on the intersections between urban processes and the politics of sexuality. But in retrospect it may well also have closed doors (or at least made them more difficult to open), as it elided politically troubling questions regarding the intersections between class and sexual identities (while implicitly celebrating "gay gentrification" as liberatory), mis-characterized gentrification as a "male dominated" phenomenon, and perpetuated the invisibility of lesbians in urban space by denying any territorial agency on their parts and ignoring the issue of access to capital as gendered.

Fortunately, we were roundly criticized for all of these mistakes, which helped open up some of the spaces our work foreclosed. The catalyzing force of critical social theories in related fields has also helped. However, in the world of planning it may be that similar dynamics of privilege, strategic positioning, patronage, mentoring, and internal critique around these kinds of issues just have never taken place (or have manifested themselves differently). It may also be that the world of planning theory, for all its cultural sensitivities and engagements with political economy, is more constrained by its ties to the world of planning *practice* and the politics of local government, which perhaps cannot so easily accommodate either abstract critical theory or on the ground interventions in cultural politics.

"Toward an Analysis of the Role of Gay Communities in the Urban Renaissance", along with related work, reflected a particular set of opportunities and constraints, at a particular point in time, within certain corners of academia and professional practice. The article opened up new areas of inquiry for some and closed areas for others. In the field of planning, it may just not have been as influential as elsewhere, due to a set of discipline-specific material and other circumstances that simply offered less room for professional and political innovations of this sort. Let's hope that this changes soon.

Revisiting "Gender and Space: Lesbians and Gay Men in the City"[2] by Sy Adler and Johanna Brenner

Although this article by Adler and Brenner was published in 1992, it continues to hold up well with impressive citation counts spread more or less evenly across the past two decades. This research added a more nuanced perspective on the differences between gay men and lesbians and their approaches to the city. The article was, in part, a response to the earlier contention by Castells (1983) that the gay neighborhoods are defined by men's need to dominate space whereas lesbian communities are defined by the tendency of women to form bonds based on social networks that are not concentrated in distinct spatial areas. Adler and Brenner appropriately critiqued this narrow understanding of gender and space, and argued that lesbian spaces clearly exist, but are rendered less visible by several factors related to the disadvantaged social position of lesbians as women in the city. Furthermore, their results indicated that residential decisions made by lesbians were directly related to their more restricted access to capital, their

---

2 S. Adler and J. Brenner. 1992. Gender and space: Lesbians and gay men in the city. *International Journal of Urban and Regional Research*, 16, 24–34.

greater likelihood of being responsible for rearing children, and their greater vulnerability to male physical and sexual violence.

Editor

****

Manuel Castells' *The City and the Grassroots* (1983) was a key text in a course Sy was teaching in the mid-1980s about urban social and political movements. Castells' observations about lesbians and space in the chapter about the San Francisco gay community were at odds with Sy's anecdotal knowledge of the lesbian situation in Portland. He proposed to faculty colleague Johanna Brenner that they jointly research whether or not there was a spatial concentration of lesbians in Portland. Johanna, who was Director of Portland State University's Women's Studies program and very actively involved with women's issues and organizations in the city, agreed that there was, indeed, a spatially concentrated lesbian community.

We determined to replicate the methods used by Castells as closely as possible. Taking advantage of Johanna's connections in the lesbian community, we secured addresses of members of Portland's two main lesbian organizations, as well as access to key informants. Looking back at the end of two decades of substantial gains for gay rights, it is stunning to recall the level of fear that gripped the lesbian community at the time of our research. Although Portland was a magnet for lesbians, violent attacks on gays and lesbians had been increasing at the time of our research, while Oregon had a growing religious right movement that during the 1990s would place three anti-gay measures on the ballot. (These were all narrowly defeated.) The two organizations were very interested in our research and wanted to support it. However, they felt they could not allow any outsider to look at, or handle, their mailing lists. We solved this problem when one of their members volunteered to go through the mailing lists and assign the addresses to census tracts. We also promised that in any publication of our results, we would neither reveal the city in which the research was done, nor the location of any concentration of lesbians we identified. We accepted those conditions and completed the research and writing on that basis.

We sent our manuscript to a Geography journal that had previously published articles related to our topic. The editors were interested in publishing it, however, they wanted maps containing identifying information about the places we discussed. We told them about the agreement we made to get the address data, and we argued that maps were unnecessary in assessing the validity of our findings. Moreover, we tried to impress upon the editors the reasonableness of this request, given the real possibility that information about the actual neighborhoods where lesbians lived could heighten their vulnerability to attack. They were quite unmoved. We then sent the piece to *International Journal of Urban and Regional Research* in part because we thought the editors wouldn't be as troubled by the absence of specific place identifiers, which apparently were considered central to defining the boundaries of geography as a discipline.

Our faculty colleagues were supportive of the research. We were invited to speak about it at seminars and in classes while we were doing the empirical work, and following publication. We were fortunate to have access to graduate student assistance for data gathering, entry and analysis. The project was a very rewarding one for both of us; we're very pleased that the paper made a contribution to what's become a rich and extensive literature.

Two decades of gay rights mobilization have substantially altered the social, political, and cultural landscape of the United States. At the same time, economic restructuring and the rise of the "post-industrial city" have profoundly shifted the urban context of lesbian, gay, bisexual, and transgendered people's lives. In the years since "Gender and Space" was first published, the academic literature on gender differences in geospatial patterns has not only expanded but also been complicated by greater attention to differences of class, race/ethnicity, and gender identity. The processes of exclusion/inclusion produced by these differences in the creation and maintenance of gay urban space have been highlighted.

In light of the profound changes in politics and the urban landscape as well as in the academic literature, were we to undertake this study again, we would probably ask different questions. We would be particularly interested in the relationship of gentrification to the shifting patterns of lesbian residence and commercial spaces. The lesbian neighborhood that we originally identified has been intensely gentrified leading to skyrocketing single-family home prices, as well as residential and commercial rents. The commercial district has also been transformed and lost a good part of its counter-cultural character, which had previously, we argued, offered a more hospitable location for lesbians than other parts of the city. Our impression is that many lesbian households have left the area to become the first wave of gentrifiers in what had been an increasingly impoverished Black working-class community in another part of the city.

It would be especially interesting to tease out the role played in lesbian residential movement by the city's urban redevelopment policies that encourage homeownership and business start-ups in that area of the city. Although one could say that there may be a new area of concentration, at least for lesbian residence, it also appears that gay men and lesbian households are more dispersed than previously and, in particular, affluent lesbians and gay men have gained access to some of the city's wealthiest neighborhoods. In addition to mapping these class effects, we would be interested in learning more about generational differences as well as life course effects on how lesbians utilize urban space. Several studies have shown a tendency for lesbian public sociality to integrate (although certainly not easily) into commercial districts dominated by gay men. This movement appears, at least in some instances, to reflect generational differences, and particularly, changing attitudes toward the value of separate women-only spaces. However, it may also be the case that in a relatively gay-friendly city such as Portland, changes over the life course may reduce lesbians' need for or interest in the kinds of commercialized "scene spaces" such as pubs, cafes, and clubs that historically were so crucial to lesbian identity and community.

The Heterosexist Project of Planning[3] Revisited by Michael Frisch

This third article by Michael Frisch was published in 2002 and was the first article, with an explicitly queer agenda, to be accepted by the Journal of Planning Education and Research, *the scholarly publication of the North American Association of Collegiate Schools of Planning. This article made a critical argument about the heterosexist nature of planning as a field and a profession. Frisch traced the origin of the planner's desire for ordering urban spaces to Patrick Geddes and Lewis Mumford who linked homosexuality to perversion, death, and disorder. He then examined the ways in which a concern for orderly urban land use often had led to zoning and formal planning documents that explicitly excluded individuals and families who fell outside the heterosexual norm. As a direct result he found that the dark side of urban planning is that it has often reinforced heterosexuality at the expense of non-normative citizens.*

Editor

****

Much has happened on this topic since this paper was written. In this piece I describe the genesis of the paper and some areas that have changed in the last decade. I conclude this introduction by raising new questions to be answered about the relationship of planning to sexual and gender minorities.

"Planning as a Heterosexist Project" was written in the late 1990s and came out of a project for a gender and planning class at Rutgers taught by Lisa Servon. Applying feminist method meant to me that I needed to explore a topic from experience. The core of the article reflects my experience in classes where it was clear that I, as a gay male, was not represented in the community analysis of planners. Worse, I realized that the "liberal" conception of twentieth century urban planning created tools of oppression. Planning exists to support the heterosexual twentieth century suburban world – the theme of a book I am currently working on. When putting the argument together I thought I would have to use only postmodern methods of revealing structured silences of important texts. Yet, upon re-reading favorite authors such as Geddes, Jacobs, and Mumford, I found instance after instance of explicit treatment of planning processes and homosexuality.

The pattern of argumentation from planning reformers and observers was intensely familiar. As an activist with ACT UP-New York in the late 1980s and early 1990s, we worked together to unpack arguments about homosexuality, AIDS

---

3   M. Frisch. 2002. Planning as a heterosexist project. *Journal of Planning Education and Research*, 21, 3, 254–66.

and life. I gained further experience with this style of rhetoric in battles over same sex marriage in my liberal Quaker religious community as well. Perhaps the hardest issue for me has been the question of critical distance. Working with social movements in my personal life created questions about the treatment of lesbians and gays within my work world of environmental planning. Too often I found cases where the public was assumed to be heterosexual. This meant health disparities, housing transition disparities and other community measures that impact LGBTs were at best overlooked. Seeing the pattern of heterosexist argumentation at work meant that I had to speak up about the assumptions. This work essentially backed up the arguments I had been making in my planning practice and social movements for over a decade.

I knew that there were many LGBT planners. At the time I was writing this article, the Gays and Lesbians in Planning Division (GALIP) of the American Planning Association (APA) was getting organized. Letters objecting to the division began appearing in *Planning Magazine*. The uproar over GALIP has calmed down. GALIP now is an established division of the APA and welcomes new members. It holds regular meetings at the annual national APA conference and sponsors workshops and mobile tours.

Laws and consumption patterns have changed in the United States since the publication of "Planning as a Heterosexist Project" (Frisch 2002). The US Supreme Court's decision in *Lawrence v. Texas* ended the tyranny of sodomy law enforcement where being homosexual was a semi-criminal state. Many states have passed state gay rights laws banning discrimination on the basis of sexual orientation. "Legal" gay marriages are available in Massachusetts, Vermont, New Hampshire, Connecticut and Iowa. Civil unions have also spread. For those without marriage, domestic partnership benefits have been widely adopted by large corporations, some state and local governments, and large non-profits such as universities and hospitals.

The rise of gay marriage has been accompanied by the two decade long lesbian and gay baby boom. As gays mainstream through marriage and parenthood, marketing gay consumption has become commonplace. Led by pop culture themes of metrosexuals, and TV shows such as *Will and Grace*, and *Queer Eye for the Straight Guy*, gay culture is mass marketed and made available for consumption by everyone. This mainstreaming and mass marketing has led to more knowledge among the public at large. Increasing levels of tolerance probably reflect this increased knowledge.

How is this new tolerance reflected in the planning practice? Perhaps the biggest change in the work of urban planners has followed Florida's use of tolerance of gays and lesbians as a measure of the creative class (Florida 2002a). Economic development planners have sought ways to attract the creative class and that has meant some attention to the LGBT community. At the very time that the "gay bar" has been identified as an endangered institution, some economic development planners want to show off their existence as part of place marketing.

The decline of fixed LGBT institutional spaces such as gay bars raises the question of community decline. Part of the heterosexist project of planning in the United States was to support concentration of identity around the nuclear family with strong gender roles. Mainstreaming of gay life may mean that LGBT partners and their kids increasingly feel comfortable living in a single family house in the suburbs. Are we (LGBTs) buying into what Bell and Binnie (2004) characterize as heteronormality when we suburbanize? Does our presence in these formally exclusive enclaves lead to their transformation or our transformation? I hope that increased acceptance would lead to new types of planning practice answering the question – what would a queer inclusive city look like? A recent MIT urban planning master's thesis examined this question (Nusser 2010). Nusser identified needs for planning queer community building institutions and queer fixed space in both Kansas City, Missouri (a moderate community in a very conservative part of the country) and in Cambridge, Massachusetts (a liberal community that has been on the forefront of LGBT rights).

Planning still operates as a technology of heterosexuality. While the progress on LGBT rights has been great, practice has been slower to follow. For example, LGBT organizations working on HIV issues have been doing community development for decades. When do our organizations get recognized as community development corporations (Frisch and Servon 2006)? There is much work to do in building inclusive planning practices.

Chapter 13
Conclusions and Reflections for the Future: Reframing Planning Practice

Petra L. Doan

The chapters in this volume have raised a number of critical questions for planning practitioners and scholars, highlighting the ways that current planning practices have treated the Lesbian, Gay, Bisexual, and Transgender (LGBT) community as invisible, immoral, and insignificant. Too often judgments about the relative importance of LGBT people have led to plans that neglect the needs of this community for safe urban spaces in which to live, work, and play. Improving the practice of planning for marginalized people, especially those who are LGBT or queer-identified, requires a reframing of planning away from the mechanical application of technical standards based on heteronormative assumptions. Truly inclusive planning should look at the behavioral expectations that underpin most models and standards, and seek to pay closer attention to questions about the whole population for whom planning is undertaken and consider carefully the impacts of planning decisions on more marginalized communities.

Recognizing the diversity of identities as expressed by local LGBT people can be challenging. Forsyth (Chapter 2) suggests using the more inclusive term – non-conforming population – which is inclusive of a broader range of people from these marginalized communities. Such broad terms are important because many individuals do not fall neatly into one single identity category but may adopt a more fluid identity, as suggested by queer theory which calls for a radical questioning of both heteronormative and homonormative identity (Hendler and Backs Chapter 4). Doan (Chapter 5) also argues that trans people often fall outside of homonormative efforts to construct queer friendly spaces and many queer identified places are located in liminal zones without clearly demarcated boundaries. With individual identities sometimes in flux and with neighborhoods without clearly defined borders, planning for LGBT communities can be quite complex. Hubbard (Chapter 10) argues that heteronormativity affects other communities of people who may not necessarily identify as LGBT because individuals who consume or produce within the sex work industry are also marginalized by efforts to make cities "family friendly."

The task of reframing planning practice therefore requires a subtle shift in approach. Rather than treating individuals and communities as static and continuing, planners must cultivate a more open and less narrowly conceived set of assumptions about the communities with whom they might be working. More fluid communities require planning processes which are adaptive and less rigidly based on assumptions about who the subjects are and what their needs might be. Planners who wish to serve the needs of all neighborhood residents could cultivate a more open orientation to discovery in order to learn about the diverse nature of local needs, instead of coming to the table with ideas and plans previously formed.

This chapter integrates suggestions from the various chapters in this volume to provide some basic recommendations about the ways that planners might better work with evolving queer communities. The intent of this volume is to reframe current practices by conceptualizing the LGBT community as an integral part of the urban economy and a vital component of urban society. A central theme in many of the chapters is that planning practice has been based on heteronormative assumptions that frequently have negative impacts on LGBT individuals. Because this heteronormativity is often invisible and deeply embedded, it is frequently difficult to overcome. Accordingly, the following sections of this chapter are organized around a series of four queries about queer communities that planners and planning scholars are invited to consider.

The contributions from the various chapters point the way forward to creating a revitalized and reframed planning practice that is truly inclusive of LGBT communities and their concerns. The critical issues raised in the chapters can be grouped into several key themes. The first query asks why planners should be concerned about the residential location patterns of LGBT people. Many plans and planning documents from around the world have for years simply ignored the presence of LGBT enclaves and acted as if they did not exist. If population subgroups are not identified in a plan, it is easy to ignore their needs and assume that they have no standing to challenge planned changes or developmental impacts. The recommendations in this section highlight the importance of visibility for sexual and gender non-conforming populations so that their needs and issues will be taken into consideration when planning future developments.

The second query asks how heteronormative and heterosexist assumptions shape planning practice. This query is important because many of the standard planning expectations about families and households contain heteronormative elements that effectively exclude same sex households, non-traditional families, and non-conforming individuals from participating in a broad range of urban services and programs. These kinds of implicit assumptions are contained in a variety of planning practices and are incorporated in many basic assumptions about the wider population. The comments under this query are intended to raise planners' awareness of their effects, and to encourage a re-thinking of what it means for planning to be fully inclusive.

The third query asks about the ways that the scale and intensity of political issues affects planning practice. Planning is often constrained by political topics, but when those politics are linked to hot button issues like homosexuality, planners may be required to walk a fine line between outraged citizens and high visibility public figures. While there is no easy answer to these queries, planners should be on safe ground in advocating for a just city that is inclusive for all citizens.

The fourth query specifically addresses the issue of urban order as it is contained in land use regulations related to sexually oriented businesses. Several of the chapters consider ways that local planning ordinances and staff have been used by the hegemonic powers to ensure a vision of "urban order" that is "family friendly." Such efforts usually involve strict regulation of non-conforming behaviors and businesses intended to "clean up" disorderly businesses and their clientele.

Why Should it Matter to Planners Where LGBT People Live?

Most of the chapters have taken as a given that a broad range of neighborhoods incorporate the residences and specific commercial enterprises of LGBT individuals. These chapters draw on a number of scholars who have demonstrated the longevity and contributions of LGBT people and their communities, but the world of planning practice continues to lag behind with little or no recognition of the vitality and importance of this aspect of the urban environment. Several chapters illustrate the importance of both gay men's and lesbians' neighborhood and residential investment decisions in urban areas (Chapter 2) and in suburban areas (Chapter 6). Previous analyses (Lauria and Knopp 1985) highlighted gay men's struggles to redevelop urban spaces in the face of harassment and discrimination during the gentrification process in New Orleans. However, Forsyth (Chapter 2) argues that although gay and lesbian neighborhoods can be important catalysts for urban redevelopment, planners should be aware that not all LGBT people have sufficient wealth to invest in urban redevelopment.

Planners need to be aware of the differences in location patterns between gay men and lesbians. Adler and Brenner (1992) found that the residential location patterns of lesbians were shaped by their experiences as women in a highly gendered urban environment. Consequently, lesbians may locate where they can afford to live safely both for themselves and for their children. Many lesbians might wish to engage in the same kinds of renovation projects as gay men, but are likely to be more limited in their ability to do so because of their lower incomes. This result means that planners should be sensitive to a broader spectrum of non-conforming residential patterns and explicitly preserve areas that provide both counter-cultural and multicultural elements that may act as safe havens for a variety of non-conforming citizens. The neglect of these areas by planners allows urban policy-makers to push redevelopment that favors the heteronormative at the expense of more marginal populations. As Adler and Brenner describe in their commentary in Chapter 12, the lesbian neighborhood they described in 1992 in Portland has been redeveloped, and its former lesbian residents have moved into poorer African-American neighborhoods.

Within the historical and persistent climate of heteronormativity, many gay and lesbian spaces have been ephemeral and difficult to track. Making these places more visible to outsiders is critical to preserving their heritage. Dubrow (Chapter 3) suggests heteronormative bias influences decisions about what parts of the built environment will be preserved. She argues that preserving historical structures and locations can be an important element of community building for now and the future and that it is vital to hold preservationists accountable. It is difficult to assess the longevity of a marginalized community if there are no markers of its existence in the built environment. While the homes of some famous LGBT individuals have been preserved, making their identities explicit is an important element of their preservation. Similarly, community landmarks for the LGBT population, which might include bars, bookstores, coffeehouses, and public cruising areas, should also be considered for preservation since they have been such important elements of queer culture. Unfortunately culture wars may discourage attempts to preserve these important minority elements of the built environment, but planners who wish to encourage diversity in urban redevelopment should be careful to ask questions about historical significance from a wide range of community members and not simply assume that all marginal areas are not worth preserving.

How Do Heterosexist and Heteronormative Assumptions Shape Planning Practice?

Heterosexist bias runs deep within the field of planning and is interwoven in many of its basic assumptions (Hayden 1982, Sandercock and Forsyth 1992, Greed 2006, Miranne and Young 2000, Spain 2001a, Fainstein and Servon 2005). Frisch (2002) critiques the notion of public order which has often been used by planners as a justification for limiting non-heterosexual uses of space starting with Patrick Geddes' linking of the "perversion" of homosexuality with the need for planning to create a rational order to discourage it (Thomson and Geddes 1912). Lewis Mumford (1944) followed Geddes' example and made direct connections between homosexuality and urban disorder. Attempts to create an orderly urban environment have often targeted LGBT bars, bathhouses, and other sex positive establishments (Hubbard Chapter 10; Prior and Crofts Chapter 11) with negative effects on the LGBT community. If planning is to become a queer inclusive project, Frisch argues that cities should embrace the "disorder" that might allow greater interaction and mixing outside of the narrow heterosexual family home (2002). He also suggests that it is essential to deconstruct the heterosexual nuclear family ideal underpinning much of urban planning, especially if gay marriage continues to be recognized by more and more states and localities. In his commentary in Chapter 12 Frisch asks whether the effect of LGBT individuals and couples moving to the suburbs has been to reinforce the heteronormative tendencies within the queer population or has contributed to a diversifying of suburban values.

Recent theoretical work that incorporates queer theory and a post-modern use of deconstruction can provide a useful lens for examining both the theory and practice of planning. Hendler and Backs (Chapter 4) suggest that planning needs to consider fluidity and permeability in plans, policies, and programs especially with reference to efforts to promote the "good" city that is often implicitly understood as heteronormative. In addition, they suggest that planners should reduce their use of binary categories in their everyday practice because these assumptions often exclude the most vulnerable who do not necessarily fit into dichotomous boxes. These authors also recommend that it is important for planners to use critical judgment in adopting "normalized standards" in the development of plans since these are often based on heteronormative expectations of behavior and the use of space.

The problem with binary assumptions is strikingly evident when planners consider the ways that dichotomous gender definitions are used to dictate the ways that men and women should behave. These expectations cause many problems for queer individuals and especially transgendered people. Doan (Chapter 5) argues that these difficulties are often experienced by LGBT people as a tyranny of gender. Planners in particular need to be aware of this tyranny in the way that public facilities are designed and operated, especially in decisions about the availability of public bathrooms that are intended for single use (without regard to sex designation). These facilities are of vital importance in enabling basic bodily necessities for gender variant individuals as well as a range of elderly and disabled individuals who may need a caregiver of either sex to accompany them. Doan also argues that efforts to ensure safe public spaces would be especially beneficial for the gender variant since they are most often the victims of hate crimes and harassment. Because trans people are more likely to be fired and less likely to be protected legally when they transition, they experience many problems in urban spaces that assume a decent income and access to resources (Doan 2001, 2007, 2010). Planners seeking to redevelop urban spaces need to be sensitive to existing populations who use those liminal spaces and not make matters worse by promoting redevelopment of spaces that are intolerant of the gender variant.

In reality, planning practice often marginalizes a broad range of non-conforming individuals. Forsyth (Chapter 2) highlights a number of areas of planning practice that must be addressed to ensure that these populations no longer suffer discrimination. Her recommendations related to housing include: ensuring that homes for the elderly are LGBT inclusive, reducing anti-LGBT housing discrimination through local ordinances, increasing sensitivity to the spiraling cost of housing due to gentrification and re-gentrification, awareness of the heteronormative nature of most family and household definitions, and making allowance for homeless LGBT youth who may be kicked out of their family homes due to their identities. She also recommends that planners work to make the city itself safer and more welcoming to LGBT individuals by making streetscape improvements to help demarcate and celebrate LGBT neighborhoods, targeting tourism promotion to LGBT individuals and families in addition to the usual heterosexual target audience, encouraging urban street festivals and major events that celebrate the LGBT population (gay pride, gay games), plus creating safe public spaces where the public display of non-heteronormative affection is permitted and harassment of LGBT individuals in public spaces is not tolerated. If planners wish to create more just and welcoming urban spaces they should consider adopting as many of these concrete measures as possible.

It is also crucial to recognize that there are many more gay and lesbian people in a region than the most visible individuals who reside in recognized urban enclaves. Anacker (Chapter 6) examines the housing and neighborhood characteristics of census tracts in the urban and suburban counties with the highest percentages of two male partners and two female partners to challenge assumptions about gay and lesbian location patterns. Her study critiques the twin myths that suburbs that are predominantly inhabited by straight couples and that in-town urban neighborhoods are predominantly gay. Anacker's results indicate that census tracts with male and female same sex partners had lower proportions of non-Hispanic whites and higher proportions of foreign born residents, suggesting that non-heteronormative couples may be attracted to more diverse environments. A truly inclusive planning practice must be careful about making assumptions about the needs of community residents based only upon stereotypes about who lives in particular neighborhoods. As Anacker has shown, LGBT people are likely to live in any part of the urban to rural continuum, and responsible planners would do well to reinforce a broad commitment to multiculturalism and seek to create environments in which such diversity will thrive.

How Do Local, Regional, and National Politics Influence Planning for the LGBT Population?

Overt discrimination is a fact of life for non-conforming populations living in cities across the globe. National political leaders sometimes try to deny that homosexuality exists in their country; for instance, Iranian President Mahmoud Ahmadinejad contended that "there are no gays in Iran" in a speech at Columbia University.[1] Other leaders have argued that if homosexual behavior exists, it must be a result of corrupt "western" influences. President Robert Mugabe of Zimbabwe once claimed that homosexuality was un-African and was a threat to Zimbabwean nationhood.[2] These polemical arguments about the LGBT population are not unique to Middle Eastern and African countries, but are replicated and in some cases encouraged by some fundamentalist churches and more conservative political groups. In Uganda, western fundamentalist groups associated with

---

1 These comments were widely reported in the United States media including CNN on September 24, 2007. Available at: http://www.cnn.com/2007/US/09/24/us.iran/index.html [accessed: January 26, 2011].

2 As reported in a local paper, *New Zimbabwe*, March 26, 2010. Available at: http://www.newzimbabwe.com/news-2109-Mugabe,+Tsvangirai+slam+homosexuals/news.aspx [accessed: January 26, 2011].

an American-based group known as The Family warned Ugandan legislators about the evils of homosexuality and one result was a recent bill proposed in the Ugandan parliament which would make persistent homosexuality punishable by death.[3] When political and religious leaders express such disdain for non-conforming populations, one result is a marked increase in levels of harassment and intolerance directed towards visible signs of non-conformity, especially at gay and lesbian bars and bookstores.

The fact that cities are seen by some observers as relative oases of tolerance, and by others as dens of iniquity, means that they have become a cultural battleground between the LGBT community and those individuals for whom their presence is a sign of moral turpitude. Urban planners are caught squarely in the middle and need to be aware of the highly charged political nature of these issues and not simply act to avoid conflict and preserve the heteronormative status quo. In their commentary in Chapter 12, Lauria and Knopp suggest that planning and planning theory are limited by connections to *practice* and the related politics of local government, both of which complicate attempts to set policy linked to contested cultural perceptions.

Often cultural and political debates occur at differing scales of governance and this adds additional complications for planners seeking to ensure fuller inclusion of LGBT individuals within the planning process. Gorman-Murray (Chapter 7) uses two examples from Australian planning practice to illustrate this point. In New South Wales (NSW) for example, state level regulations confer planning powers for community social plans to the local level, mandating the participation of seven targeted special interest groups and suggesting that several optional groups be considered including LGBT people among others. The author then analyzes the inclusion of LGBT people within local plans in NSW and found that only 22 percent of plans mention LGBT people as a target group, because planners often seek out culturally and linguistically diverse populations rather than sexual and gender minorities. However, plans from urban areas disproportionately do include LGBT individuals while plans from rural areas nearly always leave them out. Gorman-Murray finds that a variety of state level mechanisms have been effective in encouraging localities to be more proactive in including LGBT individuals and have begun to change the culture of heteronormative planning. These measures to ensure LGBT participation include: having dedicated local council staff for LGBT issues, doing anti-homophobia training for council staff, community residents, and businesses, providing support for LGBT events such as festivals, including LGBT couples in sponsored family events with child care, establishing same sex partner registers, and explicitly including LGBT groups in planning and running

---

3 The particulars of the proposed bill are available at: http://www.hrw.org/en/news/2009/10/15/uganda-anti-homosexuality-bill-threatens-liberties-and-human-rights-defenders. The role of US fundamentalists was revealed in a January 3, 2010 *New York Times* article by Jeffrey Gettleman. Available at: http://www.nytimes.com/2010/01/04/world/africa/04uganda.html.

community wide festivals and events. These activities provide excellent examples of the kinds of activities which might be used in other locations and countries to build support for LGBT inclusive planning.

Government signals about their tolerance or lack of tolerance for discrimination and human rights do make a difference to local planning processes. Planners who wish to support efforts to broaden anti-discrimination ordinances need to understand the nature of the political struggles such measures are likely to face. Chapman (Chapter 8) analyzes the ways that local politics influenced the adoption of a municipal human rights ordinance that was LGBT inclusive in Orlando, Florida. He contrasts competing urban economic development discourses which were used in the arguments before the city council. Conservative growth machine proponents argued that special rights for LGBT citizens would harm the overall economy, but the competing argument by adherents of Florida's creative cities approach were ultimately more persuasive to the council and the ordinance passed. An important lesson here is that planners concerned with economic development need to be aware of the ways that competing discourses can be used, and might provide more explicit recognition of the economic potential of LGBT individuals as evidenced by the very successful "Gay Days" at Disney.

However, it is also very important for planners to realize that not all non-conforming populations have the economic or social capital to participate fully in "creative class" activities. Muller Myrdahl (Chapter 9) critically examines Florida's creative cities hypothesis (2002a, 2005) and ponders its usefulness for planning. She adopts a framework based on the right of diverse populations to the city as proposed by Fincher and Iveson (2008). This perspective suggests that planners must go beyond simply assuming that tolerance equals gay and lesbian people; what is needed is a framework not just for evaluating the validity of competing claims from different groups, but to facilitate the marginalized in making those claims. While it is important for planners to affirm difference as a way of reinforcing and protecting variant identities, such strategies can sometimes give rise to commodification of difference and to "checklists" of difference. Even the alternative strategy that emphasizes relationships in which claims for recognition are based on appeals to justice that are open to debate and public discussion among all members of a polity (Fraser 2003: 96) may be difficult, given the high levels of homophobia and transphobia that are present in many cities today. The answer therefore is for planners to be conscious of not reducing LGBT people to one more check box on a long list. The range of identities that comprise the queer community are much too diverse to be amenable to a simple checklist. Planners who wish to be more inclusive of this population would do well to move beyond lists and boxes and seek ways to engage with this community and its needs in a more direct fashion, such as: attending community events, helping to plan pride activities, and explicitly seeking LGBT input into planning decisions.

How is Land Use Regulation Used to Constrain the Disorderly City?

Heterosexual couples are free to hold hands and be openly affectionate with one another in most countries. However, when same sex couples display affection in public (PDA), such actions often trigger harassment and even outright violence. As a result finding places to meet and express physical affection for this population has long been problematic in cities, making gay and lesbian bars, bathhouses, and other venues an important outlet for socializing. Unfortunately, in many settings urban planners have used a variety of land use regulations as a means of reducing what the heteronormative world sees as an example of the blatant disorder of homosociality. In his commentary in Chapter 12, Frisch suggests that the decline of gay bars raises questions about the longevity of the community. Another recent study (Doan and Higgins 2011) suggests that in Atlanta a major part of the redevelopment strategy for Midtown (the most identifiable gay district in the city) was the targeting and closure of gay bars that were treated as nuisances because they were not considered conducive to the kind of family-oriented development the developers wished to encourage.

In Chapter 10, Hubbard examines the regulation of sex industry premises in the United Kingdom and notes that although planning and environmental laws are framed in terms of amenity and property rights, they are imbued with assumptions about healthy and moral conduct underpinning the heteronormative approach, including prohibitions on prostitution and pornography that are seen by many as symbols of moral and spatial disorder. Because outright prohibitions for certain kinds of "vice" end up being very costly to enforce, municipalities often turn to various forms of zoning and licensing to restrict these activities to certain carefully regulated areas. In the case of the United Kingdom, a licensing system was put in place to regulate "adult entertainment" with the aim of reducing crime and disorder, promoting public safety, preventing public nuisance, and protecting children from harm. These licensing efforts are increasingly seen as mechanisms for imposing narrow heteronormative sexual morality, taste, and censorship. The author suggests that planners should listen not only to those constituents who feel morally offended by an activity, but also to the sex workers and their patrons, as well as the business owners who benefit from such activities.

Prior and Crofts (Chapter 11) extend this analysis to the Australian case and document the way that local land use regulations have historically been a significant constraint to the emergence of gay bathhouses in Sydney. For many years bathhouses were regulated under the Disorderly Houses Act (also used to regulate brothels), but the passage of anti-discrimination laws and the decriminalization of homosexuality in the 1980s meant that a bathhouse application could no longer be denied simply because its patrons were gay. As a result planning codes were developed to limit such establishments based on the supposition that such premises were disorderly and generated illegal parking, increased crime, harmed local children, encouraged prostitution, and decreased property values in the neighborhood. After examining a series of applications from several bathhouse establishments, Prior and Crofts found that these businesses were eventually permitted after evidence was presented that no prostitution was occurring (sex for money), that parking was not a problem, and that in fact there was not an increase of crime in the neighborhood. The findings of this chapter can be generalized to other situations when a planning issue shifts from a discourse of immorality to an argument about particular planning impacts. Specific counter arguments can be developed to respond to these matters of fact that may undercut the prevailing assumptions used to protect the heteronormative city. While planning can be used to bolster support for heteronormative visions of the city, its rational basis means that counter-arguments of fact can be made to dispel heteronormative bias and allow for resolution in the court system.

Towards the Creation of a Queer Inclusive City

Each of these chapters has contributed to what might be termed the queering of planning practice. What is required is a heightened awareness and sensitivity to non-normative communities of interest that may develop in urban areas. In his commentary Frisch (Chapter 12) wonders what a "queer inclusive city would look like." He goes on to note that the United States Supreme Court has ended the "tyranny of sodomy law enforcement" and there is increasing awareness of gay and lesbian issues on the part of the general public, but planning still acts to enforce heterosexuality. He is disturbed by the decline of so many gay bars and wonders what this means for the longevity of the LGBT community. Unfortunately, there is no "magic bullet" that can be used to reframe planning practice towards a less heteronormative enterprise.

One essential element, however, is the importance of a deeper understanding of the variety of LGBT individuals and communities on the part of planning academics and practitioners. Some of these communities may be visible and attractive to planners for a variety of reasons. Others may be less familiar and virtually invisible, but should not on that account be vulnerable to discrimination and eradication. Planners seeking to create a more just urban community need to adopt a more critical approach about their own preconceptions and the assumptions that underpin much of their work. Fully conscious decision-making that asks who will be helped and who will be harmed by each policy or planning change would go a long way towards mitigating the heterosexist and heteronormative orientation of much current planning practice and procedures.

List of References

Abraham, J. 2009. *Metropolitan Lovers: The Homosexuality of Cities*. Minneapolis: University of Minnesota Press.
Adkins, L. 2004. Reflexivity: Freedom or habit of gender? in *Feminism After Bourdieu*, edited by L. Adkins and B. Skeggs. Oxford: Blackwell Publishing, 191–210.
Adler, S. and Brenner, J. 1992. Gender and space: Lesbians and gay men in the city. *International Journal of Urban and Regional Research*, 16, 24–34.
Alexander, P. 1996. Bathhouses and brothels: Symbolic sites in discourse and practice, in *Policing Public Sex: Queer Politics and the Future of AIDS Activism*, edited by D. Bedfellows et al. Boston: South End Press.
Allmendinger, P. 2001. *Planning in Postmodern Times*. London: Routledge.
Alonso, W. 1964. *Location and Land Use*. Cambridge: Harvard University Press.
Altman, D. 1982. *The Homosexualization of America*. Boston: Beacon Press.
American Psychological Association. 2000. *Diagnostic and Statistical Manual of Mental Disorders, Fourth Edition, Text Revision* (DSM–IV TR). Arlington: American Psychological Association.
Amin, A. 2002. Ethnicity and the multicultural city. *Environment and Planning A*, 34, 959–80.
Amin, A. 2010. The remainders of race. *Theory, Culture and Society*, 27, 1–23.
Amin, A. and Thrift, N. 2007. Cultural economy and cities. *Progress in Human Geography*, 31, 2.
Anacker, K.B. 2009. *Analyzing Mature Suburbs in Ohio through Property Values*. Saarbrücken: VDM.
Anacker, K.B. and Morrow-Jones, H.A. 2005. Neighborhood factors associated with same-sex couples in US cities. *Urban Geography*, 26(5), 385–409.
Anderson, S. 1981. New viral cancer stirs gay fears. *The Advocate*, 324(9), 14.
Anonymous. 1999. Up Close … GALIP Chair Randy Gross. *Planning*, 65(5), 33.
Anonymous. 2006. Civil unions on way in ACT. *Sydney Star Observer*. Available at: http://www.starobserver.com.au/news/2008/04/20/civil-unions-on-way-in-act/9592.
Anthony, K. and Dufresne, M. 2007. Potty parity in perspective: Gender and family issues in planning and designing public restrooms. *Journal of Planning Literature*, 21(5), 267–94.
Atkinson, R. and Easthope, H. 2009. The consequences of the creative class: The pursuit of creativity strategies in Australia's cities. *International Journal of Urban and Regional Research*, 33, 64–79.
Aubin, T. 1987. Gay baths must do without cubicles. *Sydney Morning Herald*.

Australian Bureau of Statistics. 2005. Same-sex couple families. *Year Book Australia 2005*, catalogue no. 1301.0.

AuthentiCity. 2008. *Creative City Planning Framework: A Supporting Document to the Agenda for Prosperity: Prospectus for a Great City*. Available at: http://www.toronto.ca/culture/pdf/creative-city-planning-framework-feb08.pdf.

Baar, K. 1992. The national movement to halt the spread of multifamily housing, 1890–1926. *Journal of the American Planning Association*, 58(1), 39–48.

Badgett, M.V.L. 1995. The wage effects of sexual orientation discrimination. *Industrial and Labor Relations Review*, 48(4), 726–35.

Badgett, M.V.L. 2001. *Money, Myths and Change: The Economic Lives of Lesbians and Gay Men*. Chicago: University of Chicago Press.

Badgett, M.V.L., Lau, H., Sears, B., and Ho, D. 2007. *Bias in the Workplace: Consistent Evidence of Sexual Orientation and Gender Identity Discrimination*. Los Angeles: Williams Institute, University of California.

Bailey, R. 1999. *Gay Politics, Urban Politics: Identity and Economics in the Urban Setting*. New York: Columbia University Press.

Baird, B. 2006. Sexual citizenship in 'the new Tasmania'. *Political Geography*, 25, 964–87.

Bakker A., Van Kesteren, P.J.M., and Gooren, L.J.G. 1993. The prevalence of transsexualism in the Netherlands. *Acta Psychiatrica Scandinavian*, 87, 237–38.

Bannister, J., Fyfe, N., and Kearns, A. 2006. Respectable or respectful? (In)civility and the city. *Urban Studies*, 43, 919–37.

Barnes, T. and Hutton, T. 2009. Situating the new economy: Contingencies of regeneration and dislocation in Vancouver's inner city. *Urban Studies*, 46, 1247–69.

Barnett, B.M. 1993. Invisible southern black women leaders in the civil rights movement: The triple constraints of gender, race and class. *Gender and Society*, 7(2), 162–82.

Barnhart, E. 1975. Friends and lovers in a lesbian counterculture community, in *Old Family/New Family*, edited by N. Glazer-Malbin. New York: Van Nostrand.

Barnhurst, K.G. (ed.) 2007. *Media Queered: Visibility and its Discontents*. New York: Peter Lang.

Barr, K. 1995. Gender, sexuality and sexual orientation: All in the feminist family? *Feminist Economics*, 1(1), 121–39.

Bauman, J.F. 2002. Race, class, gender, and sexuality in planning history: A look at trends in the literature. *Journal of Planning History*, 1 (3), 225–9.

Bavinton, B., Berg, L., Harding, V. and Scamell, D. 2007. *All Love is Equal ... Isn't It? The Recognition of Same-Sex Relationships Under Federal Law*. Sydney: Gay and Lesbian Rights Lobby.

Beauregard, R. 1990. Trajectories of neighborhood change: The case of gentrification. *Environment and Planning A*, 22, 855–74.

Bedore, M. and Donald, B. 2010. Revising the politics of class in urban development: Evidence from the study of the social dynamics of economic performance. *Urban Affairs Review*, 1–35.

Beemyn, B. (ed.) 1997. *Creating a Place for Ourselves: Lesbian, Gay, and Bisexual Community Histories*. London: Routledge.

Bell, D. 1991. Insignificant others: Lesbian and gay geographies. *Area*, 23, 323–29.

Bell, D. 1995. Perverse dynamics, sexual citizenship and the transformation of intimacy, in *Mapping Desire: Geographies of Sexualities*, edited by D. Bell and G. Valentine. London: Routledge, 304–17.

Bell, D. and Valentine, G. (eds) 1995a. *Mapping Desire: Geographies of Sexualities*. London: Routledge.

Bell, D. and Valentine, G. 1995b. Queer country: Rural lesbian and gay lives. *Journal of Rural Studies*, 11(2), 113–22.

Bell, D., Binnie, J., Cream, J., and Valentine, G. 1994. All hyped up and no place to go. *Gender, Place, and Culture*, 1, 31–48.

Bell, D. and Binnie, J. 2000. *The Sexual Citizen: Queer Theory and Beyond*. Cambridge: Polity Press.

Bell, D. and Binnie, J. 2004. Authenticating queer space: Citizenship, urbanism and governance. *Urban Studies*, 41(9), 1807–20.

Bell, D. and Binnie, J. 2006. Editorial: Geographies of sexual citizenship. *Political Geography*, 25, 869–73.

Bell, D. and Jayne, M. (eds) 2004. *City of Quarters: Urban Villages in the Contemporary City*. Aldershot: Ashgate.

Bellis, M.A., Watson, F.L.D., Hughes, S., Cook, P., Downing, J., Clark, P., and Thompson, R. 2007. Comparative views of the public, sex workers, businesses, and residents on establishing managed zones for prostitution: Analysis of a consultation in Liverpool. *Health and Place*, 13(4), 603–16.

Bem, S.L. 1993. *The Lenses of Gender: Transforming the Debate on Sexual Inequality*. New Haven: Yale University Press.

Berger, V. 1991. Domestic partnership initiatives. *Depaul Law Review*, 40, 417–58.

Bergman, D. (ed.). 1993. *Camp Grounds: Style and Homosexuality*. Amherst: University of Massachusetts Press.

Berkowitz, D., Belgrave L., and Halberstein R. 2007. The interaction of drag queens and gay men in public and private spaces. *Journal of Homosexuality*, 52, 11–32.

Bernstein, E. 2007. Sex work for the middle classes. *Sexualities*, 10(4), 473–88.

Berube, A. and D'Emilio, J. 1985. The military and lesbians during the McCarthy years, in *The Lesbian Issue: Essays from SIGNS*, edited by E.B. Freedman et al. Chicago: University of Chicago Press, 279–95.

Berube, A. 1990. *Coming Out Under Fire: The History of Gay Men and Women in World War Two*. New York: Free Press.

Berube, A. 1996. The history of gay bathhouses, in *Policing Public Sex: Queer Politics and the Future of AIDS Activism*, edited by E.G. Colter et al. Boston: South End Press, 187–220.

Betsky, A. 1995. Owner of the avant-garde: A review of Philip Johnson: Life and work. *Blueprint*. February, 46–7.

Betsky, A. 1997. *Queer Space: Architecture and Same-sex Desire*. New York: William Morrow and Company.

Bier, T. 2001. *Moving Up, Filtering Down: Metropolitan Housing Dynamics and Public Policy*. The Brookings Institution: Center on Urban and Metropolitan Policy.

Billman, J. 2003. Healthier, happier and heterosexual. *Orlando Weekly*, 24 July, 24.

Binnie, J. 1995. Trading places: Consumption, sexuality, and the production of queer space, in *Mapping Desire: Geographies of Sexualities*, edited by D. Bell and G. Valentine. London: Routledge, 182–99.

Binnie, J. 1997. Coming out of geography: Towards a queer epistemology. *Environment and Planning D: Society and Space*, 15, 223–37.

Binnie, J. 2004. Quartering sexualities: Gay villages and sexual citizenship, in *City of Quarters: Urban Villages in the Contemporary City*, edited by D. Bell and M. Jayne. Aldershot: Ashgate, 163–72.

Binnie, J., Holloway, J. Millington, S., and Young, C. (eds) 2006. *Cosmopolitan Urbanism*. London: Routledge.

Binnie, J. and Skeggs, B. 2004. Cosmopolitan knowledge and the production and consumption of sexualized space: Manchester's gay village. *The Sociological Review*, 52, 39–61.

Binnie, J. and Skeggs, B. 2006. Cosmopolitan knowledge and the production and consumption of sexualized space, in *Cosmopolitan Urbanism*, edited by J. Binnie et al. London: Routledge, 246–53.

Birch, E. 1994a. An urban view: Catherine Bauer's five questions, in *The American Planner: Biographies and Recollections*, edited by D. Krueckeberg. New Brunswick: Center for Urban Policy Research.

Birch, E. 1994b. From civic worker to city planner: 1890–1980, in *The American Planner: Biographies and Recollections*, edited by D. Krueckeberg. New Brunswick: Center for Urban Policy Research.

Birch, E.L. and Silver, C. 2009. One hundred years of city planning's enduring and evolving connections. *Journal of the American Planning Association*, 75(2), 113–22.

Black, D., Gates, G., Sanders, S., and Taylor, L. 2000. Demographics of the gay and lesbian population in the United States: Evidence from available systematic data sources. *Demography*, 37, 139–54.

Black, D., Gates, G., Sanders, S. and Taylor, L. 2002. Why do gay men live in San Francisco? *Journal of Urban Economics*, 51, 54–76.

Blotcher, J. 1996. Sex club owners: The fuck suck buck stops here, in *Policing Public Sex: Queer Politics and The Future of AIDS Activism*, edited by E.G. Colter et al. Boston: South End Press, 25–44.

Bondi, L. 1998. Sexing the city, in *Cities of Difference*, edited by R. Fincher and J. Jacobs. New York: Guilford, 177–200.

Bonfitto, V.F. 1997. The formation of gay and lesbian identity and community in the Connecticut River valley of western Massachusetts, 1900–1970. *Journal of Homosexuality*, 33, 69–96.

Bontje, M. and Musterd, S. 2009. Creative industries, creative class and competitiveness: Expert opinions critically appraised. *Geoforum*, 40, 843–52.

Bornstein, K. 1994. *Gender Outlaw: On Women, Men, and the Rest of Us.* London: Routledge.

Boswell, R. 1996. The Village People: Gay community breathes new life into seedy section of Centretown. *Ottawa Citizen*, 3 November, A1.

Bourdieu, P. 1977. *Outline of a Theory of Practice.* New York: Cambridge University Press.

Bourdieu, P. 1990. *The Logic of Practice.* Cambridge: Polity Press.

Bourdieu, P. 2001. *Masculine Domination.* Stanford: Stanford University Press.

Bouthillette, A. 1997. Queer and gendered housing: A tale of two neighborhoods in Vancouver, in *Queers in Space: Communities, Public Places, Sites of Resistance*, edited by G.B. Ingram et al. Seattle: Bay Press, 213–32.

Bowes, J.E. 1996. Out of the closet and into the marketplace: Meeting basic needs in the gay community. *Journal of Homosexuality*, 31, 219–44.

Bowman, C. 1993. Hayward's thriving gay scene: Blue-collar-city takes pride in diversity. *San Francisco Chronicle*, 7 April, A15.

Bowman, C. and Cornish, B. 1992. A more perfect union. *Columbia Law Review*, 92, 1164-1121.

Boyd, N.A. 2003. *Wide Open Town: A History of Queer San Francisco until 1965.* Berkeley: University of California Press.

Boydell, S., Prior, J., and Hubbard, P. (2011). Regulating the nocturnal city (submitted). *Urban Studies*.

Boyle, F.J. (1985). *Gay Ghettos and Gentrification: Separate Issues, Misunderstood Processes – Toward an Understanding of the Gay and Lesbian Role in Gentrification.* (MS Thesis, Urban Planning). Columbia University, Columbia, NY.

Bradford, N. 2004. *Creative Cities: Structured Policy Dialogue Report.* Research Report No. F45, Family Network, Canadian Policy Research Networks Inc., Ottawa.

Brouwer, A. 1999. Letter to the editor titled GALIP serves communities. *Planning*, 65(2), 27.

Brown, G. 2006. Cosmopolitan camouflage: (Post-)gay space in Spitalfields, East London, in *Cosmopolitan Urbanism*, edited by J. Binnie et al. London: Routledge, 130–45.

Brown, G. 2007. Mutinous eruptions: Autonomous spaces of radical queer activism. *Environment and Planning A*, 39, 2685–98.

Brown, W. 1995. *States of Injury: Power and Freedom in Late Modernity.* Princeton: Princeton University Press.

Brown, W. 2006. *Regulating Aversion: Tolerance in the Age of Identity and Empire.* Princeton: Princeton University Press.

Brown-May, A. and Fraser, P. 2009. Gender, respectability, and public convenience in Melbourne, Australia, 1859–1902, in *Ladies and Gents: Public Toilets and Gender*, edited by O. Gershenson and B. Penner. Philadelphia: Temple University Press, 75–89.

Browne, K. 2006a. Challenging Queer Geographies, *Antipode*, 38, 885–93.

Browne, K. 2006b. A right geezer bird (man-woman): The sites and sounds of female embodiment. *ACME: An International E-Journal for Critical Geographies*, 5(2), 121–43.

Browne, K. 2007. (Re)making the other, heterosexualizing everyday space. *Environment and Planning A*, 39, 996–1014.

Browne, K., Cull, M., and Hubbard, P. 2010. The diverse vulnerabilities of lesbian, gay, and trans sex workers in the United Kingdom, in *New Sociologies of Sex Work*, edited by K. Hardy et al. Farnham: Ashgate, 197–212.

Browne, K., Lim, J., and Brown, G. (eds) 2007. *Geographies of Sexualities; Theory, Practice, and Politics*. Aldershot: Ashgate.

Bullough, V. and Bullough, B. 1993. *Cross-dressing, Sex, and Gender.* Philadelphia: University of Pennsylvania Press.

Burgess, E. W. 1925. The growth of the city: An introduction to a research project, in *The City*, edited by R.E. Park et al. Chicago: University of Chicago Press, 47–61.

Butler, J. 1990. *Gender Trouble: Feminism and the Subversion of Identity*. London: Routledge.

Butler, J. 1993. *Bodies That Matter: On the Discursive Limits of Sex*. London: Routledge.

Butler, J. 2004. *Undoing Gender*. London: Routledge.

Campbell, H. 2006. Just planning: The art of situated ethical judgment. *Journal of Planning Education and Research*, 26(1), 92–106.

Campbell, H. and Marshall, R. 2006. Towards justice in planning: A re-appraisal. *European Planning Studies*, 14(2), 239–52.

Canadian Institute of Planners. 2004. *Code of Practice*. Available at: http://www.cip-icu.ca/web/la/en/pa/C59DDE35F1184B5E89385E53506C19F8/template.asp.

Carey, E. 1998. No longer the fringe. *The Toronto Star*, 21 June, context section.

Carpenter, C. 2004. New evidence on gay and lesbian household incomes. *Contemporary Economic Policy*, 22(1), 78–94.

Carrigan, T. 1988. *Facts of Our Lives*. Melbourne: Outrage.

Castells, M. 1983. *The City and the Grassroots: A Cross-Cultural Theory of Urban Social Movements*. Berkeley: University of California Press.

Castells, M. 1997. *The Power of Identity*. Malden: Blackwell.

Castells, M. and Murphy, K. 1982. Cultural identity and urban structure: The spatial organization of San Francisco's gay community, in *Urban Policy Under Capitalism*, edited by N. Fainstein and S. Fainstein. Beverly Hills: Sage.

Castro CBD. 2010. *About the CBD*. Available at: http://www.castrocbd.org/content/about-cbd.

Catungal, J.P. and Leslie, D. 2009. Contesting the creative city: Race, nation, multiculturalism. *Geoforum*, 40, 701–4.

Catungal, J.P., Leslie, D., and Hii, Y. 2009. Geographies of displacement in the creative city: The case of Liberty Village, Toronto. *Urban Studies*, 46, 5–6, 1095–114.

Catanugal, J. and McCann, E. 2010. Governing sexuality and park space: Acts of regulation in Vancouver, BC. *Social and Cultural Geography*, 11(1), 75–94.

Caulfield, J. 1994. *City Form and Everyday Life: Toronto's Gentrification and Critical Social Practice*. Toronto: University of Toronto Press.

Chamberland, L. 1993. Remembering lesbian bars: Montreal, 1955–1975. *Journal of Homosexuality*, 25, 3, 231–69.

Chapman, T. (2007). *Constructing the Moral Landscape through Antidiscrimination Law: Discourse, Debate, and Dialogue of Sexual Citizenship in Three Florida Communities*. (Unpublished doctoral dissertation). Florida State University, Tallahassee, Florida.

Chapman, T., Lieb, J., and Webster, G. 2007. Race, the creative class, and political geographies of same-sex marriage in Georgia. *Southeastern Geographer*, 47, 27–54.

Chase, C. 1998. Hermaphrodites with attitude: Mapping the emergence of intersex political activism. *GLQ: A Journal of Lesbian and Gay Studies*, 4 (2), 189–211.

Chauncey, G. 1994. *Gay New York: Gender, Urban Culture, and the Making of the Gay Male World, 1890–1940*. New York: Basic Books.

Chesnut, S. and Gable, A.C. 1997. Women ran it: Charis Books and more and Atlanta's lesbian-feminist community, 1971–1981, in *Carryin' On in the Lesbian and Gay South*, edited by J. Howard. New York: New York University Press, 241–84.

Cheung, G. and Forsyth, A. 2001. Queers and planning. *Progressive Planning* [Online], 146. Available at: http://www.plannersnetwork.org/publications/2001_146/Cheung-Forsyth.html.

Clark, G.L. and Dear, M. 1984. *State Apparatus: Structures and Language of Legitimacy*. Boston: Allen and Unwin.

Clark, T.N. 2004. *The City as an Entertainment Machine*. Oxford: Elsevier.

Clarkson, J. 2008. The limitations of the discourse of norms: Gay visibility and degrees of transgression. *Journal of Communication Inquiry*, 32, 368–82.

Cody, P. and Welch, P. 1997. Rural gay men in northern New England: Life experiences and coping styles. *Journal of Homosexuality*, 33(1), 51–67.

Collins, A. 2004. Sexual dissidence, enterprise, and assimilation: Bedfellows in urban regeneration. *Urban Studies*, 41(9), 1789–1806.

Colon, I. and Marston, B. 1999. Resistance to a residential AIDS home: An empirical test of NIMBY. *Journal of Homosexuality*, 37(3), 135–45.

Colter, E.G., Hoffman, W., Pendleton, E., Redick, A., and Serlin, D. (eds) 1996. *Policing Public Sex: Queer Politics and The Future of AIDS Activism*. Boston: South End Press.

Colton, K.W.W. 2003. *Housing in the Twenty-First Century*. Cambridge: Harvard University Press.

Connell, R. 1987. *Gender and Power: Society, the Person and Sexual Politics*. Allen and Unwin.
Connell, R. 1995. *Masculinities*. Berkeley: University of California Press.
Connell, R. 2002. *Gender*. Cambridge: Polity.
Cooper, A., Law, R. and Lathius, J. 2000. Rooms of their own: Public toilets and gendered citizens in a New Zealand city, 1860–1940. *Gender, Place, and Culture*, 7(4), 417–33.
Corber, R. and Valocchi, S. 2003. *Queer Studies: An Interdisciplinary Reader*. Oxford: Blackwell Publishers.
Corburn, J. 2007. Reconnecting with the roots: A critical history of American planning and public health for the twenty first century. *Urban Affairs Review*, 42, 688–713.
Coulmont, B. and Hubbard, P. 2010. Consuming sex: Socio-spatial shifts in the place and space of sex shops. *Journal of Law and Society*, 37(1), 189–209.
Cox, K. and Mair, A. 1988. Locality and community in the politics of local economic development. *Annals of the Association of American Geographers*, 78, 307–25.
Crofts, P. 2003. Ambiguities in approaches to brothels: Disorderly houses of commercial premises? *Environmental Planning and Law Journal*, 20, 445–58.
Crofts, P. 2006. A decade of licit sex in the city. *Local Government Law Journal*, 12, 5–15.
Currah, P. 2006. Gender pluralisms, in *Transgender Rights*, edited by P. Currah et al. Minneapolis: University of Minnesota Press, 3–31.
Cusack, C.M. and Prior, J. 2010. Religion, sexuality and retribution: Placing the 'other' in Sydney, in *Religion and Retributive Logic: Essays in Honor of Professor Garry W. Trompf*, edited by C.M. Cusack et al. Leiden: Brill.
D'Augelli, A. and Hart, M. 1987. Gay women, men and families in rural settings: Toward the development of helping communities. *American Journal of Community Psychology* 15(1), 79–93.
Daley, C. and Minter, S. 2003. *Trans Realities: A Legal Needs Assessment of San Francisco's Transgender Communities*. San Francisco: Transgender Law Center.
Dalton, L.C. 2009. Introduction to the essays on influential planning books: The power of the published idea. *Journal of the American Planning Association*, 75(2), 257–59.
DaRosa, A. 1998. Gays continue Bahamian travel. *San Diego Union Tribune*, 24 May, F3.
Davidoff, P. 1965. Advocacy and pluralism in planning. *Journal of the American Institute of Planners*, 31, 331–7.
Davis, M. 1990. *City of Quartz: Excavating the Future in Los Angeles*. London: Vintage.
Davis, T. 1995. The diversity of queer politics and the redefinition of sexual identity and community in urban spaces, in *Mapping Desire: Geographies of Sexuality*, edited by D. Bell and G. Valentine. London: Routledge, 285–303.

List of References

DeGiovanni, F. 1983. Patterns of housing market activity in revitalizing neighborhoods. *Journal of the American Planning Association*, 49(22), 39.

DeGiovanni, F. and Paulson, N. 1984. Household diversity in revitalizing neighborhoods. *Urban Affairs Quarterly*, 20(2), 211–32.

Deleon, R. 1999. San Francisco and domestic partners: New fields of battle in the culture war, in *Culture Wars and Local Politics*, edited by B. Rienzo et al. Lawrence: University Press of Kansas, 100–116.

Demara, B. 1997. Jarvis Street complex sold to developer. *Toronto Star*, 15 July, A6.

D'Emilio, J. 1983. *Sexual Politics, Sexual Communities: The Making of a Homosexual Minority in the United Slates, 1940–1970*. Chicago: University of Chicago Press.

D'Emilio, J. 1992. *Making Trouble: Essays on Gay History, Politics, and the University*. London: Routledge.

DePalma, B. 1993. Two groups urging change in occupancy ordinance: Group home and gay, lesbian residents support ordinance plan. *St. Louis Post-Dispatch*, 11 November, Zone West 1.

Désert, J. 1997. Queer space, in *Queers in Space: Communities, Public Places, Sites of Resistance*, edited by G.B. Ingram et al. Seattle: Bay Press, 17–26.

DeWitt, K. 1994. Gay presence leads a revival in many urban neighborhoods. *New York Times*, 6 September, A1, A12.

Doan, P.L. 2001. Are the transgendered the mine shaft canaries of urban areas? *Progressive Planning: Special Issue on Queers and Planning* [Online] 146. Available at: http://www.plannersnetwork.org/publications/2001_146/Doan.html.

Doan, P.L. 2006. Violence and transgendered people, *Progressive Planning: Special Issue on Gender and Violence* [Online] 167: 28–30. Available at: http://www.plannersnetwork.org/publications/mag_2006_2_spring.html.

Doan, P.L. 2007. Queers in the American city: Transgendered perceptions of urban spaces. *Gender, Place, and Culture*, 14(1), 57–74.

Doan, P.L. 2010. The tyranny of gendered spaces: Reflections from beyond the gender dichotomy. *Gender, Place, and Culture*, 17(5), 635–54.

Doan, P.L. and Higgins, H. 2009. Cognitive dimensions of wayfinding: The implications of habitus, safety, and gender dissonance among gay and lesbian populations. *Environment and Planning A*, 41, 1745–62.

Doan, P.L. and Higgins, H. 2011. The demise of queer space? Resurgent gentrification and LGBT neighborhoods. *Journal of Planning Education and Research*, 31, 1.

Dora. 1980. Dora's dirt. *The Sydney Fart*, 1, Back Page.

Douglas, M. 2002. *Purity and Danger: An Analysis of the Concept of Pollution and Taboo*. London: Routledge.

Drabelle, D. 1997. Out and about in the city. *Preservation*, 49(1), 74, 76–8.

Duberman, M. 1993. *Stonewall*. New York: Dutton.

Dubrow, G. 1998a. Feminist and multicultural perspectives on preservation planning, in *Making the Invisible Visible, A Multicultural Planning History*, edited by L. Sandercock. Berkeley: University of California Press, 57–77.

Dubrow, G. 1998b. Blazing trails with pink triangles and rainbow flags: New directions in the preservation and interpretation of gay and lesbian heritage. *Historic Preservation Forum*, 12(3), 31–44.

Dubrow, G. 2001. Deviant history, deviant heritage. *Progressive Planning* [Online], 146. Available at: http://www.plannersnetwork.org/publications/2001_146/Dubrow.html.

Dubrow, G. and Sies, M.C. 2002. Letting our guard down: Race, class, gender, and sexuality in planning history. *Journal of Planning History*, 1, 203–14.

Duggan, L. 1986. History's gay ghetto: The contradictions of growth in lesbian and gay history, in *Presenting the Past: Essays on History and the Public*, edited by S.P. Benson et al. Philadelphia: Temple University Press, 281–92.

Duggan, L. 2002a. *The Twilight of Equality? Neoliberalism, Cultural Politics and the Attack on Democracy*. Boston: Beacon Press.

Duggan, L. 2002b. The new homonormativity: The sexual politics of neoliberalism, in *Materializing Democracy: Towards a Revitalized Cultural Politics*, edited by R. Castronovo and D. Nelson. Durham: Duke University Press, 175–94.

Duncan, N. 1996. Renegotiating gender and sexuality in public and private spaces, in *Body Space: Destabilizing Geographies of Gender and Sexuality*, edited by N. Duncan. London: Routledge, 127–45.

Dunlap, D.W. 1999. Stonewall, gay bar that made history, is made a landmark. *New York Times*, 26 June, 1.

Editorial. 1997. Giving the public voice. *Chicago Sun Times*, 4 November, 29.

Edwards, M. 2010. Gender, social disorganization theory, and the locations of sexually oriented businesses. *Deviant Behaviour*, 31, 135–58.

Egerton, J. 1990. Out but not down: Lesbians' experiences of housing. *Feminist Review*, 35, 75–88.

Eisler, B. 1991. *O'Keeffe and Stieglitz: An American Romance*. New York: Doubleday.

Elder, G.S. 1999. 'Queerying' boundaries in the geography classroom. *Journal of Geography in Higher Education*, 23(1), 86–93.

Elliman, M. and Roll, F. 1995. *The Pink Plague Guide to London*. London: Gay Men's Press.

Elliott, P. and Roen, K. 1998. Transgenderism and the question of embodiment, *GLQ: A Journal of Gay and Lesbian Studies*, 4(2), 231–61.

Elwood, S.A. 2000. Lesbian living spaces: Multiple meanings of home, in *From Nowhere to Everywhere: Lesbian Geographies*, edited by G. Valentine. New York: Harrington Park Press, 11–28.

Enigma Research 2006. *Economic Impact Assessment: 2006 Pride Toronto*. Available at: http://www.pridetoronto.com/downloads/Economic_Impact_Assessment_2006.pdf.

Enigma Research. 2009. *2009 Pride Toronto Economic Impact Study*. Available at: http://www.pridetoronto.com/downloads/Economic_Impact_Study_2009.pdf.

Ettorre, E.M. 1978. Women, urban social movements and the lesbian ghetto. *International Journal of Urban and Regional Research*, 2, 499–520.

Faderman, L. 1991. *Odd Girls and Twilight Lovers: A History of Lesbian Life in Twentieth-Century America*. New York: Columbia Press.

Fainstein, S. 2000. New directions in planning theory. *Urban Affairs Review*, 35, 451–78.

Fainstein, S. 2005. Cities and diversity: Should we want it? Can we plan for it? *Urban Affairs Review*, 41(1), 3–19.

Fainstein, S. 2010. *The Just City*. Ithaca: Cornell University Press.

Fainstein, S. and Fainstein, N.I. 1971. City planning and political values. *Urban Affairs Review*, 6, 341–62.

Fainstein, S. and Servon, L. (eds). 2005. *Gender and Planning: A Reader*. New Brunswick: Rutgers University Press.

Fausto-Sterling, A. 2000. *Sexing the Body: Gender Politics and the Construction of Sexuality*. New York: Basic Books.

Feinberg, L. 1993. *Stone Butch Blues: A Novel*. Ithaca: Firebrand Books.

Feinberg, L. 1996. Transgender Warriors: Making History from Joan of Arc to Dennis Rodman. Boston: Beacon Press.

Felsenthal, K. 2004. Socio-spatial experiences of transgender individuals, in *The Psychology of Prejudice and Discrimination*, edited by J.L. Chin. Westport: Praeger Publishers, 201–25.

Fenster, T. (ed.) 1999. *Gender, Planning and Human Rights*. London: Routledge.

Fetner, T. 2008. *How the Religious Right Shaped Lesbian and Gay Activism*. Minneapolis: University of Minnesota Press.

Filler, M. 1996. The architect of a master builder's store of art. *New York Times*, 2 June, Section 2, 37 and 40.

Fincher, R. and Iveson, K. 2008. *Planning and Diversity in the City: Redistribution, Recognition, and Encounter*. Basingstoke: Palgrave-Macmillan.

Finucan, K. 2000. Gay today. *Planning*, 66(2), 12.

Fitzgerald, M. 1983. Homosexuals outline fears, many voice complaints, but worry about being identified. *Daily Hampshire Gazette*, 11 February, 1, 13.

Fjellman, S. 1992. *Vinyl Leaves: Walt Disney World and America*. Boulder: Westview Press.

Flood, M. and Hamilton, C. 2008. Mapping homophobia in Australia, in *Homophobia: An Australian History*, edited by S. Robinson. Annandale: Federation Press, 16–38.

Florida, R. 2002a. *The Rise of the Creative Class: And How it's Transforming Work, Leisure, Community and Everyday Life*. New York: Basic Books.

Florida, R. 2002b. The economic geography of talent. *Annals of the Association of American Geographers*, 92(4), 743–55.

Florida, R. 2005. *Cities and the Creative Class*. London: Routledge.

Florida, R. and Gates, G. 2001. *Technology and Tolerance: Diversity and High-tech Growth*. [Online]. Available at: http://www.brookings.edu/es/urban/techtol.pdf [accessed: 24 September 2009].

Florida, R. and Mellander, C. 2007. *There Goes the Neighborhood: How and Why Bohemians, Artists and Gays Effect Regional Housing Values*. (Working paper). George Mason University. Available at: http://creativeclass.typepad.com/thecreativityexchange/files/Florida_Mellander_Housing_Values_1.pdf [accessed 19 September 2009].

Florida, R. and Mellander, C. 2010. There goes the metro: How and why bohemians, artists and gays affect regional housing values. *Journal of Economic Geography*, 10, 167–88.

Florida, R., Mellander, C., and Stolarick, K. 2008. Inside the black box of regional development – Human capital, the creative class and tolerance. *Journal of Economic Geography*, 8, 615–50.

Florida, R., Mellander, C. and Stolarick, K. 2010. Talent, technology and tolerance in Canadian regional development. *The Canadian Geographer/Le Geographe canadien*, 54, 277–304.

Fodor's Gay Guide to the U.S.A. 1998. New York: Fodor's Travel Publications.

Fogelsong, R. 2001. *Married to the Mouse: Walt Disney World and Orlando*. New Haven: Yale University Press.

Forest, B. 1995. West Hollywood as a symbol: The significance of place in the construction of a gay identity. *Environment and Planning D: Society and Space*, 13, 133–57.

Forester, J. 1982. Planning in the face of power. *Journal of the American Planning Association*, 48(1), 67–80.

Forsyth, A. 1997a. NoHo: Upscaling Main Street on the metropolitan edge. *Urban Geography*, 18(7), 622–52.

Forsyth, A. 1997b. 'Out' in the valley. *International Journal of Urban and Regional Research*, 21(1), 36–61.

Forsyth, A. 2001. Sexuality and space: Nonconformist populations and planning practice. *Journal of Planning Literature*, 15, 339–58.

Foucault, M. 1978. *The History of Sexuality, Volume 1: An Introduction*. Robert Hurley, trans. New York: Random House.

Foucault, M. 1991. Space, knowledge and power, in *The Foucault Reader: An Introduction to Foucault's Thought*, edited by P. Rabinow. New York: Penguin Group, 239–56.

Foucault, M. 1992. Governmentality, in *The Foucault Effect: Studies in Governmentality*, edited by G. Burchell et al. Chicago: University of Chicago Press, 87–104.

Franzen, T. 1993. Differences and identities: Feminism and the Albuquerque lesbian community. *Signs*, 18(4), 891–906.

Fraser, N. 2003. Social justice in the age of identity politics: redistribution, recognition and participation, in *Redistribution or Recognition: A Political-*

Philosophical Exchange, edited by N. Fraser and A. Honneth. London: Verso, 7–109.

French, R. 1986. *Gays Between the Broadsheets: Australian Media References on Homosexuality, 1948–1980*. Sydney: Gay History Project.

Frey, W.H. 2001. *Melting Pot Suburbs: A Census 2000 Study of Suburban Diversity*. [Online: The Brookings Institution, Center on Urban and Metropolitan Policy, Census 2000 Series]. Available at: www.frey-demographer.org/reports/billf.pdf [accessed: 25 September 2009].

Friedman, S. and Rosenbaum, E. 2007. Does suburban residence mean better neighborhood conditions for all households? Assessing the influence of nativity status and race/ethnicity. *Social Science Research*, 36, 1–27.

Frisch, M. 2002. Planning as a heterosexist project. *Journal of Planning Education and Research*, 21(3), 254–66.

Frisch, M. and Servon, L. 2006. CDCs and the changing context for urban community development: A review of the field and the environment. *Community Development*, 37(4), 88–108.

Fuss, D. 1991. Inside/out, in *Inside/Out: Lesbian Theories, Gay Theories*, edited by D. Fuss. London: Routledge, 1–10.

Gagnon, J. and Simon, W. (eds) *Sexual Deviance*. New York: Harper and Row.

Gates, G. 2001. *Gay and Lesbian Families in the US Same-sex Unmarried Partner Households*. [Online: Population Studies Center, the Urban Institute]. Available at: http://www.urban.org/UploadedPDF/1000491_gl_partner_households.pdf.

Gates, G.J. and Ost, J. 2004. *The Gay & Lesbian Atlas*. Washington: Urban Institute Press.

Gay Days, Inc. 2009. *What IS Orlando Gay Days?* Available at: http://www.gaydays.com/about/history.html [accessed: 3 June 2007].

Geddes, P. and Thomson, J.A. 1890. *The Evolution of Sex*. New York: Henry Holt.

Gellen, M. 1985. *Accessory Apartments in Single-Family Housing*. New Brunswick: Center for Urban Policy Research.

Geltmaker, T. 1992. The queer nation acts up: Health care, politics, and sexual diversity in the city of angels. *Environment and Planning D*, 10, 609–50.

Germain, A. and Radice, M. 2006. Cosmopolitanism by default: Public sociability in Montreal, in *Cosmopolitan Urbanism*, edited by J. Binnie et al. London: Routledge, 112–29.

Gershenson, O. and Penner, B. 2009. *Ladies and Gents: Public Toilets and Gender*. Philadelphia: Temple University Press.

Gerstmann, E. 1999. *The Constitutional Underclass: Gays, Lesbians and the Failure of Class-based Equal Protection*. Chicago: University of Chicago Press.

Gilmartin, K. 1996. 'We weren't bar people': Middle-class lesbian identities and cultural spaces. *GLQ: Gay and Lesbian Quarterly*, 3(1): 1–51.

Gleeson, B. and Low, N. 2000. *Australian Urban Planning: New Challenges, New Agendas*. Sydney: Allen and Unwin.

GLEH. 2010. *Gay and Lesbian Elder Housing: Our History.* Available at: http://www.gleh.org/index.cfm?fuseaction=category.display&category_id=13.

GlenMary Research Center. 2000. *Religious Congregations & Membership: 2000.* Available at: http://www.glenmary.org/grc/default.htm [accessed: 2 June 2007].

Geolytics, Inc. Neighborhood Change Database (NCDB) 1970–2000 Tract Data.

Godfrey, B. 1988. *Neighborhoods in Transition: The Making of San Francisco's Nonconformist Communities.* Berkeley: University of California Press.

Goldsmith, W. and Blakeley, E. 1992. *Separate Societies: Poverty and Inequality in US Cities.* Philadelphia: Temple University Press.

Golden Gate Business Association. 1999. *Great Links to Other Lesbian/Gay Web Sites.* Available at: http://www.ggba.com/pages/links.html.

Goonewardena, K. and Kipfer, S. 2006. Spaces of difference: Reflections from Toronto on multiculturalism, bourgeois urbanism and the possibility of radical urban politics. *International Journal of Urban and Regional Research,* 29, 670–78.

Gorelick, R. 2004. Baltimore needs a visible gay and lesbian community to thrive – And the gay and lesbian community needs to get with it. *Baltimore City Paper: The Queer Issue.* [Online, 9 June] Available at: at http://www.citypaper.com/special/story.asp?id=7558.

Gorman-Murray, A. and Waitt, G. 2009. Queer-friendly neighborhoods: Interrogating social cohesion across sexual difference in two Australian neighborhoods. *Environment and Planning A,* 41, 2855–73.

Gorman-Murray, A. and Brennan-Horley, C. 2010. The geography of same-sex families in Australia: Implications for regulatory regimes, in *Current Trends in the Regulation of Same-Sex Relationships,* edited by P. Gerber and A. Sifris. Sydney: Federation Press.

Gorman-Murray, A., Brennan-Horley, C., McLean, K., Waitt, G., and Gibson, C. 2010. Mapping same-sex couple family households in Australia. *Journal of Maps,* 382–92.

Gotham, K. 2002. Marketing Mardi Gras: Commodification, spectacle and the political economy of tourism in New Orleans. *Urban Studies,* 39(10), 1735–56.

Gover, T. 1993. Lesbian festival may spark tourist boom for city. *Daily Hampshire Gazette,* 21 July, 25, 32.

Grant, J. M., Mottet, L.A., Tanis, J., Harrison, J., Herman, J.L., and Keisling, M. 2011. *Injustice at Every Turn: A Report of the National Transgender Discrimination Survey.* Washington: National Center for Transgender Equality and National Gay and Lesbian Task Force.

Greater Seattle Business Association. 2010. *History* [Online]. Available at: http://www.thegsba.org/about/history/.

Greed, C. 1994. *Women and Planning: Creating Gendered Realities.* London: Routledge.

Greed, C. 1995. Public toilet provision for women in Britain: An investigation of discrimination against urination. *Women's Studies International Forum*, 18(5/6), 573–84.

Greed, C. 2003. *Public Toilets: Inclusive Urban Design*. Oxford: Oxford University Press.

Greed, C. 2005. Overcoming the factors inhibiting the mainstreaming of gender into spatial policy planning in the United Kingdom. *Urban Studies*, 42(4), 1–31.

Greed, C. 2006. Planning for women and other disenabled groups, with reference to the provision of public toilets in Britain. *Environment and Planning A*, 28, 573–88.

Green, A.I. 2007. Queer theory and sociology: Locating the subject and the self in sexuality studies. *Sociological Theory*, 25(1), 26–45.

Green Park Observer. 1983. Police at war. *Green Park Observer*, April 1983, 5.

Greenberg, J. 2006. The road less traveled: The problem with binary sex categories, in *Transgender Rights*, edited by P. Currah et al. Minneapolis: University of Minnesota Press, 51–73.

Gregson, N. and Rose. G. 2000. Taking Butler elsewhere: Performativities, spatialities and subjectivities. *Environment and Planning D: Society and Space*, 18, 433–52.

Griffin, S. 2002. *Tinker Belles and Evil Queens: The Walt Disney Company from the Inside Out*. New York: New York University Press.

Grosz, E.A. 1995. *Space, Time, and Perversion: Essays on the Politics of Bodies*. New York: Routledge.

Grube, J. 1997. No more shit: The struggle for democratic gay space in Toronto, in *Queers in Space: Communities, Public Places, Sites of Resistance*, edited by G. Ingram et al. Seattle: Bay Press, 127–46.

Grundy, J. and Smith, M. 2005. The politics of multiscalar citizenship: The case of lesbian and gay organizing in Canada. *Citizenship Studies*, 9, 389–404.

Haeberle, S. 1996. Gay men and lesbians at City Hall. *Social Science Quarterly*, 77(1), 190–97.

Haggerty, G.E. and Zimmerman, B. (eds) 1995. *Professions of Desire: Lesbian and Gay Studies in Literature*. New York: Modern Language Association of America.

Haire, B. 1999. Full steam ahead: Mardi Gras plans for the future. *Sydney Star Observer* [Online, 15 April] Available at: http://www.mardigras.com.au/media%26news/story_33.asp.

Halberstam, J. 2005. *In a Queer Time and Place*. New York: New York University Press.

Hanlon, B. 2008. The decline of older, inner suburbs in metropolitan America. *Housing Policy Debate*, 19(3), 423–55.

Hanna, J.L. 2005. Exotic dance adult entertainment: A guide for planners and policy makers. *Journal of Planning Literature*, 20(2), 116–34.

Harper, T. and Stein, S. 2006. *Dialogical Planning in a Fragmented Society: Critically Liberal, Pragmatic, Incremental*. New Brunswick: Center for Urban Policy Research Press.

Harris, C. and Ullman, E.L. 1945. The nature of cities. *Annals of the Academy of Political and Social Science*, 242, 7–17.

Harris, D.R. 1999. *All Suburbs Are Not Created Equal: A New Look at Racial Differences in Suburban Location*. [Online: University of Michigan. Population Studies Center at the Institute for Social Research]. Available at: http://www.psc.isr.umich.edu/pubs/pdf/rr99-440.pdf [accessed: 25 September 2009].

Harry, J. 1974. Urbanization and the gay life. *Journal of Sex Research*, 10(3), 238–47.

Harvey, D. 1989a. *The Condition of Postmodernity: An Inquiry Into the Origins of Cultural Change*. Cambridge: Butterworth.

Harvey, D. 1989b. From managerialism to enterpreneurialism: The transformation in urban governance in late capitalism. *Geografiska Annaler B*, 71, 3–17.

Hausbeck, K. and Brents, B. 2002. McDonaldization of the sex industry? The business of sex, in *McDonaldization: The Reader*, edited by G. Ritzer. Thousand Oaks: Pine Forge Press, 102–18.

Hayden, D. 1980. What would a non-sexist city be like? Speculations on housing, urban, design, and human work. *Signs: Supplement – Women and the American City*, 5(3), S170–S187.

Hayden, D. 1984. *Redesigning the American Dream*. New York: Norton.

Hayden, D. 1995. *The Power of Place: Urban Landscapes as Public History*. Cambridge: Massachusetts Institute of Technology Press.

Harwit, M. 1996. *An Exhibit Denied*. New York: Copernicus.

Healey, P. 1997. *Collaborative Planning: Shaping Places in Fragmented Societies*. London: Macmillan.

Hemmings, C. 2002. *Bisexual Spaces: A Geography of Sexuality and Gender*. London: Routledge.

Hendler, S. and Harrison, H. 2000. Theorizing Canadian planning history: Women, gender, and feminist perspectives, in *Gendering the City: Women, Boundaries, and Visions of Urban Life*, edited by K. Miranne and A.H. Young. New York: Rowman and Littlefield Publishing, 139–56.

Herdt, G. (ed.) 1994. *Third Sex, Third Gender: Beyond Sexual Dimorphism in Culture and History*. New York: Zone Books.

Herman, D. 1996. (Il)legitimate minorities: The American Christian right's anti-gay discourse. *Law and Society*, 23(3): 46–363.

Herscher, E. 1999. Plan for gay youth shelter in Castro unnerves some residents. *San Francisco Chronicle*, 9 August, A13.

Herson, M. and Barlow, D.H. 1976. *Single Case Experimental Designs*. New York: Academic Press.

Hertz, B. Eisenberg, E., and Knauer, L.M. 1997. Queer spaces in New York City: Places of struggle/places of strength, in *Queers in Space: Communities,*

Public Places, Sites of Resistance, edited by G. Ingram et al. Seattle: Bay Press, 357–72.

Higgs D. (ed.) 1999. *Queer Sites: Gay Urban Histories Since 1600*. London: Routledge.

Hillier, J. and Rooksby, E. (eds) 2002. *Habitus: A Sense of Place*. Aldershot: Ashgate.

Hines, S. 2006. What's the difference? Bringing particularity to queer studies of transgender. *Journal of Gender Studies*, 15(1), 49–66.

History Project, The. 1998. *Improper Bostonians*. Boston: Beacon Press.

Hobica, G. 1994. Boys in the 'burbs. *Genre*, February, 32–4, 69.

Hodge, S. 1995. 'No fags out there: Gay men, identity and suburbia. *Journal of Interdisciplinary Gender Studies*, 1, 41–8.

Hogrefe, J. 1992. *O'Keeffe: The Life of an American Legend*. New York: Bantam.

Holcomb. B. and Luongo, M. Gay tourism in the United States. *Annals of Tourism Research*, 23(3), 711–13.

Houlbrook, M. 2005. The city, in *Palgrave Advances in Modern History – Sexuality*, edited by H. Cocks and M. Houlbrook. London: Palgrave.

Howe, D. and Hammer, J. 2002. EnGendering Change: Impacts of the Faculty Women's Interest Group on the Planning Academy. Paper presented at the Association of Collegiate Schools of Planning Annual Conference, Baltimore Maryland.

Hoyman, M. and Faricy, C. 2009. It takes a village: A test of the creative class, social capital, and human capital theories. *Urban Affairs Review*, 44, 311–33.

Hoyt, H. 1933. *One Hundred Years of Land Values in Chicago: The Relationship of the Growth of Chicago to the Rise in its Land Values, 1830–1933*. Chicago: The University of Chicago Press.

Howe, M. 1994. Attacks against gays raise fears. *New York Times*, 29 May, Section 14: 6.

Hubbard, P. 1999. *Sex and the City: Geographies of Prostitution in the Urban West*. Aldershot: Ashgate.

Hubbard, P. 2000. Desire/disgust: Mapping the moral contours of heterosexuality. *Progress in Human Geography*, 24, 191–217.

Hubbard, P. 2001. Sex zones: Intimacy, citizenship and public space. *Sexualities*, 4, 51–71.

Hubbard, P. 2004a. Cleansing the metropolis: Sex work and the politics of zero tolerance. *Urban Studies*, 41, 1687–701.

Hubbard, P. 2004b. Revenge and injustice in the revanchist city: Uncovering masculinist agendas. *Antipode*, 36(4), 665–86.

Hubbard, P. 2008. Here, there, everywhere: The ubiquitous geographies of heteronormativity. *Geography Compass*, 2(3), 640–58.

Hubbard, P. 2009. Opposing striptopia. *Sexualities*, 12(6), 721–45.

Hubbard, P., Matthews, R., and Scoular, J. 2009. Legal Geograhpies – Controlling sexually-oriented businesses: Law, licensing and the geographies of a controversial land use. *Urban Geography*, 30, 185–205.

Hubbard, P.J., Matthews, R., Scoular, J., and Agustin, L. 2008. Away from prying eyes? The urban geographies of adult entertainment. *Progress in Human Geography*, 32, 361–79.

Hughes, H. 2004. A gay tourism market: Reality or illusion, benefit or burden? *Journal of Quality Assurance in Hospitality and Tourism*, 5(2), 57–74.

Hughes, H. and Deusch, R. 2010. Holidays of older gay men: Age or sexual orientation as decisive factors. *Tourism Management*, 31(4), 454–463.

Humphrey, L. 1975. *Tearoom Trade: Impersonal Sex in Public Places*. Chicago: Aldine Publishing Company.

Humphries, D. 2006a. Same-sex laws face federal resistance. *Sydney Morning Herald*, 31 March.

Humphries, D. 2006b. Gay couples seize the day … before Howard quashes civil union laws. *Sydney Morning Herald*, 8 June.

Hurewitz, D. 1997. *Stepping Out: Nine Walks Through New York City's Gay and Lesbian History*. New York: Henry Holt and Company.

Ingram, G.B., Bouthillette, A-M., and Retter, Y. (eds). 1997. *Queers in Space: Communities, Public Places, and Sites of Resistance*. Seattle: Bay Press.

Jackson, K. 1998. Islands in a sea of controversy: Caymans ban a gay cruise. *The Seattle Times*, 18 January, K1.

Jagose A. 1996. *Queer Theory: An Introduction*. New York: New York University Press.

Jarvis, H., Kantor, P., and Cloke, J. 2009. *Cities and Gender*. London: Routledge.

Jeffreys, S. 2008. *Industrial Vagina: The Global Political Economy of Sex*. London: Routledge.

Johnston, C. 1986a. Letter to David Ross regarding DA for gay recreation centre and bathhouse. *The Council of the City of Sydney*. Sydney.

Johnston, C. 1986b. Roman rumors. *Sydney's Star Observer*, 22 August, 35, 7.

Johnson, C. 2003. Heteronormative citizenship: The Howard government's views on gay and lesbian issues. *Australian Journal of Political Science*, 38, 45–62.

Johnson, D. 1997. Chicago celebrates gay lesbian neighborhood. *Minneapolis Star Tribune*, 31 August, 19A.

Johnston, L. 1971. Christopher Street: From farm to gay center. *New York Times*, July 26, 1971, 27.

Johnson, L. 2000. *Placebound: Australian Feminist Geographies*. South Melbourne: Oxford University Press.

Jolly, S. 2000. 'Queering' development: Exploring the links between same-sex sexualities. *Gender and Development*, 8(1), 78–88.

Judd, D.R. and Fainstein, S.S. (eds). 1999. *The Tourist City*. New Haven: Yale University Press.

Kahan, H. and Mulryan, D. 1995. Out of the closet. *American Demographics*, May, 40–47.

Kaiser, C. 1997. *The Gay Metropolis: The Landmark History of Gay and Life in America Since World War II*. New York: Harcourt Brace & Co.

Katz, J. 1995. *The Invention of Heterosexuality*. New York: Dutton.

Keen, L. and Stoesen, L. 1994. Gay couples come out in census data. *Washington Blade*, 24 June, 1, 24–5.

Kelly, B. 1975. Building Inspection Report For Extension of Existing Karate Club at 83/85 Anzac Pde, Kensington. Randwick Municipal Council. Sydney.

Kelly, E.D. and Cooper, C. 2001. *Everything You Always Wanted to Know About Regulating Sex Businesses*. Chicago: American Planning Association.

Kenagy, G. 2005. Transgender health: Findings from two needs assessment studies in Philadelphia. *Health and Social Work*, 30(1), 19–26.

Kennedy, E.L. and Davis, M.D. 1993. *Boots of Leather, Slippers of Gold: The History of a Lesbian Community*. London: Routledge.

Kenney, M. 1994. *Strategic Invisibility: Gay and Lesbian Place-Claiming in Los Angeles, 1970–1994*. (Unpublished doctoral dissertation). Department of Urban Planning, University of California, Los Angeles, CA.

Kenney, M. 1998. Remember, Stonewall was a riot: Understanding gay and lesbian experience in the city, in *Making the Invisible Visible: A Multicultural Planning History*, edited by L. Sandercock. Berkeley: University of California Press, 120–32.

Kenney, M. 2001. *Mapping Gay LA: The Intersections of Place and Politics*. Philadelphia: Temple University Press.

Kerkin, K. 2003. Re-placing difference: Planning and street sex work in a gentrifying area. *Urban Policy and Research*, 21(2), 137–49.

Kerkin, K. 2004. Discourse, representation and urban planning: How a critical approach to discourse helps reveal the spatial re-ordering of street sex work. *Australian Geographer*, 35, 185–192.

Kerstein, R. 1990. Stage models in gentrification: An examination. *Urban Affairs Quarterly*, 25(4), 620–39.

Kessler, S. 1998. *Lessons from the Intersexed*. New Brunswick: Rutgers University Press.

King, S. 2009. Homonormativity and the politics of race: Reading Sheryl Swoopes. *Journal of Lesbian Studies*, 13, 272–90.

Kirkey, K. and Forsyth, A. 2001. Men in the valley: Gay male life on the suburban-rural fringe. *Journal of Rural Studies*, 17, 421–41.

Klawitter, M. and Flatt, V. 1998. The effects of state and local antidiscrimination policies on earnings for gays and lesbians. *Journal of Policy Analysis and Management*, 17(4), 658–86.

Knopp, L. 1987. Social theory, social movements and public policy: Recent accomplishments of the gay and lesbian movements in Minneapolis, Minnesota. *International Journal of Urban and Regional Research*, 11(2), 243–61.

Knopp, L. 1990a. Some theoretical implications of gay involvement in an urban land market. *Political Geography Quarterly*, 9, 337–52.

Knopp, L. 1990b. Exploiting the rent gap: The theoretical significance of using illegal appraisal schemes to encourage gentrification in New Orleans. *Urban Geography*, 11, 48–64.

Knopp, L. 1992. Sexuality and the spatial dynamics of capitalism. *Environment and Planning D*, 10, 651–69.
Knopp, L. 1994. Social justice, sexuality, and the city. *Urban Geography*, 15(7), 644–60.
Knopp, L. 1995. Sexuality and urban space: A framework for analysis, in *Mapping Desire: Geographies of Sexualities*, edited by D. Bell and G. Valentine. London: Routledge, 149–61.
Knopp, L. 1997. Gentrification and gay neighborhood formation in New Orleans, in *Homo Economics*, edited by A. Gluckman and B. Reed. London: Routledge, 45–64.
Knopp, L. 1998. Sexuality and urban space, gay male identity politics in the United States, the United Kingdom and Australia, in *Cities of Difference*, edited by R. Fincher and J. M. Jacobs. New York: Guilford, 149–76.
Knopp, L. 2007. On the relationship between queer and feminist geographies. *The Professional Geographer*, 59(1), 47–55.
Knopp L. and Brown, M. 2003. Queer diffusions. *Environment and Planning D: Society and Space*, 21, 409–424.
Koehn, K. 1996. GALA festival to bring in money. *Tampa Tribune*, 5 July, Florida Metro Section, 1.
Kong, L. 2000. Culture, economy, policy: Trends and developments. *Geoforum*, 31, 385–90.
Kramer, J. 1995. Bachelor farmers and spinsters: Gay and lesbian identities and communities in rural North Dakota, in *Mapping Desire: Geographies of Sexualities*, edited by D. Bell and G. Valentine. London: Routledge, 200–213.
Krieger, S. 1983. *The Mirror Dance: Identity in a Women's Community*. Philadelphia: Temple University Press.
Krumholz, N., and Forester, J. 1990. *Making Equity Planning Work: Leadership in the Public Sector*. Philadelphia: Temple University Press.
Künkel, J. 2008. Das quartier als revanchistische stadtpolitik. Verdrängung des sexgewerbes im namen eines neoliberalen konstrukts, in *Quartiersforschung. Zwischen Theorie und Praxis Wiesbaden*, edited by O. Schnur. VS Verlag für Sozialwissenschaften.
Kweit, R. and Kweit, M. 1998. *People and Politics in Urban America*. London: Routledge.
Landry, C. and Bianchini, F. 1995. *The Creative City*. London: Demos.
Larsen, E.N. 1992. The politics of prostitution control: Interest group politics in four Canadian cities. *International Journal of Urban and Regional Studies*, 16, 169–87.
Lasker, S. 2002. Sex and the city: Zoning pornography peddlers and live nude shows. *UCLA Law Review*, 49(4), 1139–86.
Lauria, M. and Knopp, L. 1985. Toward an analysis of the role of gay communities in the urban renaissance. *Urban Geography*, 6, 152–69.

Leavitt, J. 1981. The history, status, and concerns of women planners, in *Women and the American City*, edited by C. Stimson et al. Chicago: University of Chicago Press, 223–27.

Lee, A. 1997. Discovering old cultures in the new world: The role of ethnicity, in *The American Mosaic*, edited by R.E. Stipe and A. Lee. Washington, DC: US/ICOMOS, 179–206.

Lee, A. 1992a. Cultural diversity and historic preservation. *CRM Bulletin*, 15, 7.

Lee, A. 1992b. Multicultural building blocks, in *Past Meets Future: Saving America's Historic Environments*, edited by A. Lee. Washington, DC: Preservation Press, 93–8.

Lee, A. and Lyon, E. 1992. Cultural and ethnic diversity in historic preservation. *National Trust for Historic Preservation Information Series*, No. 65.

Lee, D. 1980. *The Gay Community and Improvements in the Quality of Life in San Francisco*. (Masters thesis). University of California at Berkeley.

Lefebvre, H. 1991. *The Production of Space*. Oxford: Blackwell Publishing.

Lesbian and Gay Community Services Center. 1999. Available at: http://www.gaycenter.org/ [accessed: September 1999].

Leslie, D. 2005. Creative cities? *Geoforum*, 36, 403–5.

LeVay, S. and Nonas, E. 1995. *City of Friends: A Portrait of the Gay and Lesbian Community in America*. Cambridge: Massachusetts Institute of Technology Press.

Levine, M. 1979. Gay ghetto. *Journal of Homosexuality*, 4, 363–77.

Ley, D. 1993. Gentrification in recession: Social change in six Canadian inner cities, 1981–1986. *Urban Geography*, 13(3), 230–56.

Liberty Counsel 2007. Available at: http://www.lc.org/ [accessed: 27 June 2007].

Liepe-Levinson, K. 2002. *Strip Show: Performances of Gender and Desire*. London: Routledge.

Lind, A. 2010. Development, global governance, and sexual subjectivities: Neoliberal challenges, post-queer futures, in *Development, Sexual Rights, and Global Governance*, edited by A. Lind. London: Routledge, 1–20.

Lind. A. 2009. Governing intimacy, struggling for sexual rights: Challenging heteronormativity in the global development industry, *Development*, 52(1), 34–42.

Lind, A. and Share, J. 2003. Queering development: Institutionalized heterosexuality in development theory, practice and politics in Latin America, in *Feminist Futures: Re-Imagining Women, Culture and Development*, edited by K. Bhavnani, J. Foran, and P. Kurian. London: Zed Press, 55–73.

Linenthal, E.T. and Engelhardt, T. (eds) 1996. *History Wars: The Enola Gay and Other Battles for the American Past*. New York: Metropolitan Books.

Listerborn, C. 2007. Who speaks? And who listens? The relationship between planners and women's participation in local planning in a multi-cultural urban environment. *GeoJournal*, 70, 61–74.

Liu, T. 1991. Teaching the differences among women from a historical perspective: Rethinking race and gender as social categories. *Women's Studies International Forum*, 14(4), 265–76.

Lockard, D. 1985. The lesbian community: An anthropological approach. *Journal of Homosexuality*, 11, 83–95.

Logan, J. and Molotch, H 1987. *Urban Fortunes*. Berkeley: University of California Press.

Logan, J.R., Alba, R.D., and Leung, S-Y. 1996. Minority access to white suburbs: A multiregional comparison. *Social Forces*, 74, 851–881.

Lombardi, E., Wilchins, R., Priesing, D., and Malouf, D. 2001. Gender violence: Transgender experiences with violence and discrimination. *Journal of Homosexuality*, 42(1), 89–101.

Long, J. 2009. Sustaining creativity in the creative archetype: The case of Austin, Texas. *Cities*, 26, 210–19.

Los Angeles Times. 1995. Westside neighbors oppose plan for gay center. *Los Angeles Times*, 22 July, B22.

Lowman, J. 1992. Street prostitution control: Some Canadian reflections of the Finsbury Park experience. *British Journal of Criminology*, 32, 1–16.

Lubrano, G. 1984. Gays aren't afraid and may be a force. *The San Diego Union-Tribune*, 4 March, B1.

Luckman, S., Gibson, C., and Lea, T. 2009. Mosquitoes in the mix: How transferable is creative city thinking? *Singapore Journal of Tropical Geography*, 30, 70–85.

Lucy, W.H. and Phillips, D.L. 2006. *Tomorrow's Cities, Tomorrow's Suburbs*. Chicago: APA Planners Press.

Lustbader, K.M. 1993. *Landscape of Liberation: Preserving Gay and Lesbian History in Greenwich Village*. (Masters thesis). Historic Preservation Program, Columbia University, New York, NY.

Lynch, F. 1987. Non-ghetto gays: A sociological study of suburban homosexuals. *Journal of Homosexuality*, 13(4), 13–42.

Lynch, F. 1992. Non-ghetto gays: An ethnography of suburban homosexuals, in *Gay Culture in America: Essays from the Field*, edited by G. Herdt. Boston: Beacon Press, 165–201.

Lyod, B. and Rowntree, L. 1978. Radical feminists and gay men in San Francisco: Social space in dispersed communities, in *An Invitation to Geography*, edited by D. Langren and R. Palm. New York: McGraw-Hill Book Company, 78–88.

Mackenzie, G. 1994. *Transgender Nation*. Bowling Green: Bowling Green State University.

Macris, M. n.d. *Beginnings of the Planning and Women Division of the American Planning Association* [Online: Planning and Women Division of the American Planning Association]. Available at: http://www.planning.org/divisions/planningandwomen/history.htm [accessed: 28 August 2009].

Mai, N. 2009. Between minor and errant mobility: The relation between the psychological dynamics and the migration patterns of young men selling sex in the EU. *Mobilities*, 4(3), 349–66.

Manning, C.A. 1989. Explaining intercity home price differences. *Journal of Real Estate Finance and Economics*, 2, 131–49.

Manning, C.A. 1986. Intercity differences in home price appreciation. *Journal of Real Estate Research*, 1, 45–66.

Marcus, E. *Making History: The Struggle for Gay and Lesbian Equal Rights, 1945–1990: An Oral History*. New York: HarperCollins.

Markusen, A. 2006. Urban development and the politics of a creative class: Evidence from a study of artists. *Environment and Planning A*, 38, 1921–40.

Martin, D. and Lyon, P. 1991. *Lesbian/Woman*. Volcano: Volcano Press.

Martinac, P. 1997. *The Queerest Places: A National Guide to Gay and Lesbian Historic Sites*. New York: Henry Holt.

Martinac, P. 2010. *Stonewall Inn*. [Online]. Available at: http://www.preservationnation.org/issues/diversity/lgbt-heritage-in-preservation/sites/stonewall-inn.html.

Marcus, E. 2002. *Making Gay History: The Half Century Fight for Lesbian and Gay Equal Rights*. New York: Harper Collins Publishers.

Massey, D. and Denton, N. 1993. *American Apartheid: Segregation and the Making of the Underclass*. Cambridge: Harvard University Press.

McAlinden, A.M. 2006. Managing risk: From regulation to reintegration of sexual offenders. *Criminology and Criminal Justice*, 6(2), 197–218.

McCann, E. 2002. The cultural politics of local economic development. *Geoforum*, 33(3), 385–98.

McCann, E. 2007. Inequality and politics in the creative city-region: Questions of livability and state strategy. *International Journal of Urban and Regional Research*, 31, 188–96.

McCarthy, L. 2000. Poppies in a wheat field: Exploring the lives of rural lesbians. *Journal of Homosexuality*, 39, 75–94.

McDowell, L. 1993. Space, place and gender relations, part 1: Feminist empiricism and the geography of social relations. *Progress in Human Geography*, 17, 157–79.

McInnes, D. 2001. Inside the outside: Politics and gay and lesbian spaces in Sydney, in *Queer City: Gay and Lesbian Politics in Sydney*, edited by C. Johnston and P. Van Reyk. Annadale: Pluto Press.

McKay, A. (ed.) 1993. *Wolf Girls at Vassar: Lesbian and Gay Experiences, 1930–1990*. New York: St. Martin's Press.

McLeary, R. and Weinstein, A.C. 2009. Do off site adult businesses have secondary effects? Legal doctrine, social theory and empirical evidence. *Law and Policy*, 31(2), 217–35.

McMillian, R. 1998. *Adult Uses and the First Amendment: Zoning and Non-zoning Controls on the Use of Land for Adult Businesses*. Pace Law School, Working Paper.

McNee, B. 1984. It takes one to know one. *Transition: Quarterly Journal of the Socially and Ecologically Responsible Geographers*, 14, 2–15.

Mead, M. 1949. *Male and Female: A Study of the Sexes in a Changing World*. New York: Morrow and Company.

Mendelsohn, D. 1995. The world is a ghetto. *Out*, March, 79–83, 110, 112.

Metz, T. and Russell, J. 1998. Do the Dutch do it better? *Architectural Record*, January, 112–13.

Meyer, J. 1991. New center seen as symbol of caring for gay community. *Los Angeles Times*, 25 August, Section J1.

Meyer, M. (ed.). 1994. *The Politics and Poetics of Camp*. London: Routledge.

Meyerowitz, J. 2002. *How Sex Changed: A History of Transsexuality in the United States*. Cambridge: Harvard University Press.

Mikelbank, B.A. 2004. A typology of US suburban places. *Housing Policy Debate*, 15, 935–64.

Mill, J.S. 1869. *On Liberty*. London: Longman, Roberts and Green.

Miller, G. 1981. Councils Memerandum of The Council of the City of Sydney v. Pobina Pty Ltd and Raglana Pty Ltd regarding Club 80 at 48 Little Oxford St. The Council of the City of Sydney.

Miller, N. 1995. *Out of the Past: Gay and Lesbian History from 1869 to the Present*. New York: Vintage.

Mills, E.S. 1972. *Studies in the Structure of the Urban Economy*. Washington: Johns Hopkins Press.

Minter, S. 2006. Do transsexuals dream of gay rights? Getting real about transgender inclusion, in *Transgender Rights*, edited by P. Currah et al. Minneapolis: University of Minnesota Press, 141–70.

Miranne, K. and Young, A.H. (eds) 2000. *Gendering the City: Women, Boundaries, and Visions of Urban Life*. Landham: Rowman and Littlefield Publishing.

Mitchell, D. 1995. The end of public space? People's park, definitions of the public, and democracy. *Annals of the Association of American Geographers*, 85, 108–33.

Mitchell, D. 2000. *Cultural Geography: A Critical Introduction*. Oxford: Blackwell.

Mitchell, D. 2003. T*he Right to the City: Social Justice and the Fight for Public Space*. New York: Guilford Press.

Modlich, R. 2008. Gender and urban planning: Time for another look. *Progressive Planning*, Spring, 13–17.

Monaghan, D. 1987. Sydney after AIDS. *Sydney Morning Herald*.

Moos, A. 1989. The grassroots in action: Gays and seniors capture the local state in West Hollywood, California, in *The Power of Geography: How Territory Shapes Social Life*, edited by J. Wolch and M. Dear. Boston: Unwin Hyman.

Moran, L., Skeggs, B., Tyrer, P., and Corteen, K. 2001. Property, boundary, exclusion: Making sense of hetero-violence in safer spaces. *Social and Cultural Geography*, 2(4), 407–420.

Moran, L., Skeggs, B., Tyrer, P., and Corteen, K. 2003. The constitution of fear in gay space, in *The Meanings of Violence*, edited by E. Stanko. London: Routledge, 130–46.

Morgan, N. and Pritchard, A. 1998. *Tourism Promotion and Power: Creating Images, Creating Identities*. Chichester: John Wiley & Sons.

Mort, F. 1998. Cityscapes: Consumption, masculinities and the mapping of London since 1950. *Urban Studies*, 35(5–6), 889–907.

Moss, M.L. 1997. Reinventing the central city as a place to live and work. *Housing Policy Debate*, 8(2), 471–90.

Moulton, B. and Seaton, L. n.d. *Transgender Americans: A Handbook for Understanding*. [Online: Washington: Human Rights Campaign]. Available at: http://www.hrc.org/documents/hrcTGguide.pdf [accessed: 10 June 2010].

Mumford, L. 1944. *The Condition of Man*. New York: Harcourt, Brace.

Munt, S. (ed.) 1998. *Butch/femme: Inside Lesbian Gender*. London: Cassell.

Murphy, K. 1995. Walking the queer city. *Radical History Review*, 62, 195–201.

Murray, S. 1979. The institutional elaboration of a quasi-ethnic community. *International Review of Modern Sociology*, 9, 165–77.

Murray, S. 1992. Components of gay community in San Francisco, in *Gay Culture in America. Essays from the Field*, edited by G. Herdt. Boston: Beacon Press, 107–46.

Muth, R.F. 1969. *Cities and Housing: The Spatial Patterns of Urban Residential Land Use*. Chicago: University of Chicago Press.

Myslik, W.D. 1996. Renegotiating the social/sexual identities of place, in *Bodyscape: Destabilizing Geographies of Gender and Sexuality*, edited by N. Duncan. London: Routledge, 156–69.

Namaste, K. 1996a. The politics of inside/out: Queer theory, poststructuralism, and a sociological approach to sexuality, in *Queer Theory/Sociology*, edited by S. Seidman. Cambridge: Blackwell Publishers, 194–212.

Namaste, K. 1996b. Gender bashing: Sexuality, gender, and the regulation of public space. *Environment and Planning D: Society and Self*, 14, 221–40.

Namaste, V. 2000. *Invisible Lives: The Erasure of Transsexual and Transgendered People*. Chicago: University of Chicago.

Nardi, P., Sanders, D., and Marmor, J. (eds) 1994. *Growing Up Before Stonewall: Life Stories of Some Gay Men*. London: Routledge.

Nash, C. 2006. Toronto's gay village (1969–1982): Plotting the politics of gay identity. *The Canadian Geographer*, 50(1), 1–16.

Nast, H.J. 2002. Queer patriarchies, queer racisms, international. *Antipode*, 34, 874–909

Nast, H.J. and Pile, S. (eds). 1998. *Places Through the Body*. London: Routledge.

National Coalition of Anti-Violence Programs. 2007. *2007 Report on Anti LGBT Violence*. [Online]. Available at: http://www.ncavp.org/publications/NationalPubs.aspx.

Navarro, M. 1995. Disney's health policy for gay employees angers religious right in Florida. *New York Times* [Online, 29 November]. Available at: http://www.

nytimes.com/1995/11/29/us/disney-s-health-policy-for-gay-employees-angers-religious-right-inflorida.html?scp=1&sq=&st=nyt [accessed: 10 March 2010].
New South Wales Department of Local Government. [Online]. Available at: www.dlg.nsw.gov.au.
New South Wales Department of Local Government 1998a. *Social/Community Planning and Reporting Guidelines*. NSW Department of Local Government, Sydney.
New South Wales Department of Local Government 1998b. *Social/Community Planning and Reporting Manual*. NSW Department of Local Government, Sydney.
New South Wales Department of Local Government 2007. *Comparative Information on NSW Local Government Councils 2007/08*. NSW Department of Local Government, Sydney.
New South Wales Department of Local Government 2009. *Planning and Reporting Manual for Local Government in NSW*. NSW Department of Local Government, Sydney.
Newman, M. 1999. Marisol apartments. *Planning*, 65(4), 14.
Newman, O. 1972. *Defensible Space: Crime Prevention Through Urban Design*. New York: Macmillan.
Newton, E. 1993. *Cherry Grove, Fire Island: Sixty Years in America's First Gay and Lesbian Town*. Boston: Beacon Press.
Nicolaides, B.M. 2002. *My Blue Heaven: Life and Politics in the Working-class Suburbs of Los Angeles, 1920–1965*. Chicago: University of Chicago Press.
Nichols, T. 2004. *The City as Entertainment Machine*. Chicago: University of Chicago Press.
NALGBG. 1999. Northampton Area Lesbian and Gay Business Guild. [Online]. Available at: http://www.westmas.com/nalgbg/.
Noel, T. 1978. Gay bars and the emergence of the Denver homosexual community. *Social Science Journal*, 15, 59–74.
Northwest Lesbian and Gay History Museum Project. 1996. *Changing Space: A Historical Map of Lesbian and Gay Seattle*.
Nusser, S. (2010). *What Would a Non-heterosexist City Look Like? A Theory on Queer Spaces and the Role of Planners in Creating the Inclusive City*. (Unpublished MCP thesis). Massachusetts Institute of Technology, Cambridge, MA.
O'Leary, K. 1994. Southie plans motorcade without gays. *The Boston Globe*, 20 March, 29.
O'Malley, B. 1978. Building Inspection Report about Unauthorized Usage at 2nd Floor 2–6 Kellett St., Kings Cross. Sydney, The Council of the City of Sydney.
O'Malley, B. 1979. Report of Inspection Regarding Unauthorized Club 80 at 48 Little Oxford St., Darlinghurst at 9pm 6 July 1979. The Council of the City of Sydney.
O'Malley, B. 1983. Affidavit of Council building Inspector for Inspection of 19 Oxford Street, Paddington at 11.45pm on the 28 January 1983.The Council of

the City of Sydney v. Pobina Pty. Ltd. Land and Environment Court of New South Wales.

Orfield, M. 2002. *American Metropolitics: The New Suburban Reality*. Washington: The Brookings Institution Press.

Organization of Lesbian and Gay Architects and Designers. 1994. *A Guide to Lesbian and Gay Historical Landmarks*. New York: Old Chelsea Station.

Orlando City Council Public Hearing 2002. Amendment to add Sexual Orientation to Orlando's Human Rights Ordinance. Orlando, FL, November 18, 2002.

Orlando Gaydays. 2010. *What is Orlando Gay Days?* [Online]. Available at: http://www.gaydays.com/about/history.html.

Oswin, N. 2010. The modern model family at home in Singapore: A queer geography. *Transactions of the Institute of British Geographers*, 35(2) 256–68.

Page, S. 1989. Renting rooms in three Canadian cities: Accepting and rejecting the AIDS Patient. *Canadian Journal of Community Mental Health*, 8, 53–61.

Page, S. 1998. Accepting the gay person: Rental accommodation in the community. *Journal of Homosexuality*, 36(2), 31–9.

Palmer, K. 1999. Out in the market. *Minneapolis Star Tribune*, 17 April, H4.

Papayanis, M.A. 2000. Sex and the revanchist city: Zoning out pornography in New York. *Environment and Planning D: Society and Space*, 18, 341–53.

Parker, L.O. 2009. Just another way to be suburban: In Pr. George's, same-sex couples grow in number, visibility. *The Washington Post*, 29 June.

Pasternak, J. 1997. Chicago gays torn over a place of their own. *Los Angeles Times*, 11 September.

Pattison, T. 1983. The stages of gentrification: The case of Bay Village, in *Neighborhood Policy and Planning*, edited by P.L. Clay and R.M. Hollister. Lexington: Lexington Books.

Paul, B., Linz, D., and Shafer, B.J. 2001. Government regulation of adult businesses through zoning and anti-nudity ordinances: Debunking the myth of negative secondary effects. *Communication Law and Policy*, 6, 355–91.

Paulson, D. 1996. *An Evening at the Garden of Allah*. New York: Columbia University Press.

Peace, R. 2001. Producing lesbians, canonical properties, in *Pleasure Zones: Bodies, Cities, Spaces*, edited by D. Bell et al. Syracuse: Syracuse University Press, 29–54.

Peake, L. 1993, 'Race' and sexuality: Challenging the patriarchal structuring of urban social space. *Environment and Planning D: Society and Space*, 11, 415–32.

Peck, J. 2005. Struggling with the creative class. *International Journal of Urban and Regional Research*, 29(4), 740–70.

Perin, C. 1977. *Everything in its Place: Social Order and Land Use in America*. Princeton: Princeton University Press.

Peterson, J.A. 2009. The birth of organized city planning in the United States, 1909–1910. *Journal of the American Planning Association*, 75(2), 123–33

Phelan, P. 1993. *Unmarked: The Politics of Performance*. London: Routledge.

Philipp, S. 1999. Gay and lesbian tourists at a southern USA beach event. *Journal of Homosexuality,* 37(3), 69–86.

Philo, C. 1992. Foucault's geography. *Environment and Planning D: Society and Space,* 10, 137–61.

Phoenix, J. and Oerton, S. 2005. *Illicit and Illegal: Sex, Regulation and Social Control.* Cullompton: Willan Publishing.

Pitcher, J., Campbell, R., Hubbard, P., O'Neill, M., and Scoular, J. 2006. *Living and Working in Areas of Street Sex Work: From Conflict to Coexistence.* Bristol: Policy Press.

Planning Institute of Australia. [Online]. Available at: www.planning.org.au.

Po, Lan-chih. (1996). Feminism, Identity, and Women's Movements: Theoretical Debates and a Case Study in Taiwan. (Unpublished paper). Department of City and Regional Planning, University of California, Berkeley, CA.

Podmolik, M.E. 1997. City recognizes gay area. *Chicago Sun Times,* 17 August, 1, 8, 9.

Podmore, J. 2001. Lesbians in the crowd: Gender, sexuality, and visibility along Montreal's Boulevard St-Laurent. *Gender, Place, and Culture,* 8(4), 333–55.

Podmore, J. 2006. Gone 'underground'? Lesbian visibility and the consolidation of queer space in Montreal. *Social and Cultural Geography,* 7(4), 595–623.

Ponce, M.H. 1993. *Hoyt Street: An Autobiography.* Albuquerque: University of New Mexico Press.

Prior, J. 2000a. Interview with Len Stone. Sydney. 11 August.

Prior, J. 2000b. Interview with Dawn O'donnell. Sydney. 12 October.

Prior, J. 2000c. Interview with Denise Coussens, Owner King Steam. Sydney. 13 October.

Prior, J. 2000d. Interview with Peter Williamson. Sydney. 14 December.

Prior, J. 2000e. Interview with Craig Johnston. Sydney. 17 August.

Prior, J. 2001a. Interview with James Malone (Pseudo.). Sydney. 17 January.

Prior, J. 2001b. Interview with Fred Parkinson (Pseudo.). Sydney. 17 January.

Prior, J. 2001c. Interview with Mark Stirling (Pseudo.). Sydney. 18 January.

Prior, J. 2007. Interview with Ross Hurst (Pseudo.). Sydney. 7 October.

Prior, J. 2008. Planning for sex in the city: Urban governance, planning and the placement of sex industry premises in inner Sydney. *Australian Geographer,* 39(3), 339–52.

Prior, J. 2009. Experiences beyond the threshold: Sydney's gay bathhouses. *Australian Cultural History,* 27, 61–77.

Prior, J. 2011. Neighborhood disadvantage. *The International Encyclopedia of Housing and Home.* Oxford: Elsevier.

Puentes, R. and Warren, D. 2006. *One Fifth of America: A Comprehensive Guide to America's First Suburbs.* Available at: http://www.brookings.edu/~/media/Files/rc/reports/2006/02metropolitanpolicy_puentes/20060215_FirstSuburbs.pdf [accessed: 25 September 2009].

Quilley, S. 1997. Constructing Manchester's new urban village, in *Queers in Space: Communities, Public Spaces, and Sites of Resistance*, edited by G. Ingram et al. Seattle: Bay Press, 275–92.

Quinn, K. 2002. Planning history/planning race, gender, class, and sexuality. *Journal of Planning History*, 2002(1), 240–44.

Rankin, K. 2009. Critical development studies and the praxis of planning. *City*, 13, 219–29.

Ratcliff, I. 1999. No sex please:We're local councils!! *Local Government Law Journal*, 4, 150–63.

Ravensbergen, J. 1998. Niche marketing: Tourist bureau will target gays and gamblers in effort to fill Montreal's hotel rooms in off-season. *The Gazette (Montreal)*, 5 June, F1.

Reback, C.J., Simon, P.A., Bemis, C.C., and Gaston, B. 2001. *The Los Angeles Transgender Health Study: Community Report*. Los Angeles: Authors.

Reed, C. 2003. We're from Oz: Making ethnic and sexual identity in Chicago. *Environment and Planning D: Society and Space*, 21, 425–40.

Reed, J. 2009. Lesbian television personalities: A queer new subject. *The Journal of American Culture*, 32, 307–17.

Rendall, G.J. 1983. Affidavit of Council Building Inspector For Inspection of 19 Oxford Street Paddington at 10.45pm on the 2 April 1982 and 2.30pm 6 April 1982. The Council of the City of Sydney v. Pobina Pty. Ltd. Land and Environment Court of New South Wales.

Retter, Y. 1997. Lesbian spaces in Los Angeles, 1970–90, in *Queers in Space: Communities, Public Places, Sites of Resistance*, edited by G.B. Ingram et al. Seattle: Bay Press, 325–37.

Reyes, E. (1993). *Queer Spaces: The Spaces of Lesbians and Gay Men of Color in Los Angeles*. (Masters thesis). Graduate School of Architecture and Urban Planning, University of California, Los Angeles, CA.

Reynolds, C. 1997. Gay travelers draw ever more mainstream interest. *Seattle Times*, Travel Section, 27 May 27, D5.

Richardson, C. 1997. Social change: Rights side of the law. *The Guardian*, 26 November, 21.

Ritter, J. 1993. Oak Park welcomes gay book store. *Chicago Sun Times*, 2 December, 16.

Ritzdorf, M. 1986. Women and the city: Land use and zoning. *Urban Resources*, 3(2), 23–27.

Ritzdorf, M. 1993. The fairy's tale, teaching planning and public policy in a different voice. *Journal of Planning Education and Research*, 12(2), 99–110.

Ritzdorf, M. 1997. Family values, municipal zoning, and African American family life, in *Urban Planning and the African American Community*, edited by J.M. Thomas and M. Ritzdorf. Thousand Oaks: Sage, 75–92.

Ritzdorf, M. 2000. Sex, lies, and urban life: How municipal planning marginalizes African American women and their families, in *Gendering the City: Women*

Boundaries, and Visions of Urban Life, edited by K. Miranne and A. Young. Lanham: Rowman and Littlefield Publishers, 169–181.

Roback, J. 1982. Wages, rents, and the quality of life. *Journal of Political Economy*, 90, 1257–1278.

Roberts, M. 1997. Police bridging gap with gays. *Chicago Sun Times*, 29 August, 6.

Robinson, J. 1994. Volunteer patrol squads monitor Montrose crime. *The Houston Chronicle*, 13 June, A1.

Roeper, R. 1997. At the rainbow's end: A lot of misguided flak. *Chicago Sun Times*, 18 August, 11.

Rogerson, C. and Visser, G. 2005. Tourism in urban Africa: The South African experience. *Urban Forum*, 16(2–3), 63–87.

Rooke, A. 2007. Navigating embodied lesbian cultural space: Towards a lesbian habitus. *Space and Culture*, 10(2), 231–252.

Rose, D. 1984. Rethinking gentrification: Beyond the uneven development of Marxist urban theory. *Environment and Planning D: Society and Space*, 2, 47–74.

Rose, N. 2000. Governing cities, governing citizens, in *Democracy, Citizenship and the Global City*, edited by E. Isin. London: Routledge, 95–109.

Rosenthal, D. 1996. Gay and lesbian political mobilization and regime responsiveness in four New York cities. *Urban Affairs Review*, 32(1), 45–70.

Ross, A. 1989. Uses of camp, in *No Respect: Intellectuals and Popular Culture*, edited by A. Ross. London: Routledge, 135–70.

Ross, B. 1990. The house that Jill built: Lesbian feminist organizing in Toronto, 1976–1980. *Feminist Review*, 35, 75–91.

Ross, B. 2010. Sex and (evacuation from) the city: The moral and legal regulation of sex workers in Vancouver's West End, 1975–1985. *Sexualities*, 13(2), 197–218.

Rothblatt, M. 1995. *The Apartheid of Sex: A Manifesto on the Freedom of Gender.* New York: Crown.

Rothenberg, T. 1995. 'And she told two friends': Lesbians creating urban social space, in *Mapping Desire: Geographies of Sexualities*, edited by D. Bell and G. Valentine. London: Routledge, 165–81.

Rubin, G. 1993. Rethinking sex: Notes on a radical theory for a politics of sexuality, in *The Lesbian and Gay Studies Reader*, edited by H. Abelove. London: Routledge, 3–44.

Ruddick, S. 1996. Constructing difference in public spaces: Race, class, and gender as interlocking systems. *Urban Geography*, 17, 132–51.

Rushbrook, D. 2002. Cities, queer space, and the cosmopolitan tourist. *GLQ: A Journal of Lesbian and Gay Studies*, 8(1/2), 183–206.

Russell, P.E. 1995. *The Gay One-Hundred: A Ranking of the Most Influential Gay Men and Lesbians, Past and Present.* New York: Carol Publishing Group, Citadel Press Book.

Russo, A.P. and van der Borg, J. 2010. An urban policy framework for culture-oriented economic development: Lessons from the Netherlands. *Urban Geography*, 31(5), 668–90.

Ryder, A. 2004. The changing nature of adult entertainment spaces: Between a rock and a hard place or going from strength to strength? *Urban Studies*, 41(10), 1659–86.

Ryder, A. 2009. Red-light district. *Encyclopedia of Urban Studies* [Online]. Available at: http://www.sageereference.com/urbanstudies/Article_n227.html.

Sagar, T. 2005. Street watch: Concept and practice. *British Journal of Criminology*, 45(1), 98–112.

Saiz, A. and Wachter, S. 2006. Immigration and the neighborhood. Working Paper No. 06–22. *Federal Reserve Bank of Philadelphia* [Online, November]. Available at: http://www.philadelphiafed.org/research-and-data/publications/working-papers/2006/wp06-22.pdf [accessed: 25 September 2009].

Samuels, E. 2003. My body, my closet: Invisible disability and the limits of the coming out discourse. *GLQ: A Journal of Lesbian and Gay Studies*, 9, 233–55.

San Francisco Bay Guardian and Transgender Law Center. 2006. *Good Jobs NOW! A Snapshot of the Economic Health of San Francisco's Transgender Communities.* San Francisco: Transgender Law Center and Guardian.

Sanchez, L. 2004. The global e-rotic subject, the ban and prostitute free-zone. *Environment and Planning D: Society and Space*, 21(5), 861–83.

Sanchez-Crispin, A. and Lopez-Lopez, A. 1997. Gay male places of Mexico City, in *Queers in Space: Communities, Public Places, Sites of Resistance*, edited by G.B. Ingram et al. Seattle: Bay Press, 197–212.

Sandercock, L. (ed.) 1998. *Making the Invisible Visible: A Multicultural Planning History.* Berkeley: University of California Press.

Sandercock, L. 2000. When strangers become neighbors: Managing cities of difference. *Planning Theory and Practice*, 1, 13–30.

Sandercock, L. 2003. *Cosmopolis II: Mongrel Cities of the 21st Century.* London: Continuum.

Sandercock, L. and Forsyth, A. 1992. A gender agenda: New directions for planning theory. *Journal of Planning Education and Research*, 58(1), 49–59.

Sanders, T. 2005. Blinded by morality? Prostitution policy in the United Kingdom. *Capital and Class*, 86, 9–17.

Sanders, T. 2009. Controlling the anti-sexual city: Sexual citizenship and the disciplining of female street sex workers. *Criminology and Criminal Justice*, 9, 507–22.

Savageau, D. and D'Agostino, R. 2000. *Places Rated Almanac.* Foster City: IDG Books Worldwide.

Schlueb, M. 2002a. Gays have yet to flex political muscle. *Orlando Sentinel*, 16 April 16.

Schlueb, M. 2002b. Gay rights clashed with religious freedom. *Orlando Sentinel*, 17 April.

Schlueb, M. 2002c. City gives gay rights 1st ok. *Orlando Sentinel*, 19 November.

Schlueb, M. 2002d. Orlando votes to protect gays. *Orlando Sentinel*, 3 December.
Schwartz, K. 1998. Travel industry courts gay travellers, most of the time. *The Ottawa Citizen*, 17 January, I10.
Scott, M. 1969. *American City Planning Since 1890: A History Commemorating the Fiftieth Anniversary of the American Institute of Planners.* Berkeley: University of California Press.
Scott, J., Minichiello, V., Mariño, R., Harvey, J.P., Jamieson, M. and Browne, J. 2005. Understanding the new context of the male sex work industry. *Journal of Interpersonal Violence*, 20(3), 320–42.
Scoular, J. and Sanders, T. 2010. The changing social and legal context of sexual commerce: Why law matters. *Journal of Law and Society*, 11(1), 1–11.
Sears, J.T. 1997. *Lonely Hunters: An Oral History of Lesbian and Gay Southern Life, 1948–1968.* Boulder: Westview Press.
Sedgwick, E.K. 1990. *Epistemology of the Closet.* Berkeley: University of California Press.
Sedgwick, E.K. 1993. *Tendencies.* Durham: Duke University Press.
Seidman, S. 1996. Introduction, in *Queer Theory/Sociology*, edited by S. Seidman. Cambridge: Blackwell Publishers, 1–29.
Serant, C. 1996. Heightened crime awareness: Group takes aim at violence in gay world of Jackson Heights. *Daily News (New York)*, 21 July, Suburban: 1.
Shankle, M., Maxwell, C.A., Katzman, E.S. and Landers, S. 2003. An invisible population: Older lesbian, gay, bisexual, and transgender individuals. *Clinical Research and Regulatory Affairs*, 20(2), 159–82.
Shilts, R. 1982. *The Mayor of Castro Street: The Life and Times of Harvey Milk.* New York: St Martin's Press.
Sibley, D. 1996. *Geographies of Exclusion: Society and Difference in the West.* London: Routledge.
Sides, J. 2006. Excavating the postwar sex district in San Francisco. *Journal of Urban History*, 32, 355–379.
Silk, M. 2004. A tale of two cities. *Journal of Sport and Social Issues*, 28(4), 349–78.
Silk, M. and Amis, J. 2005. Sport tourism, cityscapes and cultural politics. *Sport in Society*, 8, 280–301.
Silk, M. and Andrews, D. 2006. The fittest city in America. *Journal of Sport and Social Issues*, 30, 315–327.
Simmons, T. and O'Connell, M. 2003. Married-Couple and Unmarried-Partner Households: 2000. *Census 2000 Special Reports.* [Online: US Bureau of the Census, Washington, DC]. Available at: http://www.census.gov/prod/2003pubs/censr-5.pdf [accessed: 24 September 2009].
Skeggs, B. 1999. Matter out of place: Visibility and sexualities in leisure spaces. *Leisure Studies*, 18: 3, 213–32.
Skeggs, B. 2004. Context and background: Pierre Bourdieu's analysis of class, gender, and sexuality, in *Feminism After Bourdieu*, edited by L. Adkins and B. Skeggs. Oxford: Blackwell Publishing, 19–33.

Skeggs, B., Moran, L. Tyrer, P., and Binnie, J. 2004. Queer as folk: Producing the real of urban space. *Urban Studies*, 41(9), 1839–56.

Smith, C. 2007. Designed for pleasure: Style, indulgence and accessorized sex. *European Journal of Cultural Studies*, 10(2), 167–84.

Smith, D. and Richardson, C. 1995. Paint the town pink. *The Independent* (London), 17 December, 4.

Smith, D. M. and Gates, G. 2001. Same-sex unmarried partner households. *Urban Institute*, 22 August.

Smith, N. 1996. *The New Urban Frontier: Gentrification and the Revanchist City*. London: Routledge.

Smith, N. 1998. Giuliani time: The revanchist 1990s. *Social Text*, 57, 1–20.

Smith, R. and Warfield, K. 2008. The creative city: A matter of values, in *Creative Cities, Cultural Clusters and Local Economic Development*, edited by P. Cooke and L. Lazzeretti. Cheltenham: Edward Elgar Publishing, 287–312.

Smith, R. and Windes, R. 1999. Identity in political context: Lesbian/gay representation in the public sphere. *Journal of Homosexuality*, 37(2), 25–45.

Snyder, M.G. 1995. Feminist theory and planning theory, lessons from feminist epistemologies. *Berkeley Planning Journal*, 10, 91–106.

Soja, E.W. 1989. *Postmodern Geographies: The Reassertion of Space in Critical Social Theory*. London: Verso.

Spain, D. 1992. *Gendered Spaces*. Chapel Hill: University of North Carolina Press.

Spain, D. 2001a. *How Women Saved the City*. Minneapolis: University of Minnesota Press.

Spain, D. 2001b. Gender and place. *International Encyclopedia of the Social and Behavioral Sciences*, 5965–9.

Spain, D. 2002. What happened to gender relations on the way from Chicago to Los Angeles. *City and Community*, 1(2), 155–69.

Spearritt, P. and Marco, C.D. 1988. *Planning Sydney's Future*. Sydney: Allan and Urwin.

Staeheli, L. 1996. Publicity, privacy, and women's political action. *Environment and Planning D*, 4, 601–19.

Stamler, B. 1997. Gay youths get place to call home. *New York Times*, 16 November, Section 14: 9.

Stein, A. and Plummer, K. 1994. 'I can't even think straight' – 'queer' theory and the missing sexual revolution in sociology. *Sociological Theory*, 12(2), 178–87.

Stein, M. 2000. *City of Sisterly and Brotherly Loves: Lesbian and Gay Philadelphia, 1945–1972*. Chicago: University of Chicago Press.

Stone, S. 1991. The 'empire' strikes back: A posttranssexual manifesto, in *Bodyguards: The Cultural Politics of Gender Ambiguity*, edited by K. Straub and J. Epstein. London: Routledge, 280–304.

Storper, M. and Scott, A. 2009. Rethinking human capital, creativity, and urban growth. *Journal of Economic Geography*, 9, 147–67.

Stryker, S. 1994. My words to Victor Frankenstein above the village of Chamounix: Performing transgender rage. *GLQ: A Journal of Gay and Lesbian Studies*, 1, 237–54.

Stryker, S. 1998. The transgender issue: An introduction. *GLQ: A Journal of Gay and Lesbian Studies*, 4(2), 145–58.

Stryker, S. 2008. *Transgender History*. Berkeley: Seal Press.

Stryker, S. and Van Buskirk, J. 1996. *Gay by the Bay: A History of Queer Culture in the San Francisco Bay Area*. San Francisco: Chronicle Books.

Sullivan, B. 2010. When some sex is legal: The impact of law reform on sex work in Australia. *Journal of Law and Society*, 37(1), 85–104.

Sullivan, N. 2003. *A Critical Introduction to Queer Theory*. New York: New York University Press.

Summers C.J. (ed.) 1993. *The Gay and Lesbian Literary Heritage: A Readers Companion to the Writers and Their Works, from Antiquity to the Present*. New York: Henry Holt.

Sunday Telegraph. 1953. Vice squad ordered to rid sydney of male perverts (growing cancer). Sydney.

Swyngedouw, E. and Kaika, M. 2003. 'Glocal' urban modernities: Exploring the cracks in the mirror. *City*, 7(1), 5–21.

Sydney Gay and Lesbian Mardi Gras. 1999. *Strategic Plan*. Available at: http://www.mardigras.com.au/pdf/stratplan3.pdf.

Symanski, R. 1981. *The Immoral Landscape*. Toronto: Butterworths.

Takahashi, L. and Dear, M. 1997. The changing dynamics of community opposition to human service facilities. *Journal of the American Planning Association*, 63(1), 79–93.

Tampa Bay Business Guild. 2010. [Online]. Available at: http://www.tbbg.org/.

Tattleman, I. 1997. The meaning of the wall: Tracing the gay bathhouse, in *Queers in Space: Communities, Public Spaces, Sites of Resistance*, edited by Gordon Ingram et al. Seattle: Bay Press, 391–406.

Tattleman, I. 2000. Presenting a queer (bath)house, in *Queer Frontiers*, edited by J. Boone et al. Madison: University of Wisconsin Press.

Tarrant, S. 2006. *When Sex Became Gender*. London: Routledge.

Taylor, V. and Rupp, L. 1993. Women's culture and lesbian feminist activism: A reconsideration of cultural feminism. *Signs*, 19(1), 32–61.

Taylor, Y. 2008. 'That's not really my scene': Working-class lesbians in (and out) of place. *Sexualities*, 11(5), 523–46.

Taywaditep, K.J. 2001. Marginalization among the marginalized: Gay men's anti-effeminacy attitudes. *Journal of Homosexuality*, 42, 1–28.

The Star (Sydney). 1983a. Club 80 faces disorderly house charge. 22 April, 4, 1.

The Star (Sydney). 1983b. Club 80 declared disorderly house. 6 May, 4, 1.

The Star (Sydney). 1983c. Adding insult to injury. 9 September, 5, 3.

Thomas, H. 2000. *Race and Planning: The UK Experience*. London: UCL Press.

Thomas, J.M. 1994. Planning history and the black urban experience linkages and contemporary implications. *Journal of Planning Education and Research*, 14(1), 1–10.

Thomas, J.M. 1998. Racial inequality and empowerment, in *Making the Invisible Visible: A Multicultural Planning History*, edited by L. Sandercock. Berkeley: University of California Press, 198–208.

Thomas, J.M. 2008. The minority race planner in the quest for a just city. *Planning Theory*, 7(3), 227–47.

Thomas, J.M. and Darnton, J. 2006. Social diversity and economic development in the metropolis. *Journal of Planning Literature*, 21(2), 153–68.

Thomas, J.M. and Ritzdorf, M. (eds) 1997. *Urban Planning and the African American Community: In the Shadows*. Thousand Oaks: Sage.

Thompson, E.P. 1963. *The Making of the English Working Class*. New York: Pantheon Books.

Thompson, S. 2007a. What is planning?, in *Planning Australia: An Overview of Urban and Regional Planning*, edited by S. Thompson. Port Melbourne: Cambridge University, 11–27.

Thompson, S. 2007b. Planning for diverse communities, in *Planning Australia: An Overview of Urban and Regional Planning*, edited by S. Thompson. Port Melbourne: Cambridge University, 199–223.

Thomson, J.A. and Geddes, P. 1912. *Problems of Sex*. New York: Moffet Yard.

Thorstad, D. 1995. Homosexuality and the American left: the impact of Stonewall. *Journal of Homosexuality*, 319–49.

Torres, V. 1996. Small business strength and support: gay associations foster networking and increase clout. *Los Angeles Times*, 10 September, D1.

Tracy, D. 2000. Strategies pay off in runoff vote. *Orlando Sentinel*, 16 April.

Tsoi, W.F. 1988. The prevalence of transsexualism in Singapore. *Acta Psychiatrica Scandinavian*, 78, 501–4.

Tucker, D.M. 1997. Preventing the secondary effects of adult entertainment establishments: Is zoning the solution? *Journal of Land Use and Environmental Law*, 12(2), 383–431.

Uebel, M. 2004. Striptopia? *Social Semiotics*, 14(1), 3–19.

United Press International 2001. *The Righteous Appear at Disney Gay Days*. [Online]. Available at: http://www.gayday.info/news/1998/united_press_international_980607a.asp. [accessed: 14 May 2007].

Urey, G. 2001. Zoning that excludes queers: What a difference a phrase makes. *Progressive Planning* [Online], 146. Available at: http://www.plannersnetwork.org/publications/2001_146/Urey.html.

US Bureau of the Census 2009. *Census Bureau Reports on Residential Vacancies and Homeownership.* [Online: US Census Bureau News]. Available at: http://www.census.gov/hhes/www/housing/hvs/qtr209/files/q209press.pdf [accessed: 25 September 2009].

Valentine, G. 1989. The geography of women's fear. *Area*, 21, 385–90.

Valentine, G. 1993a. (Hetero)sexing space: Lesbian perceptions and experiences of everyday spaces. *Environment and Planning D, Society and Self*, 11, 395–413.

Valentine, G. 1993b. Negotiating and managing multiple sexual identities: Lesbian time-space strategies. *Transactions of the Institute of British Geographers*, 18, 237–48.

Valentine, G. 1993c. Desperately seeking Susan: A geography of lesbian friendships. *Area*, 25(2), 109–21.

Valentine, G. 1995. Out and about: Geographies of lesbian landscapes. *International Journal of Urban and Regional Research*, 19(1), 96–111.

Valentine, G. 1996. (Re)negotiating the 'heterosexual street': Lesbian productions of space, in *Body Space: Destabilizing Geographies of Gender and Sexuality*, edited by N. Duncan. London: Routledge, 146–55.

Valentine, G. 1997. Making space: Lesbian separatist communities in the United States, in *Contested Countryside Cultures: Otherness, Marginalization and Rurality*, edited by P. Cloke and J. Little. London: Routledge, 105–17.

Valocchi, S. 2005. Not yet queer enough: The lessons of queer theory for the sociology of gender and sexuality. *Gender and Society*, 19(6), 750–70.

Visser, G. 2003. Gay men, leisure space, and South African cities: The case of Cape Town. *Geoforum*, 34, 123–37.

Visser, G. and Kotze, N. 2008. The state and new-build gentrification in central Cape Town, South Africa. *Urban Studies*, 45(12), 2565–93.

von Hoffman, N. 1988. *Citizen Cohn: The Life and Times of Roy Cohn*. New York: Doubleday.

Wagner, G. 1995. Gentrification, reinvestment and displacement in Baltimore. *Journal of Urban Affairs*, 17(1), 81–96.

Walks, R.A. 2009. The urban in fragile, uncertain, neoliberal times: Towards new geographies of social justice? *The Canadian Geographer/Le Geographe canadien*, 53, 345–56.

Walters, SD. 2001. *All the Rage: The Story of Gay Visibility in America*. Chicago: University of Chicago Press.

Warde, A. 1991. Gentrification as consumption: Issues of class and gender. *Environment and Planning D*, 9, 223–32.

Warren, C.A.B. 1974. *Identity and Community in the Gay World*. New York: John Wiley and Sons.

Warner, M. 1991. Fear of a queer planet. *Social Text*, 9(14), 3–17.

Warner, M. 1993. Introduction, in *Fear of a Queer Planet*, edited by M. Warner. Minneapolis: University of Minnesota Press, vii–xxi.

Weightman, B. 1980. Gay bars as private places. *Landscape*, 24,1, 9–16.

Weightman, B. 1981. Commentary: Towards a geography of the gay community. *Journal of Cultural Geography*, 1, 106–12.

Weinberg, M.S., Shaver, F. and Williams, C. 1999. Gendered sex work in the San Francisco Tenderloin. *Archives of Sexual Behavior*, 28, 503–20.

Weiss, A. and Schiller, G. 1988. *Before Stonewall: The Making of a Gay and Lesbian Community*. Tallahassee: Naiad Press.

Weiss, J.T. 2001. The gender caste system: identity, privacy, and heteronormativity. *Law and Sexuality: A Review of Lesbian, Gay, Bisexual, and Transgender Legal Issues*, 10, 123–86.

Weitzer, R. (ed.) 2010. *Sex for Sale: Prostitution, Pornography and the Sex Industry*. London: Routledge.

West Hollywood Convention and Visitors Bureau. 1999. Web site, section on Pride in West Hollywood. http://www.visitwesthollywood.com/pride/.

Weston, K. 1995. Get thee to a big city: Sexual imaginary and the great gay migration. *GLQ: A Journal of Lesbian & Gay Studies*, 2, 253–77.

Whittier, N. 1995. *Feminist Generations: The Persistence of the Radical Women's Movement*. Philadelphia: Temple University Press.

Whittle, S. 1994. *The Margins of the City: Gay Men's Urban Lives*. Aldershot: Ashgate.

Whittle, S. 1996. Gender fucking or fucking gender: Current cultural contributions to the theories of gender blending, in *Blending Genders: Social Aspects of Cross-dressing and Sex-changing*, edited by R. Ekins and D. King. London: Routledge, 196–214.

Wilchins, R. 1997. *Read My Lips: Sexual Subversion and the End of Gender*. Ithaca: Firebrand Books.

Wilchins, R. 2004. *Queer Theory, Gender Theory: An Instant Primer*. Los Angeles: Alyson Books.

Wilkinson, E. 2009. Perverting visual pleasure: Representing sado-masochism. *Sexualities*, 12(2), 181–98.

Williams, P. 2007. Government, people and politics, in *Planning Australia: An Overview of Urban and Regional Planning*, edited by S. Thompson. Port Melbourne: Cambridge University Press, 29–48.

Williams, W. 1986. *The Spirit and the Flesh: Sexual Diversity in American Indian Culture*. Boston: Beacon Press.

Williamson, P. 1999. Report submitted with DA for 'Health Club' at 21/23 Brodie Street, Rydalmere To Parramatta City Council. Unpublished. Sydney.

Willis, P. 2007. 'Queer eye' for social work: Rethinking pedagogy and practice with same-sex attracted young people. *Australian Social Work*, 60(2), 181–96.

Wilson, D. 1996. Metaphors, growth coalition discourses, and black poverty neighborhood in a US city. *Antipode*, 28(1), 72–96.

Wilson, E. 1992. *The Sphinx in the City: Urban Life, the Control of Disorder, and Women*. Berkeley: University of California.

Winchester, H.P.M. and White, P.E. 1988. The location of marginalized groups in the inner city. *Environment and Planning D: Society and Space*, 6, 37–54.

Winters, C. 1979. The social identity of evolving neighborhoods. *Landscape*, 23(8), 14.

Wirka, S. 1994. Introduction to: Housing by Mary Kingsbury Simkhovich, in *The American Planner: Biographies and Recollections*, edited by D. Krueckeberg. New Brunswick: Center for Urban Policy Research.

Witeck-Combs Communications. 2002. *The GLBT Market: The Most Unknown and Misunderstood Niche*. (Presentation). Fisher College of Business, Ohio State University. 21 November.

Witten, T.M. and Eyler, A.E. 1999. Hate crimes and violence against the transgendered. *Peace Review*, 11(3), 461–68.

Wolf, D. 1980. *The Lesbian Community*. Berkeley: University of California Press.

Wolfe, M. 1999. The wired loft: Lifestyle innovation diffusion and industrial networking in the rise of San Francisco's multimedia gulch. *Urban Affairs Review*, 34(5), 707–28.

Wolfe, M. 1997. Invisible women in invisible places: The production of social space in lesbian bars, in *Queers in Space: Communities, Public Places, and Sites of Resistance*, edited by G. Ingram et al. Seattle: Bay Press, 301–23.

Wolfe, M. 1992. Invisible women in invisible places: Lesbians, lesbian bars, and the social production of people/environment relationships. *Architecture and Behavior*, 8(2), 137–50.

Wotherspoon, G. 1991. *City of the Plain. History of a Gay Sub-Culture*. Sydney: Hale and Iremonger Pty Limited.

Wotherspoon, G. 1992. From private vice to public history: Homosexuality in Australia. *Public History Review*, 1, 148–59.

Yiftachel, O. 1998. Planning and social control: Exploring the dark side. *Journal of Planning Literature*, 12(4), 395–420.

Young, G. 2008. *Reshaping Planning with Culture*. Aldershot: Ashgate.

Zavis, A. 1997. City to renovate Chicago's gay Halsted Street. *Associated Press*, 29 August.

Zimmerman, J. 2008. From brew town to cool town: Neoliberalism and the creative city development strategy in Milwaukee. *Cities*, 25, 230–42.

Government Documents and Legislation

(6 May 1983b) Declaration of 19 Oxford Street, Paddington ... Disorderly Houses Pursuant to section 3 of the Disorderly House Act, 1943. *New South Wales Government Gazette*, 68, 2053.

(1900) Crimes Act, 1900. *The Statutes of NSW*. C. F. Maxwell (Hayes Brothers) Limited, Law Publishers and Law Booksellers.

(1943a) Disorderly Houses (Amendment) Act, 1943. *The Statutes of NSW*. Government Printer, New South Wales.

(1943b) Disorderly Houses Act, 1943. *The Statutes of NSW*. Government Printer, New South Wales.

List of References

(1945a) First Reading of Local Government (Town and Country Planning) Amendment Bill in Legislative Assembly. *NSW Parliamentary Debates (Hansard).* Government Printers, New South Wales.

(1945b) Local Government (Town and CountryPlanning) Amendment Act, 1945. *The Statutes of NSW.* Government Printer, New South Wales.

(1955a) 200 Panic in Hotel Vice Swoop. *Sydney Truth.*

(1955b) Crimes (Amendment) Act, 1955. *The Statutes of NSW.* A.H Pettifer, Government Printers, New South Wales.

(1955c) Hint Of New Bill To Deal With Homosexuals. *Sydney Morning Herald.*

(1955d) Second Reading of Crimes (Amendment) Bill in Legislative Assembly. *NSW Parliamentary Debates (Hansard).* A. H. Pettifer. Government Printers, New South Wales.

(1960) DA/ BA For Health Studio at 109 Oxford St, Bondi Junction. Sydney, Municipality of Waverley.

(1961) Marriage Act (Commonwealth)

(1968a) Second Reading of Vagrancy, Disorderly Houses and Other Acts (Amendment) Bill in Legislative Council. *NSW Parliamentary Debates (Hansard).* V. C. N. Blight, Government Printers, New South Wales.

(1968b) Vagrancy, Disorderly Houses and Other Acts (Amendments) Act, 1968. *The Statutes of NSW.* Government Printer, New South Wales.

(1971) BA For Licensed Club at 10 –14 Quay St. Sydney, The Council of the City of Sydney.

(1972a) DA For Alterations at 99–97 Belmore Rd, Randwick. *Randwick Municipal Council.* Sydney.

(1972b) DA For Health Studio and Karate Club at 81–85 Anzac Pde, Kensington. Sydney, Randwick Municipal Council.

(1973a) BA For Alterations of Existing Club at 83/85 Anzac Pde, Kensington. *Randwick Municipal Council.* Sydney.

(1973b) BA For Alterations of Existing Club at 83/85 Anzac Pde, Kensington. Sydney, Randwick Municipal Council.

(1974) DA (Application For Development Permission) For Licensed Restaurant at 10–14 Quay St., Sydney, The Council of the City of Sydney.

(1975a) BA For Extension of existing Karate Club at 83/85 Anzac Pde, Kensington. *Randwick Municipal Council.* Sydney.

(1975b) BA For Extension of Existing Karate Club into Adjoining Premises, 81–85 Anzac Pde, Kensington. *Randwick Municipal Council.* Sydney.

(1976a) BA For Internal Alterations to Create Fitness Club and Gymnasium including Sauna and Steam Room at 10–14 Quay St and 1–9 Valentine St. *The Council of the City of Sydney.* Sydney.

(1976b) DA For Fitness Club, Health Studio on the 2nd Floor at 107–109 Darlinghurst Rd, Kings Cross. Sydney, The Council of the City of Sydney.

(1976c) Minute Paper City Health Department regarding amendment of Plan For Internal Alterations to Create Fitness Club and Gymnasium including Sauna and Steam Room at 10–14 Quay St and 1–9 Valentine St. *The Council of the City of Sydney.* Sydney.

(1976d) Minute Paper Detailing Inspection of Premises For Health and Relaxation Club in Basement of 250 Pitt St. *The Council of the City of Sydney.* Sydney.

(1977) Anti-Discrimination Act (New South Wales)

(1977a) City Planning Department File Note Detailing Inspection of Advertisements at Wynyard Newsagency for The Barefoot Boy 1st Floor at 10–14 Quay St and 1–9 Valentine St. Sydney, The Council of the City of Sydney.

(1977b) City Planning Department File Note Recording Inspection of proposed Fitness Club/Gymnasium at 1st Floor at 10–14 Quay St and 1–9 Valentine St. Sydney, The Council of the City of Sydney.

(1977c) Minute Paper Detailing Complaint that 1st Floor at 10–14 Quay St and 1–9 Valentine St is being used as Homosexual Bathhouse not the proposed Fitness Club/Gymnasium. Sydney, The Council of the City of Sydney.

(1979) Prostitution Act 1979 (NSW). Sydney. *The Statutes of NSW.*

(1982a) Anti-Discrimination (Amendment) Act, 1982. *The Statutes of NSW.*

(1982b) BA For Mech. Exhaust and Air Conditioning to Kens Karate Klasses 81–85 Anzac Pde, Kensington. *Randwick Municipal Council.* Sydney.

(1982c) BA For Renovation Kens Karate Klasses at 83/85 Anzac Pde, Kensington. *Randwick Municipal Council.* Sydney.

(1982d) DA For Renovations to Kens Karate Klasses 81–85 Anzac Pde, Kensington. *Randwick Municipal Council.* Sydney.

(1982e) Discrimination and Homosexuality: A Report of the Anti-Discrimination board in Accordance with Section 119(a) of the Anti-Discrimination Act 1977. *New South Wales Anti-Discrimination Board.* Sydney.

(1983) Gays believe Raids Were Protection Payback, Inquiry told. *The Sydney Morning Herald.*

(1984a) Crimes (Amendment) Act, 1984. *The Statutes of NSW.* D. West Government Printer, New South Wales.

(1984b) Crimes (Amendment) Bill in Committee for Consideration of Legislative Councils Amendments. *NSW Parliamentary Debates (Hansard).*

(1984c) First and Second Reading of Crimes (Amendment) Bill in Legislative Assembly. *NSW Parliamentary Debates (Hansard).*

(1984d) Second Reading of Crimes (Amendment) Bill in Legislative Council. *NSW Parliamentary Debates (Hansard).*

(1986a) City Planning Department File Note Detailing Building Inspectors Recollections of Works at Roman Bath 250 Pitt St. *Sydney City Council.* Sydney.

(1986b) DA For Gay Recreation Centre and Bathhouse involving Alterations in Basement of 38–46 Oxford Street, Darlinghurst. *Sydney City Council.* Sydney.

(1986c) Letter To David Ross Requesting Details Regarding DA For Gay Recreation Centre and Bathhouse involving Alterations in Basement of 38–46 Oxford Street, Darlinghurst and Information about Existing Roman Bath at 250 Pitt St. *Sydney City Council.* Sydney.

(1986d) Report by Director of Planning And Building For the Gay Recreation Centre Plus Bathhouse in the Basement at 38–46 Oxford Street Darlinghurst. Sydney, The Council of the City of Sydney.
(1987) Copy of Leaflet Titled SAUNAS, BACKROOM AND AIDS Found in Alderman Craig Johnston Subject Files. *The Council of the City of Sydney Archives.* Sydney.
(1988) Australian Capital Territory (Self-Government) Act (Commonwealth)
(1991a) Copy of Leaflet Titled LIFELINE TO BECOME DEATHLINE in DA For Social Club (Continuation of Existing Usage) at 58a Flinders Street Darlinghurst as a Club. *The Council of The City Of South Sydney.* Sydney.
(1991b) DA For Social Club (Continuation of Existing Usage) at 58a Flinders Street Darlinghurst as a Club. *The Council of The City Of South Sydney.* Sydney.
(1992a) BA For Alterations to Existing Club at 58a Flinders Street Darlinghurst as a Club. *The Council of The City Of South Sydney.* Sydney.
(1992b) Bodyline Spa and Sauna (Sydney) Pty Ltd v South Sydney City Council. *Local Government Law Reports of Australia (LGRA).*
(1992c) DA For Gay Men's Social and Health Club 58a Flinders Street Darlinghurst as a Club, U92–00152. *The Council of The City Of South Sydney.* Sydney.
(1993) DA For Health and Fitness Centre on the 1st Floor of 2–8 Brisbane St., Surry Hills. *The Council of the City of Sydney.* Sydney.
(1993) Local Government Act (New South Wales)
(1994) Domestic Relationships Act (Australian Capital Territory)
(1995) Disorderly Houses Amendment Act, 1995. *The Statutes of NSW.* Government Printer, New South Wales.
(1996a) DA For Change of Use From Art Gallery/Yoga Centre To Gay Men's Sex on Premises Venue/Art Gallery at 8–10 Taylor St., Surrey Hills, U96–00792. *South Sydney City Council.* Sydney.
(1996b) Health and community Services Minute Paper DA Premises 8–10, Darlinghurst – Proposed Male Brothel and Art Gallery Premises. *South Sydney City Council.*
(1997a) Pride Holdings Pty Ltd. v South Sydney City Council. Before Pearlman J, 8 April. *Unreported.* Sydney, Land and Environment Court of NSW.
(1997b) Regulations Of Brothels, Local Environmental Plan, Development Control Plan, and Health Standards. *Parramatta City Council.* Sydney.
(1998) Local Government (General) Amendment (Community Social Plans) Regulation (New South Wales).
(2001a) Development Application Notice of Determination for Fit out and use of the first and second floor levels as a gentleman's club providing gymnasium, steam room, spa, massage room, television room, rest room and lounge room facilities. 357 Sussex Street, Sydney, NSW, 2000. Sydney, City of Sydney.
(2001b) Section 82A review of D/2001/285 for 357 Sussex Street, Sydney, NSW, 2000. Sydney, City of Sydney.

(2002) Development Application Notice of Determination for Fit out and use of the third and fourth levels as an extension to the first and second floor levels as a gentleman's club with gymnasium, steam room, spa, massage room, and consulting room and lounge area. 357 Sussex Street, Sydney, NSW, 2000. Sydney, City of Sydney.

(2003) Continued use of the four upper levels of the building as a sex services premises involving alterations to the existing layout. 357 Sussex Street, Sydney, NSW, 2000. Sydney, City of Sydney.

(2004) Development Application Notice of Determination for Internal alterations, change of use of the existing premises to a commercial premises to be used as a health, recreation and social center for males and associated signage. The premises is to operate 24 Hours a day, 7 days a week. 17–19 Bridge Street Rydlemere NSW, 2116. Parramatta, Parramatta City Council.

(2004) Marriage Amendment Act (Commonwealth)

(2006) Adult Entertainment and Sex Industry Premises Development Control Plan. Sydney, City of Sydney.

(2008) Civil Partnerships Acts (Australian Capital Territory)

(2009) Continuation of the use of the upper four floors of the building as a sex on premises facility plus minor alterations to an internal laundry wall. 357 Sussex Street, Sydney, NSW, 2000. Sydney, City of Sydney.

(2009) Local Government Amendment (Planning and Reporting) Act (New South Wales).

Index

Abiquiu home and studio of Georgia
    O'Keefe 60–61
'active citizenship' 140, 142
Adler, L. and Brenner, J. 13, 36, 109, 214–17
adult entertainment, UK 181–2
affection, public displays of 49
affirmative strategies 161–2
affluence
    and tourism 44–5
    see also incomes
AIDS/HIV 40–41, 42, 47, 197, 202, 205
American Planning Association (APA)
    Diversity Task Force 82
    Division of Women and Planning 5
    GALIP 7–9, 25, 82, 218
    Planning and the Black Community
        Division (PBCD) 7
architecture *see* historic preservation
Association of Collegiate Schools of
    Planning, US 5, 7
Australia
    Censuses 134–5
    governance and planning scales 130–34
    Mardi Gras 43–4
    multiculturalism 2
    same-sex partnership recognition 134–7
    social planning 131–3
        local government, New South
            Wales 137–42
    see also bathhouses
Australian Capital Territory (ACT)
    Legislative Assembly 134–7
awareness raising 50–51

Badgett, M.V.L. 27
bathhouses
    Australia 185–7, 207–8
        governance of sexuality 187–90
        history of 190–95

legal regulation of homosexuality
    195–9
planning applications and objections
    199–207
US 63, 64
Beauvoir, S. de 90–91
Berube, A. 56–7
Betsky, A. 62, 108
Birch, E. 4
    and Silver, C. 3–4, 10
Black, D. et al. 42, 107, 109, 111–12, 115
Bohemian–Gay Index 43
Bornstein, K. 92, 94
Boston, US 32–3, 57, 64, 173
boundaries, questioning of 85
Bourdieu, P. 91
brothels 178–80
    bathhouses as 198, 200–201, 204
Browne, K. 100
    et al. 14, 15, 178
business
    development and tourism 42–6
    owners and guilds 45–6
    see also sex work
Butler, J. 14, 23, 74, 75, 77, 92

Cahill, J.J. 193–4
Canada 41–2, 157, 160–61, 162
canary metaphor, transgendered people 81
Carpenter, C. 27
Castells, M. 13, 29, 31–2, 35, 49, 109, 213,
    214, 215
    and Murphy, K. 33, 79
categorization 73–4, 76–7
Catungal, J.P. and Leslie, D. 163
Chambers, A. 147
Chapman, T. et al. 159
Charbot, M. 61
Chase, C. 95

Chauncey, G. 29, 56
Cheung, G. and Forsyth, A. 80
Chicago: Halsted Street 33–4, 67
Christian perspectives 147, 148, 153, 196–7
citizen–consumers 163–4
citizenship *see* political-economy and queer citizenship, Orlando, Florida
City Beautiful Movement, US 3, 5
college towns, US 39
Colon, I. and Marston, B. 40–1
commercial sex *see* sex work
Community Development Block Grant, US 125
contamination and pollution beliefs 188–9, 190–93, 197, 201, 205–6
Corber, R. and Valocchi, S. 14
cosmopolitanism 159–60
Coulmont, B. and Hubbard, P. 180, 181
creative cities 157–8
　　alternative planning models 160–62
　　critiques 159–60
　　diverse identities 158–60
　　problematic of visibility 163–5
creative class 150–51
creativity index 151
criminality
　　hate crimes 96–7
　　and regulation
　　　　homosexuality 192–9
　　　　sex work 171–2, 177–80
cruising places 63
cultural politics of identity 146

Daughters of Bilitis 12, 56
D'Emilio, J. 12, 56
'dirt': contamination and pollution beliefs 188–9, 190–93, 197, 201, 205–6
discrimination
　　against transgendered people 95–9, 104–5
　　anti-discrimination policy, New South Wales 138–42
　　private rental housing 41–2
　　resistance to LGBT participation 7–11
Disney World 152–4
dispersed patterns 37–8

diverse identities 158–60
Doan, P.L. 14, 24, 48, 80–1, 92, 93, 95, 97, 119
　　and Higgins, H. 1, 102, 109, 110, 111, 118, 169
Douglas, M. 188–9, 202
Drabelle, D. 58
Drag culture 63
Dubrow, G. 47, 54, 80, 81

economic development *see* business; political-economy and queer citizenship, Orlando, Florida
economic exclusion 104–5, 160–61
education and income 115–18, 122–3
Eisler, B. 61
Elder, G.S. 76, 86
employment discrimination 104–5
enclaves 36–7, 102–3
eroticism in public spaces 49–50
ethnicity
　　home ownership 114–15, 122
　　quasi-ethnic community model 29–30
　　same-sex partnerships 27–8
　　US 5–7, 27–8
evolution of lesbian and gay spaces 12–13
Exodus International 147

Fainstein, S.
　　and Fainstein, N.I. 3
　　and Servon, L. 5
family, changing definition of 38–9, 80
family-oriented entertainment 152, 153
Feinberg, L. 11
feminist perspective 4–5, 29, 30, 74, 90–91, 93
　　anti-pornography campaign 182
　　see also lesbians
Filler, M. 62
Fincher, R. and Iverson, K. 131–2, 133, 134, 158, 161–2
Florida, R. 42–3, 123, 150, 151, 158–9
　　et al. 42–3, 158, 164–5
　　and Gates, G. 109–10
　　and Mellander, C. 43, 110
fluidity 76, 77, 83–4
Forest, B. 24–5

Forsyth, A. 13, 35, 36, 80, 84, 89, 93–4, 109, 111, 118, 129
　Cheung, G. and 80
　Sanderock, L. and 4, 92
Foucault, M. 24, 72–3, 74, 75, 76, 79, 187, 188
Frisch, M. 3, 78, 79, 83, 89, 93–4, 103, 129, 217–19

gay bars, US 63, 218–19
gay bathhouses *see* bathhouses
Gay Days annual celebration 153–4
gay and lesbian spaces
　challenges to 14–15
　evolution of 12–13
gay marriage *see* same-sex marriage
Gay Pride/Mardi Gras marchers 43–4, 49
Gays and Lesbians in Planning Division (GALIP) (APA) 7–9, 25, 82, 218
gender dichotomy
　historic perspective 90–92, 93
　tyranny of 89–93
　see also heterosexual normativity; transgendered people
"Gender and Space: Lesbians and Gay Men in the City" (Alder and Brenner) 214–17
gentrification
　and enclave protection 102–3
　historic preservation 67
　lesbians 35–6
　stage models of 30–1
　and urban renewal 30–4, 212–14
geography and planning: interdisciplinary approach 86, 213
Germain, A. and Radice, M. 160
Glass House, Connecticut 61–2
GLBT movement
　civil rights 74–5
　leftist politics 10–11
　sites and buildings 65
Godfrey, B. 30–31, 109
Gorelick, R. 164–5
governance
　and planning scales 130–34
　of sexuality 187–90
Grant, J.M. et al. 97–9, 102, 103

Greed, C. 92, 99, 101
Green, C. 71, 72–3, 76
Griffin, S. 153
group homes, US 39, 40–41

harassment in public spaces 48
hate crimes 96–7
Hays, Harry 47, 64
heterosexual normativity 75, 76, 77, 79–80, 85–6, 169–70, 183–4
　see also gender dichotomy
"Heterosexualist Project of Planning" (Frisch) 217–19
Hewitt, F.M. 192
historic preservation 23, 46–7, 81
　Lavender Landmarks (NTHP), US 55–70
Historic Preservation Forum 54
historical perspective
　gays and lesbians in cities 12, 29–30
　gender dichotomy 90–92, 93
　sexual identity 72–3
The History Project 57
HIV/AIDS 40–41, 42, 47, 197, 202, 205
Hogrefe, J. 60–61
Home Equity Protection (HEP) 125
home ownership and property values 107–8, 114–24
homelessness 41, 103–4
homophobia 65–6, 79, 82
homosexuality
　categorization 73–4, 76–7
　and heterosexual normativity 75, 76, 77, 79–80, 85–6, 169–70, 183–4
　legal regulation, Australia 195–9
homosociality 199, 204
household clusters *see* suburbs: same-sex partnerships, US
household size 39
housing
　affordable and appropriate 102–4
　residential zoning and 38–42
　stock 118, 119, 123
Hubbard, P. 169, 171, 176, 181, 182, 189, 207
　et al. 181, 188
human capital 42–3

identity/ies
  cultural politics of 146
  diverse 158–60
  fluidity of 76, 77, 83–4
  missing 78–83
  of planning 86
  sexual categorization 73–4, 76–7
inclusion 2–4
  local and multiscalar governance 133–4
  people of color 5–7
  and resistance to LGBT people 7–11
  women 4–5
incomes
  same-sex partnerships 26–7, 28
    and education 115–18, 122–3
  transgendered people 103
  see also affluence
Ingrams, G. et al. 56–7, 109
institutions of planning and sexuality 83–4
inter-sex conditions 95
interdisciplinary approach 86, 213
internet 101–2
interview-based research 37
invisibility/visibility issues 34–5, 163–5

Johnson, Philip 61–2
Johnston, C. 198, 199
justice ("just cities") 82–3, 161

Kaiser, C. 61–2
Kennedy, E.L. and Davis, M.D. 46–7, 56
kerb-crawling 177–8
Kerkin, K. 187
Kerstein, R. 31
King, S. 164
Klawitter, M. and Flatt, V. 26–7
Knopp, L. 13, 14, 37, 79–80, 188
  and Brown, M. 14
  Lauria, M. and 12–13, 33, 212–14

language 24
Lauria, M. and Knopp, L. 12–13, 33, 212–14
Lavender Landmarks (NTHP), US 55–70
Lefebvre, H. 145
leftist political movement 10–11
lesbians 13, 35–6, 42, 46, 111, 147–8, 162

Leslie, D. 160
  Catungal, J.P. 163
licensing and zoning of sex businesses 172–4, 178, 180–82
Listerborn, C. 166
local government social planning, New South Wales 137–42
Los Angeles 12, 47, 56, 64, 104, 109
Lowe, M.J. 58–9
Lynch, F. 107
Lyod, B. and Rowntree, L. 30, 32, 109

Macris, M. 5
Manchester, UK, Gay Village 15, 161–2
Mardi Gras/Gay Pride marchers 43–4, 49
Martinac, P. 47, 55–6, 58, 60, 61–2, 63, 65
massage parlours 178–80, 192
Mattachine Society 12, 47, 56, 64
methodological issues 37–8
Mill, J.S. 89–90
missing identities 78–83
multiculturalism 2
multiscalar and local governance, Australia 133–4
Murray, S. 30, 36

Namaste, V. 72, 73–4, 95, 97
National Center for Transgender Equality (NCTE) 97–8, 102, 104
National Coalition of Anti-Violence Programs (NCAVP), US 96–7
National Trust for Historic Preservation *see* Lavender Landmarks (NTHP), US
Navarro, M. 152–3
neighborhoods 28–38
New York 34, 46–7, 173
  RepoHistory project 57
  Stonewall Inn 12–13, 47, 54, 65, 81
Newton, C. 56
NIMBY responses 40–41, 182
Northampton, Massachusetts 35–6, 46, 111

off-street sex work, UK 178–80
O'Keefe, G. 60–61
older people's affordable housing 41
"Outing the National Register" 58–9

Page, S. 41–2
Pattinson, T. 32–3
Peck, J. 157
Pendarvis, Wisconsin 69
Pensacola, Florida 44–5
people of color *see* ethnicity
performativity 14
Perry, J. 148
Peterson, J.A. 3
Philipp, S. 44–5
Pitcher, J. et al. 177
planning, definition of 130–31
Planning Institute of Australia 131
Planning (magazine) 8, 9, 10
Podmore, J. 13, 110, 162
political activism 10–11, 12–13, 24–5
political-economy and queer citizenship, Orlando, Florida 145–6, 154–5
  body politic 146–8
  creative class 150–1
  cultural politics of identity 146
  Disney World 152–4
  traditional growth coalitions 149–50
pollution and contamination beliefs 188–9, 190–93, 197, 201, 205–6
pornography
  DVDs 180–81
  feminist campaign against 182
poststructuralism 72
power
  and knowledge relationship 72–3, 74
  tyranny of gender and gendered planning 89–93
Preservation (magazine) 58
Prior, J. 105, 188, 190, 193, 194, 197, 198, 199, 201–2, 204, 206
private rental housing 41–2
Progressive Planning 80, 83
property values
  anxieties 41
  and home ownership 107–8, 114–24
prostitution *see* sex work
protests
  against sex workers/adult entertainment 176–7, 181–2
  in public spaces 48–9
public spaces 48–50, 96–9
public toilets 99–101

quasi-ethnic community model 29–30
queer citizenship *see* political-economy and queer citizenship, Orlando, Florida
Queer Nation 49
queer theory 14, 24, 72–8
  challenges for planning 84–6
  contradictions and paradox 77–8
  criticisms 76–7
  focus on missing identities 78–83
  institutions of planning and sexuality 83–4

Rankin, K. 158, 162, 163
red light districts 171, 172–4
Reed, C. 69
relational strategy 162
residential areas
  Australia, bathhouses in 201, 204
  US
    neighborhoods 28–38
    zoning and housing 38–42
  see also gentrification; housing; suburbs
resistance 7–11
rights
  civil 74–5
  same-sex marriage 135–6
Ritzdorf, M. 38–9
Roper, E.S. 192
rural areas 37
Ryder, A. 171, 172

safety issues, transgendered people 96–9, 101–2
same-sex marriage
  Australia 134–7
  US 39, 112, 218
same-sex partnerships, US 26–8
  see also suburbs: same-sex partnerships, US
San Francisco 12, 30–2, 104, 109
  Castro CBD 34
  Compton's Cafeteria 54
  Fallon Building 66
Sandercock, L. 2, 86, 94, 131
  and Forsyth, A. 4, 92
Sanders, T. 177
Schlueb, M. 147, 148, 149–50, 151

Schwartz, K. 45
Scott, M. 189
Seidman, S. 71
Sennet, R. 83–4
sex work
 locating 171–4
 planning, UK 182–4
  adult entertainment 181–2
  off-street 178–80
  sex retailing 180–81
  street 175–8
sexual categorization 73–4, 76–7
Sheehan, P. 147–8
Silk, M. and Amis, J. 159
Simmons, T. and O'Connell, M. 27–8
social planning, Australia 131–3, 137–42
Social Reform movement, US 3, 5, 6
social stigma: transgendered people 95–6
Soja, E.W. 78
stage models of gentrification 30–31
Stanton, S. 11
Stonewall Inn 12–13, 47, 54, 65, 81
street sex work, UK 175–8
structuralism and poststructuralism 72
suburbs: same-sex partnerships, US 107–9
 household clusters 109–11
 methods and data 111–13
 results 113–24
Sullivan, N. 14, 77

Takahashi, L. and Dear, M. 40
telephone surveys 41–2
Thomas, H. 6
Thomas, J.M. 6, 7
 and Darnton, J. 159
Thompson, S. 130–31, 132, 137–8
tourism
 beaches and resorts 63–4
 business development and 42–6
 Disney World 152–4
 travel and heritage industries 67–8
"Towards an analysis of the role of gay communities in the urban renaissance" (Lauria and Knopp) 212–14
transgendered people 11
 affordable and appropriate housing 102–4
 canary metaphor 81

consequences of gendered planning 93–6
 economic discrimination 104–5
 equal access to public toilets 99–101
 safety issues 96–9, 101–2
 transportation 97, 123

unisex bathrooms 100–101
United Kingdom (UK)
 Gay Village, Manchester 15, 161–2
 see also under sex work
United States (US)
 Censuses/Bureau 26–7, 27–8, 107–8, 112
 ethnicity 5–7, 27–8
 homosexuality in cities 12–13
 inclusion 2–4
 LGBT population 25–8
 see also American Planning Association (APA); historic preservation; political-economy and queer citizenship, Orlando, Florida; residential areas; suburbs: same-sex partnerships; *specific cities*
urban renewal
 business and tourism 42–6
 and gentrification 30–34, 212–14
 see also creative cities
Urey, G. 82

Valentine, G. 13, 37, 109, 111
Valocchi, S. 72, 75
 Corber, R. and 14
violence against transgendered people 96–7, 98
visibility/invisibility issues 34–5, 163–5

Weiss, J.T. 96
Whitney, D. 62
Williams, P. 131, 132–3
Williamson, P. 204
Wolf, D. 29, 35
Wolfe, M. 32
women
 historical gender dichotomy 90–92, 93
 inclusion of 4–5
 lesbians 13, 35–6, 42, 46, 111, 147–8, 162
 see also feminist perspective

Young Men's Christian Association (YMCAs) 63
Yue, A. 157–8, 159, 163

zoning 80, 82, 103
   bathhouses 205–7
   and licensing sex businesses 172–4, 178, 180–82
   residential, and housing 38–42
   street sex work 176, 177